THE MAKING OF
SYLVIA
PLATH

THE MAKING OF
SYLVIA PLATH

CARL ROLLYSON

University Press of Mississippi / Jackson

The University Press of Mississippi is the scholarly publishing agency of
the Mississippi Institutions of Higher Learning: Alcorn State University,
Delta State University, Jackson State University, Mississippi State University,
Mississippi University for Women, Mississippi Valley State University,
University of Mississippi, and University of Southern Mississippi.

www.upress.state.ms.us

The University Press of Mississippi is a member
of the Association of University Presses.

Illustrations are from the author's collection unless otherwise noted.

Library of Congress Cataloging-in-Publication Data

Names: Rollyson, Carl E. (Carl Edmund), author.
Title: The making of Sylvia Plath / Carl Rollyson.
Description: Jackson : University Press of Mississippi, [2024] |
    Includes bibliographical references and index.
Identifiers: LCCN 2024031466 (print) | LCCN 2024031467 (ebook) |
    ISBN 9781496846679 (hardback) | ISBN 9781496854063 (epub) |
    ISBN 9781496854070 (epub) | ISBN 9781496854087 (pdf) |
    ISBN 9781496854094 (pdf)
Subjects: LCSH: Plath, Sylvia. | Women authors, American—20th century—Biography. |
    BISAC: BIOGRAPHY & AUTOBIOGRAPHY / Literary Figures | SOCIAL
    SCIENCE / Media Studies
Classification: LCC PS3566.L27 Z8494 2024 (print) | LCC PS3566.L27 (ebook) |
    DDC 811/.54 B—dc23/eng/20240816
LC record available at https://lccn.loc.gov/2024031466
LC ebook record available at https://lccn.loc.gov/2024031467

British Library Cataloging-in-Publication Data available

The Promethean spirit waxes and the human heart is light, but time and time again we crash.

—William Sheldon, *Psychology and the Promethean Will*

Oh! why were you born with that excessive, that ungovernable passion for everything that is dear to you?

—Goethe, *The Sorrows of Werther*

CONTENTS

AUTHOR'S NOTE

A word about this book's title: Sylvia Plath made her world as it made her, but how that was so continues to be occluded by the way her life and work have been presented. Biographers of Sylvia Plath labor under the burden of the obstructions Ted Hughes placed in their way by haphazardly releasing her work, by asserting the privilege of his proximity to her to suggest that only he could possibly know Plath, and by dismissing biographers as no more than interlopers. But Sylvia Plath had a life and a mind of her own before and after Ted Hughes. I say mind because this book emphasizes how she shaped her intellect around certain books she chose to read, underline, and annotate. She wrote about herself on pages Hughes never saw until after her death, and he then tried to rework those pages into his vision of her.[1] In other words, like a biographer, his commentary on Plath is the result of retrospection, speculation, and the interpretation of an archival record that he ineptly curated and fitfully distributed.

To be sure, Hughes was the Superman figure Plath sought, beginning in her earliest years.[2] That he was, in part, a fiction of her own making is neither surprising nor in itself a commentary on herself alone. As Jay Martin observes in *Who Am I This Time: Uncovering the Fictive Personality*, fictions rule—more or less—the lives of everyone. It is "neither possible nor desirable to dispense with fictions." But to "possess *only* fictions means to be possessed by them." This is the crux of Plath's plight. She built Hughes up into almost an omnipotent figure, a hypnotizing shaman that could put her to healing sleep, ease childbirth, and deliver her, it seemed, from trauma. In a March 10, 1956, journal entry she described herself as Penelope waiting for Ulysses. Yet he could just as well exert a demonic influence that she endeavored to destroy in the pyre she made of his papers, and to banish in the last days of her life. On September 18, 1956, in the home of Hughes's parents, shortly after marrying Ted, she noted in her calendar diary[3]: a "cold, nightmare rest on bed in horrid imagining of rivalry[4] & sickening voodoo forces."[5] The vertiginous romance with Hughes, and the way he soothed Plath's anxieties even as she was filled with an unnameable dread, calls to mind the film *Gaslight* (1944).[6] In that film, Paula Alquist (Ingrid Bergman), studying to become an opera singer, is entranced with Gregory Anton (Charles Boyer). Onto him she projects an idolatrous love,[7] which blinds her to his desire to dominate every aspect of her life and to drive her mad. In effect, he becomes her savior/enslaver as she seeks to overcome grief over the murder of her aunt, a great opera singer. In *Birthday Letters*, Ted Hughes propagated the myth of Sylvia Plath, undone and grieving over the loss of an overpowering father, without ever acknowledging publicly his own role in the manufacture of that myth.

Hughes never did assess and publish his impact on Plath, or why she sometimes reacted negatively to his very presence. In such instances, he retreated to formulations of what was wrong with her, not with him, relying on the support of friends who empathized with him. The consequences of his dictatorial hold over her work have been devastating, and only now are we beginning to see the entire context in which the history of Sylvia Plath was distorted.[8] That history, in this book, relies as closely as possible on her own raw data, her childhood diaries and her later calendar diaries that record, virtually in the moment, what she was thinking and feeling alongside her perfected experiences in journals, letters, fiction, and poetry. But of course we cannot be ruled by her testimony alone, which is why I have built up, as never before in Plath biography, certain figures in her life who were in a position to influence her and also to contribute a perspective on her personality and what happened to her.

Almost as detrimental to Plath biography is the example of Harriet Rosenstein, who for decades hoarded a treasury of documents, interviews, and other materials collected for a biography that was never published. She was, nevertheless, a formidable researcher and writer. Reading through her entire archive I've been impressed with the rapport she established with Aurelia Plath, Jillian Becker, Al Alvarez, Richard Murphy, and many others who knew Sylvia Plath. Rosenstein's findings, released sooner, would have significantly altered the work of Plath's first biographers. Many efforts by various scholars and biographers, including myself, to engage with Rosenstein proved fruitless, and what we now have of her crucial work is available in an archive she sold to Emory University. It took a lawsuit by Smith College to wrest Plath's letters to her therapist, Ruth Beuscher (Ruth Tiffany Barnhouse) from Rosenstein, after the therapist had lent them to the biographer. The lawsuit was a significant victory, since Smith's is the only archive to provide entirely unrestricted access to Plath's work.[9]

I have taken full advantage of Emory's impressive Harriet Rosenstein collection, which contains many important interviews conducted a decade or so after Plath's death, when memories were still relatively fresh. Heather Clark and Gail Crowther make use of the Rosenstein papers, but much of that archive has remained unincorporated in Plath biography and appears here for the first time. I have tried to minimize the cataloguing of events that sometimes congests biographies and to maximize an inquiry into the meaning of crucial moments in her life, of her reading, and of her writing. I focus on a small core of poems rather than provide long lists of titles with the brief comments on poems and stories that often stud biographical narratives.

I have written Plath's life anew based on my recent discoveries, especially in her study of psychology. Here the Smith College archive of her therapist, then known as Ruth Beuscher,[10] which I began to plumb in *The Last Days of Sylvia Plath*, has yielded important new insights. What Plath made of her studies in psychology is evident in her annotations and underlinings—here for the first time explored as a way of getting as near to the interior of her mind as a biographer can essay.[11]

PREFACE

By the time Sylvia Plath enrolled in Smith College, she had amassed a body of work and a range of experiences that will be recounted in the fresh details of this biography. Other biographers, understandably eager to get on with the mature work of her later years, have not done justice to these early records, although Andrew Wilson has made a start. To have done so would have made for biographies even longer than Heather Clark's one-thousand-page narrative.[1] And even Clark cut three hundred pages from earlier drafts that dealt with Plath's earliest years. So in this biography, more weight is given to her first two decades in order to provide a more proportional Plath. As Plath scholar Peter K. Steinberg wrote to me, "The world doesn't know, really, how truly amazing and interesting her pre-Smith and pre-Cambridge days are." So many react to Plath's life as one that was cut short and what a shame, and so on. That is understandable, but it is also the case that in thirty years she experienced more than some of us manage to absorb in sixty or more.

Because Plath, at thirty, took her own life, and because she had attempted to do so earlier while in college, it is often supposed her story is sad and that to read her is to dwell in a depressive down cycle that does one no good. In fact, many of Plath's readers find both her life and art liberating because of her powerful and exuberant expressiveness. A case can be made that her intensity wore her out, but even more persuasive is the case for her indomitable spirit that remains a compelling example for many generations of readers, young and old. There are certain accidents of history that can lead to self-annihilation, when a person feels overwhelmed, and biography is a way of explaining why that is so—why exuberance can become enervating.

I first became aware of Plath in 1973 by teaching one of her poems, "Metaphors," to a high school class. I did not know then that it was written when she thought she was pregnant, although the lines allude to her imagined condition: "I'm a riddle in nine syllables, / An elephant, a ponderous house." The poem births the transformational Plath, having fun with what metaphors do—taking in the world and making it our own, making our own language that encompasses the world and the poet's own creativity: "I'm a means, a stage, a cow in calf," meaning she is about to become a mother, which is to say more than herself, more in the world than she has ever been before. The poem can be read biographically, but it is also about poetry-making, about becoming pregnant with words. You don't have to know that Plath thinks she is pregnant, but when you do know, then you know something about what she made out of her life and what made her life great. With other poems, such as "Mussel-Hunter at Rock Harbor," I have situated the work in biography, showing how Plath addresses her brother. Of course, the poem has a life of its own without the ministrations of a biographer, but it also has other lives that emerge out of biography.

As Heather Clark shows in her recent biography, knowing the context of Plath's life can be crucial in the way you respond to her person and her work. It is vital to realize that she grew up in a household of immigrants fiercely bent on improving themselves and becoming part of the American dream of success that got underway again after the penury of the Depression and the horror of World War II. To isolate her as psychologically damaged misses the point of her existence. She was born to excel and given the encouragement to express herself by a proud family that put no limitations on her desire to succeed. She could sometimes make herself sick with worry over her program of high purpose, but that is not so uncommon among serious students of achievement, as I show in this biography.

What also made Plath sick was her keen awareness of what the Cold War was doing to her country and to the world. An early poem, "Bitter Strawberries," emerged out of her summer farm work to earn enough to help support herself in her first year at Smith College. "All morning in the strawberry field / They talked about the Russians," the poem begins. One picker says "bomb them off the map." Plath had a startling perception of how the world at large could press down on a strawberry field with a brutality mimicked in the motions of the pickers: "Cupping the berry protectively before / Snapping off the stem / Between thumb and forefinger." The idea that Plath was a self-absorbed, suicidal personality does not get you very far in understanding her life or her work or her novel, *The Bell Jar*, which begins with the narrator Esther Greenwood's traumatic meditation on the execution of the Rosenbergs that her contemporaries seem to welcome, scarcely giving it a thought. The novel had its origins in Plath's own sense of estrangement from a world that had cosseted her but also expected a conformity and complicity in the possibility of mass destruction. A society that had no compunctions about annihilating the Rosenbergs was, to her mind, bent on a Holocaust. "I get stared at in horror when I suggest that we are as guilty as Russia is, that we are war-mongers too," she told Eddie Cohen, one of the few people who understood her anomie.

On June 10, 1959, she read *The Lonely Crowd*,[2] a classic sociological study of American culture, under the spell of Alexis de Tocqueville, who first reported on the strains in this new country's individuals, poised between their quest for equal opportunity and the desire to foster a democratic community riven between calls for conformity and rebellion. In the riot of her own conflicted feelings about her mother and society, she turned to Dr. Ruth Beuscher. Plath recorded in her diary: "What to discuss with RB? Work, desire for work of meaning. To learn German. To write, be a Renaissance woman." Plath looked ahead and behind her, to the German of her parents and to the world they came from, straddling history, as did Beuscher, who had been caught in Europe during the rise of fascism.[3]

Plath had her reviving outlets—not only in writing but in friendships, socializing, cooking, exercising, and even in manual labor. She was a fully operational person, you might say—not a loner or a brooder except in her journals, sometimes, which have to be balanced by all those lively letters to family, boyfriends, fellow writers, and other professional contacts. Right from the beginning, she was a busy little girl, building huts out of the snow in the winter and with leaves in the summer, assiduously collecting stamps, riding her bike for miles and miles, performing at camp and at the pottery wheel.

Then there is the mordant humor of *The Bell Jar*, sometimes regarded as a sad or depressive work. Hardly. It is, as Heather Clark rightly insists, a protest novel, but one not written by a male poet like Goethe but by a young, vibrant woman all too aware of a society that tries to put her down or fit her into what is fashionable. Esther Greenwood will not conform— not to mother, not to society, not to employers, not to boyfriends. Esther's astringent sensibility is her safeguard, both a form of defense and attack on a society that belittles her. No wonder, then, that she feels the bell jar of a world coming down on her. Yet she is able to lift her spirits and escape suffocation—not once and for all as in a fairy tale—but with a hard-won sensibility that eventuates in the tough-minded writing of a survivor and in the triumph of a novel. It is good to know that when Plath finished her work and could take a look at the whole of it, she laughed, as she did when completing her signature poem, "Daddy." Writing gave her life back to her, so how can one not be interested in the life that made her writing possible—indeed essential.

SOURCES AND ACKNOWLEDGMENTS

Note: Plath often wrote without capitals, imitating, as she said, e e cummings, and I have not, in most cases, corrected her usage, or her misspellings and typos. In the text, I have used abbreviations in brackets to acknowledge sources when those sources are not evident in the narrative. Quotations from Plath's letters are from the two volumes edited by Karen Kukil and Peter K. Steinberg. Material derived Plath's diaries (1944–1949) are from volumes in Special Collections, Lilly Library, Indiana University. Material derived from Plath's poems are taken from *Collected Poems*. Quotations from Ted Hughes's letters are from *The Letters of Ted Hughes*, edited by Christopher Reid.

AW: Julie Goodspeed-Chadwick and Peter K. Steinberg, editors. *The Collected Writings of Assia Wevill.* Louisiana State University Press, 2021.

BHSP: Anita Helle, Amanda Golden, and Maeve O'Brien, editors. *The Bloomsbury Handbook to Sylvia Plath.* Bloomsbury Academic, 2022.

CR1: Carl Rollyson. *American Isis: The Life and Art of Sylvia Plath.* St. Martin's Press, 2013.

CR2: Carl Rollyson. *The Last Days of Sylvia Plath.* University Press of Mississippi, 2020.

CR3: Carl Rollyson. *Sylvia Plath Day by Day, Volume 1: 1932–1955.* University Press of Mississippi, 2023.

CR4: Carl Rollyson. *Sylvia Plath Day by Day, Volume 2: 1955–1963.* University Press of Mississippi, 2024.

HR: Harriet Rosenberg Papers, Stuart A. Rose Manuscript, Archives, and Rare Book Library, Emory University.

LWM1: Linda Wagner-Martin. *Sylvia Plath: A Biography.* St. Martin's Press, 1987.

LWM2: Linda Wagner-Martin. *Sylvia Plath: A Literary Life.* Palgrave Macmillan, 1999.

MGL: Andrew Wilson. *Mad Girl's Love Song: Sylvia Plath and Life Before Ted.* Scribner, 2013.

PC: Sylvia Plath. Personal calendars. Special Collections, Smith College.

PJ: Sylvia Plath. *The Unabridged Journals of Sylvia Plath*. Edited by Karen V. Kukil. Faber and Faber, 2000.

RC: Heather Clark. *Red Comet: The Short Life and Blazing Art of Sylvia Plath*. Knopf, 2020.

My debt to Peter K. Steinberg, a preeminent Plath scholar, is incalculable. Sometimes on a daily basis he answered my queries and provided significant materials for this book. Just as crucial to my work is another esteemed Plath scholar, Gail Crowther, who provided much new insight. Judy Denison, a Plath classmate, faithfully answered my questions and supplied the kind of background information about what it was like at Smith College in Lawrence House. Smith College archivist Kate Long sent many digital copies of Plath books and other materials that were a godsend during the pandemic era. Material collected on my visits to the Lilly Library of Indiana University and the Stuart A. Rose Manuscript, Archives, and Rare Book Library of Emory University for my earlier books have proven invaluable for this one as well.

THE MAKING OF
SYLVIA PLATH

PART ONE

THE EARLY YEARS

1

Where to Begin?

With the poet's birth in the Jamaica Plain section of Boston on October 27, 1932? Or with her parents, Otto Plath and Aurelia Schober Plath, married on January 4, 1932? Or perhaps, in Plath's case, with the death of her father on November 5, 1940? A biographer can simply proceed chronologically, narrating one event after another, or seek, instead, for a defining moment, when the biographical subject is marked for life—perhaps suffering a trauma in childhood that can never be overcome. Sylvia Plath's biographers—given her poems about her father, notably "The Colossus" and "Daddy"; her letters about him; and the overpowering presence of Otto Plath in *Birthday Letters*, husband Ted Hughes's interpretation of her life and death—have fastened on this father-fixation to such an extreme that Sylvia Plath's most recent and best-informed biographer has rebelled against a pathologizing of the poet, the treatment of her as if she is a mental case. Clark seeks, instead, to put Plath's early life in a much broader context as the child of immigrants in a German-speaking family, growing up during World War II, with a keen consciousness of what it meant to be German when Germans were the enemy her country was warring against. Such children of immigrants want to fit in. Sylvia as a young girl seemed well adjusted, but with anxieties about an ethnicity that set her apart from others.

However much one might want to resist a deterministic narrative of a young girl fatally attached to her dominating Daddy, the biographer has to enter the confinements of the Plath household. Aurelia Plath said of her marriage that early on she had to reconcile herself to always putting her husband first. Asserting her own will, making an effort at a separate career, fulfilling her dreams of becoming a writer—all aspirations became subsumed in serving Otto Plath's dictates and ambitions. He had his "Prussian,

3

militaristic character," and Sylvia exhibited much of his strong will, specu-lated Mel Woody, one of her intimates. [HR]¹

Aurelia had been Professor Otto Plath's former student and now subor-dinated herself in the work that culminated in his classic study *Bumblebees and Their Ways* (1934). It is not too much to say that the professor's project enveloped the household. Herr Plath deployed his research materials across the living room table as a kind of raised relief map of his scholarly terrain. He became upset if any part of this strategic plan was disturbed or displaced. Consequently, Aurelia had to memorize the exact position of every item so that she could remove pieces to clean or to use the table for some other purpose without Otto detecting any interruption of his order.

This was the patriarchal home into which Sylvia Plath, the family's first born, thrived in the watchful care of her mother, who began setting her out in the sun for an hour each morning and afternoon, initiating the sun bathing regimen mother and daughter associated with good health. [RC] By June 1933, an anxious Aurelia tracked Sylvia's weight, worried that her daughter was not eating enough—a concern that would continue. Aurelia also recorded Sylvia's words at a precious eight months ("Mama, dad, by-bye tick-tick"), and it was a big day on November 1, 1933, when Sylvia burst out with "Daddy!" No biographer can resist noting that her famous poem used that word as both a demanding child-like plea and an adult's belligerent repudiation. [RC]

Just out of infancy, Sylvia pleased her father with stories and poems—not as a subject who had to placate a tyrant but as a tyro craving the patriarch's praise. She liked to show off and became, as well, part of her mother's program for making their home as pleasant as possible. In February of 1934, Aurelia delighted in her daughter's excitement about plants and flowers: She wanted to smell them immediately. Sylvia, at this early stage, felt fully absorbed in her father's and mother's favor, surmounting her anxieties of displacement after the birth of her brother Warren on April 7, 1935, when she realized he would serve as another contribution to the family dynasty. They became playmates and confidants—and sometimes adversaries, but even then together in troublemaking: "Warren and I were bad and pushed each other underwater. Then we made friends and caked ourselves with wet sand so we had to wash off," she wrote in her diary for August 4, 1944.

2

In 1936, the family moved to a house in thriving working-class Winthrop, Massachusetts, composed in nearly equal portions of Protestants, Irish

Catholics, and Jews, with some Italian families as well. David Freeman, whose family moved to Winthrop in 1937, observed hostility to Germans and neighborhood kids putting up a Swastika flag on the flagpole of a German family. [HR]

The Plaths settled close to the home of Aurelia's Austrian-born parents, Franz Schober and Aurelia Grünwald Schober. Sylvia walked a short distance to her first-grade half-day sessions at the private Sunshine School, adjusting well to new experiences and eagerly returning home at noon to tell her mother and brother all about her activities. She did well in second-grade grammar school and enjoyed her classes. [RC] Aurelia treated her daughter's excellent academic progress like an event to be commemorated, writing a note of congratulations to her daughter on April 8, 1939, for an all-A report card. Doing well was cause for celebration. Doing well is what it was all about. That and the sheer oceanic joy captured in a photograph of Sylvia and Warren on a dock, forming in their togetherness a sort of pillar of pleasure.[2]

Not much broke the routine of these happy days, except for a category 3 hurricane that hit southern Massachusetts in September 1938, killing 564 people, injuring 1,700, and destroying thousands of trees, power lines, homes, boats, and other structures. Winthrop sustained significant damage. Plath later claimed a shark turned up in her grandparents' garden at Point Shirley. She had heard the frightening holocaust overhead and would write about it in her poem "The Disquieting Muses," remembering her father's downstairs study "windows bellied in / Like bubbles about to break." Aurelia

GREAT HEAD, WINTHROP, MASS.

Postcard of Winthrop, Massachusetts, where the Plath family moved in 1936.

calmed her children with ovaltine and cookies and had them chant against the storm: "Thor is angry: we don't care!" Words had power, too, and Aurelia used them to suppress the troubling elements that disturbed her children. Sylvia also counted on her grandparents. In an essay-memoir, "Ocean 1212," she reflected on how much she relied on her grandparents to ground her, cleaning up after the storm: "my grandmother had her broom out, it would soon be right."

In Winthrop, David Freeman played with Sylvia and Warren, along with David's sister Ruth. Sylvia continued to write to David into the mid-1950s. He said he was attracted to the "very pretty Sylvia" who had "a romantic way of acting" and a pronounced sense of her own authority. When he told her not to put wet paper in a wastebasket because it would not burn in the furnace, she replied: "This is MY wastebasket." She liked to make up stories about adventures with another playmate, Wayne Sterling, involving trap doors and secret staircases in Wayne's home. David never figured out if he was expected to believe these tales. Sometimes the children visited Grammy Schober. David remembered her heavy German accent. They played in the sand and the energetic Sylvia made up more extravagant stories. [HR]

Both David Freeman and Wayne Sterling invoked visions of Sylvia in pigtails and pinafore, an Alice in Wonderland figure. On December 7, 1938, she attended the party for Wayne's seventh birthday. For some reason Wayne never understood, Sylvia began to cry, and as he tried to comfort her, Aurelia (who was helping out with the party) hovered "watching over" them. [HR]

David Freeman's father said he thought Otto preferred Sylvia to Warren, a shy boy. David recalled Otto's tone in addressing his children: "SEEEL-VYA," Otto purred, "WRN," Otto barked. David's impression of Otto: a "stern, severe person." Aurelia also seemed "severe" until her face broke out in smiles. [HR] No one could replace Sylvia's attachment to Otto, or her desire to hear he was just as attached to her. "Dear Father," she wrote on February 19, 1940, "I am coming home soon. Are you as glad as I am?" She told him about how she had ink-stained fingers after a trip to her Uncle Frank's work room. [RC]

Mildred Norton, a family friend and neighbor, told her daughter-in-law Shirley that Otto Plath addressed Sylvia as an adult. Sylvia soaked it all up, including the technical jargon. Perhaps he enchanted her with stories about the bees, about the time he set up an experiment to see how a skunk could eat a whole bee colony, resorting to scratching their nest, snatching bees, and rolling them on the ground and between paws before eating them with a satisfying crunching sound. A review in the May 1934 issue of *The Booklist of the American Library Association* praised Otto Plath's direct observations and pleasant writing that would attract a "general reader with even a slight interest in the subject."[3] *The Hub*, a Boston University publication, advised that if "you want to spend an interesting half hour just get him to talking about birds and insects. You'll not consider it time wasted, we assure you." Yet Otto's colleagues thought of him as a loner and seemed to know almost nothing about his background or personal life, although T. B. Mitchell said that Otto told him about growing up in a German community and that he did not learn to speak English until he was twelve.[4] One of Otto's students in 1939, Norman Bailey, described Otto as a "considerate" teacher. Yet others spoke of how he ridiculed students in class. [HR] Did his behavior change in the course of a teaching career?

One colleague, Leland H. Taylor, wrote to Harriet Rosenstein that after he read the last line of Sylvia's famous first-person monologue, "Daddy," Taylor thought of the irritable Otto. No one would have called him a bastard in polite academic society, but that word fit what some of his colleagues thought of him. He seemed Germanic in his pronunciation of w's. His erect, almost rigid bearing and "very deep set and piercing eyes" could make him seem, indeed, like the forbidding father figure of "Daddy." He had an Old World formality about him that prompted Taylor to expect him to click his heels and "bend stiffly at the waist," like a Prussian Junker, and say "Ich habe die Ehre" (I have the honor) when greeting someone. Taylor mentioned Otto's hatred of his first wife, Lydia,[5] and his diatribes against evil women, along with his "anti-Semitic tendencies." It is hard for a biographer not to take such testimony to heart and wonder if Sylvia perceived her father similarly when writing in "Daddy": "every woman adores a fascist." Taylor's damaging assessment, however, came with a significant qualification: "Despite these prejudices and his unfortunate hang-ups, I feel that Plath was actually an ethical person, who would not deliberately harm anyone." Laurence Snyder, one of Otto's fellow graduate students at Harvard in the early 1920s, went further: "To many he seemed cold, distant, and arrogant, but in reality he was a warm hearted rather shy person." And apparently, on occasion, Otto behaved as a generous man, offering an interest-free loan to Ralph Singleton to "tide me over" until the end of the semester. Yet another account has Otto borrowing money from a fellow student so as not to disturb his interest-bearing savings account. While some colleagues said he had no sense of humor, at least one, Nathan Bailey, thought otherwise. Still another, George Salt, said he was "gentle," "quite unaggressive," and friendly "often to the point of being ingratiating," "emotional," "oversensitive," and "unsure of himself." As so often in accounts that rely on memory and the temperament of witnesses, what Otto Plath signified is subject to some doubt. [HR] But then, doesn't "Daddy" capture precisely that ambiguity and ambivalence—that love and hate and mystery that lots of fathers engender?

Harriet Rosenstein puzzled over Otto Plath's purported misogyny and wondered why he chose to marry again, also speculating in a letter to Leland H. Taylor that Otto's prejudices against religion and women, which came after rejecting his early training to become a Lutheran minister and divorcing his first wife, reflected a "violent generic repudiation. All women are evil; all faith is nonsense." She was aware, however, of the biographer's penchant for presuming too much: "Maybe this is too easy a generalization based on too little information, but it certainly accords with his daughter's disproportionate reactions to loss."

Did Otto Plath instill in his daughter a desire to describe and accurately reflect the natural world?[6] Her relish for school field trips is evident in the diaries she began to keep by the age of eleven. Laurence Snyder called Otto "very meticulous, even fussy, in his use of words," taking a long time to decide about the title of a paper. Should it be "The Bee-Eating Propensities of the Skunk" or "The Bee Eating Proclivities of the Skunk"? Similarly, Ralph Singleton remembered Otto speaking in a precise and clipped manner. That kind of attention to language marks the poet. Leland H. Taylor called Otto a dedicated researcher who worked to the "point of extreme fatigue"—[HR] a characteristic that could be applied to Sylvia Plath just as well.

Otto Plath's fascination with bees began in boyhood exploring fields and meadows and observing bee behavior. You can read his book today and easily imagine how he told his daughter about the "strenuous and exciting" first efforts to secure a bee colony in a large cigar box, with a layer of sand and a bore hole (which becomes a flight hole) sealed with a cork. Then he would snatch a bee nest and thrust it into the box, which he then lowered in a hole he made out of the nest site, allowing about a inch of the nest to rise above ground. Complications ensued that probably made for good stories about how to keep the colony intact. A word of advice from Otto: "Capture the bees before sunrise; they seem less pugnacious then." His talk of fugitive bees and narrow escapes provided plenty of adventure for raiders of lost bees. Otto's imperial ambition manifested itself in his accumulation of more than fifty bee colonies he would tend and observe all day, sometimes until midnight.

3

In the spring of 1939, Otto Plath, diagnosed with diabetes, began to fail, and his children were dispatched to stay with their grandparents at Point

Shirley, on the edge of the sea, which sometimes inundated the land but did not overwhelm Sylvia's indomitable grandmother who: "Kept house against / What the sluttish, rutted sea could do." From a very early age, Sylvia Plath sensed how the world could be overturned and awash with the forces of nature.

Although the children did not know what ailed their father, Sylvia's short, undated letter to him, written from her grandparents' home, reflected her concern: "I hope you are better," and then as if to cheer him up: "Over grandma's there were many ice-cakes and on every one sat a seagull! Isn't that funny (Ha Ha)." On February 20, 1940, she wrote to her mother in wonder and perhaps fear: "The waves were up to our front steps they were as high as the window!" But she was having a good time and drew a picture to prove it, showing her holding a flower next to her Aunt Dorothy Schober with a wand in her hand as if flying.

On October 12, 1940, Otto Plath lost a leg to diabetes. On November 5, he died. His hierarchical establishment collapsed. Sylvia and Warren had been kept away from Otto's suffering. What Sylvia felt then can be imagined from her later grievances against her mother, who had taken her father away from her. Aurelia believed she was sparing her children the anguish of watching their father die and the horror of attending his funeral. So Otto simply vanished from the children's lives. His death instantly became mythological—and unforgivable. It is not reasonable to expect a parent to announce his own death; what else would a child deeply attached to her father want? Wayne Sterling, who never saw Sylvia's father, spotted a photograph of Otto in Sylvia's home that looked like a daguerreotype, with the serious sharp eyes of an ancestor. [HR]

4

Sylvia cried easily, Wayne Sterling said, especially after her father's death. When he announced at school his cat had five kittens, Sylvia replied, "That's nothing. Mine had five." When he followed her home to see about those five cats, they were met by Warren who began teasing her. She cried out, "I wish I was dead." Wayne went to comfort Sylvia, but Aurelia intervened and, as always, Wayne felt her "presence." Sylvia became a loner, Sterling said, crying less but "seething" or "bristling" in unpleasant situations, withdrawing from company, "cool and distant." For the first time, she became a problem for her mother, disturbing the neighborhood by persistently teasing her playmates—although this phase lasted briefly, as did her resentment of her grandmother, who stayed in the Plath home while Aurelia went out to work.[7]

Sylvia also had a good time with neighborhood kids, picking up seashells and throwing rocks in the water. She had loving and indulgent grandparents. She did well in school. She won prizes for her writing. And her mother always encouraged her, listened to her, read to her, and took her to plays. Like many children and grandchildren of immigrants, Sylvia eagerly sought a place for herself and the acknowledgment of others that would fulfill the dreams she and her mother partnered in.

On August 10, 1941, Sylvia published her first poem, titled simply "Poem," in the *Boston Herald*, a brief evocation of sounds and sights, the crickets and fireflies of a hot summer night. The advent of Sylvia Plath in print meant she already had a public to please, a career to cultivate. The world was watching. How to speak, how to act, came in lessons from her mother, who took Sylvia to the theater to watch plays such as *The Tempest*, which is about Prospero, a kind of imagineer (to use a Walt Disney term) who can call forth a spirit like Ariel. What you put on the page could animate the world.

5

After Otto Plath's death, the resourceful Aurelia found temporary work teaching German and Spanish in a Jamaica Plain high school, but in order to support herself and her children, she had to regroup, selling her home in Winthrop and moving with her parents in the fall of 1942 to 23 Elmwood Road in Wellesley, Massachusetts. Winthrop remained, however, part of Sylvia's experience. She made return visits to play with David and Ruth Freeman and Wayne Sterling.

Aurelia had wanted to attend Wellesley College but could not afford it. She wanted her daughter to have that opportunity and looked forward to Sylvia's earning a town scholarship. Wellesley College was a Seven Sisters school, a group of historically women's colleges that included Radcliffe, Vassar, Barnard, Bryn Mawr, Mount Holyoke, and Smith. Thus Sylvia grew up with a destination in mind.

The white clapboard house in a suburban-looking neighborhood deprived Sylvia of the sea that is such an important part of her poetry and prose. She shared a room with her mother, who secured a teaching post at Boston University while Sylvia attended the Marshall Livingston Perrin Grammar School.

6

In July 1943, Aurelia suffered a gastric hemorrhage and sent Sylvia to her first summer camp at Camp Weetamoe in Ossipee, New Hampshire. She wrote her mother postcards about the bugle calls to breakfast, swimming, hiking, blueberry harvesting, boat rides on Ossipee Lake, and arts and crafts classes (making a purse for her grandmother). Sylvia's postcards are replete with dutiful, meticulous accounts of prodigious meals, the result, Heather Clark explains, of Aurelia's worry early on that her daughter was a poor eater. Sylvia sent home six photographs, after carefully calculating her expenses for laundry, food, and paper dolls (Rita Hayworth and Hedy Lamarr). She enjoyed her mother's letters and news of home. Aurelia saved all of this correspondence, abetting her daughter's urge to memorialize their lives.

Preparations for war were palpable, Wayne Sterling recalled. Winthrop was an "armed camp" with three forts, and black outs, with no lights at night along the shore. In the afternoons Sylvia and her friends would sit on the Point Shirley seawall and watch the convoys and torpedo practice. [HR] But the war was brought much closer to home during Christmas 1943, when Sylvia's Uncle Frank and Aunt Louise visited, bringing with them a friend, Gibby Wyer, who had been in the Africa Medical Corps in Egypt and in the "campaign to chase Rommel out of Africa. He was with Montgomery's 8th army," Sylvia noted in her diary. Wyer showed her a German bayonet, a German pistol, a German camera, a German belt, a German helmet, and German binoculars. Karen Goodall, who lived next door to Sylvia's Aunt Dorothy, remembered Frank Schober as a "gallant" man who doted on his niece and never tired of answering her questions—no matter how silly—about both world wars. He was also a bit of a "dandy," who wore cologne and stood out from the sober Schobers, with a "white linen strolling outfit" for good weather, complete with Panama hat and spats. [HR]

7

For Christmas, 1943, Aurelia presented Sylvia with a pocket diary. In the first entry for January 1, 1944, she resolved to be kinder to people and to curb her critical sensibility that had manifested in her negative remarks about her

Scene from the film of Charlotte Brontë's *Jane Eyre* (1943), starring Joan Fontaine (Jane) and Orson Welles (Rochester); Clayton Moore as the Lone Ranger (circa 1950s). Like Superman, the Lone Ranger is a hero in disguise, and perhaps expressive of Sylvia's desire for a rescuing figure in the wake of her father's death.

fellow campers. She recounted monopoly games, playing with paper dolls, pasting movie star pictures in her scrapbook, skating and sliding on pond ice, and snowball fights. She was pretty rugged, noting in her diary entry for March 16, 1944: "Our 2 girl army attacked the boys. As a result we were soaked when we came in . . . I got my face washed in the snow." She spent many days participating in Girl Scout activities, composing school reports (including one on Marie Curie), recording her high grades, and reading books such as *Jane Eyre* and *Gone with the Wind*. She watched the film of Charlotte Brontë's novel several times. Jane's attraction to Mr. Rochester, a kind of Superman and Lone Ranger (two of Sylvia's favorite radio serials), figured into her later search for a powerful male figure whose dangerous side she confronted in "Daddy."[8]

Reading, always reading: "I am in a reverie of happiness for I love books," she wrote on April 19, 1944. Boys could be a pesky nuisance, bumping into her sled and stuffing snow down her back, but she noticed a blond and handsome boy in class and another one "<u>so</u> handsome." She had other favorites whom she listed in her diary under the heading "Boys I like."

She also liked to jump into bed with Warren and read the funnies. Sister and brother played together often, sharing a passion for stamps: "My Jamestown Stamp offer came today and Warren and I gloated over the stamps," she confided to her diary on December 12, 1945. They liked games and winter sports, and they shared just about everything, including chores like shoveling snow. Occasionally they were "bad," to use Sylvia's word, and had fights, but judging from her diary those upsets were rare. It is not too much to say she was proud of her little brother. She went on frequent walks with her Grammy and visited the country club where her Grampy worked. She delighted in making them Christmas presents and having them there for family celebrations.

The competitive Sylvia ranked herself against her classmates, confessing her shame at receiving a B+ on her music report card. She paid attention to Sunday school sermons. She missed school days due to illness but quickly recovered. Aurelia read to Sylvia and Warren at night from *The Yearling* by Marjorie Kinnan Rawlings. Sylvia went to movies like *Lassie Come Home* and watched newsreels about the war. She played cards with Grammy and Warren. She mentioned jumping rope seventy-five times in succession and performing her first cartwheel—"(If it could be called that) and everybody laughed." She helped clean house with some satisfaction: "I feel I am being quite a help lately."

At school, Sylvia's favorite teacher, Miss Norris, assigned books and read to students works that broadened their sense of history, culture, and the world, including classes about the opera (Verdi's *Aida*), *The Blacksmith of Vilno: A Tale of Poland in 1832*, and *The Trumpeter of Krakow* (a young adult historical novel with many plot twists, set in medieval Krakow and involving precious jewels, evil alchemists, and other nefarious characters as well as plundering Tartars). Sylvia added titles like *Johnny Tremain* (set in revolutionary Boston), *When a Cobbler Ruled a King* (set during the French Revolution), *The White Isle* (about Roman Britain), and many other historical and contemporary stories in both exotic and American settings.

A diary entry for June 28, 1944, records a note Sylvia sent to her mother with a drawing of a chicken with four eggs captioned "A proud mother." The entry mentions finding a quarter and nickel and spending twenty cents on Rita Hayworth and Hedy Lamarr doll books, saving the remaining five cents for a defense stamp. This is quintessential Sylvia Plath: Her concern with domestic life, Hollywood, and the glamour of personality and fashion, and then her awareness of what is out there: the world and war. Not to mention her careful economy and keen awareness of what things cost. A concern with economizing seems to have been a family trait, remarked upon by one of Otto Plath's colleagues, who used the word "frugality" when reporting on Otto Plath's suggestion that bacon grease be saved for "use in cakes and other cookery." [HR]

8

For two weeks in July 1944, Sylvia attended Camp Helen Storrow at Buzzard's Bay, Massachusetts, averaging a letter a day to her mother, reporting on her swimming and hiking and her enjoyment of arts and crafts and of shows, masquerading with charcoal on her face as a "pickaninnny." The world was White, although for purposes of play you could be Black. Nowhere in Plath's comments on people she called Negroes is there evidence of any significant engagement with racial issues, or even much empathy for Black victims of discrimination. She grew up in the era of civil rights protests (for example, the Montgomery Bus Boycott, 1955–1956) but showed no interest in the marches for equal treatment under the law. She read newspapers but did not comment on the plight of minorities (except for Jews). She lived in a White World.[9]

Near the ocean, the all-White camp revived her memories of an early childhood by the sea. She made a ninety-page book listing her favorite actresses (Shirley Temple, Margaret O'Brien, and Elizabeth Taylor), her schedule at camp, the enormous quantities of food she consumed, the length of her walks, and other camp activities.

Sylvia's diaries, meticulously kept for almost every day from 1944 to 1949, reflect her early realization that you could broadcast your own life, as Jack Benny did on his radio show (another of her favorites). The show dispensed a running commentary on his funny failings, his desire to get ahead, and his preening, and had a cast—including Rochester, the faithful, if not uncritical African American factotum—that became Benny's retinue, commenting on his every mercenary move. Later, in London, in the last years of her life, Plath would speak of a desire to create a salon of writers, a following that would situate her at the center of literary life. At an early age, Plath realized you could incorporate yourself in a medium. You could reach out to the public and command a hearing. She would later exploit this medium in her appearances on BBC radio. Her best poetry, she would come to realize, should be spoken aloud, perfected in a voice that she worked on, transforming a regional New England accent into a broader Anglo-American style of speaking that reflected her transcontinental ambitions.

These early diaries show a sensibility already well formed and with a presentiment of destiny, which she defined in her diaries by setting down certain markers:

January 20, 1944: Today is the biggest day of my life. I had a dreamless sleep and woke as fresh as dew on spring buttercups. All day I was in another world, far better than this. I took the bus to Boston with mother and Warrie to see Shakespeare's "The Tempest" at the Colonial Theatre. It was too perfect for words. I am keeping the program as a souvenir. We took the train to Wellesley and there were no separate seats. I sat next to a young sensitive boy from the navy. He had blond wavy hair and blue eyes. In all my life I will never love anyone as I did him. Our talk was of travels, life, Shakespeare.

Later, her marriage to Ted Hughes would seem impulsive and hasty, but in fact she had been looking for just such a man almost as soon as she could write. She had a sense of the transcendent, of how art can supersede all else, before she turned twelve.

Wayne Sterling remembered that sometime in 1944, when Sylvia was twelve, she initiated a conversation about what it was like to be Jewish. She had no contact with Jews in Winthrop or Wellesley, so Wayne couldn't say what prompted her interest. [HR] Her diary entry for January 15 mentioned "trying to make a crazy statue of Hitler in the snow with no success." Perhaps that swastika on the flagpole in Winthrop had caught her attention. Her diary entry for November 25, 1945, recounted a "very interesting" Sunday School talk by a Jewish girl about Jewish customs and beliefs. "She promised to take us to a Jewish Synagogue in the future. I had a beautiful time listening to her." On January 25, 1946, a neighbor, Mr. Norton, took her to the Temple of Israel in Boston. The light in the shape of the Star of David entranced her, as did the impressive white marble pulpit and the Torah in the ark. She listened to a rabbi explaining Judaism. She was impressed. "I had a beautiful time," she confided to her diary. She drew a kiddish cup, challah, and a Star of David.

School assignments like a "problem paper" on "Roman People's Places, and Things" and the work for her Scout "World Knowledge Badge" meant that as she entered adolescence Sylvia Plath was already attuned to the history and geography that propelled her later work. By the age of twelve, Plath's school curriculum included a social studies class that covered, for example, units on the Albany Plan of Union (an early effort to unite the American colonies in a common defense) and General Braddock's North America campaign against the French during the Seven Years War. She drew several maps of the United States and mapped out important historical events like the Louisiana Purchase and the issuance of the Monroe Doctrine.

At twelve, Sylvia measured five feet three and one-half inches, weighed about ninety-five pounds, and was athletic, participating in volleyball, baseball, field hockey, and basketball, where she played the position of guard. She collected stamps from all over the world and exulted in a trip to Boston to purchase a stamp album at the Harris Stamp Company. She tended her own garden and marveled how in the spring it looked "lovely as it is full of sprouting green leaves and sweet smelling, fresh overturned earth." She watched birds. "I saw the most beautiful bird today," she wrote in her diary. "It was a little smaller than a robin and had the most beautiful blue plumage and red breast. I found out later that it was a bluebird and the first I have seen this spring."

9

On March 27, 1945, her class visited the Christian Science Monitor building where she saw the printing room and watched how the newspaper was cut and printed, an excursion she meticulously documented in her diary entry about a "magic afternoon." Some of her first articles would be published in the *Monitor*. Her own diaries, profusely illustrated—sometimes in color— suggest the importance of book making to her. In the eighth grade, on the staff of her school publication, *The Phillipian*, she was determined to put out a "super magazine."

10

The war was an ever-present part of young Sylvia's life. She played a game called "Russia" about the German invasion of the Soviet Union. On April 11, 1945, she mentioned she was put in charge of Defense Stamps at school. The next day she recorded her shock: "ROOSEVELT DIES!," adding: "He died, like Lincoln, soon—very soon before the peace treaty and end of a long, cruel war!" On August 8, 1945, Sylvia wrote in her diary: "Atom bomb!" She read that 60 percent of Hiroshima had been destroyed, but made no comment other than to report President Truman's statement that nuclear energy could be used for both destructive and constructive purposes. On August 14, at 7:00 p.m., Sylvia heard on the radio the "official word . . . that Pres. Truman has received the note from Japan saying 'We surrender unconditionally.' The end of World War II!!!!!!! How the people shouted! How the whistles blew. At night we set off firecrackers and rockets. We all thank God for answering our prayers." The war penetrated her conscious-ness in other ways too. DPs, as displaced persons were then called, appear in a diary entry describing how she joined a group of girls dressed in "old rags" who "went to one house to pretend we were refugees, but, fortunately, (for us, probably), no one was home." Does it make too much of this early effort to say she was already impersonating the persecuted, even if others would be offended and would call a poem like "Daddy" a despicable act of appropriation?

Sylvia read widely in teen and young adult novels that exposed her to many different cultures and to European and world history. On September 23, 1945, she mentions finishing *A Sea between Us*, reviewed in *Commentary*. This novel, by Lavinia R. Davis, struck close to home: "The heroine encounters the dragon of anti-Semitic prejudice early in the story during a visit to her fiancé's family in a locality resembling Cape Cod." The reviewer concluded: "For the problem of anti-Semitic prejudice, long underground in American life, to have forced its way through the pasteboard walls of a story for girls probably indicates that its pros and cons are more largely discussed today than many of us realize. It is comforting to learn even from a young ladies' handbook that our society's mores still denounce discrimination against Jews as unfair and undemocratic."

11

Wayne Sterling remembered a bike ride in which he discussed with Sylvia the suicide of a Wellesley student who had hung himself from a tree. Sylvia seemed mainly concerned with what it would be like to be "almost dead"—a curious phrase that calls to mind her later interest in D. H. Lawrence's *The Man Who Died*, about a resurrected Christlike figure, and also, of course, her own "Lady Lazarus," which suggests the speaker has a gift for coming back from the dead. Was Plath, with the early death of her father, already drawn to near-death experiences and beginning to think of life as a series of resurrections? This is the premise of Connie Palmen's biographical novel about Plath and Hughes, *Your Story, My Story*.

Plath's early diaries (1944–1947), studded with exclamation marks in many entries, and her letters and postcards from camp to her mother and Warren express an exuberant personality, eager to share her adventures and pleasures with her family. Warren and Aurelia reciprocated and Sylvia rejoiced in their "fat" and "meaty" letters that other campers envied. She made going to camp seem like a family enterprise, and that dynastic delight carries through right to her final days in England, when she wrote home wishing that newly married Warren or his wife could join her. Her desire to assemble a salon, a group of likeminded souls, is reminiscent of her days at camp when she celebrated in letters and diaries the new friends that formed a circle around her. She began diary entries "Dear Diary," as if addressing an alter ego and putting her life in order. "Dear Diary—you're one of the 'musts' for peace of mind," she wrote on October 11, 1945. Sometimes she wrote as if addressing a future self: On April 29, 1946, she announced: "Today the most wonderful thing happened!" She had sent in a "picturesque speech" to *The Reader's Digest*: "A milkweed parachute hitchhikes on a passing breeze." To her diary, she confessed "It may sound amateurish to you later, but to me it sounded pretty good."

Entering her teens, diary entries no longer are studded with quite as many exclamation marks. She was developing a remarkable vocabulary, composing a poem, "A Winter Sunset," that describes a sky of "copen shades." Ice on the trees shimmers like diamonds. Teachers noticed her talent. Mrs. Warren told her she had a "flair" for English. "She firmly believes I have a talent for oral talks," Sylvia recorded in her diary for February 12, 1946. A month later, Mrs. Warren took her aside and told her any professor would regard her work highly and she could apply to college as a scholarship student. But like most students, she tired of the school regimen: "Ugh! I am getting very eager for vacation," she confided to her diary on March 25.

Some days were just ecstatic. Coasting with Warren on the playground: "We had a super time. The hill rose shining, white and vacant. We flew down and the stinging wind brought tears to our eyes. It was glorious!" She drew a picture and wrote: "I'll never forget the feeling of those silver runners slashing through the crusty snow!" These early revelries in snow would in just a few years dissolve into the symbolism of a numbing snow/cold that would haunt her later letters and depressions. In "Tulips at Dawn," a poem written on the cusp of 1947/48, she speaks of plunging into the "depths of austere whiteness," and of "white flashes of cold" lancing her wings, a "captive / Of white worlds."

Sylvia liked to write about cooking in Food class—quite a variety of desserts, sandwiches, and main dishes—not to mention making her favorite molasses cookies at home ("yum yum"). She also took up knitting. On January 28, 1946, she recorded a visit to an Observatory: "I will never forget my first view of Saturn through the telescope! I expected a little point of light and gasped as I saw the three rings of moonlets whirling about the silvery planet." Like other bright young girls of her generation such as Susan Sontag, Plath enthused over Richard Halliburton's travel books: *The Royal Road to Romance*, *The Flying Carpet*, *The Glorious Adventure*, and *New Worlds to Conquer*. "They're full of lovely expressions and descriptions," she wrote to a friend. When a schoolmate lent her *Richard Halliburton's Complete Book of Marvels* with a picture of him on the back, she confessed: "I am in love with him. I feel as though I understand him. (Being on his fourth book.)" But another kind of adventure also appealed to her. On April 8, 1946, she had her first dream about the "lives and works" of American artists. Her imagination took another turn with mystery-horror stories like "The Mummy's Tomb," which began: "[A] gloomy atmosphere of foreboding pervaded the chill air." She added a sentence to her friend Margot's horror story: "The delicious smell of frying flesh reached my nostrils." She hoped that after camp was over, she could spend part of the summer with Margot: "Can't you just see us lying on soft pine needles," she wrote to a friend who also wrote stories, "and writing best-sellers in the quiet serenity of the woods?"

But it wasn't ever just a make-believe world for her: In a Memorial Day school assembly (May 29, 1946), a soldier spoke about "incidents of war and victory overseas, not forgetting to mention the long rows of white crosses filling the many green clearings holding the American and allied dead. It was really quite sad. Oh! but I do hope that there will be no more wars"—a sentiment she expressed many times in her diaries, and a few years later in an antiwar poem, "Seek No More the Young," inspired by Wilfred Owen and Siegfried Sassoon, depicting the "iron men" who fall limp on "spattered stone" with "eyes glazed blind." She felt "very strongly about the subject of world peace," she asserted in an April 2, 1947, diary entry: "I felt as if I had suddenly come into contact with the turbulent political world outside when Carrie showed us the paper, among those distributed by the Socialist party . . . I was gripped by a cold, tense excitement that made me and my ideas an important part of the chaos in the world today." With only the chirping of purple grackles, and the sight of her Grampy's "cheery pile" of "treasured compost," she wondered how "murder and ugly quarrels" could go on in such a "beautiful world." But then a fire engine came "screeching around the corner." She would remain the same, more than a decade later, cultivating her own garden in her Court Green country home retreat, thrusting her hands in the soil while worrying about the strontium 90 radioactive fallout in mother's milk.

12

Wayne Sterling seems to have been the first boy that Sylvia centered on. Next to his name she drew a heart in her diary entry for April 13, 1946. "Oh boy! (It's all I can say)," she added about this boy as tall she was with sandy hair and dark eyes. "Oh! is he cute!" The gentleman offered his bike to ride and accompanied her to the bus stop after her weekend in Winthrop was over. She liked the attention. At a sleepover with her friend Betsy, she spent a good part of the night talking about Wayne. Nearly a year later, it was all up with Wayne, who "really thinks he's something—poor, mis-informed boy!" A pattern, and *The Bell Jar* voice, began emerging in her choice of beaux and in beatitudes that became rebuffs but also reconciliations. She was not through with Wayne nor Wayne with her. "Wayne was unusually cool to me," she wrote in a diary entry for March 8, 1947. "In the living room he revealed the horrible truth! He had persuaded my beebee-brained brother to let him have my precious diary last night, and he had read it all in his room while the rest of us were sleeping." He quoted the worst parts about his "shallow character. . . . Mum said later he was really terribly hurt! Heaven knows I write things here that I don't mean two minutes later— but!" After her tense day of feeling sorry about "hurting anyone's feelings," Wayne called, they talked, and they "sort of made up." Sort of. Just days later Wayne rang and thought it "funny to have another boy over and call me up, yet do nothing but talk to the other boy while I wait every minute more impatiently. . . . I think he is nauseating, and if he ever reads this again and sees what I think it will serve him right for being so conceited and nosy!" She took to calling him Little Lord Fauntleroy.

13

Few writers have pinpointed the exact moment when they feel their child-hood has ended, but Sylvia Plath did in a diary entry for October 22, 1946, five days before her fourteenth birthday. She noted that she no longer looked forward to her birthday with the usual excitement. She was "growing old," even if it still seemed strange to now "take things as a matter of course." This melancholy, Wordsworthian lament, evoking the sheer joy of existence that made the child father of the man, now enveloped Sylvia Plath. The next day she wrote: "FAREWELL TO ALL DRAWINGS—THERE WILL BE NO MORE SUCH THINGS HEREIN! (SOB!)" In her earlier diaries she summed up virtually every day in a picture—really an exuberance of spirit that she would still be able to express in her drawings and writing, but with that mature sense of having to summon the "natural piety" of childhood, the intimations of immortality that protect children, for a while, from the mortal world.

She was learning things that could have been the plot of a Raymond Chandler or William Faulkner novel. Three weeks before her fourteenth birthday she met Philip McCurdy for the first time. He was raised in

Wellesley by a single mother, although he had only recently learned the true circumstances of his upbringing. He told her a riveting story about how he discovered that his sister was actually his mother, that his father was actually his grandfather. He had never met his birth father, who remained apart from his son. Single-parented Sylvia warily shared some of her own feelings about her father's death, although she was not yet prepared, as in "Daddy," to let out the horror of the story or treat it with the kind of black humor you can find in a Billy Wilder film. That poem would not find its shape and trajectory until she was far away not only from her mother but from the grandparents who, for a time, filled the void of Otto Plath's absence.

By ninth grade she had read *Wuthering Heights* and at first called it "morbid," but she stuck with it, and as she read on in her favorite spot, up in the apple tree, she had to admit it was "interesting." In the fall of 1946, she went on a Dickens kick, reading *A Tale of Two Cities*: "It is the most wonderful, magnificent book I've ever read! the characters and plot are superb. Indeed, it is a book I will always want to have to refer to." She went on to read *David Copperfield* and *Oliver Twist*. She copied Sara Teasdale's poems into her diary, including "Full Moon," invoking a "broad white disk of flame / And on the garden-walk a snail beside me / Tracing in crystal the slow way he came." Sylvia commented: "What I wouldn't give to be able to write like this!"

The reading in Dickens and a friendship with Mary, a seventeen-year-old English exchange student, immersed Sylvia in English culture, when she was not enthralled with Dumas's *Three Musketeers* and having a dreamy look at a six-foot-four Frenchman who demonstrated the rhumba in her dance class. His accent mesmerized her, and his size and speech were a combination that stood out as she graded other dance partners from "no glamour," to "wish-washy," to "perfect" to "adorable" to "ATOMIC." Closer to home, she continued to moon over Wayne Sterling and was touched when he wrote a letter to her—not something she was used to getting from even the boys who paid attention to her. She still recognized male privilege, saying after a spelling contest that it was "nice" that a boy won without expressing any regret for placing second herself. Yet she had clearly marked out her ambition. In a diary entry for January 24, 1947, she included her poem "Fireside Reveries," in which she sits, a book of poems in her lap, watching "through the living screen of fire . . . My thoughts to shining fame aspire / For there is much to do and dare." She addressed her diary on January 31, 1947: "who knows someday you might be in print. Once I start to write it is so hard to stop. There are so many things that I feel deeply about and want to get written down in here before it is to [sic] late and they have slipped away."

On February 2, 1947, she purchased a scrapbook and labeled it using India ink in "old English letters": "Sylvia Plath—1947." She pasted in snapshots of herself as a child and of her friends, filling up "every empty space" with "a more or less running account of my life history and descriptions of my experiences."

By the age of fourteen she was mastering *Julius Caesar* in English class and quoting to her classmates her Kipling favorites, including the "throbbing rhythm of": "Bloomin' idol made o' mud — / Wot they called the Gret Gawd Budd — / Plucky lot she cared for idols when / I kissed her where she stud!" The England of adventure and romance came calling long before Ted Hughes came on the scene. At a ninth-grade assembly she danced with a "tall, blonde, droolsome guy with an English accent!" She came home "very much elated" and speaking in the accents of Scarlett O'Hara: "why sho!" On May 17, 1947, she declared her ambition to win "recognition in fashion designing, journalism, book-illustrating, or something tied in with my two specialities, and THEN to go on a trip around the world, staying as long at each spot as I wish!"

14

On Father's Day June 15, 1947, Sylvia, nearing fifteen, created a "card of our iris for grampy." No mention of her father, with whom she had shared her poems and stories. The family gathered for the "grandest time!" she recorded in her diary. Was this silence about Otto of a piece with her mother's decision not to have her children attend his funeral? Nowhere in Sylvia's early diaries is there any sort of reference to the father who became the colossus of her later work.

As usual, Sylvia went away to summer camp—this time near Martha's Vineyard. She relished group activities that included biking, sailing, theatrical events, crafts, and the like. The author of *The Bell Jar*, highly critical of her contemporaries and also an observer and creator of fashion, obtrudes in her otherwise chipper diary entries and jolly missives to her mother. She liked a lot of girls at camp, she confided to her diary on July 9, 1947, but she had noted their faults that she had kept to herself. Gloria, for example, was "too insulting and boisterous" with "no scruples about anybody's feelings." Gloria had said "I was much too tall and thin in a disgusted tone of arrogance," but then Gloria was "muscular, short," and had "thick lips." Anne was usually nice but sometimes conceited and boastful. Sally was "dear" but became tiresome, calling everyone "Poopies." June was sweet but sometimes impatient and shrill. Others like Junior, Jan, and Andy gained unqualified approval. It was important to write all this down so she could "get it off my chest and act a lot nicer that way!" What the girls thought of her is hard to say, of course, but they did leave her with this parting ditty that she called "sweet": "O quite an actress is our Sherry; / Her, 'Woman, woman women!' makes us scary." Sherry, the camp name she made up for herself, allowed her, she told her diary, to be another person, and her fellow campers seemed to have understood that what they experienced had been, in fact, a persona.

She indulged in an elaborate description of the camp's final dinner and decorations complete with a "formal dance" that tuned her up for her later summer internship at the fashionable *Mademoiselle*. "I'm going to be the boy," Sylvia reported,

> and I am escorting Ann as my best girl. She is wearing a gown of white towels decorated (each) with a large pastel rose. In the back of the skirts she has a shorter towel brought to uniform length with the others by a stylish towel ruffle. She is also wearing a ruffly white blouse for a top, and I have already made the corsage which I'm going to present to her—yellow and white daisies with two lacy ferns for a background and tied neatly together with thread.

Sylvia dressed herself in dark blue slacks and a long-sleeved sailor top with her hair "done up under a rather rakish sailor hat." She made the most of her tall figure, playing the roles that men carried off with dispatch while women, she would later note, circumscribe themselves to the demure.

Sylvia Plath marked her moments, treating the end of summer camp as an eventful, even profound episode: "A chapter of my life has closed. It has been brief, but every moment has been filled with the glory of <u>real living</u>. I feel inexplicably different inside—a little too old for my outer shell." This tendency to encapsulate her life into epochs suggests the epic scale on which she lived, and how she could regard two weeks of camp, or a month in the city, as definitive of victory or defeat, progress or failure, with her fate decided in a matter of hours, or even minutes. She had a habit of experiencing all of time at once, which is to say that every moment had all of time within it and what she would make of that time. Her arrival home from camp was also telling: "The house seems dreadfully quiet and the walls seemed to crowd in on me at first, but now I'm used to it all." These periods of adjustment were never easy but could be overcome in the most ordinary ways: "It's so wonderful to be spotlessly clean again, and to <u>sleep between</u> crisp <u>white sheets</u>."

15

Already, at fourteen, Sylvia recorded in her diary certain concatenations of events that would accelerate in her middle and later years. Watching a movie, reading a book, a chance encounter with strangers would set her off. In Boston, shortly after her return home from camp, on July 12, 1947, her mother took her to see *Cynthia*, starring Elizabeth Taylor as a young girl with watchful, anxious parents.[10] Sylvia noted that the film "solved many of my own problems." What those were she did not say, but the film emphasizes the way Cynthia is invalided by her parents—her constant sneezing might have reminded Sylvia of her sinus infections and frequent colds and fevers that in fact masked a perfectly healthy young woman.

What was Sylvia thinking as she sat beside her mother watching Cynthia almost always with books in her hands? Like Aurelia, Cynthia's mother, Louise, has sacrificed her own dreams to take care of her daughter. When Cynthia declares her independence, Louise realizes that cosseting her daughter has

Scene from *Cynthia* (1947), starring Elizabeth Taylor (Cynthia Bishop), Mary Astor (Louise Bishop), and George Murphy (Larry Bishop).

"With a voice like yours, you'll be the hit of the show!"

Elizabeth Taylor (Cynthia Bishop), S. Z. Sakall (Professor Rosenkrantz), Jimmy Lyndon (Ricky Latham) in *Cynthia* (1947).

been all wrong. Cynthia seeks the adventures that her mother once sought but never acted upon. The movie seared itself into Sylvia's sensibility, telling her early on that the only way to realize her true potential involved taking risks, even though the country had been through a depression and the trauma of war—alluded to in the film during talk of shortages. Encouraged by her teachers, observing new patterns of behavior in the mass media of film and radio, Sylvia grew up in a generation imbued with, in David Riesman's words, "the possibility of change." She was also preparing her mother to accept the decision to depart from the safe environs of Wellesley for Smith College.

That *Cynthia* continued to reverberate in Sylvia's mind is apparent in her decision to enter a *Cynthia* contest, noted in her diary for September 15, 1947.[11] "Cynthia Clubs," organized for girls between fourteen and nineteen, were part of a marketing campaign for the movie that included a line of Cynthia clothes, reflecting a cultural and generational shift toward the driving force of children and young adults.[12] That shift would be noted in Riesman's *The Lonely Crowd*, which Sylvia read a dozen years after watching *Cynthia*, as she continued to struggle with her mother's constant vigilance while in therapy with Ruth Beuscher.

16

Already, Aurelia's careful monitoring of her daughter, and her daughter's constant checking in by postcard nearly every day of camp, may have contributed to Sylvia's desire to leave home and the safe environs of Wellesley. Yet the pull of home and heritage remained powerful as she watched a second film also on September 15, 1947, *The Great Waltz*, about Johann Strauss, "beautiful filmed" with "heavenly" music. "I just had tears stream down my face through till the very end," Sylvia confided to her diary. "The Waltzes really brought out the <u>Austrian</u> in me." And then, on the way home, as her bus stopped, some boys yelled "Hey Blondie!" One of them reached into the open window and pulled her hair. She blushed red when people on the bus looked at her. "NOT that I'm blonde, of course," she told her diary, "but it does something to a girl's morale to have even strange boys pay attention to her. I felt very happy about the whole evening!" Happy, not annoyed. Happy, not disconcerted. She bathed in the male gaze; it gave her a burn, so to speak, that would later energize her after Ted Hughes decamped, and she sallied out on London streets to the conspicuous delight of male passersby.

Ever the enthusiast, she began to see love in cosmic, occult terms. "If I had to pick one day of my life to live over, this would be IT!" she announced on July 15, 1947. She had come from dinner with her mother's friend, Madeline, and her son, sixteen-year-old Redmond. "Oh, Diary! I've never <u>seen</u> such a nice boy!" He was very good looking but not conceited "like <u>some</u> people I know." They liked the same things and talked about them effortlessly as she took in his dark, wavy hair and "astonishingly dark brown eyes." He put his hand over hers and *she* didn't mind. Oh, how he looked at her "sort of out of the corner of his dark eyes," so "understanding" and "natural." Tingles ran up and down her veins and she felt "sort of wobbly," nearly fainting from "sheer happiness! M-m-m!"

The next day on the way home in a downpour from her first disastrous piano lesson at the conservatory, the rain stopped as she fit the key into the front door "as if propelled by some unseen and very mocking power! ('I'm in love with someone.')" Six weeks later, she had changed her mind. She wondered: Did Redmond change or did she? After they went to see the film of *Great Expectations* together, she sounded a little like Dickens's Estella, that breaker of men's hearts, or even Lady Lazarus who "eats men like air": "He is not as interesting or talkative as before." Several months later she had a similar experience with John Pollard, who took her out on what she considered her first real date (not connected to a school activity). She found his boorish effort to become intimate "nauseating," and yet she accepted a second date with him—apparently because dating, as she put it in another entry, brought her to the attention of other boys and because, perhaps, she did not want to shy away from unpleasantness as part of what she needed to know about the world.

17

August 16, 1947: *Gone with the Wind*: "I promised myself to see the picture ever since I was a little girl and read the book five years ago," she confided to her diary. Transported to the "magic world of the past. I was Scarlett O'Hara—with all my beaus flocked around me." Afterwards she walked out of the theater's "velvet blackness" worn out after "five hours of exciting drama." It had been "thrilling and intense," exactly the kind of life she imagined for herself.

Clark Gable (Rhett Butler) and Vivien Leigh (Scarlett O'Hara) in *Gone with the Wind* (1939).

Shortly after seeing the movie, this Scarlett O'Hara of Wellesley suffered the kind of disaster that threatened her singularity: "Oh Diary! I had my hair cut today. Mother told the barber to cut off the tip ends about one inch, and he cut off three or four. My hair came out straight, bushy, not quite shoulder-length, and heartbreaking both to mother and me." At home, in tears, she lamented: "my long curly brown hair with the gleaming blonde and copper lights in it has always been considered my crowning glory." She felt she had lost a "good part of my 'looks.'" She went to Betsy Powley's, where Betsy's mother arranged her hair in a "becoming array of soft, turned-under curls." She had never appreciated her "true friends . . . until this crisis in my life." She was overjoyed to learn bridge at the Powleys, "since it is a great social asset." The Powleys took a great interest in Sylvia, and she was grateful. The Nortons and the Freemans rounded out a world that made a huge place for this girl with such huge appetites and ambitions. At a family reunion on August 31, 1947, Sylvia met several distant relatives, one of whom she said she could have kissed "when she asked me if I went to college. She said she thought that I was at least seventeen or eighteen years old!"

She wanted to feel liberated, like an adult. Who doesn't at that age? Followed by some boys, her friend Ruthie bought a package of cigarettes to impress them and offered one to Sylvia, who puffed away, feeling "very guilty and wobbly-at-the-knees." She discovered that she could fake inhaling, confessing to her diary: "I had vowed never to smoke for dozens of reasons, but the desire to impress the world over-came me for a short while." The boys yelled, "Ohh! <u>Smoking!</u>" Sylvia dropped the cigarette in a sewer, feeling "very cheap and ashamed," and perhaps dirty.

Although adventures with female friends dominated Sylvia's diaries, she mentioned her brother Warren frequently and went out of her way to include him in her games and other activities. They rarely quarreled, although Aurelia said Sylvia baited him and did not stop until he was fifteen and taller than her. [HR] Sylvia wanted Warren to discover what she liked and make it his own. She took him canoeing, observing afterwards: "I enjoyed giving him the pleasure, for I knew he liked the ride."

18

On September 4, 1947, Sylvia wrote: "Today I commenced with school once more." She was now in Bradford Senior High and noted all the subjects she was taking (English, Math, French, Latin, Art, Gym, and Orchestra)

Edna St. Vincent Millay. Photograph by Arnold Genthe, 1914. Genthe photograph collection, Library of Congress, Prints and Photographs Division.

and that all the teachers were men except in Gym and French. "The men are indeed a welcome change! I am really almost glad to get back to the old grind." One inspiring teacher stood out: Mr. Crockett (like Cynthia's Professor Rosenkrantz) introduced Plath's class to Edna St. Vincent Millay. He played the poet's own recording of "Renascence" and "The Ballad of the Harp-Weaver." "They were both so beautiful that I could hardly keep from crying," Sylvia noted in her diary. At home, she wrote a poem, one of her best, that began "Alone and Alone in the Woods Was I," and another ending "These are the wan gray shreds of the tattered day." She felt like she was pouring out her soul: "I'm full of love and exuberance for everyone in the world."

Mr. Crockett was like no other teacher Plath had encountered. One of her classmates, Pat O'Neill, could see that her teacher rejected the complacency of the wealthy in Wellesley. He assigned *Babbitt*: "Then they'd go home to their bewildered capitalist fathers," O'Neill recalled. Crockett had a passion for social justice that made students aware of a world well beyond well-manicured Wellesley. Under suspicion in 1952 during the McCarthy witch hunt for Communists in American institutions, he convinced the Wellesley Town Board that he was not a subversive. [HR]

Mr. Crockett was not only demanding but intent on developing an esprit de corps among the very best students. When Sylvia read out a paper on Matthew Arnold, Mr. Crockett called out "well said" instead of the "unhuh" that typified his response to other students. She "just about burst with pride." Half the class had dropped out. "It seems we've had quite a desertion," said Mr. Crockett, smiling. Nineteen students left made it "nice," Sylvia thought. He told them they were a "likely lot" with "a knack for our subject." Note the "our"—his way of making the class special, as though he were addressing the elect. Mr. Crockett remembered Sylvia as attentive and interested in what other students had to say. During writing assignments classmate Pat O'Neill watched Sylvia put her arms around her work, as if protecting a "very private affair." She wrote quickly and seemed to enjoy the "simple act of writing." When Mr. Crockett called time, she sat back, satisfied. Pat compared Sylvia's compositions to filling in a water color with "wide penpoints" that came down on the paper rapidly. [HR]

Sylvia visited her teacher at his home. He called her "compassionate" and "very gracious," telling Harriet Rosenstein: "In the three years I taught her I never knew her to be disheartened or sour or less than able to cope." He saw nothing neurotic in an "eminently stable girl." Mr. Crockett sensed that she played the role of a well-rounded student. A part of her, he was certain, was elsewhere, detached—way beyond the limits of Wellesley.

Of course, there were sides of her not available to her teacher's scrutiny. Karen Goodall remembered a high-energy kid who could be exhausting, the equivalent of paying attention to six children. She could be all consuming, an "energy-stealer." Judging by the diaries Sylvia was not aware of how some people found her overbearing, not simply exuberant. She enlivened friends and family, turning her grandfather, for example, into a larger-than-life presence when she spent time with him. Without Sylvia, Karen observed, her grandfather returned to his everyday, "ordinary" manner. Why Karen found this aspect of Sylvia distasteful and not life-enhancing is not clear. To those like Karen, Sylvia's high spirits seemed overdone, even fake. Karen's parents called Sylvia "high-strung."

19

Nearing the age of fifteen, Sylvia Plath was already chafing at the societal restraints that she would later throw off when she first met Ted Hughes. After a music lesson at the Boston conservatory she spotted Bill MacGorty with the "cutest six-footer imaginable!" She gave Billy the "most dazzling smile he has probably ever received." Billy included her in the conversation, and as the "handsome stranger" departed from the bus, he cast a "long look" at her, and she responded with a "little smile"—the only way to preserve her demure demeanor. She wondered, though, why she couldn't just say "I like you and let him know." She was sure he wanted to meet her, but "it wouldn't be 'proper' to pick up a 'chance acquaintance' like that, no matter how nice it would seem to be." She did, however, throw "all conscience to the winds," roaring up Paine Street with Bob Tapley and Arden Tapley in a "baby blue Ford with the red trimmings, called Henry." They were joined by two more girls and two more boys. "How we got to Arden's house in one piece, I don't know."

Just a few weeks before her fifteenth birthday she noticed a change in herself, confessing that "lately I have acquired the discomforting habit of questioning those truths which my life had been based upon—such as religion, human nature, and other laws. I am also able to see the 'other person's side' so clearly and understandingly in its own light, that I am sometimes swayed by surges of doubt."

She had a happy fifteenth birthday, going into Boston with her mother to find the right dress, with "sales ladies about me like a chorus line; exclaiming with suitable gestures: 'Oh, how becoming!' and 'My! How sweet!' and 'What a dear child!'" At five feet eight inches tall, she found it hard to imagine herself as a "dear child," but: "Maybe some tall dark MAN might think so some time." The hapless biographer cannot help but think of Ted Hughes, not yet ready for his stage entrance. That she was looking for a male consort became a subject of conversation with her friends. Reading over her diary she concluded "I must have a one track mind—as Margot puts it (sadly)—I'm 'boy crazy.' Well I can't help that! . . . It is boring, I admit to reading over my accounts of my flame for the hour when I've changed to someone else, but then! It helps to write it down."

While Sylvia's early diaries reflect many experiences not so different from her contemporaries—or even from a young woman growing up today—the normality of her life was occasionally interrupted by events she absorbed with considerable intensity and with a desire to record them as precisely as possible in her diary. In mid-December, 1947, for example, she listened intently to Mr. Rice, minister at the Charles Street jail, describe to her fellow students the criminals awaiting trial: thieves, murderers, gunmen, a "Negro prostitute," and a traitor who had broadcast over Radio Berlin. At the prison, she noted the barred doors and how she would "never forget the huge room, three stories high, that confronted us—late Bostonian sun streamed in through the high, dusty streaked windows[,] thin railed cobwebs of iron stairways clung to the walls[,] and narrow iron walks high above bordered the three stories of cell blocks." They were not allowed to speak to the prisoners. She spotted a handsome tall boy jailed for a holdup looking at her as she kept her eyes on the floor. In the chapel, women prisoners whispered and giggled supervised by "two matrons in stiff starched white uniforms." She could hear one prisoner say, "Haven't they ever seen a prisoner before." Sylvia thought the pretty Negro with a "very curvy figure" was the prostitute Mr. Rice had mentioned. During Mr. Rice's sermon in the prison chapel, the men were quiet and the women "gossipy"—"what language they used!" Sylvia visited another building with padded and solitary confinement cells, "pitch black" with no windows or benches and a slot to slide through the bread and water. The warden "playfully" shut the visitors up in solitary. "It was awful!" The highlight of the trip was a prisoner's cell that featured his two-foot-high church built out of wooden matchsticks with an interior of "tiny carved pews" and an altar with "two wee gold candlesticks." He accepted their compliments with "proud embarrassment" and wished them a merry Christmas. Sylvia had a palpable sense, nearly at the beginning of her adolescence, of what it meant to be institutionalized.

20

Sylvia relished New England winters and often recorded her delight in sledding, or as she called it, "coasting." During a blizzard in early January 1948, she watched flakes float down and land on the "black, skinny angular branches" of birch trees. The "lumpy heaps shoveled from sidewalk and driveway are molded to even, sculptured white curves by the ever shifting wind and the ceaseless falling snow. It is indeed inspiring weather." In this still enchanted world of childhood the thermally protected young poet is not quite a decade away from freezing in the land of no central heating.

Sometimes her adolescence reads like a scene from Lillian Hellman's play *The Children's Hour*, in which certain aspects of the adult world, still secreted, have to be sought out clandestinely: With Betsy, she spent an afternoon on Grammy's bed "reading aloud to each other some spicy parts from two nasty books" she had "received a while ago." Just a few days later the illicit became a scene of betrayal, right out of Hellman's film *These Three*, in which two women, bonded to one another, fall in love with the same man. Sylvia suffered a "horrible shock" when, there on a street bench, she spotted two girls and a boy—Tommy Duggan kissing Betsy, who then saw Sylvia. The "look of mingled feelings on that girl's face I shall never forget!" Sylvia confided to her diary. She greeted them "non-chalantly" while they made no move to include her on the bench. "I could have cheerfully murdered all three of them then and there." At home, she burst into tears, and then later saw the "humor of it all." "If only it weren't Betsy!" In despair she cried out: "I'll get Tommy yet." Such moments—shifting from anger and grief to humor to more anger and grief—expressed a sensibility that would suffuse her poetry and prose. She recovered at a school assembly dance. For "Ladies' choice" she picked Tommy Duggan who kept holding her "tighter and tighter" until she was almost breathless. "I'm just so 'in love' with him that it hurts," she confessed to her diary, thinking of his chin against her cheek, "so manly and rough where he had shaved. I was just in dreamland. . . . Betsy can be kissed by him everyday and twice on Sunday but I've had this one triumphant night!"

The drama with Tommy Duggan continued, relieved by her friendship with Perry Norton: "He is so pure and wonderful. It just seems unnecessary to talk when we're together because our thoughts run along the same lines. I feel so natural and perfect when I'm with him . . . I feel as if I'm walking on an elevated plane and that there is no need for the little surface boy-girl chatter . . . I can be happy as long as Perry is alive." He always seemed to be there to relieve her anxieties, to dance with her when she did not have another partner, or just to listen to her concerns. She thought others were laughing at her "awkward predicament" about Tommy Duggan: "it isn't every day that a girl makes such a fool of herself by running after a boy!" Girls were not supposed to initiate relationships, and that led to outbursts—this one directed at Tommy: "I hate him because he knows I like him!!"

As Sylvia ventured further away from home with friends—boys and girls—joy riding in Bob Tapley's car, "Henry," she decided to keep that to herself, noting in her diary for March 18, 1948: "This is the first time in my life that I haven't told mother exactly where I went." She probably didn't want Aurelia to know what Bob said, while he was driving with one hand, playing a harmonica with the other, as they rammed a snowbank: "Just call me snowplow."

21

Her own escapades had no place in her sober letter to her German pen pal, Hans-Joachim Neupert on June 14, 1948. She clearly craved an outlet far different from what was available at home. Wellesley was not enough, and she wanted not merely to learn more about the world abroad but to engage as directly as possible with this world elsewhere. She called his writing "remarkably nice" and praised his command of English. She hoped they could exchange visits. Although college-bound students study hard, she told him, others were "carefree and jolly, thinking only of parties and fun." Still, "many of us have serious aims." She let him know about the "special magazines for young people." Then she mentioned that her father had been born in Germany and came to America as a boy, became a professor of German and biology at Boston University, and wrote a book about bees. Her father was dead, so her mother earned a living by teaching, but Sylvia revealed nothing about her feelings. She asked about the stories and poems Hans-Joachim read. She hoped to hear more about Germany but wanted more: "Would you like to compare some of our ideas about religion, war, or life or science?" She provided a map of her part of Massachusetts. She likened Wellesley to a "country-like" town but with the shops found in cities. She thanked him for his map and mentioned she could follow the course of the Rhine to his home in Grebenhain and had marked it with a star to show where he lived. She liked his photograph. "I look so forward to your next letter!" Typical of her tenacity and enthusiasm, she promised to write him on the day she received his next letter.

Sylvia was quite aware of a world elsewhere—so different from her own complacent, sheltered life, she told Hans-Joachim Neupert. "Perhaps when I get out of school and into the business world, that will change." She had some notion that entry into the "business world" would have a deeply unsettling impact on her—as it did four years later in her *Mademoiselle* summer in New York City.

22

In the summer of 1948, Sylvia returned to the Vineyard Sailing Camp. She wrote postcards to her mother every day—sometimes several a day—as she had done during previous summer camps. These messages were always full of her activities without much room for gauging her emotional temperature, which apparently rose when her mother visited in mid-July. What happened is not clear, except that Sylvia saw that her mother had exhausted herself in a run uphill, an incident that provoked a scolding postcard to "Naughty, naughty, mother" and the claim: "I don't know how you'd get along without me, really." This was joking that seems more than joking, since Sylvia followed up with this admission that is as consoling as it is concerning: "The aftermath of your visit was pleasant. I feel like I've had an emotional purge—all my pent up feelings let go when I cried, and I feel so much better." What pent-up feelings, she did not say. But such fugitive remarks suggest pressures that were rarely revealed in her writing. In the main, she exulted in camp: "These two weeks are flying by on wings of jam and cheese," she wrote to her mother.

23

Sylvia realized she swayed back and forth from the minute particulars of her existence to oceanic transcendence of the mundane. "Dear Mum," she wrote from camp. "Nothing special has happened except that I have, in the midst of my petty jealousies, found myself. I am filled with complete serenity and love for you and your cheery little cards which have arrived so faithfully!" Sylvia needed constant reassurance, as did her mother, and yet between them certain anxieties could not be allayed. She relied on a network of friendships and mentors that would later be lost to her during her final days. She shared with her mother her joy at getting cards from Mrs. Freeman, Ruthie's and David's mother, and from Wayne Sterling. She couldn't be herself without them. And when she found herself, at the last, without them—or others like them—her faith in her own existence faltered.

She could not be herself without cultivating an audience. She expressed her delight in getting a letter from Hans-Joachim Neupert—in her words, an "entertaining correspondent." She wanted him to know the "special place" in her heart for the ocean. "I like the way the water changes from one mood to another—from high waves on dark, stormy days, to tranquil

Olivia de Havilland (Virginia Cunningham) in *The Snake Pit* (1948).

ripples on sunny days." She might as well have been describing her own tidal personality. She wrote a review of the 1948 film *The Snake Pit* in which Olivia de Havilland, starring as Virginia Cunningham, suffers a mental illness that cannot be separated from the institutional context of her disorienting experience. This acute perception that so-called madness cannot be sorted out from society and culture stayed with Sylvia all the way to her final days when she feared the loss of her identity if she were to be institutionalized. In her high school report she lauded the film's depiction of the "woman's fight for her sanity" and the "struggle of the individual against the institution." For Cunningham not to know herself, to suffer shock treatments that deprived her, a novelist, of memories—the very stuff of a writer's material—profoundly disturbed Sylvia. Did she know that the film, adapted from a novel, was based on the author's harrowing experience?

24

The seductiveness of sex—not just the fun of going out with boys—seems to have first received serious attention in the summer of 1949 as she was approaching seventeen. "I am awful," she wrote on July 22. "I actually wanted to go parking." What she had in mind was necking and petting and forsaking the "prim part" she found hard to play. Still, she worried about her reputation and boys losing respect for her. "Why is everyone so embarrassed & secretive about physical differences & intercourse, etc.?" she asked in her diary. "Maybe if we could talk without such inhibitions, sex problems would be easier to solve."

In August, Sylvia did a psychological, physical, and sexual inventory: "reflections on this summer": She "could stand to gain a few pounds, and my complexion could be better, not to mention my personality." But she had "assets to balance my major failings," including her considerable experience "avec les garçons"—those she had loved and lost, pointing out "there's always another one around the corner." She listed the twenty-one boys she had dates with since the fall of 1948, putting an asterisk next to "memorable occasion" and two asterisks next to "memorable guy" for a total of four memorable occasions and three memorable guys. Why the ranking? What was she looking for? She obliged herself by answering: She thrilled to the idea of a "physical complement—someone who understands. . . . Not just a single flash of perception and delight, but a continual feeling of motion, of answer to a question; of response to a seeking—a complete circuit of electric, tingling happiness." But it was hard to trust boys and to talk to them about sex, although one of them, John Hodges, earned her respect and love when he told her sex had to be a beautiful thing and not misused.

25

For long stretches in 1948 and 1949, Sylvia no longer faithfully recorded every fulfilling and frustrating day of her existence, but then on November 13, 1949, she seems to have suddenly stopped to take stock, announcing: "As of today I have decided to keep a diary again—just a place where I can write my thoughts and opinions when I have a moment. Somehow I have to keep and hold the rapture of being seventeen. Every day is so precious I feel infinitely sad at the thought of all this time melting farther and father away from me as I grow older." She considered this the "perfect time" of her life, with the "tragedies and happiness . . . all unimportant now." She described how she had made her room suited to her: "tailored, uncluttered and peaceful" with subdued colors "peach and gray, brown-gold maple—a highlight of maroon here and there," with the "quiet lines of the furniture—the two bookcases filled with poetry books and fairy-tales saved from childhood."

She evoked her present moment as "very happy, sitting at my desk and looking out at the bare trees around the house across the street—the chilly gray sky like a slate of icy marble propped up against the hills, the leaves lying in little withered heaps . . . orange piles in the gutters." She wanted to share her existence in a "wry, humorous light—and mock myself as I mock others." She dreaded the idea of growing older and marrying. "Spare me from cooking three meals a day" and the "routine and rote." She wanted to be free, to travel the world, to learn about "morals and standards" other than her own. "I want, I think, to be omniscient—and a bit insane." She thought of herself as "the girl who wanted to be God." This is a "terrible egotism," she confessed, and yet she worried that she had been "too conditioned to the conventional surroundings of this community." What vanity and what a craving for pretty clothes she had. Would she face herself at last and overcome her fears of the "big choices" looming: which college, which career? She was reluctant to forsake her mother's protection, yet she wanted to devote herself to a cause.

Instead Sylvia behaved just like other adolescents. She went out to a local dancehall, the Totem Pole, the venue for Benny Goodman, Artie Shaw, Harry James & the Dorsey Brothers, and other swing bands. One teenager described the impact of entering a "huge hall" with a large staircase on the upper level that "led down to the main dance floor and couches and small tables were interspersed on the way down."[13] The Totem Pole had three dance floors and plenty of space for intimate seating with soft lighting for a dreamy and romantic atmosphere. When Sylvia arrived, everyone was drunk and she was in a "rather gay mood myself, since I created quite a sensation (my ego cropping up again)." A good-looking blond boy ambled over to her and asked her name and then said that Edgar Allan Poe "wrote a sonnet to Sylvia once. May I kiss you?" She described this party as like a Christmas ornament: "silver, shining and frosted with red and blue and gold, inside nothing. Girls pretending to be happy with the boys they hated. Boys leaving their dates and flirting with other girls—bottles, bottles everywhere, and the high, nervous laughter. Even I found myself laughing—at myself for being part of all that. For even I was playing a part." She felt like screaming because she could not express herself.

Something was happening to Sylvia Plath that Wellesley could not address. "Today I met Patsy and was, as usual, caught up in a senseless babble of words. Talk, talk, talk. That's all we do," she confided to her diary, although this comment may be misleading, since her teacher Wilbury Crockett believed that Patsy was an "absolutely superior foil" to Sylvia. Patsy could make her intense friend see the humor of certain situations, and with an intelligence perhaps equal to Sylvia's. [HR] She needed someone to bring her out of her "tailspin." Usually, it was a boy, or several boys, that got her going again, or an idea for a story or poem. The rejections she received from editors did not deter her, especially since a few sent encouraging notes. She would just keep trying, she told her German pen pal.

She wrote a few poems under a pseudonym, Sandra Peters, including "Lonely Song," which expresses loneliness as "one of the central themes of her writing at this time," observes Andrew Wilson. Who can say, however, if such a poem is a writing exercise or a vehicle of self-expression? Heather Clark calls the poem a reveling in "romantic rhetoric." Using another name can be a form of protection; it can also be the invention of a persona, a character separate from its creator. But in a story, "Among the Shadow Throngs," another character, Terry Lane, seeks some way out of what Wilson calls her "shoddy circumstances" and failure to place her work in magazines. Impossible, then, for a biographer not to imagine Sylvia articulating in her art what came out fitfully, as well, in her diaries and letters.

These early stories had something to do with a sense that she no longer fit so well into her community and culture. "I am so tired of all the young girls here who think of nothing but party dresses and of boys who care for nothing but money and pretty faces," she wrote to Hans-Joachim Neupert. She decried the parties with the "same empty faces with painted smiles." She deplored the crudity of television and radio, no longer devoted—judging by her diaries—to those Sunday-night soap operas and comedy shows. One of her classmates, Pat O'Neill, said there was something "Old-Worldish" about Sylvia. [HR]

26

On August 24, 1949, approaching her senior year in high school, Sylvia confessed to Hans-Joachim Neupert that she felt "wistful and nostalgic": "This has been my last summer of really carefree youth—next summer I will get some sort of job and earn money in preparation for college." She preferred to go away and live on campus but might have to accept a Wellesley scholarship. The town had a "very wealthy class of people here, and in my school almost all my acquaintances come from well-to-do homes." She asked if he ever wondered about "why you are you and not someone else . . . it sounds silly to say it, but it is absorbing when you think of it." How much of her was environment, how much inherited? "I think that many of our opinions are not really our own but rather ideas that we have unconsciously borrowed from other people." Leaving home meant a testing of herself—just like her climbing a water tower even though she was afraid of heights.

At the end of September, Aurelia Plath wrote a letter to Smith College inquiring about the application process for her daughter. By early November, Sylvia had applied for admission with the full backing of her teachers and principal as a superior student—in fact, a genius. On May 10, 1950, she received her letter of acceptance. On May 30, she shared the joyful news with Hans-Joachim Neupert.

Farm work during the summer of 1950 exhausted and exhilarated her: "Now I know how people can live without books, without college. When one is so tired at the end of a day one must sleep, and at the next dawn there are more strawberry runners to set, and so one goes on living, near the earth." She enjoyed the workers, like Ilo, who talked about Renaissance painters Raphael and Michelangelo but also wanted to know what she thought of Frank Sinatra. "So sentimental, so romantic, so moonlight night, Ja?" commented Ilo. To this kind of overture, she set down her own fantasy of a moonlight night: "What is more wonderful than to be a virgin clean and sound and young, on such a night? . . . (being raped.)" It is a shocking sentiment but also expressive of how her sexuality remained a thing apart, in her imagination, and not yet exposed or violated.

Like the young schoolgirl Martha Gellhorn dreaming of one day meeting Ernest Hemingway,[14] Sylvia Plath made herself "the heroine, a reporter in the trenches, to be loved by a man who admired me, who understood me as much as I understood myself." Her cheeks burned on the day her fantasies collided with reality. She was teased with a singsong "Oh, Sylvia," as she accompanied Ilo, her coworker on the farm, to the barn to see one of his drawings. In the dim light of the barn, she climbed a ladder to see the pictures but sensed trouble and said she had to go. "And suddenly his mouth was on mine, hard, vehement, his tongue darting between my lips, his arms like iron around me." She could not remember if she screamed or whispered in her struggle to break free. He let her go and smiled as she cried. In her journal, she recorded: "No one ever kissed me that way before, and I stood there, flooded with longing, electric shivering." Ilo gave her a glass of water to calm her. Outside everyone seemed to know about the assignation as they called after her "cutie pie" and "angel face." She smiled, "as if nothing had happened."

On a date with Emile, another farmworker, she observed herself as the "American virgin, dressed to seduce." But "we play around and if we're nice girls, we demure at a certain point." She liked the "strong smell of masculinity which creates the ideal medium for me to exist in." She noted the "hard line of his penis taut against my stomach, my breasts aching firm against his chest." Later when he tried to embrace her, she told him: "You don't give a damn about me except physically." He departed after successfully getting in a long, sweet kiss. She wanted him and remarked that after "fifteen thousand years—of what? We're still nothing but animals." She wondered what *he* was thinking.

Sylvia had already questioned Aurelia with some intensity about the nature of sex. Aurelia had given her ten-year-old daughter a book, *Growing Up*, by Karl de Schweinitz, which explained in general terms the facts of life. Then Aurelia began a series of casual but explicit discussions about sex the summer before Sylvia entered Smith. She advised her daughter against intercourse, which should be regarded as a "unique experience" that went beyond momentary pleasure and took into account the "responsibilities of marriage and family." Later, Ruth Beuscher recorded Aurelia's account of Sylvia's sex education, which included Aurelia's embarrassed but determined answers to her avid daughter, telling her everything Aurelia knew about the subject, including the nature of homosexuality, which should not come as a shock when Sylvia encountered it. [HR]

Three days before Sylvia arrived at Smith, "plunged into a new world," with "confusion, dilemmas," and fighting to "find the right equilibrium for myself again," she described a date, during which she remained in "command of the whole situation." She watched, "narcissus-like," her reflection in store windows after leaving the movie palace with "glittery glass chandeliers, plush carpets and gleaming silver mirrors." She was wearing a silver bracelet given to her by Eddie Cohen, a perceptive correspondent who had written to congratulate her for the August 1950 publication of "And Summer Will Not Come Again" in *Seventeen*, her first appearance in the magazine. She regarded the bracelet as a "symbol of my composure . . . my desire to be many lives," and her vow to be "a little god in my small way." In effect, she was declaring to her date a kind of sovereignty best expressed in the stabilizing fact of print.

27

Six years earlier, in August 1944, *Seventeen* published its first issue, geared to teenage girls, a new market then when the very word teenager was just coming into currency. Romantic stories and the newest fashions encouraged young women to think of themselves as a new brand of self-sufficient entrepreneurs. Exactly when Sylvia subscribed to the magazine is not certain, but by October 1947, she was reading it in bed with a girlfriend—in effect fulfilling the magazine's efforts to foster a community of female readers sharing and swapping stories about characters that reflected their own lives or what they wanted their lives to be. By 1950, Sylvia said she had made fifty submissions to the magazine before the acceptance of "And Summer Will Not Come Again," making her an exemplary customer and creator of a new kind of culture.

The story has often been dismissed or ignored as part of Plath juvenilia, but to Eddie Cohen it sounded a self-critical note that seemed surprising in this teen periodical. The story spoke to his own self-examination at twenty-one. A bright University of Chicago dropout, Eddie had yet to find his way and thought he had found a female counterpart. Sylvia had not dreamed of reaching this kind of reader in a magazine meant for young women, but Eddie's interest was an early indicator that she could reach well beyond the genre expectations of the magazine to a broader audience. She had, in effect, seduced a male reader.

In the story, Celia is distraught after she rebukes Bruce, a handsome young man she regards as her own, when she sees him with another blonde, and he rejects Celia, saying "I hadn't figured you were like this. My mistake." He walks away. Eddie Cohen did not know that something close to this scene had occurred between Sylvia and John Hodges, handsome and athletic. Celia turns her anger on herself, as Sylvia would do to herself, and quotes lines from Sara Teasdale's wistful poem, "An End": "With my own will I turned the summer from me / And summer will not come to me again." This story presages a torment that Sylvia would visit on herself and others—later striking out at Ted Hughes when she spotted him on the Smith campus talking to a fawning undergraduate. Sylvia had a powerful need to exert her superiority that brought her into conflict with masterful males. How to control her rage in a society that permitted men to act out, but not women, would remain a besetting perplexity.

Sylvia Plath could have remained at home and attended Wellesley College as a scholarship student. Wellesley had been part of her youth. She had visited often on walks with her mother and other family members, and she had played in its environs. Certainly staying put in Wellesley would have eased the burden on Aurelia Plath, a burden Sylvia keenly took to heart and tried to assuage in her incessant reports to her mother about her health and well-being whenever away from home. Sylvia was not unhappy at home, and her returns from camp and other excursions resulted in joyous celebrations with family and friends. But she relished in her reading and brief travels the notion of a world elsewhere, and a craving for fame that required the adventuring pioneered by her hero, the writer/explorer Richard Halliburton.

Sylvia's enthusiasm for a life abroad entailed overcoming a fear of failure. No matter how often she succeeded, the next challenge seemed to threaten her equilibrium, which could only be restored by yet another achievement. That is the fate of ambitious individuals. Ambition is its own reward and punishment. Working on a sculpture that eluded her in a Smith freshman art class, she gave way to "black despair," confessing to her mother the hope that "I can make it to Xmas vacation without going completely insane—you know that sort of morbid depression I sink into." But the pressures Sylvia felt at Smith were hardly hers alone—or even evidence of some predisposition to depression. Her friend Ann Davidow confessed she could not keep up with the work at Smith. A distressed Sylvia wrote to her mother; "I got scared when she told me how she had been saving sleeping pills and razor blades and could think of nothing better than to commit suicide. Oh, mother, you don't know how inadequate I felt!" Ann's mother "couldn't see how incapable the poor girl is of thinking in this state. . . . If you were her mother, she would be all right."

28

Sylvia detected another kind of fear enveloping her generation, a fear that William Faulkner addressed directly in his Nobel Prize speech on December 10, 1950: "Our tragedy today is a general and universal physical fear so long sustained by now that we can even bear it." Only one question mattered: "When will I be blown up?" Sylvia dreaded the "great ultimate destruction" of atomic war, she wrote to Eddie Cohen, an astute and critical correspondent in whom she could confide. Channeling Faulkner, she observed that "our nerve reactions can convey worry about the future, until the fear insinuates itself into the present, into everything." So she lived "every moment with terrible intensity," seeking to restore what Faulkner called "the problems of the human heart in conflict with itself which alone can make good writing because only that is worth writing about, worth the agony and the sweat." Writing was her salvation. Sylvia, taught by her mother, had been touch typing eighty words per minute since she was sixteen, noting that "the very three-dimensional feel of this typewriter has a calming effect. It says: I'm here; you can still hold to me." Aurelia agonized nonetheless about the manic rate of her daughter's typing—sometimes as much as eight hours a day—and Sylvia sensed her mother's foreboding. She caught Aurelia "crying desperately in the kitchen," worrying, as Sylvia did,

Haven House at Smith College.

whether her "tall dreamy eye kid brother" would be "cut off before he gets a chance." Sylvia felt "a little frantic. . . . It kinds of gets you."

But neither college nor her apocalyptic concerns about a nuclear Armageddon prevented her from enjoying quiet weekends, reading *The Mayor of Casterbridge* in the library browsing room, undisturbed by telephone or visitors, with "all the comforts of home": good reading lamps, "cushioned easy chairs," and a window seat looking out on the "Holyoke range, foggily purplish in the Sunday dusk. And all the while the carillon bells are chiming out hymns and college songs." Walking back to her room in Haven House she looked at the lighted dorms in "square yellow dominos against the black" and saw "hope, opportunity, capacity everywhere."

Sylvia's letters and postcards home (sometimes more than one a day) were reassuring, addressed to "Dear Mum," "Dear Mummy," "Dear Mumsy," or "Dear Mother." She extolled the "wonderful girls" and reported: "I have a few good freshmen friends who confide their date life to me. It's so nice to live a few other lives beside your own." She looked forward to decorating her room. "There is nothing compared to living at college. I walked downtown to get some books yesterday—it's really my home. It's such fun to know what girl goes with whom and where—things you'd never know if you commuted. I love eating with a crowd & chatting at meals. in fact I love the whole place." But it was the same Sylvia clocking herself: "I'm almost 18! I get a little frightened when I think of life slipping through my fingers like water—so fast that I have little time to stop running. I have to

keep on like the White Queen, to stay in place." Sometimes she felt displaced: "Time ticks by relentlessly. Am I queer, or is it normal that I am so
snowed by being a microcosm here that I don't yet get the feeling of going
to Smith?" That kind of sudden eruption of alienation would continue to
occur at sporadic intervals for the rest of her life, so that she could in a
matter of minutes, hours, or days, turn the best of times into the worst of
times. In a remarkable journal passage written during her first month at
Smith, Sylvia, tortured by time, resembles Faulkner's querulous Quentin
Compson in *The Sound and the Fury*. She hears the seconds tick off and the
clock's "loud sharp clicks," even through the pillow that muffles the sound,
the "tyrannical drip drip drip drip of seconds along the night. And in the
day, even when I'm not there, the seconds come out in little measured
strips of time." She even wanted to smash the clock as Quentin smashes
his watch. She mentions a despair similar to that which drives Quentin to
suicide, but "I love life," she affirms: "But it is hard, and I have so much to
learn"—a part of which she puts into a poem about a clock snipping "time
in two." The clock in her room is likened to the heart beat of longing for
a "you" that is not there. This was the nighttime Sylvia, the darker side of
the bright self she personified in her daytime letters to her mother. Sylvia
never really liked reading Faulkner, and yet she was a Quentin, in certain
respects. His father had sold off some of the Compson land so Quentin
could go to Harvard; Aurelia had made comparable sacrifices for a daughter
who dared not let her down.

   Quentin had his Shreve in *The Sound and the Fury* and *Absalom, Absalom!*;
Sylvia had Ann Davidow, a freshman "free thinker" who read Eddie Cohen's
letters and said he was "wonderfully socially conscious." Ann set Sylvia up
with a blind date, a twenty-two-year-old Amherst senior, who caught on
quickly to Sylvia's performance as a Scarlett O'Hara at Smith. He told her
that she "lived 'hard,' am dramatic in my manner, talk sometimes like a
school girl reporting a theme, and have a southern accent.!'" Did she, like
Norman Mailer shifting from southern to Irish accents, depend on the mood
of the moment to reveal or conceal aspects of herself? Her date surprised
her, she confessed to her mother, by "hitting rather well on a few points of
my personality I usually keep hidden."

29

Returning to Smith after the 1950 Thanksgiving holiday, Sylvia wrote to
Olive Higgins Prouty, author of the best-selling *Stella Dallas*, made into

a motion picture and a radio serial: "I just want you to understand that you are responsible, in a sense, for the formation of an individual. And I am fortunate enough to be that person." The Prouty scholarship had been awarded to Sylvia because of poetry and stories. She was thrilled to get Prouty's encouraging response that she had a "gift for creative writing."

Sylvia's journal records the turmoil of her first semester: "I am feeling depressed from being exposed to so many lives," but it was like "grazing" at their "edges." It bothered her, especially since Ann Davidow had decided to leave Smith and Sylvia felt "bereft," since together she thought they could "face anything." She tried to restore herself with a reminder of her good fortune both physically and mentally. "What have I to complain about? Nothing much." It troubled her that in different circumstances, poorer or richer, she would have become a different person. What, really, could she attribute to her own doing? And yet she had declared herself an "I . . . How firm a letter; how reassuring the three strokes: one vertical, proud and assertive, and then the two short horizons lines in quick, smug succession. The pen scratches on the paper . . . I . . . I . . . I . . . I . . . I . . . I."

30

In January 1951, starting a second semester, Sylvia revealed a side of Smith that remained unmentionable in letters to her mother, especially the "nasty little tag ends of conversation directed at you and around you, meant for you, to strangle you on the invisible noose of insinuation. You know it was meant for you; so do they who stab you." She could hold her own in such encounters but sometimes felt "too sickened to fight back, because you know the fear and the inadequacy will crawl out in your words as they crackle falsely on the air." So she only smiled when they said "You're always studying in your rooom!"

She wrote to Ann Davidow that she was still a little wobbly from her sinus infection and cough medicine: "I swear the stuff is half alcohol." She felt lost without Ann and considered taking up bridge to connect with "Haven House humanity." She confessed that a part of her wanted to remain a sheltered child. Because her mother's purpose was to see her and Warren "happy and fulfilled," Sylvia felt compelled to "pretend to her that I am all right & doing what I've always wanted," even though she went through an "awfully black mood during vacation." Now she was "not quite so close to going utterly and completely mad." But she worried about Ann's state of mind: "you're one of the most admirable characters I've ever met."

With Marcia Brown, a lively freshman on Plath's intellectual level, Sylvia recovered some of her equanimity, as they shared their opinions on long walks and in their rooms. Sylvia went on dates most weekends but found them disappointing, writing to Ann Davidow that the American male viewed woman as a "combination of mother and sweetheart." The perceptive Eddie Cohen was another matter. He confessed his attraction to Sylvia but said dating her was out of the question because of her "tender age." His words, Sylvia told Ann, made her "feel rather good inside," but also "pretty sad when a girl has to rely on typewritten words from a guy she's never met (and no doubt would not get along with if she did) to send a little shiver of excitement and tenderness up her spine."

Sylvia Plath craved attention, and her Smith classmates were well aware of her reputation. On February 24, 1951, she wrote to her mother that someone had pinned an article about her on the College Hall Bulletin Board: "BORN TO WRITE! Sylvia Plath, 17, really works at writing." She was called "The little Wellesley, Mass blonde." Sylvia commented: "All this effusive stuff appeared in the Peoria Illinois Star on January 23." Little? Blonde? Already, accounts of Sylvia Plath filtered through to the public in distorted form. Where they got the idea she was writing a sea story puzzled and amused her: "I just laughed and laughed." Four days later she was still talking about the article and her "youthful success." She did not feel successful: "Every minute is taken up trying to keep my head above water as far as my courses are concerned." Yet she had to record all the signs of her recognition for her mother's delectation: "I think I shall start a new scrapbook about myself, what with all my little attempts at writing being blown up rather out of proportion. Imagine one awestruck girl greeted me yesterday with 'I hear you're writing a novel. I think that's just wonderful.'"

Sylvia Plath was always the writer of perpetual promise, and always the daughter obligated to report for duty. Aurelia sent long letters, which Sylvia sometimes read aloud to Marcia Brown, who described them as an extension of a "cloying," even "nauseating," home atmosphere in which Aurelia monitored her daughter's every move. Sylvia later destroyed her mother's letters. What seems obsessive about Plath's writing to her mother would probably look far different if Aurelia's letters had survived, since Sylvia's own efforts to placate her mother could then be seen in the context of Aurelia's inability, according to Marcia, to imagine why her daughter would be mad at her. Harriet Rosenstein put it in capital letters: "SYLVIA HAD TO RETREAT AND BE ALONE" away from her mother's desire to "KNOW EVERY THOUGHT AND EVERY ACTION AND ALL ABOUT EVERY PERSON AND EVERY ACTION AND ALL ABOUT

EVERY PERSON SYLVIA EVER KNEW." Mrs. Plath called her daughter "'MY LITTLE GIRL ALL THE TIME.'"

Marcia Brown depicted a desperate Aurelia Plath "struggling every minute of every day of every year to pay the bills and keep herself together—just holding on for dear life—and there is no room for color—in her tone of voice or her hairdo or her aprons or her living room or inside her head." [HR] The bitterness of her plight often surfaced, making it difficult for Sylvia to talk about her childhood. Marsha believed that her friend was ashamed of being a scholarship student, of having to rely on Olive Higgins Prouty, which, perhaps, accounts for Plath's satirical sendup of Prouty in *The Bell Jar*, a novel that relieved her of certain burdens and obligations to those who had made her beholden. Marcia went even further, claiming Sylvia "wanted to be more an upper-middle-class tweedy cashmere type at college." But this Sylvia Plath reads like the doubles she would write about in her senior thesis, representing opposing sides of the same self, grateful and resentful.

The depictions of Sylvia Plath as beautiful and buoyant also have their counterpoint in Marcia Brown's belief that her friend was never comfortable with her own body. Marcia observed that she was "round-shouldered," uncoordinated, gangly, and self-conscious about her poor posture. She didn't move well. [HR]

Sylvia wrote her mother that the flow of letters would slow because of the demands of course work, but her communications from Smith did not subside, including, as usual, an accounting of her expenses—a practice she had begun during her summer camps. Suicide was still a joking matter: "I'll write after I pass through this week," she told her mother. "Either that, or you will receive a little ink bottle full of ashes. Please scatter them on the waters of the ocean I loved so well in infancy."

Sylvia also questioned her purpose: "Sometimes I wonder whether or not I should 'go into social work'" she wrote her mother. She could earn a living, or "you could get me started secretarially next summer." Should she plan for a career? "I hate the word," or free lance, "if I ever catch a man who can put up with the idea of having a wife who likes to be alone and working artistically now & then?"

An extraordinary passage in a journal written sometime in 1951 reveals a desire to go way beyond what Smith graduates expected to make of themselves:

But the life of a Willa Cather, a Lillian Helman [*sic*], a Virginia Woolf—would it not be a series of rapid ascents and probing descents into shades and meanings—into more people, ideas and conceptions? Would it not be in color, rather than black-and-white, or more gray? I think it would. And thus, I not being them, could try to be more like them: to listen, observe, and feel, and try to live most fully.

All around Sylvia Plath, women were prepared for the plum roles of house-wife and mother, fully equipped by education and acculturation to be the homemaker-lady-in-waiting to her princely husband and his career. Yet the idea of becoming sovereign, the one in charge, never lost its hold over Sylvia, who described in her journals date after date as almost invariably failing to meet her high standards. She worried that marriage would sap her creativity. Could you be a mother and an artist?

31

In April 1951, Sylvia wrote an essay about one of her favorite poems, "Patterns," admiring the way Amy Lowell used "imagery to convey this impression of sorrow and rebellion against conventional patterns." Here was a work that spoke to Sylvia's sense of how the individual, thinking of herself as unique, considers herself a "rare pattern" even as she walks in a patterned garden that expresses her ironic realization that she is confined in the "stiff, correct brocade" of her sex against which she rebels. But, as with Sylvia, the woman in the poem understands her plight is part of a much larger lethality in which her beloved is "killed in a pattern called war." Sylvia understands that even in the garden, the impulse to pattern nature and oneself is inescapable and yet resistible in the "woman's battling against the rigidity of her gown." The woman does not cry out, yet Sylvia senses her desire to do so in the way she chafes against her clothing, "conforming to another sort of social pattern," as Sylvia did on so many occasions. One can only imagine how she identified with the woman who at one point pictures herself as naked and recollects her lover's belief that sunlight carries a blessing, as Sylvia herself seemed to acknowledge in her sunbathing reveries. Then she brought home the meaning of the poem: "So it is when I rebel against the idea of patterns which are man made . . . such as the notion of a third world war . . . I turn to read Patterns which, because of its clear imagery, intensifies and answers the emotion I myself feel." She echoed with equal feeling the poem's last line: "Christ! What are patterns for?"

"Patterns" also expresses an awareness of life-changing events. Sylvia was beginning to realize what it meant to enter a new phase of life: "I seem to grow more acutely conscious of the swift passage of time as I grow older. When I was small, days and hours were long and spacious, and there was play and acres of leisure, and many children's books to read." She regretted the loss of that world in a Wordsworthian sense, lamenting the polish and callousness of adulthood that blunted the "childlike intensity to new experience and sensations." Still, in her own view, she ricocheted between "being constantly active and happy or introspectively passive and sad."

The journals from this first year at Smith seem to reflect a sensibility easily disturbed by the unplanned and unexpected, as if Sylvia was not yet ready to adjust to events over which she had no control. When Eddie Cohen suddenly showed up, offering to drive her home for spring break, she panicked, admitting to Ann Davidow: "I just couldn't get used to the idea that this physical stranger was the guy I'd written such confidential letters to." She treated Eddie rudely and did not invite him into her home fearing her mother's disapproval. Aurelia surprised her by criticizing Sylvia's "lack of hospitality." Sylvia confessed to having been "rather shaken and surprised by the whole unexpected encounter. The thing that makes me maddest at myself is that I just ignored the fact that he'd driven night-and-day from Chicago without stopping. So I just let him drive back." She mentioned his letter complaining about cold New Englanders. But they were now writing "as if nothing had ever happened." This seemingly minor upset, however, forecasts how unnerved she would become when the circumstances of her life that she so diligently prepared for turned out unexpectedly different from her desires.[15]

Some days were a heady whirl. On May 14, 1951, writing from Smith about her weekend, she reported to her mother that the article about blind dates written with Marcia Brown got a "big spread" in the *Princeton Tiger*. In the space of a paragraph she supplied news about John Hodges, Bob Humphrey, and Ilo—the boys she had dated. With Dick Norton, she went to a performance of *The Skin of Our Teeth*, "delightful—loud & obvious, but fun," and then attended Dick's class in Contemporary Events with a "stimulating instructor." Dick, a Yale student and the older brother of Perry Norton, had thrilled Sylvia with his interest in her, but she was just beginning to notice certain irritating mannerisms. They played volleyball and then read Hemingway on a "rocky shore." Next day it was breakfast with Perry. Then out on the rocks with Dick collecting seashells. "I think I am curing him of his jovial mask which made me so cross," she wrote.

Sylvia also assessed herself, provoked, perhaps, by her return home after her first year at Smith:

I am in my old room once more for a little, and I am caught in musing—how life is a swift motion, a continuous flowing, changing, and how one is always saying goodbye and going places, seeing people, doing things. Only in the rain . . . closing in your pitifully small radius of activity, only when you sit and listen by the window, as the cold wet air blows thickly by the back of your neck—only then do you think and feel sick. . . . The film of your days and nights is wound up tight in you, never to be re-run—and the occasional flashbacks are faint, blurred, unreal, as if seen through falling snow.

She feared she hadn't done "well enough." Looking back also made her write, for the first time, about Otto Plath:

There is your dead father who is somewhere in you, interwoven in the cellular system of your long body which sprouted from one of his sperm cells uniting with an egg cell in your mother's uterus. You remember that you were his favorite when you were little, and you used to make up dances to do for him as he lay on the living room couch after supper. You wonder if the absence of an older man in the house has anything to do with your intense craving for male company and the delight in the restful low sound of a group of boys, talking and laughing.

She said little about Aurelia, except to admit she could hear her mother's voice within her and that seemed to frighten her, as if she was not herself but as if her mother's expressions were "growing and emanating" from her face. This is what, in fact, Ted Hughes would say after Sylvia had asked him to leave their home, Court Green. Now she wanted to anchor herself in her brother, reminding herself:

You fought with him when you were little, threw tin soldiers at his head, gouged his neck with a careless flick of your iceskate . . . and then last summer, as you worked on the farm, you grew to love him, confide in him, and know him as a person . . . and you remember the white look of fear about his mouth that day they had all planned to throw you in the wash tub—and how he rallied to your defense.

32

Sylvia spent the summer of 1951 earning $50.00 a week, on the go from 7:00 a.m. to 9 p.m. as a babysitter of three young children for a wealthy doctor's family in Swampscott, Massachusetts. She described her reactions as "primarily blind and emotional—fear, insecurity, uncertainty, and anger at myself for making myself so stupid and miserable." She suffered from a recurrent problem with her sinuses. The idea of cooking flummoxed her, although she began to gain confidence with a batch of Tollhouse cookies. Whenever she felt worthless, she read her fan mail from *Seventeen*, laughing "a bit sadistically" at "some gal by the name of Sylvia Plath," who "sure has something—but who is she anyhow?" The astringent Eddie Cohen had stopped writing to her after she had not answered his last letter, but his voice seemed to well up in her own caustic account of herself.

Sylvia panicked and even had her friend Marcia Brown agree they should quit their summer jobs. Marcia, treated as a member of the lower caste by her employer, had it even worse than Sylvia. [HR] But then, after Marcia insisted on her rights to a day off, Sylvia reversed herself: "You are a prisoner of sorts, and yet you have made yourself so, accepted this job for what you could make out of it." [PJ] She told herself it was better to leave with "a sense of accomplishment." Days later she scoffed at her "moanings" and grew to enjoy the nightly ritual of putting the children to bed: "Something maternal awakened, perhaps, by the physical contact with such lovely young babies? Something sensual aroused by young hands at breast, young cheeks against face, young warm child bodies under hands? Perhaps." [PJ]

She had a little time to go out on dates and to observe with "a wry smile" the languorous lives of young women from wealthy families. She envied her dates, especially the good-looking, athletic ones, remarking to her mother: "Boys live so much harder than girls, and they know so much more about life. Learning the limitations of a woman's sphere is no fun at all." What a woman could do with her "sphere," however, would eventually become the powerful means of her liberation in poetry. But in 1951, that kind of liberation seemed out of reach, thwarting her "consuming desire to mingle with road crews, sailors and soldiers, bar room regulars—to be a part of a scene, anonomous [sic], listening, recording—all is spoiled by the fact that I am a girl, a female always in danger of assault and battery."

Out at Marblehead she took a moment to let the sun seep "into every pore, satiating every querulous fiber of me into a great glowing golden peace. Stretching out on the rock, body taut, then relaxed, on the altar, I felt that I was being raped deliciously by the sun, filled full of heat from the impersonal and colossal god of nature." The sea and sun would always be her salvation. In her most vulnerable moments away from the shore and her burning star, she felt a loss of herself and full of the grime that only the sea "cleansed, baptised, purified" and the sun "dried clean and crisp."

33

Working for the wealthy had its impact. Sylvia admitted to a feeling of "presumptuousness which comes perhaps from a secret enjoyment of living with rich people and listening to and observing them. It is like hearing a supposedly confidential conversation." What to do after enjoying such privilege? "How to return to the smallness, the imperfection, which is home?" Yet she wrote to assure her mother that the opposite was true—that she longed to "lay my head in blissful peace and security under my own hospitable roof. You and grammy and grampy and Warren are so lovely to be around after long months away from all companions save Marcia." The back-and-forth of her feelings came at her again and again like the "spasmodic click-click" of the ping-pong ball she watched friends shoot at one another in a wealthy family's game room.

Journal entries during this period reflect Sylvia's strictures to herself to not waste her experience, to make the moment an occasion for writing. Some passages read like warmups for short fiction: A fat woman with a "calculating grin" moves her arms and hands "slowly, plumply, like twinging cobras." A drunken young man drops his Manhattan and it falls to the floor with a "soprano tinkle." She wrote herself into seascapes: "Gray fog shredded thin along the flat-washed duncolored beach. Small dull green waves folded over upon themselves in a slither of dirty white foam, spreading out in sheets of water, reflecting the soiled morning sky." These sentences read like pastiches of Faulkner and Steinbeck in the conjoining of words and the biological/natural language of the scene.

She kept at the writing, no matter how frustrating:

If I did not have this time to be myself, to write here, to be alone, I would somehow, inexplicably, lose a part of my integrity. As it is, what I have written here so far is rather poor, rather unsatisfactory. It is the product of an unimaginative girl, preoccupied with herself, and continually splashing about in the shallow waters of her own narrow psyche. As an excuse, she claims these are writing exercises, a means of practice at expressing herself, of note taking for future stories. Yet on the merry-go-round of time there is scarcely enough to spend pondering and attempting to recapture details. In fact, if one has not the imagination to create characters, to knit plots, it does no good to jot down fragments of life and conversation, for alone they are disjointed and meaningless. It is only when these bits are woven into an artistic whole, with a frame of reference, that they become meaningful and worthy of more than a cursory glance. Therefore, think and work, think and work.

She made friends, went to parties, and recorded it all—seemingly—including the washup after her employer's big dinner party, as she joined the downstairs kitchen crew of Helen and Lane, with whom she "charlestoned crazily" and then ladled out melting vanilla ice cream "on fresh plates" pretending "we were Alice and the White Rabbit at the Mad Hatter's tea Party." At rare moments, mistakenly thinking she was in the house alone, she sat at the piano, the "sounding of sharp chords" relieving the "great weight" on her shoulders until Mrs. Mayo shouted about the banging. She thought of her ten weeks of servitude "mercilessly crushed under a machine-like dictatorship," the same as it would be in "industry, state or organization." She longed for what she called "self-integral freedom."

But it was never the case that her definition of freedom did not include the rest of the world. She read the newspaper and noted the stalemate in Korea, the "Anglo-Iranian crisis," and the Senate's cuts in foreign aid. She could never abide the idea of an island self, of idiotic people who thought their world did not include events such as the execution of the Rosenbergs. A bell jar might be a way of describing the circumscribed world of mental illness, but it could also be a metaphor for the suffocated lives of those underneath the weight of a world they were hardly aware of.

34

At the end of August, Sylvia opened her calendar and ran into the next month: "God! all the quick futility of my days cascaded upon me, and I wanted to scream out in helpless fury at the hopeless inevitable going on of seconds, days, and years." She recorded her goodbyes to her fellow workers and friends, describing their features and stories they told her. She yearned to wrap her summer around herself like a cocoon as she prepared for "the next great phase—my sophomore year."

Some days she was down on herself:

I do not love; I do not love anybody except myself. That is a rather shocking thing to admit. I have none of the selfless love of my mother. I have none of the plodding, practical love of Frank and Louise, Dot and Joe. I am, to be blunt and concise, in love only with myself, my puny being with it's small inadequate breasts and meagre, thin talents.

I am capable of affection for those who reflect my own world. How much of my solicitude for other human beings is real and honest, how much is a feigned lacquer painted on by society, I do not know. I am afraid to face myself. Tonight I am trying to do so. I heartily wish that there were some absolute knowledge, some person whom I could trust to evaluate me and tell me the truth.

The rap against Sylvia Plath is the same as what she leveled at her self-absorbed self. Could some person tell her the truth? She had come close to one in Eddie Cohen, who would suddenly appear in her journals as the voice she longed for.[16] She expected that any man she married would demand she submerge herself into his "range of acquaintance." She wanted a passionate sexual partner and yet could not gratify herself "promiscuously," with the "male freedom" she envied. Other alternatives—women's clubs, social and political activism—promoted a sense of emancipation, but they did not seem commensurate with her desire to write. She thought she had three years to decide—exactly the time she needed to graduate, and then marry, as Smith women did. But she balked: "Why can't I try on different lives, like dresses, to see which fits best and is most becoming?" Writing to Ann Davidow after the summer of 1951 was over, Sylvia declared: "I'm just not the type who wants a home and children of her own more than anything else in the world." That would never change. She would have a home and children, but it was not, in the end, enough.

35

At the very start of fall 1951, her sophomore year, Sylvia experienced a moment of glory that seemed a dream, a wish fulfillment, putting her on the kind of stage and in a world where she was sovereign. Along with Marcia Brown, she was driven through the hilly countryside to Sharon, Connecticut, arriving with other girls in taffeta, satin, and silk and swishing up the stone steps under the "white colonial column" to attend a dinner dance in honor of Maureen Buckley O'Reilly, whose conservative ideas often got debated in Haven House in the company of Marcia and Sylvia.

At the Buckley estate, Sylvia stood "open mouthed, giddy, bubbling," assuring her mother: "you would have been supremely happy if you had seen me. I know I looked beautiful. Even daughters of millionaires complimented my dress." This was a moneyed world that left her gasping. Money is a constant theme in her letters. She notes how much she pays for necessities and thinks carefully about her indulgences. She knew nearly to the penny what it cost for her to live, to enjoy herself, and to treat others. During Christmas shopping at the end of 1951, she wrote to her mother: "There were so many little luxuries I would have liked to get for you, and Marcia!" In February 1952, in another report to Aurelia: A $150 increase in room and board. "Just as we thought we had things in hand, too!" The wording expresses what Sylvia would always regard as a family enterprise. Any failure on her part was not only her own but a blow to mother and brother. Any success was to be shared with them as well, and Warren, doing well in school, meant to Sylvia that the family standard had been raised that much higher. Children, when they came, would become part of a dynasty.

At the Buckley party, Sylvia met attractive, attentive, and accomplished Yale men but also Constantine—son of a Russian general, a Princeton senior, and a wonderful dancer—and then Plato, son of Spyros Skouros, head of Twentieth Century-Fox. Plato pointed to a Botticelli Madonna over the fireplace and said: "You remind me of her." She was dazzled by his conversation filled with allusions to Greek myth. "There is a sudden glorying in womanhood," she exulted, "when someone kisses your shoulder and says, 'You are charming, beautiful, and, what is most important, intelligent.'" She composed a rough "bit of free verse," the kind of polyphonic prose Amy Lowell patented, evoking the life of Napoleon's Josephine in "Malmaison":

> the bronze boy remembering a thousand autumns and how a hundred thousand leaves came sliding down his shoulderblades. persuaded by his bronze heroic reason we ignore the coming doom of gold and we are glad in this bright metal season. even the dead laugh among the goldenrod. the bronze boy stands kneedeep in centuries, and never grieves, remembering a thousand autumns, with sunlight of a thousand years upon his lips, and his eyes gone blind with leaves.

A jeu d'esprit, to be sure, yet so characteristic of a young writer, already steeped in history and myth, and already equipped to make a start on making her own life and observations of historic significance, fusing the fun of a moment with the cycles of nature and history.

36

Returning to Smith in the fall of 1951, Sylvia succumbed to a periodic attack of sinusitis, which made her feel like a "depressive maniac." "Manic" and "depressive" would be the terms she would continue to use to describe a despair that left her agitated and unable to cope with her writing, her studies, her very life, it seemed. Just out of the infirmary in late October, she wrote Constantine that she could not accept his invitation to visit Princeton, even though, as she told her mother, she felt the pressures of seemingly every Smith girl, who urged her to go see him, saying maybe she would "marry into Russian society, etc." Sometimes it seemed as if everything in her environment kept shoving her into a niche in which she was to think of herself as a prospective bride, the wife of a successful well-bred man, and sometimes she seemed almost ready to succumb. So turning down a date might seem a trivial matter, and yet it was one of those moments of assertion that make for a Sylvia Plath. She was trying to balance between "possibilities of future life, or present tasks," she wrote her mother. She needed a respite. It felt like a renaissance just to breathe again, and turning down an alluring date also gave her a measure of breathing room. Like other Smith students, she watched and waited: taking her turns sitting at a desk in Haven House monitoring entrants and spending a hour once or twice a week waiting on tables as part of her obligations as a scholarship student.

Although Sylvia had written to Ann Davidow about her estrangement from fellow students who looked askance at her unwillingness to socialize—to play bridge, for example—by November 1951, as her calendar notes, she was a bridge player. Sylvia Plath did not want to be a loner, even though she did not want to conform. Her interest in journalism, in the show of social life, reveal a sensibility that if not exactly gregarious—to use her word—enjoyed the company of her cohort and learning about the world at large. She resembled, in good measure, Esther Greenwood, her heroine in *The Bell Jar*, who keenly feels her singularity and yet desires an intimacy with her contemporaries and participates in their parties, even as she can be quite caustic about them.

Sometimes, as Sylvia wrote to Hans-Joachim, she wondered if her brother and their generation would be able to live a normal life span or "will be killed, and the land destroyed." Her seeming absorption in her studies, in writing, in boys, in friendships, in family matters never meant she was not aware of the larger forces and arguments that ruled lives and governed institutions. On October 29, 1951, she attended William F. Buckley's lecture at Smith about his new book, *God and Man at Yale*. She could see he relished his command of the audience as he advanced a contrarian argument that academic freedom was totalitarian. A university wouldn't hire a racist to teach racism, he argued, so talk of exploring all sides of a question was bogus. Inculcating the right values, not entertaining all points of view, remained higher education's paramount purpose. He attacked the self-interestedness of the academic community, with faculty members owing fealty to their departments and not to those who "paid the bills" and supported the institution. She wondered about the incipient fascism of a system that relied on those who had the money and could enforce their ideas.

37

No entry in a Sylvia Plath journal or one of her letters can tell us what she was like in class, but fortunately one of her professors, Robert Gorham Davis, described her to biographer Linda Wagner-Martin. [LWM1] He remembered her smile, not one for "the photographer," not one that sought acceptance or expressed ambition, but an expression of "happiness at what was being offered, being shared . . . I was conscious of Sylvia from the beginning before I knew the quality of her work, because she was always attentive, always looking up at me as I spoke, always smiling. I can still see her very clearly." Perhaps he felt flattered; perhaps Sylvia, knowing it or not, was flattering him, but her letters demonstrate a tremendous desire to share herself with others and to learn from them. She was always asking Ruthie Freeman, Hans-Joachim Neupert, Ann Davidow, Marcia Brown, and others to tell her about their lives, and she wanted to enjoy their successes and commiserate with their failures. Her journal is full of personality sketches and observations of all sorts of people, her specimens of what life could be like.

Professor Evelyn Page described an "agreeable" student who addressed her writing assignments and requests for revision with "professional flexibility"— a rare reaction in Page's experience. Her notes on Plath's writing suggest that first drafts were overwritten but that the student learned to manage this weakness and improve. [HR]

38

Throughout the fall of 1951 and into the early months of 1952, Sylvia saw a good deal of Dick Norton, his brother Perry, and the Norton family. She seemed to be in training for the life of a doctor's wife as Dick took her to a cancer clinic and what was then called a "lying-in hospital," a carryover euphemism from Victorian days. "BABY BORN!" Sylvia announced in a calendar entry for January 1, 1952.

Sophomore year became a grind. "Smith is a damn, heartless, demanding machine at times," she wrote to Ann Davidow. By February 1952 she longed for spring break and also brooded over what she had learned about Dick Norton. She had been shocked to discover that her "blond god" was not a virgin. Marcia Brown called him the caricature of an all-American boy that she found "repulsive" and supposed Sylvia had been attracted to him as the epitome of honesty and virtue. Marcia always had the urge to put her hand over her mouth to restrain her own disgust with the mom and apple pie sentimentality. [HR]

Sylvia admitted her envy of males. "I resent their ability to have both sex (morally or immorally) and a career." She would "gladly go to bed with many of the boys" she dated but feared having a baby and getting "too emotionally involved, or getting found out (I'm no good at fooling people—too transparent.)" She did not want to get trapped in an early marriage. She still dated other guys, preferring the tall ones so she could wear heels. She theorized that her devotion to art, study, and writing was a sublimation of sexual energy.

To Constantine, she revealed her state of mind: "Life about now is as scintillating as that in a state penitentiary." Leaving out what she had learned about Dick Norton, she described her maternity ward visit, "life in the raw," that would make "terrific background material for those short stories I'm always trying to write. My collection of rejection slips would wallpaper several rooms, but the few things I have had published made me determined to keep on battering on the editor's doors." She mentioned her "great curiosity about mental Asylums" and wanting to work in a hospital. She also wanted to hear about the life of a "suave Princetonian gentleman" and "enchanting Georgian!" She romanticized him as a "dashing Cossack" or a "Napoleonic warrior," and also, perhaps, as an alternative to medical school Dick Norton.

There were other alternatives, as well, and even if they were fleeting, they contributed to her sense of destiny. On a bus trip home in March 1952, she sat next to a "lanky, tall and attractively nice looking" young man, and they talked "solidly for the rest of the trip." He was a PhD student in entomology at the University of Massachusetts. She told him about Warren, her summer jobs, "destiny, hypnosis, dream significance, chance, future plans." Then they went to a restaurant and talked another hour over sandwiches and coffee. She reported to her mother: "It dawned on me during the course of conversation that daddy majored or taught entomology." It turned out the young man knew Otto Plath's book about bees. "Life seemed too strange for words," Sylvia thought: "his name was Bill something-or-other, and for a few hours I told him about most of my life and ideas and I think I loved him for talking to me. It just shows what wonderful people an uninhibited girl can run across."

At nearly the same time as this encounter on a bus, Plath wrote a story, "Though Dynasties Pass," about a one-legged Korean War veteran on crutches on a train in conversation with a young woman with an art book who might have been Sylvia Plath. He has the estranged affect of a soldier going home, the kind of alienated character that Hemingway and Faulkner wrote about, but in this case the story turns on the young woman's under-standing that the soldier, for all his misgivings, must make contact with his sister again, establishing the familial connection that was so vital to Plath. He looks at the young woman's book and confesses he does not understand what the artists are getting at, and she replies: "these guys, they don't want to paint apples in the same old way, so that's why they use all those blobs of color . . . to make people get excited and see things fresh and all." He is disarmed and, you might say, refreshed by her simple, direct explanation. It is such a good example of how Sylvia wanted to include the world in her prose and make readers see her and her art in new ways. The young woman wants to know about his family, just like Sylvia wanted to know about her friends' families or even the circumstances of a stranger she met on a bus, establishing a bond that brought home to her so much of the world. The Korean War gets hardly a line in the story, but it is an important one—a response to her question about what it is like: "Oh, not much different," he says. "Flatter and muddier, that's all." It is the same world for everyone, yet he fears his sister will not understand. But the young woman won't have it and tells him he has to see his sister right way and not check into a hotel as he had planned. She asks him to imagine how his sister would feel knowing he has not returned home immediately. His face lights up at her forceful advice and admonition. And she tells him: "You look good when you get excited." Unlike an earlier incident when a woman offended him by offering him a seat, this young woman sees only his reaction to her and forthrightly tells him about it. It is a marvelous story that ends with him departing the train and banging on her window a final goodbye—a sure sign of elation at the exchange between them. This is what Sylvia Plath knew literature could do—act as a liberating force. The story's title alludes to a Thomas Hardy World War I poem, "The Breaking of Nations," and seems to have these lines in mind that follow a terse depiction of the disaster of war and why it cannot conquer life: "Though Dynasties pass. / Yonder a maid and her wight / Come whispering by: / War's annals will cloud into night / Ere their story die."

39

Although Sylvia had her slumps, her detailed Smith calendars reflect an irrepressible cub reporter persona, which she summed up for her mother at the end of April 1952: "You are listening to the most busy and happy girl in the world." She had just been elected to Alpha-Phi Kappa Psi, an honor society for the gifted in dance, drama, literature, music, or painting. Sylvia worked diligently on her drawing at Smith, and her saturation in modern painting pervades her poetry. Aurelia, with tears in her eyes, recalled a visit with Sylvia to the Smith Museum of Art. Aurelia admitted her ignorance about art until Sylvia went over each painting meticulously, opening up a world that had been closed to her mother. There is a point when the mother becomes the child, and the child becomes the mother, Aurelia told Harriet Rosenstein, affirming this was "true, good, and necessary."

In the spring of 1952, Sylvia reports for the *Daily Hampshire Gazette* and the *Springfield Daily News* on five events in four days, including a talk by poet Ogden Nash, three lectures on the European student, and a Friends of Smith meeting about "fascinating Smith alums with great book collections." She got these assignments because she worked fast and had an "angle." She was looking forward to W. H. Auden's course in creative writing next year. "Honestly, mum, I could just cry with happiness—I love this place so, and there is so much to do creatively, without having to be a 'club woman.' The world is splitting open at my feet like a ripe juicy watermelon." The reference to club woman reflected Sylvia's refusal to segregate herself like certain women interested in education and culture but often scorned as earnest but tiresome dilettantes not fully integrated into society—similar to career women, another negative term in Sylvia's lexicon.

40

Near the end of her sophomore year, Sylvia Plath did an inventory: "I will still whip myself onward and upward (in this spinning world, who knows which is up?) toward Fulbright's, prizes, Europe, publication, males. . . . From the inactive (collegiately), timid, introvertly-tended individual of last year, I have become altered. I have . . . directed my energies in channels which, although public, also perform the dual service of satisfying many of my creative aims and needs." She continued reporting campus events in articles that appeared in the *Daily Hampshire Gazette* and the *Springfield Daily News*. Her calendar reveals many hours spent in Press Board meetings and many more hours reporting on local events. On the Honor Board, she judged student infractions. She had made all sorts of efforts to engage with her community and to analyze her own state of mind.

A long journal entry probed what it meant to have sex and to mate and to achieve balance rather than domination. She wondered if Dick Norton's assertiveness was part of a "mother complex." Sylvia had been close to Mildred Norton, Dick's mother, who had taken a course in German from Otto Plath. The Nortons were virtually Plath family members, signified by Sylvia's calling Dick's mother "Aunt Mildred." Sylvia cited Philip Wylie's book on momism, *Generation of Vipers*, mentioning Dick's "ruling" matriarch" and his desire to "assert his independent virile vigor." She resented his "superiority complex," which she had as well, but his "patronizing attitudes" were "extremely offensive." His comments about family life inhibiting her creativity she viewed as a fear he sought to implant in her. She considered a vow not to marry, "JAMAIS, JAMAIS!" She wondered: "How many men are left? How many more chances will I have? I don't know. But at nineteen I will take the risk and hope that I will have another chance or two!"

In the meantime, she had to contend with the drudgery of a waitressing summer job in the Belmont Hotel, three shifts a day clearing tables and cleaning up, shunted into a side room for inexperienced staff. On really taxing days, she napped between shifts and fell into such a deep sleep she labeled her time-outs a "coma." To relieve the stress, she wrote letters, sunbathed, and swam between shifts. She turned down an extra job of handing out linen because it would have boosted her hours to seventy a week. Her body, she knew, could not hold up, and, as at Smith, she knew driving herself harder would result in a physical breakdown.

Then on June 10, 1952, her mother sent a telegram announcing that Sylvia had won a $500 *Mademoiselle* prize for her story "Sunday at the Mintons." After her elation, she began to wonder: Would Dick Norton recognize "his dismembered self!" That would be her concern with other fiction—notably *The Bell Jar*, which made no compromises with niceness or convention as she pilloried boyfriends, her mother's friends, and others in proximity to her astringent sensibility. "It's funny how one always, somewhere, has the germ of reality in a story, no matter how fantastic," she told her mother. But she was also proud of creating a character, Liz, who "isn't always ME," proving she was beginning to use her "imagination to transform the actual incident. I was scared that would never happen—but I think it's an indication that my perspective is broadening."

So what exactly had Sylvia Plath accomplished in "Sunday at the Mintons"? The story is about Elizabeth Minton and her "supremely fastidious brother," Henry, now in retirement and waited upon by his servile sister. Sylvia had reassembled Dick Norton as a pontificating older man, "invariably so clear, so precise" and condescending to his daydreaming sister. Sylvia clearly had had enough of Dick worship and had begun to resent his lectures, his careful arranging of their dates, his insistence on the superiority of science—all of which she exaggerated in Henry's moralizing and sanctimoniousness. Sylvia feared being caught up in male-pattern hegemony—her language in this story recalls Lowell's poem "Patterns," as Elizabeth goes about, "her full lavender skirt brushing and rustling against the stiff, polished furniture." Henry reduces the world "to scale," to his beloved maps, while Elizabeth dreams over "pictures of the mountains and rivers with queer foreign names." She has it in her to be Sylvia, a world traveler and achiever, but she has bent to her brother's rule even as she is irritated by his clock and compass and the "relentless exactness" of his mechanisms. If not in reality, then in imagination, she seeks a release from his complacent, patriarchal tyranny. She conceives of a scene in which she has jettisoned Henry. She loses her mother's amethyst brooch in the terrific wind and implores him to retrieve it from the rocks. The bulky Henry "bent slowly, majestically, puffing a little from his heavy dinner" and is overcome by a "great bulk of green water moving slowly, majestically inward." He is pictured as a "colossus astride the roaring sea," the image of brotherly/fatherly majesty that would become the title poem of the only poetry collection Sylvia published—but Henry goes down into the elements that can no longer be reduced to his "maps and the sea serpents drawn decoratively in the middle of the Atlantic Ocean." Sylvia could hardly restrain the humor in the disappearance of this pretentious man Elizabeth compares to a porpoise. Elizabeth thinks "sympathetically of Henry and how he never could digest shellfish." This hilarious revenge fantasy ends when Elizabeth is tugged out of her daydream by Henry, who tells her it is getting late. She sighs in submission and says, "I'm coming." In *Mademoiselle*, as Sylvia Plath very well knew, transgression could be portrayed only as a dream so as to keep intact the status quo of male privilege while giving young women at least some outlet for their rebellion. Winning this prize, Sylvia said, encouraged her to apply for a guest editorship at the magazine for the following summer.

41

Sylvia Plath relieved herself of daily cares by going to the movies—in this case with a Princeton undergraduate. She commemorated the date in a remarkable passage that melded her exhilarating experience with that of millions of others. Her journal entry is like that moment in *Jane Eyre* when Jane turns to the reader and says: "millions are in silent revolt against their lot." The seeming triviality of Sylvia's complaints about her summer job had another meaning: the recognition that like so many people she did not want to wait, to bow down in service, to simply do the job demanded of her. And like so many other people in the summer of 1952, she went to the movies—in this case to see a double bill: *Quartet* (based on Somerset Maugham stories) and *Kind Hearts and Coronets*. It was like attending a continuous mass: "one may stay through the beginning of the second to achieve full continuity" in the "democratic twilight" of the theater. She described what happened in the semidark:

> Mamie and Joe nuzzle each other playfully, fondly in response to the sermon of a screen kiss, there is no one to be censorious, no one who really minds. For this is the altar at which more Americans spend their time and money, daily, nightly, than ever before. Here the mystic incense of the traditional popcorn, chewing gum and chocolate, of mixed perfume and whiskey smells is neutralized and cooled by the patented air-conditioning system. And here people can lose their identity in a splurge of altruism before the twentieth century god. His messengers, his missionaries are everywhere. Dark in the room above your heads, one runs the machine; reel after vibrating reel of divine life circles under his direction onto the mammoth screen, playing forth the drama, the life force, the Bible of the masses. Rave notices are circulated in the newspapers. Everybody reads them. Sex and slaughter are substituted for the sin and sulphur of the pulpits, now quite antiquated. Instead of watching a man dictate manners and morals, you watch the very workings of these manners and morals in an artificially constructed society which to you, is real. Which, to all the worshipers, is the most wonderful and temporary reality they could ever hope to know. [PJ]

She was quite aware of the technology of this "wonderful and temporary reality" as projected through machines that both excited and cooled the audience on a summer night when in most places and homes such relief from the heat and such suffusing of romance were not to be had.

As to herself and her date, that part of it had to be told in the third person as she observed their coupling: "his arm rested for a little on the back of her chair, and his hand, now and then, tightened appreciatively on her shoulder, and she wanted very badly for him to hold her in his arms because it was a long while since she had been made love to, and then it had been quite thoroughly and wonderfully." She wrote about "disciplining" her libido as she seemed to be channeling her screen favorite, Scarlett O'Hara, by falling into a "drawling southernly" accent. At the end of the night, her date said she was "sweet and nice." She replied "huskily," in another bravura movie moment: "Sometimes I have to be told." Then he wanted to make love to her, but she gently withdrew, settling on another date with him the next day in Boston, where she had her first scotch and soda, watching the waiter mix it in relief that she did not have to deal with the "tray full of glasses and bottles and colored plastic sticks" and all the "glassy glitter and tinkle."

The heady, troubling early summer of waitressing and dates came to a halt in late June in what Sylvia called "a final fatal sinus infection"—as if something in her had died. Back home she compared her period of recovery as the "lifting a bell jar off a securely clockwork-like functioning community, and seeing all the little busy people stop, gasp, blow up and float in the inrush, (or rather outrush,) of the rarified scheduled atmosphere—poor little frightened people, flailing impotent arms in the aimless air." That spectacle of the "repetitive rut," as she termed it in her journal, would, of course, eventually lead to one of her masterpieces, *The Bell Jar*.

Another image of the bell jar occurs in a March 24, 1952, letter to her close friend and college roommate, Marcia Brown. For the first time in her correspondence Sylvia expresses a wariness about her mother: She asked herself why she took the job and admitted "I think I did it to get away from mother & Wellesley, as much as I hate to admit it. I love her dearly, but she reverberates so much more intensely than I to every depression I go through. I really feel she is better without the strain of me and my intense moods—which I can bounce in and out of with ease." It is tempting to picture Aurelia's worried look in reaction shots in the movie of Sylvia Plath's life, followed by a shot of a receptive Marcia Brown, reading Sylvia's epistolary lament: "I miss our periodic urge-talks!" Sylvia had, by way of compensation, the attention of Art Kramer, a twenty-five-year-old Yale graduate who liked to talk politics—giving her an Adlai Stevenson speech and telling her about Whittaker Chambers's recently published autobiography, *Witness*. Sylvia thrived on these conversations and said he stirred up her "lethargic intellect," since she was in a babysitting world that had no call for big words.

Sylvia recovered from her infection and delighted in a new babysitting job near the Cape with a Christian Science family, the Cantors, who took her

into their confidence and made her part of the family. The Cantors would
remain important in Sylvia's life. She confided in Mrs. Cantor, explaining
how she just had to get away from her mother. Mrs. Cantor would later
see this was so, when Aurelia came to live with the Cantors for almost
two months during Sylvia's recovery in McLean Hospital after her suicide
attempt. Mrs. Cantor realized that Aurelia resented her husband for leaving
the family in debt and not providing for their future. The pressures Aurelia
felt had built up around her daughter. Aurelia needed "a lot of comfort,"
Mrs. Cantor told biographer Harriet Rosenstein in a remark that helps to
explain why Sylvia was so assiduous about informing her mother on an
almost daily basis about her plans. Aurelia, however, had been made to feel
she had no choice, telling Wilbury Crocket that shortly after Otto's death,
Sylvia had demanded she sign a statement declaring she would never marry
again. Aurelia felt bound by her promise, Crockett said. [HR] Aurelia, seeking to console her child, gave her a kitten, she told Harriet Rosenstein, and
the delighted and grateful child mentioned she knew her father did not like
cats, so the present was all the more precious. Aurelia implied that Sylvia
adjusted well to her father's death, and that her feelings changed only after
psychiatrists with "Oedipal theories" made "villains of parents."

  While working for the Cantors, Sylvia attracted the attention of Bob
Cochran, three years younger, a precocious suitor who adored her. She loved
what she called the subtle power of a woman that men succumbed to in their
need to idealize the beloved. "Oh, I bite, I bite on life like a sharp apple.
Playing it like a fish, I am happy," she wrote in her journal near the end
of summer: "And what is happy? It is going always on. There is something
better to be done than I have done, and spurred by the fair delusion of
progress, I will seek to progress, to whip myself on, to more and more—to
learning. Always." Ambitious in every sense of the word, in every aspect
of her life, she amazed Mrs. Cantor, who wondered at how Sylvia knew so
many boys, who showed up at the Cantors prepared to please Sylvia. Dick
Norton visited often and struggled to remain a contender. He had taken
up poetry and talked about Hemingway with her.

42

Sylvia was never not a writer. She sought out Val Gendron, who published
in the pulps and popular magazines. Sylvia wanted to know how it was done
and showed Val some of her work, and Val was impressed and offered to
recommend Sylvia to her agent. In her journal, Sylvia recorded Val's advice:

"Beginning writers work from the sense impressions, forget cold realistic organization. First get the cold objective plot scene set. Rigid. Then write the damn thing after lying on the couch and visualizing, whipping it to white heat, to life again, the life of the art, the form, no longer formless without frame of reference." To write better was to live better: "Always persists the credulous human vision, of something better than that which is," Sylvia wrote as she packed up to leave her summer job and prepare for a third year at Smith.

After a long talk with Mr. Crockett, her high school mentor, Sylvia thought of graduate study in England, Oxford or Cambridge. England would be her "jumping-off place" for travel on the continent. She planned to study philosophy, write stories, and write a novel. Although she declared her love for both Norton brothers, she considered the idea of falling in love and having "an affair with someone over 'there.'" Crossing the Atlantic seemed essential to proving to herself what she could achieve, even if she returned home to resume the life she had left.

43

On September 26, 1952, Sylvia Plath began her third year at Smith, with courses beginning in "full force." In Lawrence House, she tended to study on her own, "in her room, rather than in the library." A friend, Claiborne Phillips, sometimes saw her at her desk, and sometimes "cross-legged on her bed with her hair falling down around her face, obscuring it except for the very front. She sat that way on her bed when I would come in her room to talk, hunched over, sometimes with an elbow on one knee as we talked." To Harriet Rosenstein, Phillips recalled Sylvia's "slim body and animated expression" in the "late afternoon sun shining in through the window" and a "companionship of loneliness together": "I think we were both very lonely but didn't know how to break through to each other." They did not share childhood memories, or much about their lives before Smith: "our earlier lives seemed remote."

Sylvia requested several items from home. Like other scholarship students she was required to work an hour per day as part of her room and board. She waitressed at lunch. A complimentary letter from Olive Higgins Prouty signaled continued financial support for Sylvia's studies. Her course work for the year included medieval literature, modern poetry, Milton, and physical science. She decided to drop art because of a heavy schedule. A letter from Eddie Cohen about plans to marry a divorcee with a two-year old son provoked a paradoxical response: "What a wonderfully sordid life."

The steady, almost daily recitative that Sylvia sent from Smith to her mother—mainly a celebration of her good fortune—proved unsustainable in her journals, in which she had only herself for an audience: "God, if ever I have come close to wanting to commit suicide, it is now, with the groggy sleepless blood dragging through my veins, and the air thick and gray with rain and the damn little men across the street pounding on the roof with picks and axes and chisels, and the acrid hellish stench of tar." Yet suicide—a word she used casually—seemed a remote option and a capitulation to cowardice:

> To annihilate the world by annihilation of oneself is the deluded height of desperate egoism. . . . There is no integrating force, only the naked fear, the urge of self-preservation. I am afraid. I am not solid, but hollow. I feel behind my eyes a numb, paralyzed cavern, a pit of hell, a mimicking nothingness. I never thought, I never wrote, I never suffered. I want to kill myself, to escape from responsibility, to crawl back abjectly into the womb.

Some of these words Sylvia would later repeat in one of her last desperate letters, but earlier depressive episodes hardly seem prophetic. How many young women and men in college do not encounter the self-doubt, the desire to return home—as Ann Davidow did? Sylvia spoke for herself but for many like her who still want to read her because she confronted her anxieties:

> I do not know who I am, where I am going—and I am the one who has to decide the answers to these hideous questions. I long for a noble escape from freedom—I am weak, tired, in revolt from the strong constructive humanitarian faith which presupposes a healthy, active intellect and will. There is no where to go—not home, where I would blubber and cry, a grotesque fool, into my mother's skirts—not to men where I want more than ever now the stern, final, paternal directive—not to church which is liberal, free—no, I turn wearily to the totalitarian dictatorship where I am absolved of all personal responsibility and can sacrifice myself in a "splurge of altruism" on the altar of the Cause with a capital "C."

It is noteworthy that she saw the social, psychological, and political implications of her depression and was not willing to consign the management of her identity to others. Near the end of her life, she would again reject the idea of returning home—even the idea of awaiting deliverance from a "paternal directive," a Daddy, or an institution. In "Among the Bumblebees," a story written at Smith at this time, a dying father, once powerful, declines and becomes remote, signaling Sylvia's lifelong fear of abandonment and the dread that her "whole being" was, as Linda Wagner-Martin comments, "centered in the 'core of himself.'" [LWM2] Yet aside from this story, Sylvia continued to view her life in larger terms. She would not surrender to a more constricted kind of existence that Elizabeth tolerated in "Sunday at the Mintons." She was leading herself to the larger statements of poems like "Daddy": "I can begin to see the compulsion for admitting original sin, for adoring Hitler." [PJ]

Unlike most of her classmates and contemporaries, Sylvia Plath had a sense of destiny, which sometimes stymied as much as it propelled her, since she worried about a correlation between success and suicide: "Why did Virginia Woolf commit suicide? Or Sara Teasdale—or the other brilliant women—neurotic? Was their writing sublimation (oh horrible word) of deep, basic desires? If only I knew. If only I knew how high I could set my goals, my requirements for my life!" In the meantime, she had to pretend, as she did for her mother's sake: "Masks are the order of the day—and the least I can do is cultivate the illusion that I am gay, serene, not hollow and afraid." [PJ]

Sylvia had a long discussion with a nurse in the infirmary who talked about nursing school, her boyfriend, and his brother's suicide and was told "Some people can take just so much and no more." [PJ] Two days later in a letter to her mother Sylvia referred to herself as a "depressive maniac." In her journal for November 18, 1952, she cried: "You have forgotten the secret you knew, once, ah, once, of being joyous, of laughing, of opening doors." The next day, she did allow her mother part way into her state of mind, writing in a long letter that she was eager to get home for a rest given her "very frustrated mental state." She worried about her science course: "I have practically considered committing suicide to get out of it." The course had become a symbol of all she wanted to avoid—the "barren dry formulas" that were the antithesis of her dedication to art, now acknowledged in her inclusion in *America Sings: Anthology of College Poetry* (1952). The science course paralyzed her: "I don't give a damn about valences, artificial atoms & molecules." She considered seeing the school psychiatrist.

A month later, restored over Thanksgiving, Sylvia entertained Dick Norton's suit, which now included sending her his fiction and poetry—"bless the lad for trying," she wrote her mother. She entertained a newcomer, Myron Lotz, an impressive athlete pitching for a Detroit Tigers minor league team and a "brilliant scholar" from an Austro-Hungarian immigrant family. Even

Marilyn Monroe (Nell Forbes) in *Don't Bother to Knock* (1952).

more encouraging was a rejection from the *New Yorker* that said "PLEASE
TRY US AGAIN." She was "thrilled to bits."

She closed out the year with Perry Norton and Myron Lotz, including a
drive with Lotz into the country and a walk past a mental hospital hearing
people screaming, "a most terrifying holy experience, with the sun setting
red and cold over the black hills . . . I want so badly to learn about why
and how people cross the borderline between sanity and insanity!" That
borderline was like the ha ha of Jennifer Dawson's novel, that recess of
land separating the asylum from the rest of the world that she was reading
about in the last days of her life.[17] How to make it over into sanity out of
the snake pit of an asylum and across the ha ha was already imprinted in the
imagination of a young woman still on the happy side of that divide. How
the world could seem alien to a young woman in mental distress had also
been the theme of *Don't Bother to Knock*, a film Sylvia saw on September 13, 1952. It featured Marilyn Monroe as a disturbed young woman trying to overcome the trauma of her fiancé's death. What may have lingered
in Sylvia's imagination was the sense of acute isolation that the mirror-
gazing Monroe accentuated by her reveries in front of a mirror that swallowed her up just as thoroughly as the self-consumed speaker of Sylvia's
poem "Mirror."

The thrill-seeking Sylvia reported to Aurelia her first half-hour flight in a two-seater plane at the invitation of the pilot while Myron Lotz waited on the ground. She watched the mountains "reeling up into the sky" and the clouds floating below as the pilot did a "wing-over." "Never have I felt such ecstasy!" she exulted as she took over the stick and made the plane climb and tilt. But she still suffered from insomnia and made an appointment with the school psychiatrist about her science course.

44

In late December 1952, on a visit to Dick Norton, now in a tuberculosis sanitarium in Saranac, New York, Sylvia broke her left leg skiing rather recklessly down a steep hill. Was she just after adventure, or seeking some dramatic departure from her anxieties over the formulaic world of science and Dick Norton? She joked to her mother that her fractured fibula caused no pain but was hard to "manipulate while charlestoning."

In the winter of 1953, an exhausted Sylvia had to hobble to class and spent much time in her room with an inarticulate roommate, Mary, "a brilliant science major . . . a rather forbidding, cold personality," remembered Enid Epstein, Sylvia's close friend. [HR] Sylvia seemed almost driven mad by her "stultifying" science course—the very subject Dick Norton so prized but which she dreaded. In her journal, she described this period as the nadir, a winter solstice of suffering. "Mary Ventura and the Ninth Kingdom" ably captures this dour period. She puts her protagonist on a train to death, envisaged as a trip north into the cold, the "gray streams of ice between the cracks in the stones. The frozen surface caught the light from the car and glittered as if full of cold silver needles." The Ninth Kingdom is the "kingdom of negation, of the frozen will." The protagonist of the story manages to get off the train and save herself, but it is a near thing.

Sylvia also felt she had escaped from the train of academic nemesis by launching a successful petition to audit her science course so that she would no longer have to study the tiresome textbook and sit for tests. She relieved her stress by dwelling on Myron Lotz, an athletic and intellectual Yale student that had become a replacement for Dick Norton, whom Sylvia now despised for his competitiveness and jealousy, which brought out the same in her. She no longer desired Dick and could not imagine living with him. He shriveled in her estimation, short and stocky, not the "Giant, superman: mental and physical" she yearned for in her journal. Just then another titan arrived: "the most handsome, tall, learn, curly brown-haired boy," she confided to her mother. Gordon Lameyer was a senior at Amherst majoring in English whose mother attended Sylvia's Smith Club talk. He looked "most promising," she concluded.

The break with Dick Norton signaled a passage in Sylvia's life, the moment when she realized that she would choose only the very best man to "heighten" her, as she put it, suggesting that she sought a mate who would help her to aspire higher than seemed possible with Norton and other young men she had dated. It is difficult not to think of Myron Lotz as a kind of dress rehearsal for Ted Hughes. She liked the "tender and rough sex play" with Myron. [PJ]

"Do I want to crawl into the gigantic paternal embrace of a mental colossus?" she asked and answered herself in a journal entry: "A little maybe. I'm not sure." She looked forward to the possibility of a "creative marriage now as I never did before." Approaching the spring of 1953, she was reading, quoting, and feeling like Gerard Manley Hopkins: "The world is charged with the grandeur of God." She had begun to think of life after Smith: graduate school, a Fulbright to England, a job in publishing, and then marriage?

This point in a Smith College student's education, heading into her last year, meant finding a lifetime mate—that is what Adlai Stevenson, the Commencement speaker, said a woman had been educated for: a husband and family that she could nurture, applying all she had learned to household management. Although Sylvia Plath had no immediate plans for marriage, every date now seemed especially susceptible to her dreams of an ideal marriage partner, and that cultural imperative to mate, saturated with her sexual fantasies, culminated in a villanelle, "Mad Girl's Love Song," published in the *Smith Review* in the spring of 1953. Women were supposed to hold back, remain virgins, and it had upset Sylvia that Dick Norton felt no such diktat to abstain. Women could be seduced, but her own desire to seduce the inexperienced Myron Lotz had to be hidden, vouchsafed only to her journal. But a poem could say it all by being, just that, a poem, relinquishing—if only in her imagination—societal restraints, expressing, at once, both her active control over her love and her submission to it: "I dreamed that you bewitched me into bed / And sung me moon-struck, kissed me quite insane. / (I think I made you up inside my head.)" What possessed Ted Hughes to leave this poem out of *Collected Poems*?[18] Only later in *Birthday Letters*, decades after her death, would he begin to countenance how much she had made of him herself, and how much that making of him cost her: "I shut my eyes and all the world drops dead." The poem ends with a wistful recognition of mortality and the evanescence of love, lost and awaiting a return as "I grow old and forget your name." What time could do to experience, turning the yearning for love into a fading memory, haunts the poem and maddens its singer, for it is a work that cries out to be made into a song, a lyric that you can't, in fact, get out of your head, a mad song, bringing into Sylvia Plath's poetry, Peter K. Steinberg observes, madness, a subject, he notes, that "would be integral to Plath's work." The poem is an astonishing performance for a poet, still an undergraduate, "the best I've written yet," she told her mother. In the rigid structure of a villanelle, Sylvia seemed to right herself out of the misery of looking at how her leg had withered after the cast had been taken off and her worry that a delayed visit from Myron Lotz might result in their not getting together at all.

45

Three years before her sudden, dramatic marriage to Ted Hughes, Sylvia Plath thought of herself in quite another way, telling her mother that "love is difficult to define, but it is a very slow growing rational thing. I have to know a great deal about anybody, and be able to predict reasonably the future life I'd have, before I could ever commit the next 50 years of my life." Love was on her mind as she worked in April on a story for submission to *True Story*, which specialized, as Kathy Newman puts it, in "conflicts over money, class, and work."[19] Narrated by Jenny Martin, "I Lied for Love" drew on details from Sylvia's summer work on a truck farm. Like Sylvia, Jenny is unnerved by the way the male laborers' looks dress her down, making her feel naked. Jake's "slick, secret smile" makes her cheeks burn. She is rescued by an Estonian, Ivan (modeled after Ilo), with a bayonet scar on his chest from fighting overseas. Just as Jake, who has discovered Jenny alone, is about to rape her—the scene becomes more of a bodice-ripper than a *True Story* romance—Ivan arrives and strikes the "selfish savage beast" to the floor. Nothing so dramatic had happened in Sylvia Plath's account of her own experience, but her story required, she supposed, this melodramatic turn—with a Superman, who carries the shaken Jenny to her father who fires Jake and warns his daughter not to trust boys—any boys. They only want to get their way and to do her dirt. Her father has wanted to keep her innocent, which seems the point of an earlier scene when he is shocked to see Jenny wearing the dress of her dead mother, Marianne. Unnerved by his daughter's sudden grown-up appearance, without the pigtails he has cherished and which she has cut off, he strikes her unconscious, and when she awakes he profusely apologizes, although it is evident he cannot cope with his daughter's impending maturity. She, in turn, is treated as a country bumpkin when she enters high school and is made to feel uncomfortable

Barbara Stanwyck (Stella) and Anne Shirley (Laurel) in *Stella Dallas* (1937), written by Olive
Higgins Prouty.

by her wealthier classmates in a scene foreshadowing the class conflicts of
"Superman and Paula Brown's New Snowsuit," a story Sylvia would write
a year later under the guidance of critic Alfred Kazin.

In "I Lied for Love," Phil Forester plays the role of Superman-savior, the
kind of tall, dark, and handsome boy that Sylvia mooned about in her early
diaries. Phil, the seeming epitome of the gentleman-hero, bows low to her
when he first notices Jenny at a jewelry shop counter where she is working.
She has to lie to her father when she goes out with Phil to become part of
his "rich, fast life," just as Sylvia raced around in a blue convertible with her
high school classmates. Now Jenny is accepted as a peer among Phil's friends,
as she speeds along in his blue convertible. She subdues her conflicted
feelings about deceiving her father and memories of Jake's ugly advances
as Phil kisses her tenderly and presents her with a gift of perfume, the first
tribute she has received from a boy. Her best friend, Mary Jackson, warns

Jenny that dreams of marriage are foolish since Phil's family will surely want him to marry a society girl. In this story, Sylvia Plath places herself in the world of Olive Higgins Prouty and *Stella Dallas*, in which wealth rules and romance among unequals leads to disaster. But Jenny cannot help herself in her drive to get away from lowly farm life. She worries about forsaking her father, just as Sylvia dreaded abandoning Aurelia and that modest home on Elmwood Road, and all that Sylvia no longer cared to share with her mother and the smaller world Sylvia had left behind.

"I Lied for Love" is a sublimated story about the ambivalence of adolescence—made all the more agonizing because of the heroine's consciousness of class and what she leaves behind. Who knows what the setting of Prouty's Brookline estate triggered in her protégé's own storyline? Why did Sylvia have to write so often—sometimes twice or more a week and even twice a day—to her mother from Smith? What thread in her childhood did she fear losing, what gain had to be amalgamated in the mother-daughter nexus? As willful as Jenny is about her destiny, she cannot tell her story without feeling the pull of her father's desire to sequester her in the family compound similar to what Aurelia had arranged for Sylvia. Mary Jackson tells Jenny that she is all her father has. The same could be said for Aurelia, although Sylvia made "I Lied for Love" more excruciating by eliminating the presence of a brother for Jenny. But the parallels abound: Jenny's hard working father has a heart attack; Aurelia had been hospitalized with ulcers.

For Sylvia's first meeting with Prouty in December 1950, she came prepared having read Prouty's class-conscious novels, which is perhaps why she confessed to Prouty her mixed feelings about a high school sorority—her desire to belong and at the same time her distaste for that kind of exclusivity. "Seems to me there's a story there," Prouty commented. Writing for *True Story*—quite aside from Sylvia's ambition to write for all kinds of audiences and cash in—seems also to have been a showing of solidarity with the less privileged, and with the kind of sentimental but socially engaged fiction Prouty published.

Whatever strains informed stories like "I Lied for Love," everything seemed to fall into place by the late spring of 1953 when Sylvia began earning money as a journalist for the *Daily Hampshire Gazette* and editing the *Smith Review*, which she thought under Sally Rosenthal's editorship had been too provincial. Sylvia wanted to make it a national magazine, according to Sally, who became angry at Sylvia's criticism. To Sally, Sylvia could be charming but also a demanding perfectionist, and in a world of her own that seemed way beyond what Smith had to offer her. [HR] But as Sue Weller, another Smith classmate said, Sylvia could "lift me out of myself," showing the way to a world far greater than most undergraduates could have imagined. [HR]

Sylvia covered the appearances of actor Charles Laughton and poets
W. H. Auden and Dylan Thomas, and she pressed ahead with submissions
to the *New Yorker* after an encouraging rejection letter and publication of
three poems in *Harper's* magazine. Her grand destiny seemed assured when
she was awarded one of the highly competitive summer guest editorships
at *Mademoiselle* in New York City, where she would stay, for the first time,
in a hotel. She wrote to her mother during one of her typical busy days
at Smith: "I'll have the chance to see what it's like living in the Big City,
plus working on a magazine!" She vowed to be as "cooperative and eager"
at the magazine as she was with the Cantors, and to write a piece for the
Christian Science Monitor about her month at the magazine. She seems to
have had at least some idea that she would need to be on call, meeting relentless deadlines, working all day in an office, with strenuous demands like
those that had depressed her during her brief employment at the Belmont
Hotel and with the Mayos. To her brother Warren, Sylvia described the
guest editorship as a five-day schedule of "grubby work" but also going to
theater openings in "4 gala weeks." She described her junior year at Smith
as a "charmed plathian existence," save for "five or six really tense times."
But what if each day and week included such tensities? She does not seem
to have contemplated that question.

46

In the midst of explaining to her mother why the mother-dominated Dick
Norton could never have been her choice as a mate, Sylvia also noted that
Myron Lotz was "emotionally insecure and uncertain of who he is." This first
sign that he was not to be her ideal mate also signaled her own continuing
quest for security, if not yet a desire to settle down in a marriage. Her own
doubts about herself seem to have been allayed by all the good news, and
yet she had some premonition she did not express to her mother: Sylvia was
about to undergo a trial, a passage into a new territory that excited her but
that she had to negotiate by making that vow to be "cooperative and eager."
She had not yet experienced the strain that vow would make on her appetitive
sensibility, and she could not acknowledge—not to her mother and apparently not to herself—that part of her passage into the next phase of her life
was also an embarkation from the mother ship. All Aurelia ever received from
her daughter was the assurance that she was Sylvia's indispensable mainstay.

On June 3, 1953, Sylvia gave her mother an accounting of her first three
exhausting and exhilarating days of her *Mademoiselle* month in New York

The "exquisite Barbizon" where Plath resided during her month in New York City.

City. She began with describing the "exquisite Barbizon": "green lobby, light cafe-au-lait woodwork, plants, etc." The elevator "whooshed" her up to room 1511: "Green wall-to-wall rug, pale beige walls, dark green bed-spread with rose-patterned ruffle, matching curtains, a desk, bureau, closet, and white enameled bowl growing like a convenient mushroom from the wall. Bath, shower, toilet, a few doors down the hall. Radio in wall, telephone by bed—and the view!" From her window she looked down on gardens, alleys, the Third Avenue elevated train, the United Nations, and a "snatch of the east River." From her desk at night a "network of lights, and the sound of car horns" serenaded her with the "sweetest music. I love it." She seemed pleased with her fellow guest editors, attractive and well turned out. They had already been to Richard Hudnut for their hairdos and makeup. Only a nosebleed at breakfast spoiled her fun. She was surprised not to be named fiction editor but claimed she loved being managing editor because of the "all-inclusive" work. Perhaps at first this was so, but the demands of the job would soon drain and frustrate her. Her interview with novelist Elizabeth Bowen would appear in the August issue of *Mademoiselle* along with the interviews the other guest editors had with fashion designers and beauty experts. Sylvia's was the only interview with a writer. She had prepared by reading Bowen's work, especially *The Death of the Heart*, a masterpiece that would have its impact on *The Bell Jar*. But Plath's piece had been honed to three sentences with bits of Bowen's words used like sound bites about herself as a "failed poet" who preferred the short story form and believed young writers needed "criticism and encouragement." No transcript of the Plath-Bowen interview, or notes about it, seem to have survived.

Letters home reflect a narrowing of ambition as Sylvia pinned all her hopes on getting into Frank O'Connor's Harvard summer school short story course. Exactly why she thought this course was so crucial to her development as a writer is not clear, but it seems that she regarded him as her contact with the wider world of publishing and professional writing that she had first encountered with Val Gendron. Sylvia wanted to work every day on her fiction, and the O'Connor course would not only structure those writing days but give her the feedback that went beyond the rejection slips, even when they included some words about her writing.

To Myron Lotz, Sylvia wrote about staying at a hotel "for circumspect young women." It was also the site where women from everywhere, it seemed, came to "start an entirely new life," as Paula Bren, a historian of the Barbizon, puts it, and take "fate in her own hands." Circumspect meant the Barbizon was a sanctuary, a place of protection against the men who prowled about, seeking to get past the front desk, which was as watchful as what Plath had experienced at Smith. This was the domicile of aspirants to fame in the worlds of fashion, art, acting, and publishing, an establishment in cahoots, in fact, with Betsy Talbot Blackwell, editor-in-chief of *Mademoiselle*, to chaperon young women to success. This was heady stuff for out of town hopefuls, some of whom succumbed to the stress, "lonely enough," Bren reports, to "commit suicide: often on Sunday mornings"—perhaps after the pressures of the week and after a Saturday night date failed to materialize or had gone wrong, leading to the Sunday of sorrow. *The Bell Jar* recounts the disastrous efforts of young women to break out, to discover New York on their own, before returning to what was called a "secular nunnery." In the 1950s, New York "without a male companion was a restricted experience. Being a woman alone, without a date, limited where you could go and what you could do," Bren writes. This was a time when a woman could not walk into a bar alone without exciting the suspicion she was there for trade. And don't forget these *Mademoiselle* hopefuls were contestants, having competed for the select group of twenty that Plath contracted in her novel to a biblical twelve, apostles of a "star formation," which had the guest managing editor at the apex of a *Mademoiselle* group photograph. Plath was expected to play the role of working woman so often assigned to the acerbic Eve Arden in Hollywood films. Sylvia would not, in the main, be writing. The Plath who had shied away from elective office in school and the administrative roles that would have sapped the energy for writing now had to direct the traffic of talent.

Of course, Sylvia was excited by meeting so many writers, publishers, and poets, listening to managing editor Cyrilly Abels converse on the telephone with "important people," and "learning innumerable things about magazine work and human beings." The parties, the shows, the ballet, the museums, a Yankees baseball game were a thrill, but she also noticed: "Lives drip away like water here, not even making a dent in the acres of concrete." Then on June 19, all this pell-mell partying and event-going put off Sylvia Plath, so that she would be unable to recover her bearings. Sick "at the stomach" over blaring headlines announcing the execution of the Rosenbergs, she watched a "tall beautiful catlike girl who wore an original hat to work every day," the very image of a *Mademoiselle* petted protégé. This model of fashion, Sylvia wrote in her journal, "rose to one elbow from where she had been napping on the divan in the conference room, yawned and said with beautiful bored nastiness: 'I'm so glad they are going to die.' She gazed vaguely and very smugly around the room, closed her enormous green eyes and went back to sleep." Hardly a sentient human being—more like, indeed, a cat. No one in this habitat paid attention or appreciated "how big a human life is, with all the nerves and sinews and reactions and responses that it took centuries and centuries to evolve." She heard no protests over this "appalling thing" that would happen that night: "it is too bad that it could not be televised," Plath noted in her journal, "so much more realistic and beneficial than the run-of-the mill crime program. Two real people being executed. No matter. The largest emotional reaction over the United States will be a rather large, democratic, infinitely bored and casual and complacent yawn." New York—the world—was never the same for her.

Sylvia signed off her letter to Myron Lotz: "your bucolic newyorker"— perhaps reflecting how much the city rushed her along. She was hardly a rural maiden, but the pace undid many a writer, like William Faulkner, who sent home for help from his wife who joined him as high up in a building as he could afford on one of his early noisy visits to New York. Then, too, New York was "abominably hot," she wrote her brother, "perishing for the clean unsooted greenness of our backyard." She was just plain worn out and unable to digest all that had happened to her. The change from the hectic schedule at Smith to the frenzy of New York City had been too much. "I have been ecstatic, horribly depressed, shocked, elated, enlightened and enervated." To think of it all at once, she confided to Warren, would split open her mind. She used the word "bucolic" again to emphasize what a rube she had been but also perhaps to signal how the city had depleted the oxygen of her imagination.

47

Almost as soon as Sylvia arrived home, she went for a swim at Morses Pond, the very epicenter of her childhood, commemorated again and again in her childhood diaries. This one-hundred-acre site is where she went pic-nicking and water sliding with her friends, caught fish, biked, sunbathed, and boated with Dick Norton. She had broken through the pond's winter ice and "christened" it with her bare feet. It had been her relief on muggy days. She swam in water over her head and had stood on her hands under water. In the deeper part (twenty-three feet) she had done her high dives. Morses Pond had been the scene of so many rendezvous and farewells. This time she had with her Gordon Lameyer, who had sought her out as both beauty queen and intellectual icon. He was her Gary Cooper, remi-niscent of the actor who had played in *The Wedding Night* (1935), whom the writer Tony Barrett modeled after F. Scott Fitzgerald. Gordon discussed his favorite, James Joyce, and his esoteric novel *Finnegan's Wake*. They read poetry together.

July 1: The entry in her calendar for Harvard Summer School is crossed out. She had not been accepted into Frank O'Connor's class on the short story. *She* had been crossed out. What to do? She picnicked with Marcia Brown along the Charles River. She spent more time with Gordon Lameyer and with Warren. She played tennis. She cleaned the car. On July 4, she put one word in her calendar: "decision." What did it mean? She tried to concentrate on shorthand lessons with her mother. She relieved her anxiety about staying home by going out with Gordon. But many days in her cal-endar were blank like the pages she could not fill with her fiction or poetry. She worked part-time in a mental hospital—not the best setting for a young woman fascinated with human psychology but also dreading the institu-tionalization that she had read about in *The Snake Pit* and then watched in the film adaptation starring Olivia de Havilland. She had dinner with Mrs. Prouty on July 27 but had nothing new to show to her benefactor. "Shockt" was the word in her calendar for the first brutal shock treatments given to her without any sort of sedative. Now she had fewer social engagements, and nothing at all listed for the week leading up to August 24 and her attempt to end her life. She was exhausted, no longer able to swim, her friend Pat O'Neill noticed. They sat on a raft, with Sylvia staring down into the water. [HR] Her days were full of deceit, her nights haunted by the truth. She could not sleep. New York had made her feel small.

The Elizabeth Bowen interview in the August issue of *Mademoiselle* had been shrunk to three pathetic sentences. She felt like a fraud who had let everyone down. She did not see how she could return to Smith now that her mind was a "blank." Worst of all, she had let herself down. She left her confession in a desk, admitting her guilt, and then went below, to the lower depths of the house, to end her existence. She later told Pat O'Neill, whom she had known since tenth grade: "If Mr. Crockett only knew the ways of compromising yourself." The artist's high ideals he had touted had been crushed in New York, and it was all about selling yourself, with "chromium-plated relationships . . . carried on to the clink of money." [HR] O'Neill's choice of words was apt, since in the 1950s chrome plating was replacing nickel on automobiles that became all shiny surfaces. The guest editors were, quite literally, the next year's models—to be replaced in the next model year as part of an incessant turnover of talent.

How Sylvia Plath tried suicide and how she was found became national news that she only began to absorb in the slow stages of her physical and mental recovery in the last four months of 1953. That recovery story, the significance of being found, grew in importance gradually, when she began to realize what kind of impact she could have on the world. The story of how Warren found her under the house, and of her return to life, however, has to be delayed in order to recount how Sylvia was sure she had lost herself and had become lost to the very world whose interest in her became part of her rebirth.

For eight days after Warren had rescued her, Sylvia remained in the Newton Wellesley Hospital before she was transferred to the psychiatric ward of Massachusetts General, where she became worse as the inmates taunted her, saying she should be in a "special ward for suicides." After Sylvia turned suspicious and delusional, Mrs. Prouty paid for a transfer to McLean Hospital on September 14 as a patient with a "psychoneurotic disorder" and a "depressive reaction." Aurelia was interviewed by Dr. Ruth Beuscher as part of the effort to establish an understanding of the patient's background and the reasons for her breakdown. A family history, recorded by Beuscher, described Sylvia's grandfather as "easy going," her grandmother as "homey," and Aurelia as highly intelligent, quiet, reserved, and trustworthy. Aurelia described herself as tense and worried about the family's financial security. She explained her unhappy marriage with Otto, made worse by the twenty-year gap in their ages, with few outings and no entertaining. A capsule biography of Otto mentioned his great fondness for his children, especially Sylvia, but that during his illness he had become short tempered and the household had become tense, although after his death, the presence of the grandparents had relaxed the atmosphere.

Aurelia told a happy story about her pregnancy and even her labor and delivery, which she called "cooperating with nature." Otto joined in her mood as she breast fed the baby, eight pounds and six ounces at birth, for five months. A month later Sylvia was teething, then walking at eleven months, and talking in sentences five months later. Toilet training began early and was entirely successful, although Sylvia had a tendency to become constipated and Aurelia resorted to suppositories. This superintending of bowel movements—a concern if Sylvia did not evacuate every day—went along with an initial lack of appetite that improved shortly after Warren was born. Sylvia grew up fearless, friendly with many playmates, and excelled in school, with happy periods at summer camp. Aurelia made it a practice to be frank about the facts of life so that sex was not a mystery to her children. She also explained the history of Sylvia's relations with Dick Norton and how he had "fallen" from her daughter's idealization of him when he confessed to his own sexual adventures. Sylvia had been frank with her mother, admitted she had "petted to orgasm" with Dick, but in effect she had followed her mother's counsel not to have intercourse, although she longed for the physical sensation of sex in a marriage, which she nevertheless dreaded because of its "responsibilities." Aurelia could think of no serious mental disorder before her daughter's suicide attempt and then described the harrowing days of confusion, indecision, and panic in July and August that were so unlike her daughter, who read a book on abnormal psychology and diagnosed herself as insane.

Dr. Ruth Beuscher, a young trainee, seemed to enjoy Sylvia's confidence after other senior members of the staff had not been able to help her. Later Sylvia described her as "only 9 years older than I, looking like Myrna Loy, tall, Bohemian, coruscatingly [sic] brilliant, and most marvelous." The reference to a movie star, ignored or passed over quickly by other biographers, is a key to the recovery of a young woman fascinated with stardom and who believed in the magical, healing properties and make believe of Hedy Lamarr and Rita Hayworth paper dolls, projections of a Sylvia Plath who would later model herself as Betty Grable for a magazine spread in a Cambridge University publication. Loy played both glamorous roles and those of compassionate mothers, as in *The Best Years of Our Lives*, and it was important to Sylvia to be in the care of a therapist who looked the part and was cinematically satisfying.

Myrna Loy, a Hollywood star. Plath believed Ruth Beuscher looked like Loy.

According to Ruth Beuscher's notes, Sylvia felt betrayed and trusted no one. She remained unwilling to talk and even exhibited signs of retardation, leading to the conclusion she was suffering "delayed adolescent turmoil." Beuscher left a detailed record, beginning on September 22: "Pleasant, friendly cooperative. Attitude superficial. Probably still suicidal." A week later, Sylvia's mood had improved and she was "more active" and interacting well with fellow patients. She had begun reading books in the hospital's library and taking long walks. She shied away from group activities but no longer resisted the idea that she would recover. But the positive signs were intermittent and an entry for October 6 reports episodes of depression, confusion, and suspicion. The next week Sylvia alternated between pleasant moods and a taciturnity that admitted of no discussion, except for her "shortcomings and self-deprecatory ideas." Beuscher believed her patient was still hiding tremendous hostility. Two weeks later, Sylvia kept expressing a sense of emptiness and then her rage as she described one of her visitors as "that old bat."

On October 27, Aurelia brought Sylvia flowers on her birthday, and her daughter threw them in a wastebasket. Sylvia claimed she had done so because there was no vase. But Beuscher thought otherwise and wondered how to deal with Plath's hostility so that it was not directed at herself. The therapist thought her patient might still be suicidal, even though she responded well to occupational therapy, including weaving and pottery making. On November 10, Sylvia finally expressed the desire to get well but doubted she would, since she still seemed empty-headed. Beuscher thought she remained suicidal. The depressions deepened and by November 24, Beuscher prescribed chlorpromazine, which made Sylvia drowsy and tired, which she interpreted as part of her depression and not a response to the drug.

On December 8, when suicide seemed a "real risk," Beuscher decided on electric shock treatment, convincing the head of psychiatry, Eric Lindemann, that "Sylvia's overriding sense of guilt and unworthiness could only be purged by the 'punishment' of shock treatments."[20] The first shock treatment, administered two days later, resulted in a "dramatic recovery." Now Sylvia became "cheerful, thoughtful, and cooperative." By the sixth treatment, however, she had had enough, and after one more session, Beuscher discontinued the shocks, agreeing to Sylvia's request that she be permitted visits home. She also longed to loll around in some "sunny tennis clime for a while"—much more therapeutic than enduring the New England winter that had done in Quentin Compson. Sylvia's story "Tongues of Stone" captures the moment of rebirth: "And in the dark the girl lay listening to the voice of dawn and felt flare through every fiber of her mind and body the everlasting rising of the sun."

Ruth Beuscher believed that her own bond with Sylvia Plath had made it possible for her patient to trust her and begin the route to recovery. Without question, Beuscher, who had conflicting feelings about her own mother, believed that Plath had bonded with her.[21] Sylvia had a spent a month declaring love for her mother, but the therapist suspected otherwise, and after some prodding, as she vouchsafed to Harriet Rosenstein, Sylvia revealed her hostile feelings. The therapist traced these feelings to an early rivalry for Otto Plath's affection, especially since Otto was old enough to be Aurelia's father and Aurelia acted almost as much as Sylvia's sister as her mother. Beuscher has been much criticized for indulging her patient, but it was never the therapist's intention to leave Sylvia with such negative feelings but rather to explore and resolve those feelings, as she had done with other patients and with herself.

On December 28, from McLean Hospital, Sylvia felt well enough to write to Eddie Cohen explaining what had happened to her. She began by denouncing her junior year at Smith, treating herself as a kind of imposter "skipping by" while friends were forging ahead with their educational and marital plans. Even worse, that summer she could not concentrate on shorthand or her literary work. Unable to sleep, and under psychiatric care, she had a terrible experience with outpatient "shock treatments." Because of her horror of mental hospitals, she decided to use her "last ounce of free choice and choose a quick clean ending." Better that than be a burden to her family. She would leave behind "illusions left among my profs, still poems to be published in Harper's, still a memory at least that would be worthwhile." Her body kept bobbing to the surface when she tried to drown herself, which is why she decided to take fifty sleeping pills and sequester herself in the basement, leaving a note that she had taken a "long walk." Her brother had rescued her after hearing her "weak yells," the result of her waking up after vomiting up the pills. All she could recall afterwards were nightmare days of "flashing lights, strange voices, needles"—depicted in her brilliant story "Johnny Panic and the Bible of Dreams." She was angry at those who would not let her die but insisted on dragging her into the "hell of a sordid and meaningless existence." In "Tongues of Stone," the depressed character, "the girl," sees herself as "a parasitic gall on the face of the earth," with the "backwaters of her mind" breaking out "on her body in a slow, consuming leprosy," her "dead brain folded up like a gray, paralyzed bat in the dark cavern of her living skull." What puts the girl in such a suicidal state is not explained, except for this suggestive passage, describing the period just before the suicidal act: "the girl had lain awake listening to the thin thread of her mother's breathing, wanting to get up and twist the life out of the fragile throat." Homicide or suicide seem to be the alternatives. The desire to erase herself, and to become unseen, had become inexorable: "There was nowhere to hide. She became more and more aware of dark corners and the promise of secret places. She thought longingly of drawers and closets and the black open gullets of toilets and bathtub drains. On walks with the fat, freckled recreational therapist she yearned toward flat pools of standing water, toward the seductive shadow under wheels of passing cars."

Now, however, Sylvia seemed eager to escape the surveillance at McLean, certain that she had improved enough to make it possible to resume her courses at Smith for the winter/spring semester of 1954, while remaining in touch with Beuscher and continuing sporadic consultations with her, exploring the ramifications of her suicide attempt and its impact on the world. She mentioned to Eddie Cohen that she had received letters from "all over the United States from friends, relations, perfect strangers and religious crackpots." Most of these letters have not survived, but Plath scholar Peter K. Steinberg tracked down well over two hundred notices of her suicide attempt in thirty different states and Canada. Sylvia's story struck some nerve in the culture that she would later explore in *The Bell Jar*. Just as she had planned, the suicide attempt had accomplished its purpose: leaving behind the memory of a promising poet. She had made her mark, a showing, a drama of her self. Her suicide effort had been successful, which is perhaps why when she spoke of it later to Anne Sexton, she did so without regret and did not say she would not do it again. "Lady Lazarus" boasts that suicide is "the theatrical / Comeback in broad day."

48

Articles published over three days that reported the search, the discovery, and the aftermath of Sylvia's suicide attempt included her photograph with sketchy details about her "mysterious disappearance." Aurelia, identified in many articles as a Boston University professor, told the *Boston Herald* about a note her daughter left around 2:00 p.m, August 24, 1953, mentioning she was going for a long hike and would return home the next day. Presumably, the note would give Sylvia enough time to end her life. Aurelia said that "as a girl," Sylvia "liked to be alone and enjoyed taking walks by herself." But perhaps because the note said Sylvia would return the next day, a suspicious Aurelia called the police at 6:00 p.m. One article, preserved in Olwyn Hughes's papers, appeared in the *Boston Traveler*, with a photograph of Sylvia, mentioning the "100-man" search party, including twelve policemen, assembled in an effort to find the "brilliant Smith College student." The *Boston Daily Record* reported that her "favorite spots for walking are the Public Garden and the Esplanade along the Charles River where police of the Back Bay and Joy St. stations went to look for her." A State Police bloodhound, "Big Sid," had been hampered by heavy rains the night before. Colonel Rex Gary, "a former Army Intelligence officer" and family friend, had joined the search. Some newspapers provided bulletins during the next two days: "Day-long search fails to find Smith student," reported the Amesbury, Massachusetts, *Daily News* on August 26. The *Daily Hampshire Gazette* noted that Plath had been an active college correspondent for the paper. It had been supposed, at first, that Plath's return home might have been delayed by an injury to her ankle since it had been broken in a skiing accident. Aurelia doubted it, since Sylvia always telephoned her when she was late.

The next day it was widely reported that a missing bottle of fifty sleeping pills had been found, with the implication that the search was on for a possible suicide. The *Albany Times-Union* noted she had been a "literary contributor" to national magazines and that she had been "despondent" over a writer's block, and quoted from "Mad Girl's Love Song": "I shut my eyes and all the / world drops dead." The *Albuquerque Journal* provided additional details about the search for "Pretty Sylvia Plath," including "a large number of Boy Scouts, in the hunt near the Plath home and around Lake Waban, Morses Pond," and a "five-mile stretch of woods that runs from the vicinity of the Plath home to the Weston [Massachusetts] line." Aurelia explained that her daughter had been depressed because she felt "she was unworthy of the confidence held for her by the people she knew." Other accounts had Aurelia saying Sylvia had been "nervous" and "under a doctor's care." Some publications, such as the Athol, Massachusetts, *Daily News*, provided a little more of Aurelia's reaction to her daughter: "For some time she has been unable to write either fiction, or her more recent love, poetry. Instead of regarding this as just an arid period that every writer faces at times she believed something had happened to her mind, that it was unable to produce creatively any more." The Beverly, Massachusetts, *Evening Times* reported that Sylvia had been "advised to devote less time to academic activities in the interest of her health" and gave this description of her "wearing a blue denim skirt and a blue jersey blouse. She is five feet nine and weighs 140 pounds. Her hair and eyes are brown." The paper quoted Aurelia as having questioned Sylvia's friends, and all had agreed she was "depressed and that it was very apparent that suicide was on her mind." The police had contacted Smith students all over the country in hopes of clues to her "mysterious disappearance." Aurelia told the *Boston Globe:* "It sounds peculiar, but she has set standards for herself that are almost unattainable. She's made almost a minor obsession of fulfilling what she believes to be her responsibility to her sponsors, and I am gravely concerned for her." Even though a doctor had said Sylvia suffered from "nervous exhaustion," Aurelia insisted the disappearance was "completely unlike her" and asked that a photograph of Sylvia be published to aid in the search. After nearly two days and with no trace of the "pretty Smith College poetess," the *Boston Herald* quoted police chief MacBey as saying "It doesn't look good." Sylvia had not taken any clothes or money with her, Aurelia said, suggesting her daughter was no runaway: "There is no question of a boy in the case."

The next day, Sylvia's grandmother, doing the wash, heard groaning, and her brother Warren traced the sound to underneath the house. The newspaper announced that a groggy Sylvia had been discovered after a forty-hour search wrapped in a blanket on the dirt floor of the cellar, a

LAKE WABAN. WELLESLEY COLLEGE.

A postcard of Lake Waban at Wellesley College, one of the locations where Boy Scouts helped search for Plath.

twenty-by-ten-foot space with cement walls, the entrance blocked from view by "a pile of kindling wood," which Sylvia had carefully constructed to show no sign of disturbance. The *Baltimore Sun* described the entrance to the suicide site as a "2 1/2 foot opening about 5 feet above the cellar floor." Warren and a police officer had crawled into the space to bring her out. The Asheville, North Carolina, *Citizen-Times* quoted Police Chief Robert McVey, who said "an empty water jar and a container of eight sleeping tablets were found by the girl's side" with forty tablets missing. The Attleboro, Massachusetts, *Sun*, in a piece titled "Home All Along," reported that Sylvia was in "critical condition," but another hospital source, quoted in the *Bangor Daily News* called her condition "fair." By August 27, 1953, the day after she had been found, the *Boston Globe* reported she was "out of danger." Other publications varied in their wording, calling her condition "satisfactory" and "fairly good." The *Burlington Daily News* noted that at the Newton-Wellesley Hospital, she "would not tell why she took 40 to 50 sleep capsules." *The Townsman*, a Wellesley newspaper, reported that Sylvia had "swallowed what is considered a lethal dose of sleeping pills." The Plath family, the paper noted, wished to express its "sincere thanks" for all who had participated in the two-day search. The same day the *Boston Evening American* ran a headline "Pill Girl 2 Days in Cellar," almost as if she had become a freak in a side show. The *Daily Oklahoman* headlined: "Sleeping Beauty Found at Home." Already, the mythological Sylvia Plath of poetry and of biography had been born, offering the miracle or trick of her recovered self to the world that is proclaimed in "Lady Lazarus."

There is no telling how much Sylvia read into the articles sent to her that appeared in newspapers from Massachusetts to Maine, New Hampshire, Vermont, New York, Connecticut, Maryland, Delaware, Rhode Island, New Jersey, Pennsylvania, Virginia, Washington, DC, Alabama, South Carolina, Tennessee, Louisiana, Florida, Oklahoma, Texas, Missouri, Ohio, Michigan, Illinois, Iowa, Wisconsin, Minnesota, New Mexico, Utah, California, and Canada. What she did read showed the impact she had on the world that went in search of her. It was like reading her own obituary. She had become a cynosure with the world trailing after her, asking, like her doctors, why she had wanted to end her life.

49

Perhaps the unspoken reason for the intense interest in Sylvia's Plath's disappearance and the drama of her depression had to do with what Aurelia told the *Boston Globe* about her daughter: She had been "unfailingly dependable." Here was, as the *Globe* put it, a "brilliant beautiful Smith College senior from Wellesley," a town of the wealthy and well-educated, gone missing. If someone like Sylvia Plath, with supposedly so much to live for, did not want to stick around, what about everyone else? Her fate is reminiscent of Edwin Arlington Robinson's "Richard Cory," "a gentleman from sole to crown / Clean favored and imperially slim," and "schooled in every grace," who on a "calm summer night, / Went home and put a bullet through his head." Sylvia included the poem in an anthology of poetry she had compiled for Mr. Crockett.

Although Sylvia had gashed her face and would carry a scar, the relief in the press was palpable in the announcements that she had been found "uninjured," "in good condition," or with "no apparent serious injury." Was there more to the story? What about all those parents, grandparents, and siblings—everyone on the edge of survival? As they poured over the details of Sylvia lost and found, issued in slow release form over three days, what did they read into the misadventure and rescue of this variously described "honor" and "scholarship" student? Some headlines, as in the *Des Moines Register* were evocative, "College Poetess Hunted in Woods." The headline, accompanied by a photograph in the Charleston, West Virginia, *Gazette*, seems, in retrospect, a foretelling: "OBJECT OF SEARCH." An "All-Out Quest" announced the *Gloucester Daily Times*.

What had happened to Sylvia Plath? She had returned home from the disequilibrium of New York City and discovered that she could not concentrate—on anything, not on learning shorthand, not on her writing, not on what she had proposed to do with her senior year at Smith. New York City had been her maximum opportunity, and in her view she had failed to measure up. That she was depressed was not, in fact, a judgment on her, although she looked at it that way. Her letdown was also the letdown of other young women who returned home from that heady New York City month; her letdown was also what many young people experience in the passage from one phase of life to another.

Sylvia was one of those superachievers, people of high ambition, who are often disappointed in their progress, so that they feel, however unreasonably, that they are behind where they should be. They have been caught up in what Gail Sheehy calls, in *Passages*, the "wunderkind pattern." In New York City, the whole world had seemingly opened up for Sylvia Plath, and then, as often happens to others at such moments, she was overwhelmed and scared like someone in the "period of provisional adulthood."

And yet Sylvia seemed to have returned to her exuberant self, arriving home from McLean in January 1954 for a weekend visit. Neighbor Karen Goodall remembered Sylvia shouting to her grandparents: "I'M HOME." They represented a profound source of stability and affection. Alison Smith, a Smith classmate, remembered how Sylvia gave her grandmother a "passionate hug" when she entered the house. [HR]

As she gained confidence, Sylvia began writing to her college and family friends to say she was gradually easing back into the "outside" world. On January 13, 1954, Ruth Beuscher noted that her patient's return to Smith was "contingent" on seeing the Smith psychiatrist, Dr. Booth, "twice a week," but added that Sylvia's attitude was "good" and her "insight" into her own condition was also "good." In concluding remarks, Beuscher observed that Sylvia had transferred her hostility to her mother to herself in "violent" and "primitive" feelings certain to make Sylvia frightened of herself. The purely rational and academic approach to problems had failed her and had opened up massive doubts about her own identity. At the same time, the conventional pressures of practicing the feminine role had intensified Sylvia's disturbance, as she tried to negotiate her sexual desires and what society expected of her. The more she tried to please her mother the more she felt dominated by her mother, losing a sense of what her own values and standards ought to be. Repressed feelings about her father had brought out a "sado-masochistic" tendency. To counter Sylvia's retrogression, Beuscher had encouraged her to act out, to voice her anger, as she would later do in "Daddy" and *The Bell Jar*. What Aurelia would later deplore as unkindness on her daughter's part seems, in view of Beuscher's therapy, the lifting of the bell jar that had come down on Sylvia, so that she could declare her independence. But Beuscher also counseled that this independence would take time to develop—as indeed it did, fully emerging in Sylvia's only published novel and the poetry of her last year. She was a late developer emotionally, a young woman who did not menstruate until she was sixteen—a fact that Beuscher found significant in assessing her patient's conflicted behavior with her mother, teachers, and other authority figures. It came as an enormous relief to Sylvia, Beuscher reported, when she realized she did not have to make important decisions just yet, that she could bide her time as she came to understand what she truly wanted for herself. She needed to play out the "conflict of wills" that had marked her dating and not settle too quickly on a permanent mate.

Ruth Beuscher's concluding paragraph in her report, written in the third person and quoted here in full, reveals the tremendous power the therapist now wielded, a power that some biographers have criticized: "During the last interview held with this patient, she spontaneously remarked: 'You have been like a mother, but without any of the disadvantages.' This was precisely the role which the therapist had tried to assume, and it was felt that this line of approach was very successful with this patient." The passive voice, "it was felt," presumably encompasses therapist and patient. It does seem like a very self-satisfied statement disguised as an objective fact, which is why Beuscher's sanguinity has been assailed. But would another approach have worked with Sylvia Plath? No one else at McLean had been able to reach Sylvia, no other therapist had revealed to the patient the psychodynamics of her condition.

50

Sylvia began classes at Smith in the second semester, commencing at the end of January 1954, maintaining a lighter schedule that would delay her graduation until the following year. She resumed her friendship with Claiborne Phillips, a classmate with a special interest in public affairs. Phillips recalled a scene with Sylvia sitting cross-legged on Claiborne's bed and telling her about her breakdown. Her memories of McLean already had attenuated and seemed "unreal" and "like a dream." She recalled a sense of numbness and slowly coming alive on the sanitarium's lawn, and then feeling restored while working with clay as part of her therapy. Claiborne said it was not the kind of friendship that led to an understanding of how Sylvia had come to terms with her suicide attempt. Instead Sylvia read to her parts of Gordon Lameyer's letters, sharing her excitement about him. [HR]

With Smith classmate Elinor Friedman, Sylvia was more explicit, calmly saying that in her disgust she had tried to bash her head in when she realized the pills had not killed her. On the way to McLean, she had tried to jump out of the car in front of a bus. What brought her to life was Ruth Beuscher's "great revelation . . . about being herself and a woman." Friedman did not explain to Harriet Rosenstein exactly what that meant, but it would seem—given what Claiborne Phillips reported—that part of Plath's recovery had to do with expressing herself sexually, which she was able to do more freely after her return to Smith.

Sylvia had expected some awkwardness about her return but was met with "such love and warmth" that after only a week she had settled in nicely. Professor Elizabeth Drew had hugged and kissed her in a welcome back, and Lawrence House students, many of them freshmen and sophomores, took her reappearance in stride and saw, in some respects, a new, more sociable, bridge-playing Sylvia not quite so driven as in her first three years. She kept no calendar this time—perhaps because she had fewer appointments and classes to record. She wrote to Mrs. Cantor, quoting Mary Baker Eddy: "We are sometimes led to believe that darkness is as real as light; but Science affirms darkness to be only a mortal sense of the absence of light, at the coming of which darkness loses the appearance of reality." Sylvia's darkness had dispersed "like a mist or fog, showing the clear, wonderful outline of the true world, and the true self." But she had to deal with unfinished business—"shocking feelings" about her mother to which she alluded in a February 16, 1954, letter to Philip McCurdy. Even in bright, cheerful moments, Sylvia sensed an undertow not visible on the surface of her feelings. It was the time of year when Smith girls were planning weddings while Sylvia demurred, saying to McCurdy she had no taste for diamonds and church ceremonies. She favored some kind of pagan rite that she had seen enacted in a New York theater in a "Rites of Fertility" scene in Tennessee Williams's *Camino Real*.

Stimulated by Christian Science, she questioned what is real. So did Tennessee Williams. Sylvia saw his play *Camino Real* performed on May 2, 1953, telling her mother it was the "most stimulating, thought-provoking, artistic play I've ever seen in my life!" Then she read a revised version while she recovered from her suicide attempt in late 1953 or early 1954.[22] She kept a *New York Times* review of the play by Brooks Atkinson and underlined his verdict: "<u>a sensitively composed fantasy about the hopelessness and degeneracy of life in the world today.</u>" The corruption and cruelty the critic singled out seem akin to her view of the world after returning from her

New York City *Mademoiselle* month, a view confirmed during those first dispiriting days in the asylum. Did she identify with the play's American innocent, Kilroy, who succumbs to what Atkinson calls a "moral plague," with an "angel of death" delivering his requiem? She underlined the sentence in Williams's foreword: "A cage represents security as well as confinement to a bird that has grown used to being in it." Some theatergoers had run from the bleakness of the play, checking out before the final scene, Williams noted, but Sylvia Plath had stayed, watching what, in a sense, would happen to her.

The play's set evoked the world out of which Sylvia had emerged. She underlined: "the loud singing of the wind, accompanied by distant, measured reverberations like pounding surf or distant shellfire": memories of her own earliest shoreline existence, the portents of what was to come? Into the scene Williams placed a phoenix, "painted on silk," intermittently "softly-lighted," since "resurrections are so much a part of its meaning"—for Sylvia too after her own resurrection. Don Quixote, the hero of perpetual delusions and dreams, appears as a "desert rat" at a barrier gate raised so that he can enter a walled town, a compound that might as well be an asylum where wild birds are tamed and put in cages. Sylvia underlined: "the spring of humanity has gone dry in this place."

She also underlined the gypsy's announcement over a loudspeaker: "Do you feel yourself to be spiritually unprepared for the age of exploding atoms?" That the ending of the world might coincide with Sylvia's own extinction did not seem like such a stretch in this play that spoke to her own fears. One of her frustrations may well have been that her interest in abnormal psychology reflected not only her own anxieties but those of a world that refused to recognize its own uneasiness, made imminent as audience members walked out on a play that put their cosmic disquiet on stage. Sylvia bracketed the gypsy's speech that put the question: "Do you wish that things could be straight and simple again as they were in your childhood?"

The question is posed as the American Kilroy recovers from a shipboard illness and encounters Casanova, confined in this unnamed place that is policed by guards who forbid the "exchange of serious questions and ideas, especially between persons on the opposite sides of the plaza." This is the McCarthyite period that Sylvia protested and marked with a vertical line in the margin next to Casanova's words. Without possessing the coin of the realm, Casanova informs Kilroy, whose pocket has been picked, he will be separated into his chemical components with countless others, and his individuality—the romance of existence, in other words—will be annihilated. "You have a spark of anarchy in your spirit," Casanova tells Kilroy, "and that's not to be tolerated. Nothing wild or honest is tolerated here! It has to be extinguished."

Casanova is worried that he will not receive a letter that will include a check so that he can remain in a hotel. Otherwise, he will be thrown out into the street and swept up by street cleaners who will shovel him into the chemical flux—perhaps a symbolic way of describing the drugs that subdue the originality of selfhood. The worry over money—a constant refrain in Sylvia's letters and lessened only slightly by Mrs. Prouty's benefactions—made it seem like she was constantly on a precipice, manifested in the play by the "narrow and steep stairway" to the Arch of Triumph, otherwise known by the ambiguous sign: the "Way Out." Poised on the stairway's top step, Kilroy cannot decide if he is on the verge of nothingness or plentitude: "It's too unknown for my blood," he says.

The roving Casanova asks his new companion Kilroy: "Travelers born?" Kilroy answers: "Always looking for something!" The American has the same vehement desire for a life abroad that propelled Plath but that Casanova characterizes as "Satisfied by nothing!" Here was a play that put her plight right in front of her. Kilroy keeps looking for a way out, underlined two different times in Sylvia's copy of the play, as he shouts he is a free man and has equal rights—disputed by Gutman, who runs the show and insists Kilroy wear the clown clothes of a circus Patsy. This is what happens when the vagrant self is stripped of its identity and incarcerated.

A "Nursie" appears in search for a patient, Esmeralda, who has taken flight, as Sylvia had once contemplated doing by springing from the car that took her to the state hospital. The Nursie cries out for the patient she has made into a caged pet: "Where is my lady bird, where is my precious treasure?" Sylvia Plath knew all about what it meant to be petted into passivity. Williams supplied stage directions that had actors plunging into the aisles and the seats, breaking down the distance between audience and stage, between the characters in confinement and the audience in its own theater cage. No wonder some theatergoers could not bear to stay for the whole show, to see Kilroy subdued, silenced, and forced to don the Patsy costume. The irony of that World War II phrase "Kilroy was here" is now manifested in a character who is no longer free and no longer a self. Sylvia put a double vertical slash next to this Gutman speech: "And these are the moments when we look into ourselves and ask with a wonder which never is lost altogether: 'Can this be all? Is there nothing more? Is this what the glittering wheels of the heavens turn for?' "[23]

It gets worse on the road of reality. Sylvia underlined Gutman's evocation of mental breakdowns that could happen to even the bravest and most privileged risk-takers: "Adventurers suddenly frightened of a dark room.

Gamblers unable to choose between odd and even. Con men and pitchmen and plume-hatted cavaliers turned baby-soft . . . When I observe this change, I say to myself: 'Could it happen to ME?'—The answer is 'YES' And that's what curdles my blood." *Camino Real* showed Sylvia Plath that her agony was not hers alone, and that art could address that agony.[24]

Sylvia took a special interest in Camille, underlining the description of her as a "sentimental whore" who makes the "mistake of love." She is another of the play's fugitive "legendary" characters, describing a "resort," actually an asylum with rows of iron beds, from which she has escaped, as from her death, which she describes with this assertion: "the last thing you know of this world, of which you've known so little and yet so much, is the smell of an empty ice box"—a morgue. Camille accuses Casanova of giving up because he is in terror of what is on the other side of the walled compound, what she calls "Terra Incognita." When Casanova proposes that they stay, Camille responds: "Caged birds accept each other but flight is what they long for." Sylvia was no courtesan, yet like Camille, she had entertained men like Dick Norton who would have caged her up, so to speak. Sylvia underlined Camille's words and later delivered them as part of her audition for the Amateur Dramatic Club at Cambridge University, which won her the part of a whore. Sylvia reveled in the role, "insisted on it as a theme of humor," Jane Baltzell remembered, and would say the word " 'whore' with peculiar gusto." [HR]

At a prophetic moment in *Camino Real* Casanova confesses to Camille, sounding like the Ted Hughes whom Sylvia would enchant: "you've taught me that part of love which is tender. I never knew it before. Oh, I had mistresses that circled me like moons! I scrambled from one bed-chamber to another bed-chamber with shirttails always aflame, from girl to girl, like buckets of coal-oil poured on a conflagration! But never loved until now with the part of love that's tender." Camille doubts that Casanova means what he says. Distrust is her only way of guarding against betrayal, she tells him, in a line that Sylvia marked with a vertical slash. What Camille fears is that they will cage themselves like a "pair of captive hawks." Sylvia bracketed the line and perhaps delivered it at her Cambridge audition for the Amateur Dramatic Club as part of a long speech that included the passage "squinting at cards and tea-leaves. What else are we offered? The never-broken procession of little events that assure us that we and strangers about us are still going on! Where? Why? and the perch that we hold is unstable." This is the world of tarot and ouija boards that Ted Hughes would consult with Sylvia Plath to descry their destiny.

Did Sylvia ever reread this play and shudder at her bracketing of Camille's sorrow? The lines could be addressed to Ted Hughes, the author of *The*

Hawk in the Rain: "What is it, this feeling between us? When you feel my exhausted weight against your shoulder, when I clasp your anxious old hawk's head to my breast, what is it we feel in whatever is left of our hearts?"

Did Sylvia Plath make a full recovery? She underlined: "There is a time for departure even when there's no certain place to go." A limping Lord Byron confesses that he has reneged on his promise as a poet and declares that only by leaving Camino Real can he possibly recover himself. He departs along with a collection of caged birds. *Camino Real* emphasizes that resurrections are recurrent. So are relapses. The gypsy tells Kilroy, in another line Sylvia underlined: "We're all of us guinea pigs in the laboratory of God. Humanity is just a work in progress." Kilroy responds "I don't make it out." The Gypsy asks "Who does?" and follows up with a declaration that would have resonated with Sylvia's childhood: "The Camino Real is a funny paper read backwards!" Kilroy, a former Golden Gloves champion, has been knocked out, so to speak, by life and no longer knows how to play the hero, the Superman of Sylvia's childhood.

Kilroy is swept up by the street cleaners, dead from an enlarged heart but, in effect, dead because he has outlasted his ability to box and his claim to greatness, which nonetheless, Sylvia underlined, should be remembered, along with the recognition that "laurel is not everlasting." Or is Kilroy only dreaming, since he rises from the dissection table to reclaim his heart, wondering if what he has experienced is a dream. His posthumous self recalls the living Kilroy. It was like that for Sylvia, that near death that seemed so distant, or like a dream, in her own afterlife, when she resumed classes at Smith in early 1954. Kilroy is one of those "fading legends that come and go in this plaza," says Esmeralda, whom Kilroy has been courting. At the play's enigmatic ending, the man of La Mancha appears and drinks at the previously dry fountain that has begun to flow. He declares: "The violets in the mountains have broken the rocks!"—the sign, perhaps, of another resurrection.

Tennessee Williams called his play a "poem on the romantic attitude toward life"; in his biographer's words, it was "a rallying cry against the status quo. The message to his audience was to resist inertia and seize every opportunity to expand one's horizon."[25] *Camino Real* is, in effect, a dramatic realization of William Sheldon's Shelleyan view of the Promethean life that Plath was about to read in *Psychology and the Promethean Will*. The play demonstrated for her both the peril and promise of transgressing traditional boundaries that she would later encounter in David Riesman's *The Lonely Crowd*.

A fellow McLean patient, Jane Anderson, said Sylvia had left the hospital too soon, before a full scale therapy had been accomplished. Sylvia's February 25, 1954, letter to Jane is full of high spirits but may have seemed to the doubtful Jane a coverup. Sylvia had acclimated to Smith in a week, she claimed, and the past was fading fast. "I felt conspicuous at first during the discussions of suicide in these books"—her class was reading Dostoevsky—and "felt sure that my scar was glowing symbolically, obvious to all (the way Hester's scarlet letter burned and shone with a physical heat to proclaim her default to all)." But she had "adjusted" to Smith routines, including, like the other students in Lawrence House, attending house meetings. "We took our mending," Judy Denison told me. "I mended my wool socks over a light bulb (we wore wool kneesocks with the charcoal Bermuda shorts, as in my photo of Sylvia—no synthetics in them so they needed a lot of mending). I can't remember what we discussed—social stuff related to house, like should we have a party & invite guys from Amherst, house chores, napkins, who knows what."[26]

In her letter to Jane Anderson, Sylvia even entertained the idea of writing her Russian paper on the "theme of suicide, feeling that I have somewhat of a personalized understanding of the sensations and physical and mental states one experiences previous to the act." She referred to her "new easygoing feelings," hiking and biking with Marcia Brown, good bull sessions in Lawrence House, dating seven boys in four weeks, and going to movies. She felt that her "escapade" had made "no lasting scar" but served as an advantage in understanding herself and others. She regarded psychiatric help at this point as "really superfluous." "Escapade" was the word she had used before in alluding to her suicide attempt and would use again in a letter to her mother, treating her trauma as something she had gotten over. She consulted Dr. Booth, Smith's psychiatrist, once a week, but there was no deep exploration of her feelings. She called herself "consistently 'happy' rather than spasmodically ecstatic." She encouraged Jane to give this letter to Ruth Beuscher. "I would like her to know how I am getting on."

Sylvia could not foresee, of course, how her moods and experiences would change her views. She did not regard her experience at *Mademoiselle* a suitable subject for a novel!

51

In April 1954, an exhilarated poet sent home her first poem in nearly a year, "Doom of Exiles," which concluded: "Still, stubbornly we try to crack the nut / In which the riddle of our race is shut." Her letters allude to reading philosophy and talking about it with friends. She wrote relatively little about her own feelings as she continued to open up to the world.

Her life changed on April 19, 1954, when she met Richard Sassoon, whose father was a cousin of Siegfried Sassoon, the poet who had inspired her antiwar poetry. This Sassoon was "a thin, slender Parisian fellow . . . a British subject, and a delight to talk to . . . I find he's another of those men who are exactly as tall as I, but they don't seem to mind it, and I certainly don't." At five feet eight, he was an inch shorter than Plath. She was his first love, according to Richard Wertz, one of Sassoon's Yale roommates. [HR] Sassoon and Plath, friends and lovers, arranged trysts at Elinor Friedman's home, about forty miles from Smith. It is a pity her letters to him have gone missing, but without doubt his letters reveal an aura of sophistication, a delight in word play, and a romantic temperament that beguiled her. His refusal to speak to biographers, except for some limited cooperation with Andrew Wilson, has meant that his full part in Plath biography has never been adequately represented. At the outset of Plath's encounters with Ted Hughes, Sassoon remained a vital part of her imagination, and his abrupt withdrawal from her, and her futile search for him in Paris, constituted a psychic blow and a gap in her identity that Hughes could not fill, notwithstanding his huge presence in her life and work. For Plath, as for her biographers, Sassoon is the man who got away.

Harriet Rosenstein almost caught up with Richard Sassoon. He answered her letter, saying her approach was "perceptive and happily without aggressive personal projections." But what he had to share was quite personal, part of a relationship almost "hermetically intimate and very inter-subjective so to speak." He did not elaborate but seemed to be alluding to how both of them came to one another out of their own very private needs, which accounts, perhaps, for his wariness. Only a meeting with Rosenstein could determine the extent of his cooperation. But something happened—connected with Sassoon's move from Berkeley, California, to Boulder, Colorado—and a meeting never occurred. Instead, Sassoon wrote a long letter analyzing Rosenstein, suggesting she was locked up and unable to sort out her own mission amid biographers' projections of Sylvia that had put the person he knew out of reach. He no longer thought he could help Harriet, concluding that his time with Sylvia had been confusing and egotistical, and "adolescently hysterical." Yet he insisted the relationship had been "significant" and "extremely rich." It has to be wondered: Who was locked up more? Rosenstein or Sassoon? He said he might be able to answer some questions, but he resisted the idea of a recorded interview. In a succeeding letter, he enclosed a poem about Plath, calling himself her "man-child lover." The poem expresses his youthful inability to deal with her pressing question: "Will I be great in my art?" All he could say to answer was "Either that or happiness." Did he sense some kind of split in her, the person and the poet, that could not be bridged? The poem evokes his sense of being lost to her, as she was lost to herself: "In less than a decade she'd hit / the psychic center / and fame and suicide."

Richard Sassoon published an opaque and convoluted meditation on Plath (without naming her) in a story, "In the Year of Love and unto Death, the Fourth—An Elegy on the Muse," in *Northwest Review* (Winter 1962). As in his letters to Plath and to Harriet Rosenstein, he swaddled himself in verbiage, conveying the impression of a writer who either did not know what he wanted to say or found the saying so painful it had to appear in a protective wrap, which Rosenstein, like any conscientious biographer, tried to decipher and annotate. He began, straightforwardly enough, with an unnamed "her" declaring: "So that no matter what happens, I shall always very simply love you." For purposes of biography, lucid bits of the story retrieve what Sylvia was like with him, how she spoke with a "fusion of severity and coquetry," perhaps because of the "urgency and brevity" of their meetings. For Sassoon, the memory of their vulnerability seems to have been overwhelming as they coupled like "two reared over-bred horses that need help." The word choice is extraordinary: reared as in bred, but also reared as in raised up needing, perhaps, help in their physical and mental intercourse, or what Sassoon called in his letter to Rosenstein their intersubjectivity. "I cannot tell where your body begins and mine ceases," she told him. For Sassoon, as well, the encounter with Plath remained, it seems until the end of his life, impossible to encompass.[27] Richard Wertz believed Sassoon regretted losing Plath and cursed himself for not being available to her when she went looking for him in the fateful period just after she met Ted Hughes. But to Wertz, high-energy Sylvia had burned out Richard.

Harriet Rosenstein looked elsewhere, beyond Richard Sassoon's labyrinthine prose, interviewing Connie Taylor Blackwell, Smith College class of 1956, who dated a friend of Sassoon's and learned about Richard's involvement with Sylvia and his pretentious view of himself as a writer, even though he had published nothing. Sylvia seemed to show no awareness of his sense of inferiority, or that her published record as a writer intimidated him, but it was obvious to Blackwell. To Claiborne Phillips, he seemed "unsure of himself and non communicative." She was annoyed at his habit of "looking beyond" her face when talking to her. Was Sylvia serious about Richard? Phillips asked. A defensive Sylvia indicated she was not and that her psychiatrist had liberated her from "old hang ups about sex." She was not worried about hurting him by taking a hedonistic view, and that worried Phillips. [HR]

Richard Sassoon's embarrassment showed as he tried to outdo her and become "mythic." Playing the role that Plath required of him proved exhausting. Connie Taylor Blackwell observed in Sassoon a melancholy that verged on the suicidal. In 1974, she told Rosenstein that she remembered him sitting on a ledge at Yale's Calhoun Hall, saying "he couldn't stand life any longer." He was given to such histrionic scenes, according to a friend who knew him later in Berkeley.[28] His roommate, Mel Woody, said Sassoon lacked "ego-strength." On July 5, 2017, he killed himself.[29]

Richard Sassoon was part of a hard-driving group of students with high ambitions and who, like Plath, felt the stresses of competition and often talked about Kierkegaard and suicide. Connie Taylor Blackwell confessed to Harriet Rosenstein that she had her own suicidal crisis, what she termed a "small crack-up" in her senior year. It was one of those passages in life when what comes next—life after college—posed a problem that increased the anxieties of students who expected to achieve great things. They congregated around Yale's Elizabethan Club, drinking Sherry and smoking clay pipes—an obvious counter culture rebuff to the massive drinking that went on at Yale that resulted in "pig nights" that featured getting girls drunk. A few female students like Plath and Connie Taylor Blackwell were admitted as honored Club guests. "Everyone's emotions were so heightened," Blackwell remembered, calling the Club an "intellectual womb" quite apart from the rest of Yale and Smith. Women like Blackwell and Plath found the Club a refuge from a campus life in which they felt their intensely intellectual interests isolated them. Studying in England, Blackwell observes, was the natural next step for Plath.

Did Plath read Richard Sassoon correctly and supply the very mystique both sought to create? She called him a "very intuitive weird sinuous little guy whose eyes are black and shadowed so he looks as if he were an absinthe addict . . . all of which helps me to be carefree and gay." Absinthe, one of the preferred drugs of poets, supposedly stimulated creativity, and Plath's reference to it suggests that in Sassoon's presence she experienced a kind of joyous relief and elevation of spirits in quite a different way from the later rough-and-tumble of Ted Hughes. Sassoon would take her to plays, brought her fine wine, and became a kind of exotic drug of esthetic enlightenment that she craved and could not obtain elsewhere. He had grown up in Tryon, North Carolina, and though she did not apparently see him as a southerner, did he not have in his manner and voice some of that soft courtly manner that contrasts so vividly with Hughes's northern heartiness? For all her attraction to big, strong men, nowhere does Plath seem to have regarded Sassoon as offensively effete. On the contrary, his refinement soothed and accentuated her own sensitivity. He had swiftly moved to the top of her list. Sylvia told her mother that she preferred her "French boy Dick Sassoon," quoting French poetry to her, rather than "lugubrious Myron" Lotz. To her friend Philip McCurdy, she described her involvement with a "satanic relative of siegfried sassoon" (she liked to eschew capitals à la e e cummings). Richard spoke to her half the time in French, and she seemed under a spell, treating him as a transgressive type, preferring "cloistered velvet rooms, pale with roses, light wine, a volume of baudelaire or vigny or rimbaud and a nuit d'amour," whereas "I occasionally want good healthy vulgar american sun, sweat and song . . . entendu?" The ellipses are hers, inviting her interlocutor to use his imagination as she slid back into French, returning to Sassoon's spell, as if he were some character out of the Poe the French found so decadently fascinating. She could hardly write a letter during this period that did not include French words and phrasing.

Sylvia had also attracted Richard Sassoon's roommate, Mel Woody, with whom she argued about sexuality and fertility. Her time with Woody began as a platonic exchange of ideas but eventually turned erotic and "torrid," yet short of intercourse, he told Harriet Rosenstein. Sylvia sent him her parodies of Housman, Shakespeare, and other poets while continuing her correspondence with Gordon Lameyer, whom she treated as a kind of Richard Halliburton figure because of his travels in the navy. She entertained yet other males—some of them like Philip McCurdy and Perry Norton she regarded as her "psychic" brothers. She resumed contact with Ruth Beuscher, seeing the therapist outside of an office, and even shopping together with her, as Beuscher later told Harriet Rosenstein. Shopping was part of the therapy. Beuscher said as much. "Always feel happy shopping; gives me a sense of 'things' somehow: taste color and touch, and a certain power and plentitude," Sylvia wrote in her journal.

She wrote to Gordon Lameyer on June 12, 1954, about an afternoon hour session with Ruth Beuscher, the first of bimonthly visits during the summer, enjoying "analyzing and philosophizing with her." Beuscher had been in Europe during the fascist takeover in the 1930s and had written about it. How much she shared with Plath is impossible to say, but more than treatment of a patient seems to have been on Beuscher's mind. She would become an ordained minister and would write about the important spiritual content of therapy. Plath's own interest in Christian Science and her study of religion at Smith prepared her for spiritual discussions with Beuscher. In a letter to Gordon Lameyer, Plath reported that at Beuscher's home they discussed "religion, philosophy, honesty, selfishness, and a lot of other potent, and perhaps more intimate, topics." Even when these two women could not see one another, at virtually every crucial stage, they would share Plath's progress and prognosis—not simply in terms of herself but of the world history both women were bound up in.

52

In late June 1954, Sylvia returned to Winthrop with her mother and to memories of childhood as they visited the Freemans (the father had just died). For Gordon Lameyer, she drew streets and houses and the ocean: "lawns that were continents, rocks that were fortresses, alleys that were secret passages to magic worlds," an Eden of dreams that never were reality. She remembered David Freeman, the "superman of my lois lane days." She visited her old house and the golden rain trees her father had planted, "now flourishing giants." She discussed with David their attitudes toward death, which were remarkably the same, although she did not say what they were, perhaps because it was a subject not yet prepared for the page. She met up with other old friends and John Hodges, whom she had not seen in years. On June 23, 1954, she had a "delightful" therapy session with Ruth Beuscher. Were the "good old days" part of what they talked about? Was she revisiting, in a phrase she used in a letter to Lameyer, her "portals of discovery"? She seemed also to be including him in a projection of what her future would be like—what, in fact, she would do for Ted Hughes, when she wrote to Gordon: "do let me be your typist!"

After a meeting with Dick Norton, the first in six months, she was seeing "patterns and problems" in her life (the influence of Beuscher?). "I had lived so hard and so much and deep that never again could I go back to the same small country of his [Dick's] personality which once, years ago, I had seen as vast and glittering with promise." What this meant, of course, is that she was raising the stakes for herself—at every moment making a return to the home of her past impossible. She contrasted forging her "plastic plathian phenomenon" to the rigid Dick. She wrote all this to Gordon Lameyer, as if, perhaps, he had enough height for her. Richard Sassoon, who makes no appearance in these letters, was off in Europe and perhaps, for now, seemed unreachable or not quite fitted out yet as a consort, for what she called her "scarlett-o'-hara,-molly-bloom elemental eve nature." She made up Joycean words, describing her " 'colloquacious' Cape Cod landlady," saying her neologism was not as good as his "bikeening." With Sassoon, she spoke French; with Lameyer she tried out a language like that found in *Finnegan's Wake*, one of Gordon's favorites. She said she loved him "more than the alphabet and roget's thesaurus combined."

To Mel Woody, she wrote of an "amusingly ectoplasmic umbilical cord between us," and about her excitement over Harvard Summer school made possible by a scholarship. She even mentioned the possibility of auditing Frank O'Connor's nineteenth-century novel class, which led to a reference

Lois Lane and Superman.

to her suicide attempt the previous summer as a "cataclysmic downward gyre" plummeting her to "symbolic death." The "center did not hold because there was none, or rather (as you wrote), too many." Now she understood the "black and sustained hells a mind can go through." She did not write as someone recovering from a near-death experience, but as one who understood that descending into such depths of despair was always a possibility for "a mind"—hers and others.

53

By July 1954, Sylvia resumed a detailed calendar of her studies in German and English, her social activities, and meetings with Ruth Beuscher every two weeks. She alluded to a perplexing, disturbing date with brilliant, mesmerizing Edwin Akutowicz, a mathematician and Harvard PhD, which resulted in a sexual encounter that put Sylvia into the emergency room with excessive bleeding. It was a reckless affair, since Sylvia was aware that Edwin had been aggressive with her roommate, Nancy Hunter, yet Sylvia seemed almost to court this disaster, as if in fulfillment of her desire to be as bold as men were, to mate in the rough way she would later describe in her letters about Ted Hughes. She said as much in an August 5 letter to Gordon Lameyer, reveling in the "burlesque coarseness of existence," adding: "somehow, with all the difficult and dark things that have happened to me, I seem to be able to maintain a healthy, productive optimism, which eventually manages to work out crises and problems, transmuting them into positive events, such as art of instructive philosophical development." She had given herself an "(I think) unnecessary, yet indicative, test," with a "traumatic shock last week." What Gordon Lameyer made of this murky letter is impossible to say, but given an unscheduled call to Ruth Beuscher after the encounter with Akutowicz, it seems that at the least Plath needed help in reckoning with what had happened to her and was, perhaps, fencing it in with her epistolary circumlocutions. She wanted to take control of her own sexuality and did not see herself as Akutowicz's victim. Indeed, she saw Akutowicz several times after their bloody encounter—much to the horrified surprise of Nancy Hunter, who called the six-week summer at Harvard a "succession of crises." [HR]

Plath may have turned to Edwin Akutowicz as a result of what happened with Nancy Hunter, who told Harriet Rosenstein that Syl (as Hunter called her) expected Nancy to "put the pieces back together. She asked considerably more of me than than I was able to do and the frightening thing was that I was tempted to do it. She wanted me to hold her together physically." Hunter then used words that repeat Ted Hughes's description of his own predicament near the end of Plath's life: "it was either her or me," Hughes insisted: "I couldn't make a choice because if I chose her, I perished, and if I chose me, she perished, and I had the guilt for it on my conscience for the rest of my life." The pressure was on. Aurelia had reminded Nancy they would be at Harvard on the anniversary of Sylvia's suicide attempt: "You've got to watch her on that day," Aurelia instructed Nancy. On the day, a frantic Aurelia could not reach Sylvia and berated Nancy, who told her Sylvia was out on a date with Gordon Lameyer. "You were supposed to take care of her!" Aurelia exclaimed.

Like Ted Hughes, Nancy Hunter developed a deterministic view, saying Plath was a "parasite" and "screwed up," and writing about "alienation and disintegration." But Hunter, like Hughes, seemed caught in her own contradictory reactions to a roommate who unquestionably was an overpowering presence, but one that for others, like Marcia Brown, for example, had been electrifying and uplifting. [HR] How much of Hunter's withdrawal from Plath was a matter of her own insecurity is impossible to sort out. According to Hunter, Plath had stolen Akutowicz from her in order to "supersede" Nancy in that relationship. Sylvia was always doing that, Hunter claimed, taking what was Nancy's and making it Sylvia's. Listening to Hunter on the phone, Rosenstein concluded: "Nancy protests that she didn't care, but her voice is full of rancor." This was the period of Nancy's own "emotional downfall," she confessed to the biographer. After Harvard summer school, the friendship between Sylvia and Nancy attenuated, especially after Sylvia rejected Nancy's version of what had happened during their summer together. The aggrieved Hunter called herself Plath's "junior partner." [HR] But the narrow scope of Hunter's recollections emerged when she declared Plath showed no interest in politics, in McCarthyism, which reveals Hunter's ignorance about some sides of Plath's interests. She remembered only the Sylvia Plath who was clothes conscious and materialistic. But to Richard Wertz, much of Nancy's hostility to Sylvia had to do with envy. Nancy simply could not match Sylvia in talent. Mel Woody concurred, saying Sylvia overpowered Nancy and made her feel insecure. [HR]

Plath told Edwin Akutowicz about her sorrow over losing the father she adored, and she regarded Akutowicz, as she confessed in her notes for *The Bell Jar*, as her "Dream-father." [RC] Did her summer study of German evoke memories of her father as well? She records none in a journal or calendar, but Nancy Hunter remembered Sylvia talking about Otto Plath. In her letters Sylvia mentioned her faltering efforts to master the language, efforts that would continue into the last year of her life, listening to lessons on BBC radio, with unsatisfactory results.

After the rencontre with Edwin Akutowicz, Plath went to a Cambridge gynecologist and had a complete "pelvic examination," she told Gordon Lameyer, saying it was "comforting to have a definite and competent doctor's advice, and even if I regret the unsavory way I discovered about my manyarteried insides, I'm glad to get the deluge over with so that I will be healthily prepared for a natural and completely understood sexual life." Her calendar entry for August 27, 1954, notes that she had a "long good talk" with Beuscher about "domination, paternalism, sadism." What a combination! The father/dominating figure and the female desire to be dominated would lead to the famous line in "Daddy" about every woman adoring a fascist. And she wasn't quite done with Akutowicz, meeting him in late October at Rahar's in Northampton for a beer and "afternoon of dubious

macchiavelian [*sic*] merit." To her mother, she described him as "very peculiar, archaic, but amusing."

54

In the month leading up to her return to Smith, an exuberant Plath had
played with poetic forms and began writing sonnets, including "Suspend
This Day,"[30] with references to Dufy, Seurat, and Matisse and ending with
the lines: "Suspend this day / so singularly designed, / Like a rare Calder
mobile in your mind." The poem is akin to her loving and punning letters to Gordon Lameyer, to whom she remained grateful as the chevalier
servant who had written long, adoring letters to her during her recovery in
McLean. She sent her daring "Circus in Three Rings" to the *New Yorker*. She
portrays the speaker of the poem as a ringmaster of her "extravagant heart"
with a whip that has a "fatal flair," defending her "perilous wounds" with
a chair. As in so many of Plath's letters that work out a kind of precarious
balancing act between her fluctuating moods, the poem's speaker declares
"my demon of doom tilts on a trapeze." There you get her death-defying
swing in an exuberance built on suffering that is, like the Calder mobile,
up in the air thriving on its intricate construction, which is Plath, which is
her poem.

55

By late October 1954, the return to Smith for a final year seemed just as
hectic and calendar-crowded and rushed as earlier years. Here is a sample
for October 22:

  7:00–8:00: Waits on tables at breakfast as part of her scholarship
     obligations
  8:00–11:00: Works on German translations
  11:00–12:00: German class
  12:00–1:00: Shakespeare class
  1:30: Coffee with Elinor Friedman
  2:00–4:00: A conference with Alfred Kazin about her fiction
  2:30: Hands in chapter of her senior thesis on "The Double"
  4:00: Meets her friends the Freemans

5:30: Takes a bus to Amherst to meet Gordon Lameyer and his friends
10:00–4:00: Works on Golyadkin paper as part of her studies of
    Russian literature

She did not often stay up until the early hours of the morning to finish a paper, but she thrived on a regimented schedule, telling her mother that she was having a "wonderful year" and that she worked best "under a healthy tension."

Sylvia worried about her mother, prone to ulcers, teaching in the evening since she would have no time to rest. Aurelia went into the hospital for tests, and a worried Sylvia urged her again to take a holiday and recuperate. As for herself, she was getting together the transcripts, statements of purpose, and other items required for graduate school applications and a Fulbright Fellowship at either Oxford or Cambridge. She hoped a letter of support from Dr. Booth (the Smith psychiatrist) would "compensate for my mental hospital record." A letter from Ruth Beuscher would leave "no doubt as to the completeness of my cure." Robert Gorham Davis agreed, observing that "you would never have inferred from her manner what she had been through." He did not think she was masking her true feelings and never saw any sign of moodiness. She responded well to others. [HR] A classmate, Jane Truslow, who later married one of Sylvia's lovers, Peter Davison, noted that Sylvia was "no shattered creature." Jane had a negative view of Sylvia's return, calling her a "princess" who had her roommate Mary waiting on her and manipulated every opportunity offered her at Smith.

Jane Truslow was annoyed at Sylvia's "gushing," which later put off Smith classmate Lisa Levy (Smith Class of 1955), who admitted she resented the way Sylvia commanded attention. Enid Epstein thought the opposite: Sylvia was surprised at the interest in her and did not think of herself as "greatly admired." It is a pity that Harriet Rosenstein, who spoke with both women, never put them in a room together to reveal how their reactions to Sylvia mirrored themselves. There were many different cultures and personalities at Smith, Marcia Brown said to Harriet Rosenstein, so it is no wonder that the perceptions of Plath should play out differently in the temperaments witnesses brought to their testimony.

Jane Truslow and Lisa Levy were, in certain respects, doubles who shied away from Sylvia even as they replicated her behavior. Lisa thought of herself as a rebel and called Jane "troubled" like herself. During one lunch Jane sat in Lawrence House with her head down and unable to speak. The next day she disappeared and was found three days later wandering in the woods. She was hospitalized. Something similar had happened to another student as well, Lisa recalled. A professor had also shot himself. "People were cracking up left and right in that place. Nobody paid attention, nobody

helped, nobody understood," Levy told Harriet Rosenstein. No wonder a
senior thesis on Dostoevsky and doubles became so appealing to Plath. Lisa
remembered how hard it was to get Sylvia to engage with her. To Lisa's questions and comments, Sylvia replied with her own, and Lisa retreated, certain
she could not get through. Sylvia seemed to be conducting interviews, not
conversation. She had no interest in leveling with Lisa. Levy's reactions
contradict Enid Epstein's, who said Sylvia was "genuinely interested in what
others were doing, and always marveled at their talent." Enid and Sylvia
both worked on Press Board in their junior years, and Enid remembered
Sylvia's respect for articles written by Sally Rosenthal and Nora Jonson.
At the same time, in private, Enid enjoyed Sylvia's ability to slice apart a
personality in a sentence. [HR]

Lisa Levy watched in horrified fascination as Sylvia Plath bewitched the
faculty, and Levy wondered what that meant to Plath, to become such a star
at such a young age. Did she feel she deserved it, or was she tormented by
high expectations? Certainly Sylvia's letters provide some ballast for Levy's
speculations. It is perhaps why Claiborne Phillips wondered if she was "one
of the few people in Sylvia's life interested in her as a person and not for
her talent." Although Phillips did not use the word, she seemed to think
of Plath as a star who was the "most ruthless exploiter of her talent." For
all her visibility on campus and contacts with students and faculty, Phillips
thought of Sylvia as a "loner"—a curious word but one often applied by
stars, like Marilyn Monroe, to themselves. Who, the star thinks, values
me for myself, not my fame? Smith students came up to her and gushed
about her success, the thrill of the moment. Elinor Friedman remembered
Sylvia's fascination with stars and with a classmate, Joanna Barnes (Smith
class of 1956), who had become a movie actress.[31] Barnes did not know Plath
well, but they were in classes and extracurricular activities together, and
Barnes was impressed with her presence: "Physically, she was a knockout.
Tall, masses of sun-streaked hair and a smile that could light downtown
Pittsburgh for at least a week and a half. The whole effect might have been
overwhelming, were it not for her extreme reticence and softness." Plath's
fascination with movie stars, already evident by the age of twelve, when
she began pasting movie star images in a scrapbook and playing with paper
dolls of Hedy Lamarr and Rita Hayworth, may well have contributed to
shaping the persona Barnes evoked. Barnes watched Plath as she returned
for her final year: "she managed to appear unchanged, though I think all of
us were more acutely aware of the turmoil behind that sunny facade, which
had previously only appeared in her work."

Lisa Levy, trained as an actress, provides a remarkable study of Sylvia in
the flesh, beginning with Plath's posture, which Lisa called "devious": She

held her head to one side, "a kind of phony giving-in," with "broad, very tight shoulders," as if someone had taken a doll and done "weird things to it." Below those wide shoulders her body curved in an expression that suggested opposing emotions—a seductiveness that at the same time might mean "don't touch me." This impression recalls what Gordon Lameyer said to Harriet Rosenstein—that Plath came on "passionate, yet was 'shocked' when sexual advances went beyond a certain stage." He recalled that after her release from McLean and recovery he had "tried some not-nice sexual move" that outraged Sylvia, who called him "lascivious." Lameyer called her response "harsh" but also "literary." To Lisa Levy, that "don't touch me" behavior was often the way women of the time conveyed their seductiveness. But to Levy, more was at work in that strong torso: stubbornness, drive, and "an incredible tension," with mixed signals coming from the surprising fluidity of the hands, which Levy likened to a Circe, a sorceress with a voice like a whine—so different from the poet Plath in her later recordings. That was another "*person*," Levy emphasized.

Others, like classmate and friend Elinor Friedman, called Sylvia a superb listener who took in everything Elinor had to say, energizing Elinor, whom Sylvia treated as a "Hebrew princess." Sylvia looked at Elinor and saw the history of people who had overcome suffering. Elinor felt Sylvia's identification with her was also a way of overcoming her own Germanic background, her "WHITENESS."[32] Aurelia recalled Sylvia said during this period: "I wish I were good enough to be a Jew." [HR]

56

Sylvia had colored her hair blonde during the summer months but now had dyed it back to brown to "look demure and discreet." She chafed at a hectic schedule with little time for writing poetry, although she continued to submit work to magazines such as the *Ladies' Home Journal*, the *Atlantic Monthly*, and the *New Yorker*, undeterred by rejections. "I am very happy in spite of the fact that I have so much work to do," she wrote to Gordon Lameyer on October 8, 1954. Jon Rosenthal, an Amherst student who met Sylvia at this time, recalls he was told about her suicide attempt and yet he found her "radiant" and "hardly his conception of a suicidal type." [HR]

Warren visited Sylvia at Smith and she arranged dates for him and his friends. But she worried about him. He seemed "vague and negative too much of the time." She stressed the importance of her "healthy bohemianism" period that countered a "clock-regular, responsible" manner. Warren needed a social life, a change of scene, and companions to counteract his "introverted habits." As for herself, "if only england would by some miracle come through, I would be forced shivering into a new, unfamiliar world, where I had to forge anew friends and a home for myself, and although such experiences are painful and awkward at first, I know, intellectually, that they are the best things to make one grow." The word "shivering" leaps out for anyone aware of how the English cold would creep into her almost like a supernatural force.

Sylvia admitted to her mother that the fall of 1954 had not been easy for her. Still worried about money, she took a job on Monday afternoons reading Hellenic history to a blind Smith professor. A late period had made her feel "very blue," plus a cold had "thrown" her off. She studied German several hours a day but made little progress, in her estimation. Her divided personality is reflected in her thesis on the double in Dostoevsky and her interest, as she told her mother, in "reflections (mirrors and water), shadows, twins."[33] She would look later in life for women who doubled her, so to speak, rivals but also representations of her own ambitions and imprint on the world. Like another famous college student, the suicidal Quentin Compson, she went around her world shadowed by her own acute consciousness of existence and of time, expressed in her remarkable poem "Mirror." We don't know what the Hamlet-like Quentin was studying at Harvard, but Sylvia was immersing herself in a Shakespeare class and in the plight of his tragic heroes. One of her classmates watched Sylvia take almost verbatim notes on Professor Dunn's lectures. [HR]

Sylvia recovered her spirits after a meeting with renowned critic, Alfred Kazin, now teaching at Smith. She sat in his class and then turned in an assignment, looking, perhaps, for a sign of authority, a kind of blessing, that Frank O'Connor had not been present to provide in that summer crisis of 1953. She was "beat but beatific," she told Gordon Lameyer, because Kazin admonished her that it was her

> holy duty to write every day, spill out all, learn to give it form, and [he] is going to let me go off on my own every week, only asking that I turn in lots and lots and not to bother with the regular class assignment. He is extremely critical and encouraging, and the fortuitous accident of interviewing him is something I'll praise fortune for all my life long. I adore him!

Kazin represented a kind of authority she could not find otherwise on the Smith campus. He would recall in his memoir, *New York Jew*, that she told him nothing about herself, although he became aware that she was a "pet" of the English department. If you knew Kazin, as I did, you hear the scorn for academics in his remark. He was not emotive, and I can't imagine Plath wanting to confide anything about her personal life to him. But that seemed fine with her, since he represented not a comforting faculty member but that literary world outside of campus that only a few other faculty members, like Robert Gorham Davis, regularly published in the *New York Times*, could connect her to. Cyrilly Abels at *Mademoiselle* could mentor Plath in the ways of publishing, but, unlike Kazin, she was not a *writer*.

Alfred Kazin's encouragement of her writing buoyed her, as did Smith College's stalwart Mary Ellen Chase's effort to send Sylvia on a Fulbright to Oxford or Cambridge. On her birthday, she wrote to Gordon Lameyer: "I am tempted to borrow trouble in the way of metaphors and liken myself to an agéd eagle who has just been run over by time's wingéd chariot," managing to work in allusions to both T. S. Eliot and Andrew Marvell in one sentence. She referred to her own paradoxes, "hard for anyone to understand," adding: "I am serene and happy, despite the heavy pressure of thesis, German, Shakespeare, et. al." She held on to her love for Gordon Lameyer, even if she did not have the time to see him as much as they both desired. She wrote to him more than she did her mother, although letters to Aurelia clocked in at about once a week. She did not tell her mother about her airplane adventure, with "all the little planes lined up looking like gaudy painted toy gliders, and that Icarian lust came upon me again," she confessed to Gordon. She took flight, "the shadow is parting from the earth . . . me screaming about how this is the fourth dimension and god isn't it a fantastic day. . . . All very naughty and dashing."

57

In the late fall of 1954, Plath worked on "Metamorphoses of the Moon," identified in her calendar as a "poem on analysis." It is a masterpiece of occlusion. Nowhere is there even an allusion to sessions with Ruth Beuscher. But the Plath who went up in the plane, braving all, turned in her imagination to herself as a World War I pilot who "dares all heaven's harms / to raid the zone where fate begins." We know that with Beuscher she talked about her mother, the shocking death of her father, and how her youthful aspirations had resulted in a breakdown. But confronting that past had not led to a resolution; no "duel," as in a dogfight, had led to conquering her adversarial feelings. She remained in the "mute air," the thinning atmosphere of a flight toward an outcome that, like the sky in the poem, "holds

aloof" from the "falling man" who is asking, inventing, and hoping "in vain."
What knowledge she had gained is likened in the poem to the "bitten apple"
that ends the "eden of bucolic eve," a phrase that calls to mind her yearning
for the bucolic surroundings of her Wellesley home in those last peripatetic
Manhattan days. What she came to understand in analysis had its own "slow
disaster" breaking through the "skull's shell" that "like a cuckoo in the nest
makes hell." She reckoned with her powerful need to idealize, to seek saviors,
as in her adoration of Alfred Kazin, in deflationary lines such as "What prince
has ever seized the shining grail / but that it turned into a milking pail?"
Analysis, it seems this poem is saying, is a process of disenchantment: "our
eyes glut / themselves on clay toes and short clubfoot / which mars the idol's
sanctity." In such lines we are on the way to the ambivalence of poems like
"The Colossus" and "Daddy," which amplify and shrink the Byronic father,
depriving the poem's speaker of an innocence, a fairy tale, so that the intelligence of the "fake" made into a paragon "hangs itself on its own rope." Like
the speaker of the poem, Plath remained poised on "perilous poles that freeze
us in / a cross of contradiction, racked between / the fact of doubt, the faith
of dream." The idea of a freeze, of not being able to thaw out her feelings,
which would become an insurmountable burden of her last days, is upon us
in this poem. The "freeze us" is important, for she tried her best to make this
poem about more than herself, about how the quest for heroes that begins so
early in life can bring us down when, as the poem puts it, we look through
the "scrupulous telescope" that turns the "mica mystery of moonlight" into a
"pockmarked face." None of this is to say that Sylvia Plath was suicidal. The
poem is not a premonition of her own death, but it is a leading indicator, you
might say, of the terms and conditions she knew needed more exploration,
whether or not her conflicting emotions could be resolved. The poem is as
much a sign of her strength of mind and purpose as it is of the misgivings that
troubled her. She continued to see or to call Beuscher at least once a week.

The stimulating meetings with Beuscher and the intense sessions with
Alfred Kazin coalesced in an autobiographical story Plath wrote for his class,
"Superman and Paula Brown's New Snowsuit," which she read aloud in his
home "over coffee and lovely pastry." She told her mother excitedly, "everybody analyzed it," and Sylvia "stayed afterwards to help with the dishes,
and talked to the beautiful blond mrs. kazin, whose second novel is coming
out this winter." Elinor Friedman called Ann Birstein "a bitchy competitive
person." [HR] Birstein, as I knew her twenty years later, was a formidable
figure, with a wry sense of humor that rivaled her husband's astringency. You
can spot it in a short memoir about Plath she published in *Vogue* (October 1,
1971). Birstein sensed no "aroma of death," even though she knew about
Sylvia's suicide attempt. It was not "uncommon," in Birstein's experience, for

a young woman to crack "under the strain of hard work and the pressures of an exclusively female society and having to be resuscitated and reassured, like young men anxious about their masculinity."

The force of Alfred Kazin and Ann Birstein, this couple *at home*, is perhaps the origin of Plath's desire for a powerhouse marriage and a later quest to establish a London salon, a literary and domestic audience that would feed and gratify her imagination. Her receptiveness to literary analysis, her desire to talk out her life with Beuscher, and the historical dimension she now included in her fiction resulted in a new power to reckon with her life and place in the world that culminated in *The Bell Jar* and her last poems.

Plath scholar Peter K. Steinberg calls "Superman and Paula Brown's New Snowsuit" a "deceptively simple story." That is part of its charm but also the writer's way of drawing you into what it is like for a fifth grader to experience her first awareness of history and her place in it. The story is set during World War II. The unnamed narrator has won a prize for drawing Civil Defense signs. This apparently minor detail is, in fact, crucial, since the contest is part of the war effort, and the child is made to feel part of a society committed to its survival. She lives near Logan Airport and dreams of flying, awaking with a shock, "like Icarus from the sky." The words are a premonition of her fall, a loss of innocence. In her dreams, Superman teaches her how to fly. Even better, he is practically a family member since he resembles Frank—the name of Sylvia's uncle. In this story, Plath does not bother to change names or locations, reminding her mother in a letter that the story is based on an incident they both remembered. During the day the narrator, like Plath, has a childhood companion, David Sterling, who joins her in "Superman dramas." They alone conquer the air in games that "made us outlaws, yet gave us a sense of windy superiority." They pride themselves on their singularity and do not realize the consequences of going it alone. They require a villain and choose a Jewish boy, Sheldon Fein, who invents tortures they have to overcome. The family sits by the radio, where Sylvia listened to her Superman programs, with Uncle Frank—the "strongest man," David admits, he had ever known. But now instead of entertainment there is foreboding and reports of "planes and German bombs," with Uncle Frank saying "something about Germans in America being put in prison for the duration." Mother says over and over again about the story's missing Daddy: "I'm only glad Otto didn't live to see this; I'm only glad Otto didn't live to see it come to this." The drawing of Civil Defense signs, the fire drills, and talk of bombing in the school's dark cellar make little children in the lower grades cry: "The threat of war was seeping in everywhere." Everyone, in short, has to be on guard.

In this tense atmosphere, the narrator has to deal with Paula Brown, "bossy and stuck up," and wealthy, although that is only implied in the description of her beautiful clothes that include a powder blue snowsuit "embroidered with pink and white roses and bluebirds" and leggings with "embroidered straps." She even has a "little white angora beret and angora mittens to go with it." All this the narrator observes at a birthday party for Paula that is followed by a trip to the movies to see *Snow White*, an entertainment perfectly in keeping with the fairy-tale world of children, but the narrator's mother does not realize it is a double bill with a war movie about Japanese torturing prisoners of war. No longer does the narrator have to imagine villains or torturers: "Our war games and the radio programs were all made up, but this was real, this really happened." The narrator tries to block her ears and "shut out the groans of the thirsty, staring men," but she cannot tear her eyes away from the screen. The narrator runs to the girl's room and vomits up her cake and ice cream. Later, in bed, she can no longer dream of salvation: "No matter how hard I thought of Superman before I went to sleep, no crusading blue figure came roaring down in heavenly anger to smash the yellow men who invaded my dreams."

Outside on a Saturday, children are playing Chinese tag (the tagged player has to hold a hand on the tagged part of the body). Paula Brown tags the narrator on the ankle and the narrator does the same to Sheldon Fein as they run into the street close to where a car has made an oil slick, which Paula Brown slides into, smearing her beautiful snowsuit and mittens. She accuses the narrator of pushing her. The children take her side and taunt: "You did it." The narrator from a German family has become the scapegoat even as she shouts "I did not!" She is attacked with snowballs. She has become a different kind of Snow White. She returns home, greeted by her adoring Uncle Frank: "How's my favorite trooper?" He is about to be drafted and includes his beloved niece in his war effort. She has almost no time to recover before the doorbell rings, and her mother is heard talking to David Sterling, the narrator's playmate. Then the mother asks her daughter: "Why didn't you tell me that you pushed Paula in the mud and spoiled her new snowsuit?" The narrator again denies the charge, now made, ironically, by the mother who worried Germans would be scapegoated. The mother says, "but the whole neighborhood is talking about it," and the consensus is that they should buy Paula a new snowsuit. Even worse, Uncle Frank visits her in her room to say "very softly": "Tell me honey . . . you don't have to be afraid. We'll understand." He sighs when she again denies that she is guilty. He says they will pay for another snowsuit "just to make everybody happy, and ten years from now no one will ever the know the difference." But of course the narrator has not forgotten anymore than Sylvia Plath forgot in the letter to her mother. The end of the story is a chilling obliteration of childhood in terms of the childhood that has just been violated: "Nothing held, nothing was left. The silver airplanes and the blue capes all dissolved and vanished, wiped away like the crude drawings of a child in colored chalk from the colossal blackboard of the dark. That was the year the war began, and the real world, and the difference." The accusation has been enough to render the narrator a criminal—not even believed by her Superman uncle. We are not far from the world of Esther Greenwood and the Rosenbergs, where the times try those who do not fit in, and the charge sheet—if it is alarming enough—leads to anomie, and an alienation of the self from society.

What must that evening at Alfred Kazin and Ann Birstein's have been like? Reading aloud to a group for the purposes of analysis. At the very least, it was a way to share Plath's fiction of reality in front of a receptive audience, a group awaiting her word, representing a world in which she could have an impact that is denied to the narrator of her story. For certain, Plath was inspired by telling her story, becoming the center of attention, and by her belief that her story's narrator no longer can imagine for herself. For Sylvia Plath the world became a larger, more threatening place the deeper she dove into her childhood, when everything was possible and then nothing—no suffering could be impossible—save what she could rescue in the annealing of her art.

Aurelia Plath plays a minor, plaintive role in "Superman and Paula Brown's New Snowsuit" reflective of her daughter's ambivalent attitude toward her. "I have a very attractive, but nervous mother, whom I see as little as possible," Sylvia wrote to a friend during the Christmas holidays of 1954, adding "I do love her, and am not contemplating matricide." Aurelia began to shrink in her daughter's imagination as a figure of narrow proportions and unequipped for a writer's struggle to explore and command the world's attention. On the way to what would become *The Bell Jar*, Aurelia's character would appear as an inhibiting, retrograde force—a part of what made Sylvia Plath possible, to be sure, but also lacking in the magnificence that a writer like Plath ruthlessly pursued.

Jon Rosenthal visited the Plath home that Christmas of 1954 and saw a very different Aurelia Plath, "quite attractive" and "almost statuesque," but also "stoical and fidgety," and part of a rather crowded household with several small rooms. Sixteen years later, biographer Harriet Rosenstein formed a similar impression: "Mrs. Plath is attractive, slim youthful. Marvelous luminous large eyes. Holds self proudly. Nervous, at times contained, at times over-eager. Enthusiasms excessive particularly raptures over flowers." Much the same description of Sylvia was given to Rosenstein when she interviewed her college classmates at Smith and Cambridge.

But Sylvia's life seemed so much bigger than the "tidy, unimpressive" house Rosenstein entered. Sylvia seemed so much bigger than her mother, Jon Rosenthal thought, even as Sylvia seemed to take no notice, never treating him as less than her equal: "She never put me down." She was "physically demonstrative," Rosenthal told Harriet Rosenstein, and a "very warm person," but they did not have intercourse, even during a ski trip, when he was feeling rather reckless and driving fast on slippery road, disturbing Sylvia who jumped into the back seat. Two hours later she jumped back into the front seat and gave him a big kiss and explained that his fast driving had bothered her because she had been close to death and did not want to ever be that close again. Later they talked about her suicide attempt, and she explained how hard it was for her because so many people had put her on a pedestal, and that made it difficult for her to reach others. The jumping back and forth in the car was quintessential Sylvia, Rosenthal said: "That's the kind of person she was: she was very out-front. If she felt that way, she was there. If she didn't, she wasn't there. Which is one of the very appealing things about her because there were no games. There were so many games between men and women in those days." Rosenthal, recovering from some horrendous experiences in the military, seemed to find her company restorative.

58

After a brief "vacation," just before the beginning of her last Smith semester, Sylvia wrote to her mother: "I rested and played and whirled until I really wanted to come back to Smith." She had splurged on a plane ride to New York City: "I kept my nose pressed to the window watching the constellations of lights below as if I could read the riddle of the universe in the braille patterns of radiance." To a college classmate, Enid Epstein, she wrote: "I am becoming a fatalist and think that somehow this postponed senior year was necessary for me to grow more slowly in time." She wanted to see stories by Enid, who said that Sylvia thought of herself as a "backwoods type" compared to Enid's New York City sophistication. Sylvia, worried she was not good enough, often turned to Enid, also published in *Seventeen*, for reassurance, writing: "I'm so deep in rejections that I am hardly equipped to criticize!" She had put off the idea of marrying Gordon Lameyer, now that she was deeply involved with Richard Sassoon, her New York City squire, given no acknowledgment in her letters to her mother or to Lameyer.

In New York City, Sylvia reveled in her time in a police station reporting a stolen suitcase that had been taken from Richard's car. She acted as though crime was her beat and Richard her partner "as explosive as ever," she wrote his rival, Mel Woody. In that letter her offhand reference to herself as a lady suicide suggests how much of her own experience was turning into material for her to write in poems like "Lady Lazarus."

59

In Sylvia's last semester, she seemed enveloped in the male trinity of Albert Fisher, Alfred Kazin, and George Gibian—all three of whom went well beyond the calling of teachers to inspire and guide their students. These were three quite different personalities, but all of them exuded an allure and air of authority. Fisher, who had an Irish, tweedy look, had affairs with students and liked to talk about sex. [HR] Sylvia joked he might initiate an affair, although he does not seem to have done so. She was grateful for his offer to tutor her about poetry and to deal with her own poems. Gibian treated her thesis as a master work and also brought her into his home, where she babysat for him. She did not tell him about how her work on Dostoevsky and the double, the subject of her senior thesis, had special relevance to her own experience, but he noted that she was interested not only in the literary treatment of the double but also in the psychological and anthropological studies of the double and twins. Physically, she appeared to him like any other Smith student: healthy, tall, and good looking. [HR] Kazin promoted a professional engagement with her ambitions, going out of his way, outside the classroom, to treat her as an aspiring writer.

It may have been her absorption in this troika, and this fathering of her talent, that served as a prompt to write a villanelle she first titled "Dirge" and then revised as "Lament." The poem's refrain "the sting of bees took away my father" brings him back to earth, to mortality, from the heights of a man who mangles the "grin of kings" and ransacks the "four winds." Something about this swarm of insects, seemingly so small yet lethal, haunts the poem, making a mockery of the man who "scorned the tick of the falling weather." This consciousness of the tick of time, of a decline signaled by atmospheric changes and changes in personality, is evident in a letter Sylvia received from Aurelia shortly before composing the poem. Sylvia responded to her mother's letter about Otto Plath's colleague whose " 'personality' was criticized by his students—as with daddy, disease twisted an otherwise good nature." Nature can be part of the undoing of the self, attacking the pride in personality, that goes before the fall. Otto had left his disease untreated (he thought it was cancer) and then succumbed to diabetes, losing a leg first and then his life, sting by sting, so to speak, as the disease advanced on him.

The ambivalent reaction to her father coincided with strains in her dealings with her mother. Like many parents, Aurelia worried about her child's future and discouraged what she considered impractical plans. Sylvia rejected this conventional thinking, the slotting of herself into the security of traditional education and career preparation, even though she had been considering graduate school—a choice her mother endorsed. The strain between them is evident in a letter Sylvia wrote on February 10, 1955, dismissing her mother's objections to taking a teaching job in Morocco. Sylvia had rejected the idea of learning shorthand because she wouldn't take the kind of job that would interfere with her writing. She was excited about the "vitality of this small international community" in Morocco, where she would be among those trying to set a good example and spread good will, as explained to her by Mr. Shea, an American consulate representative and head of the school there. How could her mother not see that this experience abroad would be a

> thousand times more advantageous for my languages and growing interest in international politics than "courses" at a sweet American desk? . . . After a year in England, or a year in Morocco, who knows what I wouldn't be equipped to do? . . . The international outlook is the coming world view, and I hope to be a part of that community with all I have in me. I am young enough to learn languages by living, and not the artificial acceleration or plodding of "book" courses. I want people opposite me at tables, at desks, not merely books.

She was attracted to Morocco's "cool, dark climate with a hot sun"—a not inconsiderable enticement since she had always associated good health, physical and mental, with the sun. Mr. Shea was "like the intelligent, loving, liberal father I have always longed for, and I can think of no man except Mr. Crockett who so much made me think that there are saints on earth, with a radiance and love of service and helping others to grow which is almost superhuman." Then, too, she wanted to "counteract McCarthy." She believed that "new races are going to influence the world in turn, much as America did in her day, and however small my part, I want a share in giving to them." She and Sue Weller would know in late April or early May if their applications had been successful. She had the full approval of Professor Fisher who had recommended her for the job, which was also endorsed by the Smith Vocational Office. She had gone to the trouble of explaining so much because to her mother her "goals in life" seemed "strange."

This is the Sylvia Plath on the way to *The Bell Jar*, which opens with an invocation of the Rosenbergs as a stain on American history, and the emergence of a voice that is at odds with the political and cultural Cold War status quo, which depended on, in her view, an intolerance and parochialism—not to mention a provinciality—that is treated with such disdain in the novel. Sylvia's harsh view of friends and family, including her mother, that appears in the novel's characters constituted a welling up of protest against the conformity of a community that did not honor dissent and saw it only as the subversion of societal norms. Aurelia Plath, to her daughter's dismay, had voted for Eisenhower, the centerpiece of a collage Sylvia had made with the President as the general of a hostility against those at home and abroad that did not acknowledge American hegemony. As much as she owed her mother, as much as she owed her society and all those who had made the success of a scholarship girl possible, her gratitude could not, in her estimation, require her to submit to the prescribed patterns that so many of her Smith College contemporaries followed.

The fulcrum of Plath's singularity had been Ruth Beuscher, who had lived abroad during the advent of Nazi-occupied Europe and wrote about its decimation of the human spirit, and who believed that the psychology, the politics, and the religious beliefs of the individual had to coalesce in the formation of a successful identity. Sylvia said as much in a letter to her mother when she noted she saw her desire to serve abroad as "serving my religion, which is that of humanism, and a belief in the potential of each man to learn and love and grow: these children, their underdeveloped lands, their malnutrition, . . . all these factors are not the neat rigid American ideals," but there was so much to learn from such factors even as she taught them.

But Morocco was wiped off Sylvia Plath's map on February 14, 1955, the day she wrote to Ruth Cohen, the Principal of Newnham College Cambridge, accepting her admission as an "affiliated student at Newnham College to read for the English Tripos."[34] She planned to arrive at the university in October 1955 even if her Fulbright application was not successful. Now even her mother had to be satisfied: the "whole english dept. here is behind me and against machine-made american grad degrees." In March, she met a Cambridge graduate, Chris Buxton, who presented an "enchanting picture of spring boating & may 'balls' & gardens there."

60

Plath's fascination with Edwin Akutowicz continued, perhaps as a result of her opening up to him about her father. Akutowicz had known her intimately in a way no other older male could rival, notwithstanding her contacts with Alfred Kazin and Albert Fisher, and with older male figures close to her family, like Dick Norton's father. No other man at this point could speak to her, as Akutowicz evidently did during a dinner in Lakeview, Massachusetts, on April 9, 1955, which Sylvia described in her calendar as a "very dear time." She had been reckless with Edwin during her Harvard summer, but a poem she was working on suggests she wanted it that way. In the highly coded "Circus in Three Rings," somewhat decipherable by reading her journals,[35] images of Akutowicz and Sassoon, whom she had called "satanic," fuse in the invocation of Mephistopheles as an elusive figure that is both a projection of her own daring sense of herself as the ringmaster of her fate and of her "demon of doom," so that she has to defend herself, flourishing a whip with a "fatal flair" from "my perilous wounds." Such words hardly encompass her dating merry-go-round. She continued to see Gordon Lameyer. All of Sylvia's Smith College friends agreed he was the very image of all-American handsome. After a Sunday with Richard Sassoon in New Haven, on May 15, 1955, she returned to Northampton, where Gordon met her at the train station. She had her courtiers on both ends.

"Circus in Three Rings" also seems to emerge out of Plath's reading of William Sheldon's *Psychology and the Promethean Will*, a book recommended by Ruth Beuscher and that Plath read twice. Beuscher trained with Sheldon and corresponded with him for several years. His playful letters to her reveal that she had the kind of flair that also attracted Sylvia. From Columbia University, he wrote to Beuscher on June 18, 1955: "You haunt Bard Hall.[36] I go over there once and a while, but the place is a barren disappointment without the brilliant slinky flapper who used to catalyze both the juvenile and institutional somotonia of the place."[37] In an earlier note to her, he claimed: "Have known only five bright women in my life and you are almost two of 'em."[38]

Sheldon addressed himself to what he called humanity's "divided soul."[39] Plath underlined his observation of "two elemental wishes; a wish to harness and restrain; and a wish to freely express the direct desires of the biological self." This dichotomy of purpose is what Ruth Beuscher explored in her therapy, acutely aware of how women of Plath's generation had been required to withhold themselves, "save" themselves for marriage. Plath underlined Sheldon's view that the "roots of much emotional bafflement go back to sexual frustration." The choice of the words "go back" suggests a kind of atavism, a reversion to feelings human beings have always had but that have been repressed in the material (political and economic) conditions of society. Beuscher had to work hard to break down Sylvia's defense system that initially would not allow her to confess her hostility to her mother's well-intended but nevertheless repressive regime. To restore the whole person, Sheldon argues, is to recognize that the Western world has "recoiled in mortal fear from contemplation of its own soul." The three rings of Plath's poem—self, society, and soul—get whipped up in the "circus tent of a hurricane / designed by a drunken god." Beuscher via Sheldon counseled Plath not to ignore the religious dimension of suffering, which would mean recognizing that an individual's agony meant more than itself, that her suffering was our suffering, or our suffering was hers, performed, as in a metaphysical circus, Plath realized, in a public spectacle, which is the poem, an expression of exuberance that belies the "rose of jeopardy" flaming in her hair. A day by day reading of her calendar explains the wielding of a whip, the tilting of a trapeze, the revolving rabbits around Mephistoph- eles who promised so much to Faust. As in the poem, Plath often treated her own life in letters and journals as magical, death-defying, exhausting, and exhilarating. When *Atlantic Monthly* accepted "Circus in Three Rings" for its August 1955 issue, Sylvia wrote her mother: "That fortress of Bos- tonian conservative respectability has been 'charmed' by your tight-rope walking daughter!"

Tight-rope walking suggests, of course, a precarious balance, an escape from death that, in Plath's case, also engendered art. Did she see her own escape and rebirth in the example of Stefan Wolpe?[40] On March 29, 1955, on the bus home to Wellesley, Sylvia had a "wonderful talk" with the composer and superb pianist. He believed, as Plath did, in an art that simulta- neously appealed to all levels of listeners. A Jew, and a Communist, he fled Nazi Germany when Hitler came to power, and he had to keep running from fascism in Europe until he settled into a teaching position at radically innovative Black Mountain College, the home of modernists and abstract expressionists like Willem DeKooning and Franz Kline, both of whom became Wolpe's friends. Listening to Wolpe may have been one of instiga- tions of a poem like "Daddy," a kind of escape fantasy denunciation that results in a Declaration of Independence. The next day, at home, she arose late and after breakfast began to play the piano.

61

On May 20, 1955, Sylvia learned that she had been awarded a Fulbright and felt like she was "walking on air." On June 6, on a "lovely blue day," she graduated from Smith College. The Commencement speaker, Adlai Steven- son, supposed, in Sylvia's words, that "every woman's highest vocation is a creative marriage." Exactly what Sylvia thought of that "hypothesis," as she described it to fellow poet Lynn Lawner, she did not say, but she remarked that Stevenson was "most witty and magnificent." She picnicked afterwards at Quabbin Reservoir with her mother and grandparents. The next day at Mrs. Prouty's for tea, she wrapped up a crucial phase of her life that her benefactor had helped to bankroll. Like many writers before her—Hemingway is perhaps the best example—she would not hesitate to satirize a mentor as part of declaring her independence. Home, family, teachers, lovers, and friends were fair game, not because Sylvia was ungrateful, or meant to be unkind, but because no form of obligation could interfere with the writer's sovereign imagination.

With Aurelia in the hospital for an operation on her ulcer, Sylvia stayed close to home in the summer of 1955, reconnecting with childhood friends like the Freemans, dating Gordon Lameyer, seeing Richard Sassoon, and spending time with others like serious George Gebauer, who seemed under her spell. She sunbathed, swam, picnicked, and cleaned house while listening to records, which stimulated an "ineffable nostalgia." [PC] For what, exactly, Sylvia did not say, but it would seem she was revisiting her childhood and upbringing and storing up energy for her foray abroad, which she prepared for in letters to Rhoda Dorsey, a Smith graduate now at Cambridge, and to Cambridge faculty.

62

On June 18, 1955, Sylvia appeared at the dedication of the Babson World Globe on the campus of Babson College in Wellesley. The Globe was meant to

> impress upon students and other viewers an appreciation of the world as a whole . . . stimulating an interest in world geography, history, economics, transportation, and trade. . . . When it was dedicated in 1955, the Globe measured 28 feet in diameter and weighed 25 tons. It was engineered to rotate on its own axis. . . . The Globe was the largest of its kind at the time and drew tens of thousands of visitors to campus each year.[41]

As she watched the globe rotate, perhaps she thought of a letter she had written on April 11 to Claiborne Phillips about seeking a "new world to conquer and be conquered by."

At the same time, she wrote and revised poems, sending them out to a variety of publications, including the *Saturday Evening Post, Woman's Home*

Companion, Ladies' Home Journal, the *New Yorker,* the *New Orleans Poetry Journal,* and the *Atlantic Monthly.* She spread her talent and her person as widely as possible, socializing with editor Peter Davison, first introduced to her by Alfred Kazin, taking Davison to bed (that's how he came to describe it), and then summarily leaving him by the end of the summer. He felt "devoured" and never got over the idea that he had been used, abetted by his wife Jane Truslow's dislike of Sylvia evident in Harriet Rosenstein's interview with her. But Sylvia never supposed commingling with Davison, "British and tweedy," had been serious. [PC] Even in their most intimate confiding moments, she presumed that this liaison was temporary while she prepared to leave the country. This did not mean she did not genuinely enjoy herself with Davison, as she indicated in her calendar entry for August 7: "good love." [PC] Davison's grievance against Sylvia may have been due to what Ruth Beuscher called her "cold-blooded" relationships with men. She enjoyed sex with them and "realistically evaluated what she wanted in men and went after it." [HR]

63

"Platinum Summer,"[42] an unpublished story Sylvia worked on in July and August of 1955, reflects her deep immersion in a Hollywood sensibility that had been forming since her preteens, when she began cutting out those paper dolls of Rita Hayworth and Hedy Lamarr, relished Elizabeth Taylor's performance in *Cynthia,* mooned over Cornell Wilde in *Centennial Summer,* and then had her moments of Hollywood proximity dating the son of movie mogul Spyros Skouras, a scion who inspired in "Platinum Summer" the creation of Ira Kamiroff. He is introduced as if motion pictures have given birth to him: "son of Kamiroff Pictures, Inc." Sylvia's blonde persona appears in the story as Lynn Hunter, with perhaps a touch of Lynn Lawner, a Wellesley undergraduate poet Sylvia had met at a poetry contest and described in letters as "attractive" and "lovely." They had shared a room at the contest and exchanged several letters. Given Plath's penchant for seeking out doubles of herself, Lynn Lawner, the person, transformed into a character, came made to order.

Being blonde had in itself magical properties in the lexicon of Plath's culture. "Is it true blondes have more fun?" an advertisement for Lady Clairol hair coloring asked, beginning in 1956. But of course that ad was building on a long-standing vision of the blonde beauty stemming all the way back to James Fenimore Cooper's *The Last of the Mohicans* and popularized in Anita

Loos's novel *Gentlemen Prefer Blondes*, adapted for the screen with Marilyn Monroe, who is evoked in a Plath poem, a journal, and in letters. For Sylvia, being blonde became a cynosure as early as 1944 when she noticed "a blond and handsome boy" in class; a sailor with "blond wavy hair" on a train; "a tall, blonde, droolsome guy" at a ninth-grade assembly; some boys yelling at her at a school bus stop, "Hey Blondie." At a dance a "good looking blond boy ambled" over to her saying Poe had written a sonnet to a Sylvia. "May I kiss you?" he asked. "And Summer Will Not Come Again" features a scene in which Celia is upset because she sees her boyfriend Bruce with "another blonde." In the January 23, 1951, issue of the Peoria, Illinois, *Star* she was called "The little Wellesley, Mass blonde." She had been shocked to discover that her "blond god," Dick Norton, was not a virgin. Alfred Kazin's wife, Sylvia noted, was a "beautiful blond."

No wonder Sylvia thought a story titled "Platinum Summer" was a sure winner. Her heroine knows that Ira exploits his Hollywood connections to seduce girls with "stars in their eyes," but Lynn had a "Douglas Fairbanks streak when it came to opening Pandora's Box." In fact, she had a taste for "rare esoteric films in foreign languages." In a sentence Plath invokes the swashbuckling hero of silent cinema and Louise Brooks as the salacious Lulu in Pabst's famous film. For good measure she threw in a premed character, shades of Dick Norton, and made Lynn a waitress at an ocean resort hotel like the Plath who waited tables at The Belmont. Becoming a platinum blonde has accelerated Lynn's social life with the "speed of a roller coaster."

Lynn is aware that Ira regards her as no more than, in Hollywood terms, a hot property. For all her initial attraction to him, he repels her when she learns he has paid off Lynn's boss to take her out against the rules of guests fraternizing with the help. His confession has taken the joy out of her joy riding with Ira in his convertible (Sylvia's own favorite vehicle for summer romance). Lynn, like Sylvia, has vowed this summer to leave her T. S. Eliot behind and just have fun. But the story, actually, counts on knowing something about Eliot and modern psychology. Lynn addresses her roomate, Happy, "Listen Adler," to which Happy, a "psych major," responds, "Polly or the psychiatrist"—references to both the famous New York City madam and Alfred Adler, the Austrian psychiatrist, a pioneer of the term "inferiority complex." This story may have had too much recondite material—no matter how lightly it was treated—for a popular publication. The *Ladies' Home Journal* rejected it, even though beginning with Alfred Hitchcock's *Spellbound* (1945), psychiatry became a part of the romance of mass culture. But erudite banter in a magazine story with references to Dalí and Machiavelli?

In the story, in spite of her intelligence and education, Lynn has been transformed, you might say, by a magazine that urges: "BE A NEW WOMAN . . . EMPHASIZE ONE FEATURE. MAKE IT A TRADE-MARK." So she had glossed herself into a blonde. As with Sylvia, it was just a matter of "bringing out the natural highlight in her hair." Just as Plath's hair had been her crowning glory, so Lynn's "brightening lotion" makes her walk as though she were "wearing the Crown Jewels," with "more prospects lined up than Princess Margaret." But the trouble is the one person she wants to entice, Eric, a premed student working as a bus boy, is enamored of his laboratory skeletons. After he fails to show up for a date and is seen going off with a wealthy hotel guest, Lynn accepts Ira's invitation to sail on a yacht that becomes the scene of seduction with kisses that make her think "T. S. Eliot was never like this."

When Lynn next encounters Eric, he is apologetic, but she turns away only to slip with a tray in her hands and, she thinks, breaks her leg. Eric drives her to a bone specialist, observing, as Dick Norton might have said to Sylvia, that Lynn should "stop flinging yourself at life with such a vengeance. You collect danger signs like the little boy in the Charles Addams cartoon. But even *you* can't lead a charmed life all the time." It turns out that Eric, working as a bus boy, has been paid for, just as Ira paid Lynn's boss so Ira could date the help. Eric's boss has ordered him to chauffeur "Miss Smith-Biddleford." Lynn realizes that Ira has made sure Eric was out of the way so that Ira could have Lynn to himself on the yacht.

Lynn is examined by Doctor Lewis, a "plump jovial man," with the "cheerfulness of a professional endomorph," the body type that William Sheldon had identified before he wrote *Psychology and the Promethean Will.* The injury brings her closer to Eric, who asks her why she has dyed her hair. To match how she feels inside, she tells him, to which he responds: "You're definitely an effervescent platinum blonde inside and, what's more, you can feel it without the stage props." He places a brown head scarf over her hair, asking her how she feels. "The same," she says. "Only better." It is ironic, she realizes, that only by turning herself into a blonde could she get him to value her natural self, smelling of pine needles, Eric tells her after she dyes her hair back to brown. It is a small detail—those pine needles—but perhaps recalling those days when she was thirteen, with her girlfriend Margot, reveling in "soft pine needles in a large clearing enclosed by pine trees. The needles covered a rocky ledge which was very smooth. We had a lovely time." Or that time when they were fourteen and she wrote to Margot: "Can't you just see us lying on soft pine needles and writing best-sellers in the quiet serenity of the woods?" Sylvia associated those pine needles with rebirth, the sense of an emerging new self, "Today is the most wonderful Saturday yet," she wrote in her diary on January 25, 1947, "the air is soft, and a mild spring wind wafts the scent of pine-needles and rich life earthier about the world."

Lynn has won Eric over, who only worries:

> "With that impulsive streak of yours, you'll always need someone masterful around to keep you from going quite wild."
>
> "Someone like a lion tamer?"
>
> "Someone," Eric illustrated by kissing her masterfully on the mouth, "exactly like me."
>
> And to Lynn's amazement, right there on the front porch with her brown hair and sprained ankle she felt as if she were wearing the Crown Jewels. Absolutely anybody could see she was phosphorescent all over.

The story has an obligatory happy ending, with a kiss that Dick Norton was never able to deliver, a kiss Ira knows how to apply but only to the "color wheel" of girls he promised to make starlets. The "lion tamer" here is a man, not the poet herself who wanted to organize the show, as she revealed in "Circus in Three Rings." If Sylvia yearned for that kind of male, protective embrace, it would have to come from a member of the opposite sex who had more to offer than had, as yet, been conceived in her imagination.

64

Writing on all levels and reaching many different audiences geared Sylvia up—a propulsion she needed as she welcomed but also dreaded what her stay abroad would bring her, comparing herself, in a letter to Gordon Lameyer, to Henry James's heroine, Isabel Archer, wondering if she would grow through "struggle and sorrow." She was already showing a certain susceptibility, dancing with Rick Hanzel, an "exquisite dancer" with "fantastic teutonic bone structure," who was "intensely serious about life" but could also "go absolutely wild with a deadpan mambo." Aurelia had arranged for dance lessons at a Fred Astaire studio, and Sylvia gratefully obliged her mother, supposing that she could now command the dance floor, sailing on the *Queen Elizabeth*. She was preparing for the dips and rocks and backbends.

As if to gird herself in an American identity she visited her friend Sue Weller in Washington, DC, taking in all the customary sites: the Capitol, the Supreme Court, the Library of Congress, and the National Gallery of Art, where she lingered to absorb the Flemish and Florentine art. But the Lincoln Memorial transfixed her: "Such a colossus, in such clean, enormous, simply carved white stone. I felt shivers of reverence, looking up into that craggy, godlike face." She did not often experience a visceral sense of what it meant to be an American or appear to anticipate how that conception of a god-like hero would define central aspects of her life and work.

65

Just before departing for England, Sylvia walked by the sea with Warren, perhaps remembering their early shoreside upbringing; sunbathed in her backyard; said her goodbyes to Ruth Beuscher, with whom she continued to have a "wonderful rapport"; called and met with other friends she had made during her Harvard summer; went to those who had stood by her like Mrs. Prouty; checked in with personal and professional contacts like Peter Davison; and spent time with childhood playmates like Patsy O'Neill, who joined Sylvia for an evening by the fire with another colossus, Mr. Crockett. It is as if Plath was gathering all of her experience, what she had known to be good in her life, and embraced it all once again as she set off into the much anticipated unknown. On September 11, 1955, she had herself photographed in front of her Wellesley home, saying her goodbyes to her "dear family" over a champagne and roast beef dinner.

PART TWO

THE MIDDLE YEARS

1

On September 14, 1955, Sylvia Plath boarded the *Queen Elizabeth*, accompanied by Warren and Peter Davison. She walked the deck. She danced and talked with "young prep school boys." She enjoyed their company as much as her meetings with prominent figures aboard ship. The next day she had a "lovely tea" with Anthony Wedgwood Benn, an inveterate diarist and British Labour MP, later known as Tony Benn when he shifted to the far left of his party. She probably heard about British politics and society from Benn, a well-placed scion who later renounced the peerage he had inherited from his father so he could continue to serve in the House of Commons. He had a passion for reform. She may have enjoyed his already developing sense of loyalty to the Labour movement even if that meant dissenting from party policies. Although a backbencher, he had important committee assignments and had access to the Labour Party leaders, including Hugh Gaitskill, a prime minister-in-waiting. Benn had an anticolonialist bent, expressed in his support of his "poverty stricken brothers in Asia and Africa," as important to him as "our social defenses at home." Sylvia still hoped to get to Morocco, for the summer, to teach at the American school that had so impressed her. Benn supported the CND (the Committee for Nuclear Disarmament) and their marches of public protest, which Plath observed on one occasion.[1] Like Plath, he deplored McCarthyism; in speeches he launched all-out attacks on McCarthy, and he supported Americans in Britain who had been blacklisted in their own country because of their alleged Communist connections. Benn's politics would have appealed to Plath, who became an outspoken critic of Britain's botched takeover of the Suez Canal. Judging by her letters to Aurelia, Plath had already rejected the Conservatives and found the Liberals "vague." That left Labour taking tea with her. Sylvia, already an accomplished journalist at Smith and who had interviewed Elizabeth Bowen for *Mademoiselle*, would have come to this tea prepared.

In short, Anthony Wedgwood Benn and Plath had much to share with one another in conversation. Meeting a significant figure like Benn bolstered Plath's sense of access to the wider world she had read about in books, treasured in her childhood stamp collection, and now would experience firsthand. The transatlantic Tony, married to an American, Caroline Benn, often made trips overseas so that his children could see their American grandparents, so it is just as likely that Plath spoke with him about family matters, putting together the personal and political. What we know about her suggests as much: history, as she would show in *The Bell Jar* and in certain poems, is part of everyone's life whether they know it or not. Benn felt the same way, organizing political talks with sailors in the engine rooms of the ships on which he sailed. This urge to create a community of interests, expressed in Sylvia's desire later on to create a London salon of writers, is what made meetings with engaging figures like Benn so appealing.

2

An uninhibited Sylvia shocked at least one of her fellow Fulbrighters, by making love with Carl Shakin, a Jewish New York University engineering student on his way to a Fulbright at the University of Manchester. [RC] In her calendar she noted the "stars & good love." They continued their affair when the ship docked in Cherbourg, spending an afternoon in a park and bicycling through enchanting, "quaint streets." The next day, docking in Southampton, an *Evening Standard* photographer took pictures, and then she traveled with Carl through "D. H. Lawrence country," arriving at Waterloo Station, taking a bus to Regents park, then tea with Carl, and off to a performance of *Waiting for Godot*. These were dazzling days to commemorate as part of her chosen destiny.

The Fulbright program always begins with a round of lectures and social activities acclimating new Fulbrighters to their host country—in this case, of course, a tea with what Plath called "famous celebrities," the literary critic David Daiches and the novelist C. P. Snow, whom she regretted not meeting. Orientation included lectures on politics, nationalization, the colonies, and education, which she had perhaps been first introduced to by Anthony Wedgwood Benn. She visited the National Gallery, viewed the "famous Reading Room" and the Elgin Marbles at the British Museum, walked

An aerial view of Cambridge.

through Trafalgar Square and Regents Park, ate at fine restaurants, went to plays, drove through the still bombed-out areas of London, and browsed the Charing Cross Road bookstalls "for hours." It was, as she wrote to her mother on September 25, 1955, a "whirlwind" of activity and like "walking in a dream." She mentioned her "shipboard romance" with Carl, who had just departed for the University of Manchester.

Ensconced in a cozy room in Whitstead, in Newnham College, Cambridge, Sylvia wrote her mother two long letters about her thrilling meetings with white South African students and about her "dear Scottish" house mother, Mrs. Milne. Yet Sylvia's sense of loneliness and strangeness would remain the gravamen of her gaiety abroad. She dreamed every night of Aurelia and Warren, telling her mother this meant she missed them, but the dreams were about their getting rid of her "forever." She sought out Dick Wertz, Sassoon's Yale roommate studying at Cambridge, noting that he had the kind of close relationship with Ann Davidow, her first-year roommate, that Sylvia had enjoyed with Perry Norton. That kind of brotherly bonding, of reinforcement, meant the world to her. In its absence, the universe closed in on her. She had left London with the telling need to send a "slew of postcards to all the people who had been most dear: the Crocketts, Cantors, Freemans, Prouty, et. al." But at the same time she was keen to immerse herself in a new culture, to "find out about politics, and religion."

3

Sylvia wrote her mother in early October about shopping for furniture and other items to make her room feel like home. Lectures would start soon and all was "poised on the threshold, expectant, tantalizing, about to begin." Her studies for two years would be assessed in six written exams at the end of that time. Her subjects included tragedy, classic French playwrights, the English moralists, and philosophy and literary criticism beginning with Aristotle and ending with D. H. Lawrence. She planned to "slowly spread pathways and bridges over the whistling voids of my ignorance." She was scheduled to attend lectures by F. R. Leavis (a "malevolently humorous little man"), Basil Wiley, and David Daiches. Attendance at daily lectures from 9:00 to 12:00, as recorded on her calendar, resembles the same kind of structured days she thrived on at Smith.

In the damp cold her sinuses plugged up. She had to wait for some time in this wet world for medical attention, dealing with a hardened nurse who dispensed only aspirin, but a kindly National Health Service doctor prescribed effective nose drops. Auditioning successfully for the Amateur Dramatic Club (ADC) revived her. She performed a "sarcastic speech on true love by rosalind in 'as you like it' and, for contrast, the part of the aging camille (my cough and difficulty in breathing was a help here) in tennessee williams' wonderful 'camino real,'" she reported to Gordon Lameyer.

Sylvia's copy of *As You Like It* is heavily underlined—obvious evidence of a close reading.[2] Rosalind, self-described as "more than common tall," disguises herself as a man, Ganymede, and behaves accordingly—an enviable role for five-feet-nine-inch Sylvia to play, who had envied the male's freedom of action. Rosalind presents herself with a "swashing [swaggering] and martial side." The Sylvia Plath who had put aside so many dates, so many self-regarding suitors, marked with a vertical line Rosalind/Ganymede's dispatch of the "love-shak'd" Orlando, who has none of the lover's marks upon him:

A lean cheek, which you have not; a blue eye and sunken, which you have not; an unquestionable spirit, which you have not; a beard neglected, which you have not; but I pardon you for that, for simply your having a beard is a younger brother's revenue. Then your hose should be ungarter'd, your bonnet unhanded, your sleeve unbutton'd, your shoe unti'd, and every thing about you demonstrating a careless desolation. But you are no such man; you are rather point-device [faultless] in your accoutrements, as loving yourself than seeming the lover of any other.

Sylvia underlined Rosalind/Ganymede's quip to Orlando: "<u>Men have died from time to time and worms have eaten them, but not for love.</u>" Marriage is found wanting in Rosalind/Ganymede's underlined words: "<u>Men are April when they woo, December when they wed; maids are May when they are maids, but the sky changes when they are wives.</u>" Yet Rosalind is full of passionate yearning: "how many fathom deep I am in love! But it cannot be sounded. My affection hath an unknown bottom, like the bay of Portugal."

Securing a coveted place in the ADC elated her. She praised the producer for his "stroke of intuition" in casting her in a significant role as Mrs. Phoebe Clinket, a "mad poetess in an 18th century farce," *Three Hours after Marriage* by John Arbuthnot, Alexander Pope, and John Gay. She did not say more

Miss Ada Rehan (Rosalind, disguised as Ganymede) in *As You Like It*. Antique print, 1891.

about what that intuition meant to her. Was she thinking of her suicide attempt, or her mercurial temperament? Or was it her "bat-like figure" on a bike "in her flapping black Cambridge gown" that had attracted the producer's attention? Or was it something else about her that had prompted that "stroke of intuition," and why did it gratify her? She had been approached in the street by a Cambridge man who had said how much he enjoyed her stage work and how her voice filled the room. Was this brash American, with her animal spirits, author of "Mad Girl's Love Song," already called "mad" in the offhand way of the British? The stage direction appealed to a person who did not mind making a spectacle of herself: "Enter Clinket and her maid bearing a writing-desk on her back. Clinket writing, her head dress stain'd with ink, and pens stuck in her hair." How much was already known at Cambridge about Sylvia's writing ambitions? Dr. Arbuthnot, a physician, probably authored the line about Clinket suffering from a "procidence [prolapse] of the pineal gland, which has occasioned a rupture in her understanding. I took her into my house to regulate my oeconomy; but instead of puddings, she makes pastorals." Was Sylvia, with her stuffed-up nose, just the right choice, a figure akin to Clinket who had, apparently, some problem with blood flow in the brain that accounted for her eccentricity? Clinket explains: "Madam, excuse this absence of mind; my animal spirits had deserted the avenues of my senses, and retired to the recesses of the brain, to contemplate a beautiful idea." This ecstatic poetess describes her play as "so proper to excite the passions! Not in the least encumber'd with episodes! The vraysemblance and the miraculous are linked together with such propriety." Undaunted by rejections of her writing, she defends herself: "I may perhaps be excell'd by others in judgment and correctness of manners, but for fertility and readiness of conception, I will yield to nobody." Clinket is paired with Sir Tremendous, who pronounces her sentiments "most divine," as would another Sir Tremendous soon to occupy the stage of her imagination.

Now she was getting written invitations to tea from several ADC members and also from a strapping nineteen-year-old, Mallory Wober, whose playing of Scarlatti's sonatas impressed her. He included a map to their rendezvous. She wondered how he knew she had no sense of direction. Sylvia would often latch on to people who provided her with an orientation. Next to them she experienced a profound ignorance, saying, for example, that she knew nothing about music—a seemingly puzzling comment from a person whose childhood included a devotion to hours and hours of playing the viola and the piano and to periods of intense listening to music.[3] But her study of religion and psychology, which had coalesced in her reading of William Sheldon's *Psychology and the Promethean Will*, convinced her that she was right to doubt her understanding of the world as manifested in art and music and politics—all of which had to be united in thought and feeling resulting in a conception of the religious experience he italicized and Sylvia underlined as "*a universal craving in the human make-up: It is the craving for knowledge of the right direction—for orientation.*"

Deciding on drama as her extracurricular activity revealed a good deal about her need to command the stages of her existence and to see herself as a character inviting the attention of those who could guide her even as she shaped them to her desire. Perhaps Mallory Wober reminded her of Bob Cochran, another suitor three years younger than her. Wober was in this respect the perfect choice, falling under her spell yet already well versed in the ways of Cambridge just as Bob had been at the Cape.

4

Some days Sylvia seemed to spend more time with men in restaurants than in the lecture hall learning about tragedy and literary criticism. On October 28, a "cold, frosty day," her schedule included the following:

9:00: Redpath lecture
10:00: Leavis lecture
11:00: Bradbrook lecture
12:00–1:00: Tea with Richard Mansfield
4:30: Tea with John Lythgoe
6:00: Sherry with Brian Corker at Pembroke College
8:00–10:00: Dinner at Copper Kettle with Richard

She found university food insipid, so to combine a date and good food was most appealing.

Two types of English women put her off, she wrote in a letter to Elinor Friedman: the "fair-skinned twittering bird who adores beagling and darjeeling tea and the large, intellectual cowish type with monastically bobbed hair, impossible elephantine ankles and a horrified moo when within 10 feet of a man." Jane Baltzell, another American at Cambridge, said she agreed with Sylvia, adding, according to Harriet Rosenstein's notes: "A disproportionate number of physically odd women: cross eyes, humps, etc. Women took 'almost classically neurotic' postures; wore clothing haphazardly, almost like in asylums. The shrill shrieky voice seemed almost fashionable." Sylvia and Jane "giggled at all this."

The men treated Sylvia "like a queen," she boasted to Mrs. Prouty: "I find myself building up the beginnings of an agreeable salon of actors, producers, writers, embryonic lawyers, scientists, and so on." As at Smith, she encircled herself with admirers and rated them as to their looks and demeanor, indulging some "weak" Englishmen as well as their more robust brethren. Some of this reporting came with an air of condescension, as if the queen, indeed, was speaking. Part of the theater's attraction to her was exactly that of the salon, the companionship in producing a play, with everyone, including electrician and wardrobe mistress, an intimate part of the collective effort. The absence of such a society would take an enormous toll on the last days of her life.

Another new friend, perhaps as exotic to her as Richard Sassoon, was Nathaniel LaMar, "from exeter and harvard who wrote the story creole love song in the atlantic!" It was later selected for *The Best Short Stories of 1956* volume. She described a "lovely light-skinned negro, and I look most forward to talking to him about writing, etc." At the end of October they had a tête-à-tête over tea, and she felt an instant rapport. Up to this point she had little contact with African Americans—meeting some at parties on the Cape, but that was about it. Her conversation with Nat, as she called LaMar, on October 31, 1955, may have been the first time she had ever had such an intimate contact with a Black man.

Was Nat Lamar's color that put him into two worlds part of what attracted him to Sylvia? He was the son of a widowed schoolteacher and had gone to a Negro elementary school in Atlanta, thinking he would never "make it"—until the Fund for Negro Students had financed his education at Exeter.[4] Like Sylvia, he had been raised by a single mother and was a scholarship student, class poet, summa cum laude at Harvard, and now on a fellowship at Cambridge. To Sylvia, he had appeared as a kind of wonder, and yet in his aspirations and journey away from home not so different from herself, another displaced person, like Mallory Wober, a Jew, who did not quite fit into the English scheme of things.

Nat LaMar became part of the romance plot of Sylvia's sojourn in Cambridge. Whatever she learned from him, it did not touch her deeply in terms of race consciousness, a topic she never appears to have thought much about. She was surprised later, in the spring of 1962, when Ann Davidow wrote to her about civil rights demonstrations at the University of Chicago, which Sylvia thought of as the "most progressive of places racially."

Sylvia grew up in a segregated society, went to school without people of color, and read textbooks like *The Rise of Our Free Nation*, the very title of which presumed a union of values that, in truth, had yet to be realized. "Negroes" entered the book's narrative as having been "brought" to Virginia in 1619. Slavery thereafter is treated as an economic system that naturally took hold in the agricultural South even as it was abolished in the industrial North. Sylvia read about the events leading to the Civil War but was never exposed to the mechanics of slavery. No account of the slave's life ever entered her history book. Slave revolts are mentioned in a sentence. What did a young student—even as bright as Sylvia—make of this tepid text? None of her school assignments recorded in her diaries come anywhere near the subject of Civil War or civil rights. And here is what happened to Reconstruction:

> Many Southern white people feared the effect of granting the privi-leges of citizenship and the vote to Negroes. Some of them formed secret societies to prevent the Negroes from exercising their rights. Members of such societies usually dressed up in long white robes and rode about the country at night. These robed men frightened Negroes and warned them to stay away from voting places and to behave as white men wished them to do. One such society was the Ku Klux Klan. When Southern whites gained control of their own states, they found other ways to keep Negroes from sharing fully in government.

History is so well masticated here that nothing is left of the terror waves and lynchings that decimated African American communities, many of whom fled North. What is the significance of those sacerdotal white robes—not sheets? Did any teacher, for a moment, do some explaining, providing some concrete details? Negroes were frightened? What did that mean? Was it worse than Halloween? And what were those other ways that prevented Blacks from exercising their franchise?

Where was Sylvia Plath on May 17, 1954, when the Supreme Court decided *Brown v. Board of Education*, striking down separate but equal? Her diary is silent for that day, and it is not likely she had that decision on her mind, or what it meant to this young woman who had participated in minstrel shows at school and during her camp summers. She described on July 10, 1945: "Our minstrel show was a great success! I dressed like a little pickanninny girl and when one of the darkies danced I had to say 'I love dat man!'" As a young reader, she does not seem to have understood how retrograde *Gone with the Wind* was.

So Nat LaMar appeared as a wonder. Nothing in her experience, or in her learning, prepared her for the existence of such a paragon. That is what Sylvia sought—models of accomplishment and ambition. Not until 1956 was an African American woman, Barbara Chase, chosen as a *Mademoiselle* guest editor, and even then there were "serious concerns," reports Paula Bren in her history of the Barbizon Hotel that housed the *Mademoiselle* young women in New York waiting for their big break: "as of yet, no fashion magazine had ever published a photographic image of a black woman on its pages." Would the magazine's southern readership cancel their subscriptions?[5] But Chase made the cut and walked into a hotel and into a culture that seemed to her as segregated as the South, although Chase chose not to behave as an inferior. As a result, she nonplussed the women in charge who were not prepared for her sophistication and treated her like the wonder who had appeared before Sylvia Plath in a Cambridge tearoom. But the *Mademoiselle* mavens lost their nerve when it came to presenting Chase at a fashion show because the big buyers would make a "big fuss." Chase remained backstage. "They literally hid me," she recalled. She appeared as hardly more than a smudged image in a *Mademoiselle* group photograph of guest editors. This is the same Barbara Chase-Riboud who published the acclaimed novel *Sally Hemings* (1979).

What it meant to Sylvia for an accomplished African American to materialize before her she never quite said, but she was enchanted at the sudden deep connection to Nat LaMar. Did his light color make a difference? Nat, as she called him, was "very much like me, enthusiastic, demonstrative, and perhaps trusting and credulous to the point of naivté," Sylvia reported to her mother. In virtually the same breath she described her reaction to the surrealist film *The Cabinet of Dr. Caligari*: "it shocks one into new awareness of the world by breaking up the conventional patterns and re-molding them into something fresh and strange." Nat, too, might be included in that sentence. She was looking for revelation. "I remember her as like a hummingbird going from person to person," Nat LaMar told Andrew Wilson: "she felt compelled to get to know as many people as she could, and her neck was on a kind of swivel all the time. It was as if, 'Who is the next person coming into this room? I must talk to them in case they are worth knowing.'" She told her mother she considered LaMar "a wonderful sort of psychic brother," whom she planned to meet in Paris after the end of classes in December. She later told Elly Friedman she had a brief affair with him. [RC] But LaMar presented the relationship to Andrew Wilson as "platonic." He described them as following "parallel paths." She talked about her past, LaMar recalled, with a certain "allure," as a necessary experience. To Anne Stevenson, he put it differently, emphasizing Sylvia talked about herself with "rapt clinical objectivity, like a lepidopterist dissecting an impaled butterfly." She also seemed to view Nat as a necessary but not sufficient experience—like Mallory Wober. She wrote to her friend Elly Friedman, calling them "dear, sweet boys (mostly jewish and negro) . . . but none I could marry." Why? Because they were "jewish and negro" or too dear and sweet? Or both?

Even with so many new men in her life, Sylvia Plath longed for Richard Sassoon, sending him a letter in mid-November, 1955: "In the beginning was the word and the word was sassoon." The English boys, she wrote to her mother, are "babies compared to him." She saw bits of Sassoon in her dates, but none of them added up to much. She had shared a kind of intimate sexual and aesthetic experience with Sassoon that left her wanting more. She had underlined an italicized passage in William Sheldon's *Psychology and Promethean Will* that articulated what she was looking for: "*a compatibility between inner feeling and outer experience—a wish for the marriage of feeling and intellect, and a potential keen delight in the achievement of it.*" Those forays with Sassoon to New York City, eating in fine restaurants, going to plays, and visiting museums, had not been simply entertainment. On the contrary, those moments with him were the anticipation of something more: "a potential keen delight" in the union of their thoughts and feelings. Sheldon's "marriage of feeling and intellect" expressed to perfection her sexual and cerebral selves that coalesced with Sassoon. Sheldon emphasized "warming and vitalizing the aesthetic experience" that led to the "growth of the soul"—a word he deliberately invoked because, like Ruth Beuscher, he believed modern psychology had ignored spiritual matters in such a way as to imperil any ability to deal with the whole person, the personality attempting to shape its own character. Again, his choice of words—"warming and vitalizing"—had a sensuous affect. What those English boys lacked—and they did seem like boys to Sylvia—was precisely Sassoon's intense mode of seeing and feeling. Not that she did not try with her Cambridge consorts, confessing to Mallory Wober: "There is something quite mystical that happens to me when I think of you." And also something sensual, as she recorded in a calendar entry for November 20: "MALLORY—talk, music & love." She said in a letter to him: "Now, Mallory (I like to say that name out loud, because it has just the right number of syllables to give it so many kinds of dramatic expression)." She wanted him to ask her to "demonstrate some time."

Sheldon did not call himself a romantic psychologist, but Plath's carefully and copiously underlined copy of *Psychology and the Promethean Will* seemed to track Sheldon's Shelleyan trajectory, which had to be uppermost in her mind as she studied the Romantics in her first months in Cambridge. It wasn't just the weather that was damp and cold; it was the men who did not have Richard Sassoon's heat. They could be charming and witty and knowledgeable, but they were not fired with the enveloping romance that Sheldon captured in his evocation of the "total occurrence of consciousness in which feeling and realization became one, or intermingle." In the margins, Plath put a star next to those words and what followed: "Whenever a thing is both perceived and felt, there is the experience of the soul; and whenever a thought and feeling become indistinguishable, there is the soul. Soul means oneness, unity, union between the inner wish and outer reality." In other words, Plath's notion of one—unity and union—was, as Sheldon insisted it had to be, romantic and religious.[6] She joked about her quest for sublimity, but she was serious about it all the same, sending Mallory Wober an importunate note asking him if she could come to his room and "listen to music & you & calm my most hectic & tormented psyche," transforming herself into a "sedate femme du salon." She signed herself "Your ramping jade." She had at the time a small part in a play, *Bartholomew Fair*, as a "rather screaming bawdy woman," she reported to her mother.

Classical music had a special, sanctified place in *Psychology and the Promethean Will* that Plath seems to have taken to heart in hallowed Cambridge. "In the music and the dignity and the great age and tradition . . . an urban mind may experience for a moment some fleeting twinge of that sense of significance and at-one-ment." He singled out an aesthetic preference for music coupled with the "selection of friends" as a way of "quickly reaching the deeper levels of consciousness." With Mallory Wober, Plath was practically following Sheldon's program of therapy. Music, he believed, "can be shown to be of greater use than dream material in the analysis of the motivation of a personality." They spent an afternoon in her room as he played a rented Hammond organ "singing our favorite hymns (he introduced me to a wonderful one with words by john bunyan beginning: 'he who would true valor see') and christmas carols he also played bach and scarlatti, and as we ate tea on the floor by the fire, we heard tchaikovsky's magnificent 1st piano concerto & beethoven's." She wrote her mother that she had begun playing the piano again.

Music revealed Sheldon's conception of the Promethean will, which contended with conflict within the self and society. The Promethean mind is "built up not by eliminating conflict but by intellectualizing it" and developing character in response to conflict. What bothered Sylvia about Cambridge, particularly the female dons, is that they seemed shriveled and part of a static, incarcerated life. Her theater work reflected, as she told her mother, her desire to "be out on the stage too, and create in any way, no matter how small." Sylvia wanted to move out of academic life and into the "world of growth & suffering where the real books are people's minds and souls," which meant finding friends and being able to say, like Yeats, "'It was my glory that I had such friends' when I finally leave the world." Mallory Wober's "coal-black hair, elegant strong bone structure, scarlet cheeks, blazing black eyes, with a wonderful feeling of leashed strength" is how she pictured Dmitri Karamazov. She found an "aesthetic delight in just looking at him." He nursed her during one of her colds and accompanied her to the Advent Service at the exquisite King's Chapel, which Sylvia described, noting its "cobweb lace of fan-vaulting" and the choir boys "singing in that clear bell-like way children have: utterly pure and crystal notes." She had never been moved like this before.

5

Richard Sassoon's one-day visit on December 4, 1955, provoked a melancholy mood. She had tea with him and his former college roommate Dick Wertz, and noted in her diary "sherry & long sad talk—'you can't go home again.'" What exactly transpired she did not say in the letter to her mother mentioning Sassoon's visit but providing no details—a surprising omission for her. Evidently the joy she had taken in him had abated. Was it because of something he said, or his manner of speaking? Was he beginning to pull away from her? Even in her terse calendar jottings she made sure to mention moods that seemed worth recording. What was she sighing over? She let Elly Friedman know in a letter: Sassoon had "shrunk," like Gregor Samsa in Kafka's "Metamorphosis," to "an insect, to my utter horror. BANG." At nineteen, Mallory Wober, she had concluded, was too young for her. What both men lacked is what William Sheldon had extolled: the Promethean spirit. For Sylvia, this meant a man who braved the world's conflicts and did not become what Sheldon called a "waster" reaching for quick resolutions of perennial problems. The fully developed self had to fight through conflict, explore the nature of opposing forces, and Wober was not ready to confront that kind of struggle, and Sassoon had shied away from it. Sassoon had brought on a sad mood, although she did not blame him for it, only saying in a letter to him that if she did not stop identifying with the seasons, and find a "core of fruitful seeds in me . . . this English winter will be the death of me."

6

In a deeply revealing letter to Elly Friedman, Sylvia described her runaway adventure with a horse, Sam, bolting into traffic, causing an uproar that made her feel positively giddy as she hugged Sam's neck "passionately." She enjoyed the sight of screaming children and women. "I am here today. Black and blue, to be sure, but with a new religion: I mean to marry Sam any day now." It was a joke, of course, but also no joke. Sam had disturbed the universe in precisely the way Mallory Wober and Richard Sassoon could not. And what Sheldon meant by the religious experience was exactly the experience of oneness—in this case between woman and horse. This would not have surprised Sheldon, who believed that only adults still capable of reveling in a child-like closeness to animals and nature had the prospect of developing into full Promethean human beings, capable of adding knowledge to the world. To Gordon Lameyer, who also read the story of Sam, she confessed: "Never has every fiber of my mind & body been so simply & passionately concentrated, since I flew down the ski slope to fracture my fibula: nothing in the world mattered but keeping from under the flying hooves of that runaway horse!"

7

Sylvia's concern, she confessed in a Christmas letter to Mrs. Prouty, was over-stimulation. The term carried more weight than might be supposed. William Sheldon observed that "everywhere young minds are swamped and confused with too much stimulation." It was difficult to "grow a soul in the teeth of overstimulation." In fact, "overstimulation is the real destroyer of the human soul." Sylvia, under some duress, welcomed the end of the Cambridge term and a few weeks to collect herself. Sheldon recommended "reminiscent contemplation," so that a consciousness could feel "in tune with itself." Sylvia did as much in her long Christmas letters, thinking about, as she told Mrs. Prouty, the "most important elements & cutting out the inessential" and to "go on reading and enjoying slowly, and not want to devour the University Library at one desperate gulp." So far she had little time to examine herself or to concentrate on her own poetry and prose. One of Sheldon's observations hit home, and Sylvia underlined it: "to maintain an orientation in the face of overstimulation is like trying to remember a half-learned poem in the midst of a bombardment."

There is some evidence that under Ruth Beuscher's care, which included a meticulous reading of Sheldon, Plath had begun to reevaluate what she had considered so good about her childhood. She marked up Sheldon's attack on summer camps, which overstimulated and "hysterically delighted children" or made them feel "inferior and left out of things." He had seen as much in the treatment of several patients. Better to allow children to work through their shyness and reserve rather than speed up their socializing. Sylvia—not one to remain silent about objections to what she read—underscored Sheldon's sentiments, perhaps reconsidering the powerful push her mother had given her. Paraphrasing the Promethean that Sheldon had lauded, Sylvia observed: "The constant struggle in mature life, I think, is to accept the necessity of tragedy and conflict, and not to try to escape to some falsely simple solution which does not include these more somber complexities." Would she have the strength to meet the Promethean challenge? It was a question she put to Mrs. Prouty, who, after all, had seen Sylvia at her lowest point in McLean and who had superintended her recovery followed by tea and sherry in Prouty's living room and country club. "I have constantly to remind myself"—Sylvia used the phrase twice in her letter to Prouty, as if to slow herself down, and repeat to herself what she might otherwise neglect in the pell-mell of her existence.

8

Sylvia wrote twenty Christmas letters and picked out Christmas cards that she thought would appeal to her correspondents, telling Mallory Wober "I never realized quite so intensely what wonderful people I have known." In December 1937, not long after she had learned to read, Sylvia wrote her first poem, "Thoughts": "When Christmas comes smiles creep into my heart. / I'm always happiest when I'm singing a song or skipping along." In the Christmas of 1943, Aurelia gave Sylvia her first pocket diary. That Christmas was "the most joyous one I had," she wrote in that diary, "because my Uncle Frank and my Aunt Louise came home from Spokane Washington to stay until New Years Day." She woke up on December 24, 1944, in great excitement looking for the Christmas services announcing a full account of Christmas in her new diary. On December 24, 1945, after putting presents under the tree, she watched her Grampy, who had to work on Christmas Day at the country club "have his Christmas as he won't be here tomorrow. Grampy was touchingly happy with all of his gifts as we made him the center of attention for, I believe, the first time in his life." The next year, saying she could not wait for Christmas, she drew a picture of the living room decorated for Christmas. She described how the colorful "Christmas lights and window candles gleamed mellowly through the dusk" and the "expectant 'waiting' feeling in the air." At Christmas, Aurelia would play Christmas songs, Sylvia delighted in creating Christmas booklets and cards, making a Christmas wreath with Warren, and happily wrapping Christmas presents in Scouts. She even made Christmas cards for Warren to send to his friends. She sang Christmas songs in music class and made a Christmas border for her teacher's blackboard, and she loved school assembly Christmas programs and participating in Sunday School Christmas pageants and later in Christmas cotillions. Sylvia often made her own Christmas presents for her family and reveled in shopping for presents when she could not make them. She thought it was just "divine" to put up a Christmas tree and decorate it with lights and ornaments. She would spend a day with friends as they showed and treasured their Christmas presents.

Perhaps sensing Plath's longing for home, the Jewish Mallory Wober played Christmas carols for her. She basked in the welcoming Mallory Wober's family gave her when she visited them in London and wrote to him: "all this is Christmas wrapped in my heart." To be home for Christmas reified her place in the world and what she could do for others. The month after Christmas was a letdown: "I cannot remember any month as long as this one." Christmas seemed a "dim dream," she wrote in a diary entry for January 31, 1947. To be alone, without her family, at the end of the Christmas holiday season would become, in the last month of her life, unbearable.[7]

9

Feelings for Richard Sassoon seem to have revived as he showed her around Paris, easing her into all of it by speaking French and taking her to areas like the Place Pigalle that she could not have ventured into alone. For her Sassoon was Paris, a place and a person that Sylvia regarded as a second home, "a mythical place which promised light and delight and deep experiences." Dave Haslam observes in *My Second Home: Sylvia Plath in Paris 1956*: "Maybe we all have such places in our minds. Where we imagine uncaging ourselves and discovering the secrets of life." This was the cinematic city of *An American in Paris*, the salon of Joyce and Hemingway and so many other writers and artists, a city with a "permissive reputation," Haslam reminds us, where James Baldwin could be free to be himself. It was the city of celebrated exiles.

It is not too much to say that Richard Sassoon treated Sylvia like royalty, squiring her to the Louvre and indulging her at the best restaurants. "Ate like a queen," Plath reported to her mother. The grandeur of Paris—Notre-Dame, the Champs-Élysées, the Tuileries—enchanted her, with Sassoon along as her courtier. She confessed to her mother that he was only man she had loved, but she feared for his "particular nervous, intense fluctuating health." Brilliant and intuitive, he had come closest to her ideal, but his "spells of black depression . . . would mean living in daily uncertainly." She called him a "holy person." He did not look "at all like the kind of man I could be fond of; but he is, and that's that."

On the way to Nice with Richard Sassoon, she described the "good weight" of him sleeping on her breast. They arrived and she satiated her longing for the sea, promenading arm in arm with him, climbing a hill to get a glimpse of Italy. As always, the sun restored her spirits, which had been dampened by rainy England and shriveled by the London cold. She returned to Cambridge in early January seeking again the solace of Nat LaMar over many coffees and teas. They seemed aligned, as she observed, by her experience with Alfred Kazin and LaMar's with Archibald MacLeish.

Then the reverie with Richard Sassoon ended as he broke up with her, saying he had to be his own man, establish himself before he could think of committing himself to her—and even worse he wanted to continue another affair with a Swiss woman. The abruptness of his announcement stunned Sylvia, who would spend the interval between Christmas 1955 and Easter 1956 trying to find a way for him to come back to her, even as she continued to encourage the attentions of the Cambridge fellows who never seemed quite up to the mark, never able to excite her imagination of the Sassoon who had displaced all other men in her exilic existence. She would spend several months thinking that no matter what he said, she could win him back, even while admitting her own doubts about how well he could hold up to the kind of full life she projected.

10

Anticipating a visit from Aurelia in the summer of 1956, Sylvia set out for her mother her state of mind and expectations. She described a heavy schedule of reading, lectures, and translation leaving little time to write. She had rejected the idea of an academic career and the single life of female academics who seemed a sorry lot to her, isolated from the mainspring of life and socially maladroit. At the same time, she did not want to be one of those "career women." Wise cracking and sardonic Eve Arden played those roles effectively in the movies, but she did not attract the romantic interest of the leading male characters or become the cynosure of the plot, which is where Sylvia wanted to be. But she could not do it alone, and teaming up seemed the best way to dominate the world's attention. "I do hope someday

I meet a stimulating, intelligent man with whom I can create a good life," she wrote her mother, "because I am definitely not meant for a single life."

Excited to be living on the edge of the Continent she felt "smothered at the idea of going back to the States!" She would consider returning only if she had a husband. "I really think I would do anything to stay here." She was considering applications for Saxton and Guggenheim fellowships to prolong her stay abroad. But waiting for someone she could "honestly marry" was "so hard." In the meantime, she bolstered herself at teas and tête-à-têtes with Christopher Levenson, an editor of a Cambridge magazine, *Delta*. Like Nat LaMar, Levenson was warm and intuitive and also far more robust than most of the Englishmen she met.

In letters Sylvia never lingered long to assess her state of mind. A February 6, 1956, letter to her mother is an exception:

> In the last two years we have certainly had our number of great tests (first my breakdown, then your operation, then grammy's) and we have yet been extraordinarily lucky that they were timed in such a way that we could meet them. I am most grateful and glad that I banged up all at once (although I am naturally sorry for all the trouble I caused everyone else), for I can't tell you how my whole attitude to life has changed! I would have run into trouble sooner or later with my very rigid, brittle, almost hysterical tensions which split me down the middle, between inclination and inhibition, ideal and reality. My whole session with Dr. Beuscher is responsible for making me a rich, well-balanced, humorous, easy-going person, with a joy in the daily life, including all its imperfections: sinus, weariness, frustration, and all those other niggling things that we all have to bear. I am occasionally depressed now, or discouraged, especially when I wonder about the future, but instead of fearing these low spots as the beginning of a bottomless whirlpool, I know I have already faced The Worst (total negation of self) and that, having lived through that blackness, like Peer Gynt lived through his fight with the Boyg, I can enjoy life simply for what it is: a continuous job, but most worth it. My existence now rests on solid ground; I may be depressed now and then, but never desperate. I know how to wait.

Was she as settled as she said? "I know how to wait" is revealing—as if she were telling herself so to make it so. She might be waiting but she was also searching, expecting an outcome that went way beyond what Nat LaMar or Christopher Levenson could offer her. In speaking of "we" in her letter, Sylvia also identified a crucial element in her own sense of survival. What happened to her had happened to her family, and it would be consideration for her family that would weigh heavily in the way she began in her last days to reflect on her life.

11

Gordon Lameyer was planning to join Sylvia for some travel in Europe when she had a break from her studies, and she wrote to him to check in on her overburdened mother teaching and also nursing Sylvia's grandmother, recovering from a stomach cancer operation. Sylvia knew her mother would not want her to worry, but Sylvia wanted the truth from an outside observer. She, in turn, did not want to worry her mother, but even so letters home reflected some anxiety: "Occasionally, I am chastened and a little sad, partly because of the uncertainty of the coming years, and the cold whispers of fear when I think of the enormous question mark after next year (which is still not finally financed)." The "cold fears" were not merely metaphorical; she reacted viscerally to the lack of central heating and mentioned her discomfort often. She was awaiting approval of a second Fulbright year and concerns about money were never entirely assuaged. She made her distress more explicit in calendar diary notations: "frozen tears & suffering," "very depressed & antagonistic and hollow," "close to blackness again," "terrible tearful frustration and & desire for R. or C." Richard Sassoon or Chris Levenson? In little more than a week she would meet Ted Hughes for the first time. He would begin—although not all at once—to virtually cantilever Plath out of her cornered feelings of desire and disappointment. The *New Yorker* rejected a story, "The Matisse Chapel." She was nowhere near a breakdown, however, as she noted: "somehow new stoic courage." On February 22, 1956, she started the day with "new resolution to be accessible and sweet."

In a two-part article for the *Christian Science Monitor* (March 5 and 6, 1956) she observed that for all its modern conveniences and conveyances, Cambridge seemed rooted in the past. To her American sensitivity staying there was like "turning back a time machine." It even had a haunted quality evoked in the "ubiquitous large ravens . . . hunching darkly in trees, muttering perhaps, if one listens closely, 'Nevermore.'" That amusing conceit treated lightly the fact of her own melancholy. She did not minimize the charms of the town—the green peace and sweetness of the life there—she had related as much in her letters, calendar diary, and journal. But she also expressed her view that the students were less mature socially than their American counterparts—which is one reason why Americans like Nat

LaMar and Dick Wertz and farther away in France, Richard Sassoon, were essential to her, although that personal part of her life did not make it into the article. She missed the frank give-and-take of American teenagers, she told her *Monitor* readers. She could not write of England without mentioning the "penetrating cold."

In her calendar diary she recorded an "awful wet cold" and "no sleep— great depression." Part of the problem was her dread that Richard Sassoon could not live up to her expectations. She accepted him "even in the heart of his weakness, whom I can make strong, because he gives me a soul and mind to work with." He did not swim or ski or sail and do all the physical business that made Gordon Lameyer attractive, although she thought Gordon had a weak mind. She addressed herself to Sassoon in her journal vowing to make him "invincible on this earth. Yes, I have that power. Most women do, to one degree or another." But it exhausted her to prop up Sassoon: "still I hope there will be some man in Europe whom I will meet and love and who will free me from this strong idol." Europe, not England, where she doubted the strength of the male stock. She was at an impasse with the men around her: "I am sick of Mallory, Iko, John, even Chris. There is nothing there for me. I am dead to them, even though I once flowered." She had one of her once a month colds that left her shivering and looking like hell with an ugly red nose and feeling sorry for herself, telling her mother she wanted someone to baby her and bring her broth. "I sometimes despair of ever finding anyone who is so strong in soul and so utterly honest and careful of me," she lamented: Nothing approached that "depth of experience when you work or live side-by-side with someone, sharing the daily texture of life." On February 24, 1956, a day away from meeting Ted Hughes for the first time, she had already, as she had prophesied in "Mad Girl's Love Song," made him up inside her head.

The next day, she went to see "fatherly" Dr. Davy, a psychiatrist. They had a long talk about her past and how isolated she felt because those around her seemed so immature. She followed up this therapy with one of her soothing dinners with Nat LaMar, who had not wearied her. At night, on an upswing she went to the famous St. Boltoph's party celebrating the literary journal that published, in her words, "really brilliant" poetry and "taut, reportorial and expert" prose. Her American friend Jane Baltzell knew some of the contributors. Baltzell spotted Ted Hughes sitting in the corner looking like an "eagle in a pet shop, bored, melancholy, discontented, a malcontent." Moody, drinking, not doing much of anything, and "full of contempt for publishers, editors, jostling for fame, all that," according to Baltzell, who thought he might even have stopped writing if it had not be for the advent of Sylvia Plath. [HR]

Sylvia arrived at the party with an English friend, got drunk, and met Ted Hughes. So much has been written about their fateful encounter that it is perhaps better to quote her three-word calendar diary: "mad passionate abandon." No other American woman, no other English woman, is likely to have accosted Ted Hughes with such ferocious flirtation, responding to his filching of her earrings by biting him on the cheek. Having read some of his violent poetry, she had come prepared to retaliate and to conquer.

Jane Baltzell recalled first meeting Sylvia, noticing her "almost comically American appearance: even a bit gauche. A tourist with a capital T." Baltzell said Sylvia was "an embarrassment in her complete unabashed Americanness." She had practically advertised herself as such, having her Smith bike shipped over with her Smith license plate. And she rode that bike like a young girl, "hurtling along." Even at rest, in class, she had a leg "swinging incessantly." She had the "sheen of energy," a "radiance." [HR]

Sylvia had been looking for more than succor, which is what the available men had to offer. She was looking to be lost—and found. So was Hughes. Iko Meshoulem, who knew both Sylvia and Ted, said, "There always seemed to be a party at which Ted was saying goodbye to one girlfriend and starting up with another." In fact, Sylvia and Ted had heard about one another, and the party became their raucous rendezvous. They were, in other words, already performing for one another. Both were at a crossroads. Hughes, in her estimation, was further along as a poet, but he already sensed that she would be his equal as she boldly quoted his poetry back to him. For all his budding brilliance, Ted drifted—few publications to his credit and clueless as to how to proceed. Sylvia took charge and saw the way ahead. He had quit studying literature for a Cambridge degree because he believed literary criticism slaughtered what it pretended to preserve. The idea of an academic career positively revolted him, and Sylvia had already decided the life of a don or a professor was not for her. But the idea of sallying forth on her own was daunting, and she did not want to be another celibate Marianne Moore. Both poets realized they could fast track themselves by joining together. This is to get a little ahead of their story, to be sure, but that first meeting—no accident—set down certain markers.

Not that Plath saw her future all at once. Hardly. She had gone to the party just after writing about Richard Sassoon in her journal. He was not ready to settle down and brave the big world she was counting on. And yet Richard knew "that joy, that tragic joy," she had not found in any other man. "I long so for someone to blast over Richard." Was Ted the one? She had her doubts—not about Ted exactly, even though Hamish Stewart called Ted the "biggest seducer in Cambridge."[8] No, it was Ted's menagerie she feared. Hamish called them "phonies," and she imagined them talking and laughing about her as the "world's whore." [PJ]

Not only did Richard Sassoon remain on her mind, but after that first bout with Hughes, perhaps feeling especially transgressive, she violated Cambridge's midnight curfew. Goaded by Hamish Stewart she climbed the locked gates of Queen's College—usually a sport for males, but she accepted his challenge to get over the gates and accompany him to his room where they had sex. In her calendar diary for the next day, she wrote "exhausted & chastened after orgy." It took her all morning to recover, still in shock and trying to process in spurts what had happened to her: "weary & gray—chills—simply spent—desperate re work—obsessed re Ted—dark giant—lust & anger—nap." [PC] The rest of the day she recovered in the company of her own cohort—with "dear sweet" Chris Levenson for coffee by the fire, then with Mallory Wober for a sumptuous dinner, followed by some time with Jane Baltzell and Derek Strahan before retiring to bed with a hot milk.[9] Sobered up, there would be time enough to confront what her first encounter with Hughes portended.

It is a pity we do not have a Hughes diary entry for that first meeting comparable to Plath's. He went looking for her, and when he did not find her went to the trouble of making sure that one of his brotherhood let her know of his whereabouts. She was America, as Hughes would later declare in *Birthday Poems*, which to him meant the promise of breaking out of his English rut—the same rut Sylvia had deplored in letters home about Englishmen.

The encounter with Ted Hughes resulted in a poem, "Pursuit," which begins with a panther that "stalks me down / One day I'll have my death of him." In her journal, Sylvia notes that she dedicated the poem to Ted, and the invocation of a "black marauder" seems a result of the passionately brutal encounter with him.[10] And yet Richard Sassoon told a close friend he thought the poem was about him, and Plath said as much in her journal.[11] In her March 6, 1956, letter to Sassoon, she affirmed that her poems were "all for you." At this point, he remained very much a fixture of Plath's imagination, a projection of her desire for a strong, fearless man. The panther of "Pursuit" is lithe and taut with an ardor that "snares" and a voice that "spells a trance." Sassoon wrote Plath incantatory letters: "And I have made you smile, I have made you laugh—perhaps I have even made you cry—was this not me! and me alone?"[12] Sassoon knew that he was the only man who had truly inhabited her mind and body. No man had ever written to her in his plaintive, soulful way. Her letters to him are similarly incantatory: "I have been gliding on that wind since noon, and coming back tonight, with the gas fire wailing like the voice of a phoenix, and having read Verlaine and his lines cursing me, and having just come newly from Cocteau's films 'L' Belle et La Bête' and 'Orphée,' " she wrote on March 1, 1956.

The idea that Verlaine was speaking directly to Plath reveals how the universe of her life and imagination appeared to her. Richard Sassoon, in fact, was a figure out of Cocteau, an Orpheus (Jean Marais). She wrote in her calendar: "magnificent—Jean Marais: Richard." Watching *La Bête*, rendered in English as *Beauty and the Beast*, you have to wonder if Plath saw her life working itself out as an allegory, with Hughes playing the Beast. Perhaps that image of a lissome panther, rather than representing brute strength, is what Sassoon took away from the poem, which also allowed Hughes, who later sculpted a jaguar, to suppose he was Plath's intended. After all, she had often played one man off of another, frolicking with Sassoon, then writing Gordon Lameyer charming letters.

Like the work of Tennessee Williams, the films of Jean Cocteau served Sylvia as a way of framing her own existence. The handsome Jean Marais has the beauty that could turn beastly in his performance as Orpheus treating his wife contemptuously as he falls in love with the seductive emissary of death. As the Beast he seduces Belle by evincing a nobility that she draws out of him. She releases what he himself calls the good in him—as Ted would say Sylvia did. Belle becomes increasingly devoted to the Beast, expressing a wonder at her own reactions, which turn into beatific expressions that one can almost see in Sylvia's evocation of Ted in her diaries. But Orpheus, the poet, is also Ted, both of whom never quite give all of themselves to their adoring wives. Yet those wives persist in believing they can save the Beast from himself. A crucial moment in *Beauty and the Beast* defines the way Sylvia would resolve her own doubts about Ted: Belle declares, with significant satisfaction: "He would never eat me." She compares his impact on her with hypnosis—one of Ted's specialities.

Jean Marais—so malleable in his performances—bridged the divide between Richard Sassoon and Ted Hughes in Sylvia's imagination, so much so that she wanted to will strength into Sassoon. And he knew she still wanted him as her Orpheus, although like Orpheus, her letters reveal that Sassoon was retreating from her, like one of those elusive Cocteau cinematic figures. The Frenchified Sassoon would have no trouble seeing the roles she thought he had it in him to play. In a short time she would go looking for him in Paris. Both Hughes and Sassoon were, at any rate, fierce projections of Plath's imagination reified in the films that seemed to enact her destiny: "I made your image wear different masks," she wrote Sassoon,

and I played with it nightly and in my dreams. I took your mask and put it on other faces which looked as if they might know you when I

Jean Maraise (Orphée) in Jean Cocteau's *Orphée* (1950); Maraise (the Beast) and Josette Day (Belle) in Cocteau's *La Belle et La Bête* (1946).

had been drinking. I performed acts of faith to show off: I climbed a tall spiked gate over a moat at the dead hour of three in the morning under the moon, and the men marveled, for the spikes went through my hands and I did not bleed.

Such miracles happen in a life conceived as a surrealistic film.

Sylvia could not pry herself away from Richard Sassoon and wanted him to do it: "Break your image and wrench it from me. I need you to tell me in very definite concrete words that you are unavailable, that you do not want me to come to you in Paris." She said to him "save me from death," a reversal of the "death of me" phrase in "Pursuit," as though Sassoon represented a remedy for the encounter with Ted Hughes, which Sylvia had announced in her journal: "Then the worst happened." Sounding like she was in a Cocteau film, she concluded her March 1, 1956, letter to Sassoon: "I must get back my soul from you; I am killing my flesh without it." Or was her craving for Sassoon just as lethal?

12

To her mother on March 3, 1956, Sylvia casually mentioned meeting a "brilliant ex-Cambridge poet" at a wild party: "will probably never see him again," although she has written her "best poem" ["Pursuit"] about him, the "only man I've met yet here who'd be strong enough to be equal with." By March 4, she was writing to Gordon Lameyer to let him know she was dreaming about him, continuing a pattern of spreading out her succession of suitors as widely as possible, making each one her favorite: "I can make all my vacation plans revolve around you, and would like very very much to do so."

But the old routine of triangulating her romances was not working, as her calendar entries for March 6 reveal: "Richard's letters—crying— revelation—1st saintly letter, 2nd disgusted him." She wrote him a "long letter re eternal love & weakness in wish for immediate love & joy in this world—decided to go to Paris whether he'll see me or not." This was not the girl who wrote in her early diaries about boys circling the block, or waiting downstairs at Lawrence House, for her appearance. Even worse, she had no female confidants. Jane Baltzell had proven unreliable, marking up Sylvia's books and accidentally locking Sylvia out of their shared Paris hotel room all night. They were too much alike in a key respect: Both wanted to be "queens among our men," Baltzell told Harriet Rosenstein. In short, when

Ted Hughes robbed Sylvia Plath of her earrings, he was staking a claim as her consort. Yet even after their torrid tête-à-tête, she wrote to Richard Sassoon on March 6: "I know now how deeply, fearfully and totally I love you, beyond all compromise, beyond all the mental reservations I've had about you, even to this day."

It is tempting to get lost in the blow-by-blow bursts of Plath's letters in this period and to wonder exactly what world she was living in. It is the kind of question Cocteau is always presenting in his films. Letters home suggest she was delightfully immersed in her studies, yet to Richard Sassoon she wrote of her longing to join him, to forsake Cambridge, and settle in Paris and accompany him to his classes at the Sorbonne. He evidently replied (judging by her letters) that she was asking more of him than he could deliver. In her replies she wanted to know why he had to be so much like Brand, Ibsen's intransigent idealist. What she meant by his idealism she explained in a letter to Elly Friedman, referring to Richard

> coming like rhett butler from his slambang hedonist life through love that is holy, sassoon, not saying "I don't give a damn" and leaving her on the stairs holding a piece of red dirt, but saying: "two years of army (it may kill him) and I must make a fortune and only then found a family, and always in the holy skies our love is and will be: someday; meanwhile, I must be noble and give you your freedom."

Sylvia compared herself to proud but also shamed Phèdre in a Racine play she had just read as part of her study of tragedy. She was also Hawthorne's Rappacini's daughter "fatally unable to live in the normal world, and a death-menace to those who wanted to approach her from this world." "This world"—what was that? It's the kind of question that haunts Cocteau's films and also her projection of what literature taught her to experience. Jay Martin, in *The Psychologies of Political Exile*, has a term for such sensibilities: "fictive personalities." Goethe, Martin argues, invented such personalities like Werther, whose suicide prompted many suicides of his generation and lit up those like Napoleon, no less, who "replace their own identities with an identity from the media," the media, in this case, of books. At every crucial stage of his life, Napoleon identified with the characters he had read about, contemplating suicide in the mode of Werther when not reversing himself and identifying with Caesar's desire to conquer. To compare Plath, who had already crowned herself, to Emperor Napoleon is no stretch.[13] Like him, a voracious and voluminous reader, she "needed so many preformed identifications to fill in" what was lacking from "ordinary sources." Think, of course, of her watching *Gone with the Wind* and saying she *was* Scarlett O'Hara.

Sylvia confided to Elly Friedman that she could only imagine a figure coming along like Jean Marais who might transform her and "break richard's image & free me." Like another fictive personality, Quentin Compson, daydreaming that he could act with the honor and prowess of a chivalric knight and failing, she walked about that other Cambridge, declaring: "I miss being of the world around me: a kind of schizophrenic living in cambridge with her clocks and books and running naked on the bay of angels in her head with sassoon."

Perhaps it is around this time that Sylvia came to Iko Meshoulem's room, "in tears, flushed, distraught, hysterical." She spoke of having to choose between two men—maybe more than two men, including Mallory Wober and Ted Hughes, but perhaps Richard Sassoon as well (Meshoulem could not remember other names). "You must forgive me," Sylvia said. "I'm very high. Make love to me. You must make love to me." Iko admits he was "highly stirred," but felt loyal to both Mallory and Ted and also fearful of the pregnancy that might have resulted from intercourse. She then fell into an exhausted sleep and never mentioned the incident to Iko. [HR]

Plath was reading D. H. Lawrence's *The Man Who Died* and believed in her mystic union with Richard Sassoon when they visited Vence, where Lawrence died.[14] Richard, as she made plain in her journal, was connected with her rebirth: "I was the woman who died, and I came in touch through Sassoon that spring [of 1954], that flaming of life, that resolute fury of existence." Dorothea Krook, lecturing on Lawrence, brought Sylvia, like the character in the story, also back to life—or as Plath said to her mother, Krook was a woman—at last a woman in Cambridge!—she could "grapple" with. Together the two of them could take on the world. After a long journal entry on March 8, 1956, in which she despaired of making Sassoon her own, she could not end the evening without asserting her sovereignty in a scene right out of Shakespeare: "Come my coach. Goodnight, goodnight."

What did Dorothea Krook make of Sylvia Plath? In retrospect, Krook provided an evocative scene with Sylvia sitting on a sofa in the "golden Platonic light," striking the Jewish Krook as Jewish. What exactly made for that Jewish look, Krook did not say, except for noting how Sylvia scrutinized her, discovering, perhaps, that they were kin. Their religious-like rapport is captured in Krook's memoir of the "sacred ground on which our minds met."[15] Sylvia's "charming American neatness and freshness," combined with something deeply moving and receptive about her, inspired Krook, as it had Ted Hughes. Years later, when he visited Israel where Krook was then teaching, she was astonished at the taciturn man she had met in Cambridge. He greeted her with a warmth that apparently arose from his memories of what Plath and Krook had shared. Krook and Plath lingered over Plato, and Krook let go, "spreading one's wings to the argument" in a manner that she had done only with a half dozen students in thirty years of teaching. That Krook and Plath were on a higher echelon became apparent when Smith mentor Mary Ellen Chase visited Cambridge and told Krook that it was hard to know who Sylvia was talking about "whether it's Plato or Mrs. Krook she admires most."

What exactly made for this fascination with Plato was more than Krook could remember. It is perhaps enough to know that these two dwelt together in spirit, with Krook becoming Plath's ideal of the writer/scholar/woman. As with Ruth Beuscher, there was no mind/body split, and no devastating disintegration of that union that would eventually sunder Sylvia and Ted. The best Krook could do is remember the topics they lost themselves in: the nature of love and beauty, justice, "the pleasant and the good," "knowledge and opinion, the contemplative intelligence, the practical intelligence, the Platonic rationalism, the Platonic mysticism." Perhaps even more importantly Krook explored these topics by "reviewing my personal life's experience for illustration, or proof"—very much as Ruth Beuscher had done. But with Krook, Sylvia—perhaps constrained in her role as student—held back her own personal experiences, as if—in Krook's retrospective judgment—she could transcend her troubles by devoting herself to the mastery of texts, never sharing with Krook any of her poetry.

Krook watched as Sylvia brought her happiness with Ted to an "idyllic pitch." What would happen, Krook wondered "if something should ever go wrong with this marriage of true minds?" Contemplating the resulting suffering left Krook breathless. Krook's memories were poignant, especially because Sylvia wanted more from her than Krook was able to give, and the result, after Sylvia's death, led to remorse, as Krook vouchsafed to Harriet Rosenstein. Krook felt "very bad" about rejecting Sylvia's invitations to socialize:

> so bad, that once, when she had asked me again and I had again to say I couldn't, I said to her : "You do understand, don't you, Sylvia ? What the claims of my life are; how they leave no room for, let's call it, the pleasures of society. . . . When I've the time I haven't the strength, when I have the strength I haven't the time. . . . If I took time off, I wouldn't be able to do the things you've been so kind and generous about : the lectures, the pupils, the research and writing, the kind of thinking, living, that has to go into them to make them worth anything and life going on all the time, you understand—never stopping for a moment, to give a breathing space for art. . . . I simply can't fit in anything more just now, unless I tear myself to pieces. . . . You do

understand, don't you, the price one has to pay?" I don't suppose I used these exact words, but I did speak these thoughts, or something like them, just this once. She answered, "yes, yes, I do understand"—with a kind of vehemence and a shiny light in her eyes which persuaded me she really did. The remembrance of her understanding has been a comfort I have clung to in the years since her death, when I have often been haunted by the thought that I was perhaps another of the people she loved who betrayed and abandoned her.[16]

Who can say what more Krook could have done for Plath? But, later, when Plath had to confront the pressures on her while teaching at Smith, and what it would cost her, did she remember what Krook told her? Sylvia knew what it meant not to stop for a moment and to commit oneself to the society of scholarship. Visiting Cambridge, Massachusetts, for a fortnight in the autumn of 1957, Krook called Sylvia after Krook's letters were "slow in reaching her." Krook recalled that she was "excited and moved, and so was I. I can't remember anything we said; I only remember it was the last time I heard her voice."

13

At the same time that Dorothea Krook became a guiding light, Sylvia wanted to open up to her mother, to share her breakthrough. She sent Aurelia two poems, "Pursuit" and "Channel Crossing." The first she called Blake-inspired and about the "beauty of death, and the paradox that the more intensely one lives, the more one burns and consumes oneself," and the second reflecting a "turning away from the small, coy love lyric (I am most scornful of the small preciousness of much of my past work) and bringing the larger, social world of other people into my poems." Her crossing to France survives in the poem as a "brief epic," confronting the havoc of the waves, an onslaught that "making harbor through this racketing flux / Taunts us to valor." She sought a heroic stage in her own life and work that she submerged into the "we" sailing "toward cities, streets and homes / Of other men, where statues celebrate / Brave acts played out in peace, in war."

Returning to Richard Sassoon seemed an imperative: "Oh, mother, if only you knew how I am forging a soul! . . . all pales to nothing at the voice of his soul, which speaks to me in such words as the gods would envy. I shall perhaps read you his last letter when you come; it is my entrance into the taj mahal of eternity." This language about the soul hearkens back to *Psychology and the Promethean Will* and the "total pattern of conscious experience where feeling and thought intermingle. This, I think, is what we mean by the experience of the soul," Sheldon surmises. "Channel Crossing" meant so much to Plath because it expressed her refusal to turn away from what Sheldon calls the "awful questions" people "find in their own souls," avoiding the kind of existential crisis Sylvia was now ready to face head-on instead of, in Sheldon's words, "shouting it down, by making a noise, by turning on the radio, by anything." Many people, of course, seek salvation—but not immediately, not in such urgent words that Sheldon spoke to Plath: "Modern man has lost the courage . . . to grow a soul," Sheldon declared, and she took that denunciation as a challenge. For all the learning available at Cambridge, her letters and journals show that something was missing, especially in the desiccated women dons who were not complete human beings. "Are these woman . . . better for their years reading and writing articles on 'the Political Tragedies of Jonson and Chapman' or books on 'The Fool' and fear the bright brilliant young ones like Dr. Krook?" [PJ] She put her finger on their detachment from the human spirit when she underscored Sheldon's admonition: "At the more educated levels of life people have lost touch with their souls." But Sheldon said it was more than that and Plath underlined his breathtaking announcement: "The whole Western world has recoiled in mortal fear from the contemplation of its own soul, as it once recoiled from sexual reality." The ordained Ruth Beuscher had said to Plath there had to be a therapy of the soul, a conviction of Sheldon's that Plath marked in the margin of *Psychology and the Promethean Will:* "For years psychologists have shouted down the soul with an intensity which recalls the puritan shouting down his sexual consciousness." The nexus of sexuality and spirituality in Sheldon and Beuscher has to be factored into Plath's own sexual development and her rejection of what it meant to grow up as a good girl.

"Channel Crossing" exemplified a Sheldon passage Plath underlined: "Happiness is essentially a state of going somewhere whole-heartedly, one-directionally, without regret or reservation." It is a paradoxical happiness, to be sure, because the poem ends with the frightening acknowledgment that "we walk the plank with strangers." If that seems scarifying, it is also, in Sheldon's view, so liberating that he put it in the italics that Plath underscored: "*For in one of its elemental aspects the human soul may be defined as the capacity for imagining pain, and whatever stunts this capacity stunts the whole personality.*"

Sylvia's sense of pain and conflict was Promethean. There was no other way to develop—as Sheldon had insisted: "The inability of the undeveloped mind to tolerate and intellectualize conflict constitutes the deepest bafflement of civilization." With a vertical slash she marked this insight in the margin. Intellectualized conflict is what Sylvia, writing to her mother, expected from her new supervisor, Dorothea Krook: "The one woman I admire at Cambridge! I should grow amazingly by fighting her logically through Aristotle, Plato, through the British philosophers, up to D. H. Lawrence!" Plath was on Sheldon's cutting edge: "It is possible that the only really significant thing that man is now doing lies in the extension of his understanding of conflict." She wrote as much to her mother: "I want you to understand that my battles are intricate and complex, and that I am, without despair, facing them, wrestling with angels, and learning to tolerate that inevitable conflict which is our portion as long as we are truly alive." What was this life Plath wanted but what Sheldon italicized and she underlined: the "*struggle for character . . . the central conflict of life.*"

The next day a "huge joy" galloped through her when she was told that "Lucas and Ted threw stones at your window last night." She sat, now in full fictive mode, "spider-like" waiting for Ted to call on her, like Penelope waiting for Ulysses. [PJ] It was in terms of conflict that she imagined Hughes coming after her: "Another day of hell. He is on the prowl." A friend knocked on her door to say he saw Luke and Ted on the street that "very morning." She was sure they would not come. But then she learned they had mistaken her window and thrown mud at her friend Phillipa's

Vivien Leigh (Blanche DuBois) and Karl Malden (Mitch) in Williams's *A Streetcar Named Desire* (1951).

instead. She imagined them rolling in the mud "treating me like that whore, coming like the soldiers to Blanche DuBois. . . . They refused to face me in daylight. I am not worth it. I must be when if they ever come. They will not come." She wanted to "rave out in the streets and confront that big panther, to make the daylight whittle him to lifesize." [PJ]

14

What was Hughes playing at? Perhaps not enough attention has been paid to his timidity, after Plath had clutched him at that party. He seemed big enough to satisfy her, but then he had run away—pleading another date but then returning, like a little boy, throwing mud at her window, and sort of hanging around, as he had been hanging around Cambridge, aimless and yet treated like an authority by his cohort. Sylvia had boasted to her mother that "the boys" treated her as a second Virginia Woolf. But exasperated by Ted's dilatory courtship, she was ready to gun him down in the street.

Finally, on March 20, 1956, Lucas Myers, an emissary from Ted Hughes, extended an invitation to meet him in London on her way to Paris for an end-of-term holiday. Sylvia did not seem to realize that Luke disliked her and resented acting as a go-between, although his loyalty to Ted had the effect of making his hero seem all the more desirable to Sylvia, as in the case of those receiving an audience with an eminence: "invitation from Ted!" she recorded in her calendar diary.[17] Even so, she seems to have spent little time thinking about a rendezvous with him and concentrated instead on her mission to win over the retreating Richard Sassoon.

Just then Plath received a letter from Jane Anderson, who had suffered a mental crisis and became a friend during Sylvia's treatment in McLean. Sylvia could write to Jane as someone who had shared her trauma, and she looked forward to Jane's visit to Cambridge. Jane had shared her plans to become a psychiatrist after getting her medical degree and apparently had trouble with college admissions because of her breakdown. Sylvia empathized: "I, too, have felt the handicap of having a record in a mental hospital, and probably was the only Fulbright student to have a letter of recommendation written by her psychiatrist!" To Jane, Sylvia sounded the Sheldon clarion call: "Each month of reliable living & growing, I think, is a solid step away from McLean. . . . There is much fighting and inner struggling going on all the time, a kind of forging of the soul through conflict, and, often, pain, but behind it all, there is this Chaucerian affirmation which holds fast." The holding fast in a fictive personality requires the curative of literature. Even her successful eye operation—occasioned by a splinter—became the story of "oedipus and gloucester getting new vision by losing their eyes, but me wanting, so to speak, new vision and my eyes too. the doctor quoted housman cheerfully: 'if by chance your eye offend you, pluck it out lass and be sound.'" But it was not the eye but the splinter that had been plucked out to a rejuvenated Sylvia's delight. Although she would study another year at Cambridge, she confessed the "heavy critical atmosphere" dominated by F. R. Leavis "can be deadly," and she was looking forward to more creative work to "find my voice." This uneasiness about the oppressiveness of literary criticism would be reinforced by Ted Hughes. Part of her disaffection with status quo Cambridge had to do with a growing awareness of "arabs & jews arguing here, south african communists who are going back to fight the totalitarian white government that keeps the colored people in appalling chains."

15

By March 23, 1956, Sylvia was in London making the rounds with friends and then meeting up with Lucas Myers and Ted Hughes, spending an exhausting night with him that she found "disturbing," according to her calendar diary for March 24: "wounded & shaken" from a "ruthless" Ted. He had "called me wrong name." He had said "Shirley" during intercourse, the name of the woman he had been with when he first met Sylvia.[18] Did she wonder if it wasn't her that he was fucking, that she was just doubling for his intended target? Was Sylvia just another Shirley, another woman to be wounded? Three days later in Paris, she was still recovering from the "sleep-less holocaust night with Ted." A powerful word to apply to lovemaking, a laying waste to the body and to the spirit, suggesting a demonic possession, the kind of violent eroticism associated with Dracula. She worried about her victimhood, imagining Ted's friends were already referring to her as his "mistress or something equally absurd." [PJ] But she was getting used to the idea, writing in her journal for April 5: "I lust for him, and in my mind I am ripped to bits by the words he welds and wields."

Right from the start, Sylvia knew, as she would later tell Jane Anderson during Jane's visit to Cambridge, that coupling with Hughes was hazardous, but he was a "sadist" she could manage.[19] A sadist? That word reverberates, a single word she put down in a calendar entry for April 5, 1956. Plath had at that point significant sexual experience with Peter Davison, Richard Sassoon, Carl Shakin, and men at Cambridge. She had been sexually assaulted in

New York during her guest editorship at *Mademoiselle*, fictionalized in *The Bell Jar*. She had bled profusely after her rough consensual sex with Edwin Akutowicz, and shocked after what seems to have been his digital rape of her during Harvard summer school, but she used no words for those incidents similar to those she had applied to Hughes. What she felt in the moment with Ted appears to have been a horror worse than she had ever suffered with any other man—perhaps mitigated by taking to an extreme the Sheldonian determination not to turn away from conflict and pain. What had been lacking in her previous liaisons had been a power dynamic, a confrontation with an overwhelming force that she would seek to absorb and amplify.

But put aside for the moment the singular psychology of Plath's behavior and take into consideration Assia Wevill, another exile in England arriving from Germany, then Israel, thrice married and even more conversant than Plath with the rigors of love making. Assia said after her first coupling with Hughes that he had raped her.[20] An attraction to such abusive men drove Rebecca West to therapy after she diagnosed herself as sadomasochistic.[21] Plath referred to "my sadistic-masochistic temperament" in a letter to Marcia Brown. What disturbed West was the idea that she could make herself, in the words of one theorist, a "more or less obliging prop for the enactment of man's fantasies." Some women, you might say, enjoy that sort of thing, but "such a pleasure," Luce Irigiray claims, "is above all a masochistic prostitution of her body to a desire that is not her own, and it leaves her in a familiar state of dependency upon man."[22] In a journal entry for February 18, 1953, Sylvia wrote: " 'Oh, I would like to get in a car and be driven off into the mountains to a cabin on a wind-howling hill and be raped in a huge lust like a cave woman, fighting, screaming, biting in a ferocious ecstasy of orgasm. . . . ' That sounds nice, doesn't it? Really delicate and feminine." Why the quotation marks? Was she quoting someone else, or wryly commenting on her own daydreams, which were the subject of that entry? On the advice of Ruth Beuscher, when the marriage to Hughes broke down, Sylvia read about sadistic and masochistic personalities in Erich Fromm's *The Art of Loving* and, of course, would write in "Daddy": "Every woman adores a fascist." This famous line packs all sorts of connotations, including, it seems, personal ones. At Cambridge, during a day of sickness, Sylvia poured out to fellow student Evelyn Evans the remorse she felt about having a German father, which she connected to the fate of the Jews. "She felt that through her father she was guilty." [HR] Did that mean, then, that rough sex was a form of punishment, a holocaust of the culpable self?

What would have happened if Richard Sassoon, a very different object of adoration, had been there in Paris to welcome her? It might have made all the difference after her fraught intimacy with Ted Hughes. She wrote in her journal for March 26, 1956: "Overcome by a disastrous impulse to run to Sassoon as formerly; I took myself in leash & washed my battered face, smeared with a purple bruise from Ted and my neck raw and wounded too, and decided to walk out toward Richard's." But Sassoon's landlady told her he would not return until after Easter. Sylvia left a note for him, writing in tears, she noted in her calendar diary. She wandered until she found the restaurant where they ate on her first night in Paris, and felt "growing pride & affirmation at independence." Exactly why she felt liberated, she did not say, but perhaps seeking Sassoon confirmed her own will to exert herself and confront his rejection. She walked along the Seine to Notre-Dame and went by the bookstalls, feeling good, then enjoying a supper with Giovanni Perego—an Italian Communist journalist she had met in transit—and his friends.

Sylvia Plath made the best of Richard Sassoon's loss by encircling herself, as she always did, in the salon of her own desirability. Already she was composing letters on Perego's typewriter. At home and abroad—as soon as she was old enough to travel by herself—she chatted up males and females alike, this time in the aftermath of the failure to find Sassoon, to create a continental world with him. After extolling Perego and his friends and learning about the colonialist British in Africa, she told her mother on March 26: "Perhaps the hardest & yet best thing for me is that Sassoon isn't here." She exulted in being on her own, no longer subject to his moods. Giovanni guided her, she reported, "like a kind father." In her letters, she had been voicing a need for fatherly figures like Alfred Kazin to spur her along. Perego consoled her as she tearfully told him her troubles. A chance meeting with Carl Shakin, her romantic conquest aboard ship on the way to England, had amazed and perhaps unsettled her. Alone in her hotel room she meditated. She was bound to have a "tragic life," but one with a "comic face." That gave her the idea for a story to work on in the morning. Her life and her writing crossed over as she walked both banks of Paris. Her days there were a wandering and a wanderlust, as she homed in on herself and her troubles, finding, as Jay Martin says Dante eventually did, "a home in . . . authorship."

Always, away from home, Sylvia seemed to grow on herself. This crisis-nexus between Richard Sassoon and Ted Hughes, the pain of parting and the promise of a new, if dangerous, liaison depressed and invigorated her. You can see it in her day-by-day up-and-down calendar accounting of her Easter in Paris as she arose rebuffed and yet reborn.[23] She was nearing the age of twenty-five, the same age as the Dalai Lama when he left Tibet. His departure was the making of him, Jay Martin observes, since Tenzin Gyatso, remaining in Tibet, would have been suffocated by Chinese oppressors. In

exile, he "came of age," Martin observes, "he became free of Tibet, of out-
worn rituals and formalities, of China. Exile endowed him with the world."
Such comparisons may seem overblown, yet, Martin reminds us that like his
seven subjects—Ovid, Dante, Napoleon, Pushkin, Trotsky, Einstein, and
the Dalai Lama—millions of displaced peoples are experiencing "depression,
anxiety, confusion, identity diffusion, feelings of oppression, narcissistic
strivings, creative release, and (sometimes) the ecstasy of freedom in exile."
Sylvia Plath experienced all of this and more—sometimes, it seems, in a
single day—and understood the political implications of her expatriation.

     Sylvia Plath was on the exilic trajectory that Martin charts in his world
historical figures—rejecting a town scholarship to Wellesley College in favor
of a bigger rival, Smith, but already presuming that her time at Smith would
simply help to launch her invasion of England, where she could jettison
American conventions or be as free to be an American as she liked without
conforming any more than she liked to the culture she had left behind, a
culture that simultaneously thrilled and disturbed her. She had written to
her German pen pal about all she was learning at Smith and her enjoyment
of the parties, dating, and socializing, but she had to add a Korean conflict
proviso: "this war-scare bothers me so much that i can never completely
forget myself in artificial gaiety. . . . I think of us as of the Roman Empire
and feel that this is the fall, perhaps, of our new and bright civilization." A
decadent England was too small for her, but it was a beginning, especially
when she found someone so much bigger than the English lads that bored
and delighted her by turns but could not ride her to ecstasy.

     She turned toward England and Ted Hughes, whatever her dread and
desire, at times, to return to the womb, to mother, to the conveniences of
her native land. Hughes, this disaffected Cambridge graduate, lurked, she
realized, on the edge of success. She had already read enough of his poetry
to prophesy his destiny as a great writer, but he needed a push, which also
pushed her to exceed her own expectations. He spoke to an expatriate sentiment she began announcing in her letters home soon after she arrived in
Cambridge. She was not sure she would ever want to return to the United
States—at least not as a permanent resident. She saw just how decrepit
England was, yet she also realized she could fill it with her spirit in a way
not available to her in America. In her various English male companions
she sought a bonding to this new country of her imagination when she
was not adding to her colonizing of Nat LaMar and Mallory Wober, who
became subsumed in this assertion in a letter to Jon Rosenthal: "My best
friends here are Jewish or negro," as if Wober and LaMar represented the
multitudes of her Cambridge imperium. Did she ever think back to Dick
Norton's comment that she had "negroid" features? She told her mother:

"Actually, I have no desire to go back to America at all! The nearness of the continent, with its stimulating variety of people and customs and country in such a small, available space, is a constant delight." The intimate, human scale of interaction enchanted her as she negotiated the interstices of English culture and the promise of more on the European horizon. She wrote in her journal about conquering the countries she visited and of the "historic moment" in which she departed one country for another.

That Sylvia colonized Mallory Wober is evident from the testimony of those at Cambridge who knew both of them. He never got over her, they told Harriet Rosenstein, who caught up with him one day in a "forced march" through Hyde Park, Belgravia, and Sloane Square. He was a reluctant interlocutor but revealed, nonetheless, the almost magical impact Sylvia Plath had on him. When she entered a Cambridge gathering—"concert, meeting, whatever—heads turned," Wober told her. "One sensed a special presence there."[24] Not everyone, of course, reacted this way to Plath, but

Sappho. On display in Castello Sforzesco, Milan, Italy.

Jewish Wober did as one who gravitated toward a woman who needed his adoration. She was his Sappho, even as Wober said Sappho was her model. His comments also evoke his worship of a genius whom he thought had not yet found her own creative terrain.

Sylvia Plath embodied exile, and like Pushkin joined what Jay Martin terms the "tradition of displaced beings" that included Albert Einstein, who "chose the time, place, and duration of his exile. Germany did not exile him; he exiled Germany. The fierce individualism that made him choose to be an exile had its origin in his earliest childhood." Change the name and country and you have Sylvia Plath. Like Susan Sontag as a child, trying to dig her way to China in the backyard of her Tucson, Arizona home,[25] Plath charged ahead. Even as a child she built up her own playworld that included constructing her own huts away from town, sought a German pen pal, collected stamps from around the globe, read children's biographies and novels, and watched movies set abroad and in various periods of history.[26] She listened closely to her Austrian grandparents. History was often brought home to her. On December 27, 1943, Uncle Frank visited and introduced a friend, Gibby Wyer, in the Africa Medical Corps in Egypt and in the "campaign to chase Rommel out of Africa. They went from El Alamein to Tunis," Sylvia wrote in her diary.

Sometimes Sylvia had treated herself as an alien in wealthy Wellesley, demonstrating an estrangement that comes out in stories such as the one about Paula Brown's new snowsuit and the Superman-savior that was her ready-made for the advent of Ted Hughes. After considering and rejecting American graduate school education, Sylvia Plath had suited up for a life abroad—like Dante, in Martin's words, "embracing exile itself."

16

From Paris, Sylvia went on to Munich and Venice and Rome, escorted by Gordon Lameyer—as much for his utility as an escort to fend off preying men as for a friendship now more fraught than fruitful. She mourned the loss of Richard Sassoon as she visited the typical tourist sites in a chilly Venice, a warmer Rome, but with a fractious Lameyer no longer willing to placate her moods. They had some kind of "devastating encounter" near the Laocoon "grotesques," as she called them in her calendar diary. For sure, they were all twisted up in her suffering and his frustration.

By April 13, 1956, Sylvia was back in London and waking up the next day after a "Bloody exhausting night of love-making" and "terrible dreams."

Coitus was like something out of the painful ecstasy of St. Teresa in Bernini's Rome. She went back to bed and peaceable sleep, later that day longing for the "magnificence of Ted" on the train back to Cambridge. But it would not last, she told her journal: "Ted: you have accepted his being: you were desperate for this and you know what you must pay: utter vigilance in Cambridge." He had replaced the "void" of Richard Sassoon in her guts, but she suspected that Ted "has no love for you." She should consider herself "lucky to have been stabbed by him. . . . Let him go. Have the guts." She would cook, play, and read for him but work for "Krook, Varsity & home." She had just been invited to join the staff of *Varsity*, the Cambridge University paper, resuming her interest in journalism that had marked the early part of her time at Smith.

Sylvia found it difficult to resist the "temporary sun" of Ted's "ruthless force." These early reports on his bad behavior in her calendar diary are not promising. She is disgusted by his "brothel talk" and "lack of care," and she walks away from him in "horror" and revulsion as from a character out of Cocteau. Yet she remained with him, evidently deciding that only beside him could she measure herself and triumph: "incredible feeling of own faith & integrity that will come through," she jotted in her calendar diary, "Ted cannot ever annihilate me—I see his flaws, egoism, bombast." Sheldon had counseled that the only way was to work through conflict—not avoid or minimize its significance. With Ted Hughes she encountered the supreme test of this Promethean doctrine. And in some ways she felt superior to his banging around, breaking a bottle, and indulging in chaos like a "naughty irrepressible boy" in a "contest of wills."

Sylvia's April 17, 1956, letter to her mother said more, perhaps, than Sylvia realized, while at the same time reflecting a remarkable prescience: "The most shattering thing is that in the last two months I have fallen terribly in love, which can only lead to great hurt: I met the strongest man in the world, ex-Cambridge, brilliant poet whose work I loved before I met him, a large hulking healthy Adam, half French, half Irish, with a voice like the thunder of God; a singer, story-teller, lion and world-wanderer & vagabond who will never stop." Ted Hughes was a Yorkshireman but it suited her mythology to think of him as a superior bifurcated Richard Sassoon: a French Celt. Like world wanderer Richard Halliburton, her childhood adventurer-hero, Ted had come to liberate her. But she had written to herself that she had to be "vigilant." Ted had no boundaries, and was, in some ways, hardly a man—more like a mythological figure, part man, animal, and god, with one of her favorite words for him: "hulking," which could mean well-built but also clumsy, a brute, a beast right out of Cocteau, whose work she took with her on sketching tours of Paris. What dread might Aurelia have felt in reading her daughter's expressions of exaltation and loss: "The times I am with him are a horror because I am then so strong & creative & happy, and his very power & brilliance & endless health & iron will to beat the world across is why I love him and never will be able to do more, for he'll blast off to Spain & then Australia & never stop conquering people & saying poems." He spoke to her own frightening Napoleonic desire to conquer. Could she hold onto him? Wasn't that what she wanted to find out? Which is why she could not just let him go. "Ted reads in his strong voice, is my best critic, as I am his," she told her mother. He seemed to reciprocate, writing to her in verse on April 9, 1956: "Ridiculous to call it love. / Even so, fearfully I did sound Your absence, as one shot down feels to the wound, / Knowing himself alive." He could beat the world, but she had her own weaponry, and could bite.

The romance quickened with walks in the country. Ted pointed out forest wonders in a voice booming better than Dylan Thomas's. They made love under cooing pigeons. Ted did not walk into a room: he stalked up to bookshelves and with derrick-like hands pulled down the great poets to read and then outdid them with his own verse. His understanding of nature lore outdid Natty Bumppo—or so you would gather from reading her calendar diaries and letters. In her poem "Metamorphosis" she pictures him: "Haunched like a faun." All nature seems to watch the "changing shape he cut." Hughes had released from her a fount of poetry and no longer appeared as a danger to her: "I see right into the core of him, and he knows it, and knows that I am strong enough, and can make him grow." There it is: For all his power, he still needed hers. She also governed herself with a precarious conceit: "I can teach him care," she told her mother in all her pride of discovery, no longer afraid of what he was: "a breaker of things and people" in this "sick small insular inbred land." She was bound to him in her Nietzschean desire to "breed supermen," and in her Sheldonian commitment to "accepting sorrow & pain but living in the midst of Hopkins, Thomas, Chaucer, Shakespeare Blake, Donne, and all the poets we love together." In effect, she had completed her fictive self by coupling with Hughes and her literary canon, and setting him, on no less than a world stage: "thought of Bulganin[27] & Ted," she wrote in her diary for April 22, 1956, after meeting a Russian delegation at a reception in London.

17

In her April 21, 1956, *Varsity* article, "An American in Paris," Sylvia relayed her impressions using "we," as if she had headed some kind of expedition to the city. It is odd to read "we borrowed" Giovanni Perego's Olivetti type-writer, as if several sets of fingers played across the keyboard. She apparently meant the plural pronoun as a way of putting herself forward as a typical American, although how many Americans could have discussed De Chirico, De Stael, Melville's novels, and Verlaine's poetry, as she did with Perego, is doubtful. She presented a travelogue/fairy tale that of course had no place for Richard Sassoon. The article seems written in the ascension of spirit she had experienced on her return to Hughes, so that her purchase of a "most enormous blue balloon" from a "brown wrinkled gypsy woman who vanished in a puff of smoke immediately" excited children who followed Plath "like the Pied Piper, wide-eyed, reaching up and saying in wonder: 'Balloon!'" This Richard Halliburton kind of gambol she enhanced with people who "smiled and grew benevolent; cats stared with yellow eyes from first floor balconies." High and low, she had the world's attention.

Ted Hughes was not out of place in this carnival of the spirit. They went to the circus, and that alone inspired her to write her mother: "Ted is incred-ible . . . he has not changed his clothes since I met him two months ago, but wears always the same black sweater and corduroy jacket with pockets full of poems, fresh trout and horoscopes." What could Aurelia make of this sensitive ruffian who sought to chart the stars that governed human existence? She was not to worry, Sylvia said in her most Sheldon-like mood: "I have learned to make a life growing through toleration of conflict, sorrow, and hurt." And her poetry was the better for it: "my voice is taking shape, coming strong; Ted says he never read poems by a woman like mine: they are strong and full and rich, not quailing and whining like Teasdale, or simple lyrics like Millay: they are working sweating heaving poems." She sought to prove her new power to her mother by enclosing a poem, "Complaint of the Crazed Queen," about a hulking giant "with hands like derricks" who tramples her "dainty acres," is "puissant on his prowl," and then quits the queen at "cock's crowing," causing her to search in vain among "all doughty men / whose force might fit / shape of my sleep, my thought." Like the Queen's giant, Ted was a commanding dream come true, if still in stilted phrases like "puissant on his prowl" an alliterative fantasy that Plath built up in letter after letter.

18

By May 3, 1956, after "miraculous" lovemaking with Ted, Sylvia had resolved all misgivings in his favor, reporting to her mother: "I have passed through the husk, the mask of cruelty, ruthlessness, callousness, in Ted and come into the essence and truth of his best right being: he is the tenderest, kindest, most faithful man I have ever known in my life." The calendar diary, in medias res, told a somewhat different story of fights that became ecstatic makeups. Richard Sassoon had now been entirely expunged. Everything, she thought, had prepared her for this rendezvous with Ted and the reckoning with her "best right self."

Ted could also be restful to be around. On May 4, 1956, she told her mother it was easier to write with him in the room. "I can tell you, if you will sit tight on it that within a year, after I graduate, I can think of nothing I'd rather do than be married to Ted." The next day she forced the issue: "got guts to face Ted in honest Brave statement of concern for next year." Whatever he said, it was enough for her to make a break with others that she cryptically recorded in her calendar diary: "nice if tense & last breakfast with Nat. Keith [Middlemass], etc." Why last? Nat LaMar told Andrew Wilson that after the advent of Ted Hughes, Sylvia had no time for him or other male friends at Cambridge.[28] She needed to signal the new dispensation, because that same day she recorded "life together—vision of this face of Ted: my one man." He confirmed Sylvia's project of redemption: "Ted says himself that I have saved him from being ruthless, cynical, cruel and a warped hermit because he never thought there could be a girl like me and I feel that I too have new power by pouring all my love and care in one direction to someone strong enough to take me in my fullest joy." But an actual day (May 8) yielded somewhat different results: "fine afternoon passing from flash of resentment at Ted's drunkness last night" to "excellent love & talk" to "dear Ted: god I love him." A cryptic calendar diary reference to a "blonde one" seems to have contributed to Sylvia's annoyed surveillance of her one man. But on May 10 she noted, "after noon of best love yet: created wedding plans."

The psychological dynamic between Plath and Hughes seems to function like Anna Freud's description of "altruistic surrender," in which gratification is derived from a "projection of one's own wishes into another, followed by identification with the gratification which that other person experiences."[29] Sylvia had tried to build up Richard Sassoon into the idea of what she thought he should be. With Ted Hughes, it was much easier work because of his own powerful sense of self-worth. She could thrive on his power, investing in him positive qualities that resulted in ennobling him. Altruism, Anna Freud observes, "enables both the altruist and his or her objects." In short, Ted felt empowered since Sylvia provided him with a platform—plans for sending out his poetry to important magazines and publishers—beyond the ken of his provincial coterie in Cambridge. That she might be fictionalizing him, and that he might be doing the same for her—which is how his Cambridge cronies tended to view the coupling—did not matter. As Jay Martin observes: "there is a very close connection between fictive personality and the capacity for inventiveness, originality and creativity." Both writers, of course, had already succeeded (sometimes) on their own terms, yet both remain dissatisfied with themselves. But with one another they could collaborate in what Anna Freud called the ego's mechanism of defense. Both believed the best protection for themselves was to commit absolutely to shielding the other.

Sylvia's descriptions of these exhilarating early times with Ted seem the projection of a fictive self, of a world she imagined and inhabited and accepted as real. Reading Eugene O'Neill, she exclaimed in her journal: "I am Nina in 'Strange Interlude'; I do want to have husband, lover, father and son, all at once. . . . And I cry so to be held by a man; some man, who is a father."

All this absorption in Ted did not preclude a full involvement in Cambridge life that is reminiscent of her early days of journalism at Smith. She enjoyed attending meetings of *Varsity*, writing articles about what it was like at Smith and on current fashions, which included modeling a swimsuit that Ted helped her pick out at a shop in town. *Varsity* replaced her exhilarating Amateur Dramatic Club performances. She went at it all—reporting and lovemaking, and debating cheerfully with her supervisor Dorothea Krook, pell-mell, not so different from what she recorded in her earliest diaries, full of accounts of writing, playing, colloquies with teachers, reading, dates, and dialogues with boys—sometimes all occurring on the same day.

19

On May 22, 1956, Ted wrote for the first time about Sylvia to a member of his family, the one he felt closest to: his sister Olwyn Hughes. He told her that Sylvia was first rate, and a promoter of his poetry: "She is Scorpio Oct 27th, moon in Libra, last degrees of Aries rising and has her Mars smack on my sun, which is all very appropriate." Appropriate? Are we then all settled about what this means? How about Mom and Dad? Even after the June 16, 1956, wedding, no word from Ted to his parents. He had a lot of explaining to do that Sylvia had been offering to her mother almost from the moment she met Ted. Where was he, really, in his charting of the universe?

It was a Promethean daily coupling, according to Plath, a struggle through "wrong love and hard talk . . . criticism of selves," and a "sense of

growing through hardness & hurt" and "another conquering," monitored
in her calendar diary. Because we have so much of her testimony, and so
little of his, it is hard to calculate who was more moody, who was in the
wrong, and how they righted their relationship. She wanted to publish
him to the world, telling her mother: "He has just never bothered to try
to publish (outside the Cambridge magazines)." Later he would resent her
drawing him out into a world that opened up to him even as he continued to scorn the professionalism that made his career possible and the
vulgarity of the popularity she courted and that his Cambridge friends
sneered at. "A tearful talk re public opinion." Sylvia recorded in her calendar diary for May 27—perhaps alluding to the snide reaction to her
swimsuit modeling.

In poetry, Sylvia evoked a consecrated world with Ted that set society
aside. In "Bucolics," a couple are as one, pitching their coats on nature's
green bed and making love all afternoon until the sweet wind changes
its tune and "blew harm: / Cruel nettles stung her ankles raw." The male
stamps the stalks that "caused his dear girl pain." He departs, as Ted was
wont to do in their early Cambridge days, while she grieves his loss and
her pain—she "stands burning, venom-girt, / In wait for sharper smart
to fade." Nettles in "Wreath for a Bridal" protect the couple, cloistered
by green leaves as cows moo an approval joined by the sun "surpliced in
brightness." The wedding, in effect, occurs with congregant cows and the
sun itself officiating. Virtually every sunny spring day in Cambridge, Sylvia
was sunbathing for blessings, baking the cold out of her, as she remarked in
her calendar diary. Beyond the boundaries of Cambridge the "owl voice" in
the poem tells them "yes" and the avian assembly "laud these mated ones."
The couple is a "pair" that seeks "single state from dual battle," parrying
"scruple" for "wedlock wrought within love's proper / chapel." "Watchful
birds" people the "twigged aisles" mimicking a church wedding and bridal
procession and provide the choir as "two burn one in fever." Knit together
like the "teeming" land that will sprout with "fruit, flower, children," the
poem ends with "each step hence go famous." No less than Adam and Eve
and their progeny emerge out of this poem, which is a bravura performance
of destiny and fame—the one that Sylvia already boasted about in a letter to her mother on May 18, forecasting a marriage to Ted that would
issue in seven children and recognition of his greatness. Children were,
in fact, the locus of the poet's posterity that Plath always seems to have
projected: "still we persist in hopefully faithfully bringing forth children
into the world." She had once dreamed of going to Morocco and teaching "these children, their underdeveloped lands" and the "new races" that

were going to "influence the world." Now, with Ted, she would create her own race.

The "dual battle" mentioned in "Wreath for a Bridal" was virtually a daily occurrence, with flareups and what Sylvia call fratches, followed by making up and making love. The couple seemed to thrive on friction. After fighting through a steak and mushroom dinner on June 2: "great love on park bench." In "Crystal Gazer," a poem she was writing at the time, Plath mused about past, present, and future, "time's three horizons." Gerd, the crystal gazer is called on to tell "How we shall do together, / Well or ill." She gives the ball a spin and presents an image of "two stalwart apple trees / Coupled by branches intertwined," with "springing all about, / Staunch saplings." Here was the House of Plath and Hughes with her projected seven children. When asked about hardship, Gerd foretells "rough storm . . . May wreak / Some havoc on tender limb and / Yet Strengthen that orchard thereby." But the poem does not end in fruition. Gerd's mind is "Plague-pitted as the moon" and, piercing "time's core," she envisions "love blazing to its gutted end— / And, fixed in the crystal center, grinning fierce: Earth's ever-green death's head."

Why didn't this poem give Plath pause? It had begun well predicting the couple would weather their storms, but the ending was a grisly paradox with grinning death ever green in the sense that death, and the gutted end of love, was as inevitable as a perennial. Mrs. Prouty had written to Sylvia to say that Sylvia's letter, written on May 27, 1956, should have served as a warning. Ted was unreliable (as unfaithful and fascinated with other women as Dylan Thomas) and violent. A man his age (twenty-six) was not likely to change. What Sylvia felt, Mrs. Prouty assured her, would not last. It was love's first flash of intensity—that was all. Mrs. Prouty needed no crystal ball or horoscope to predict certain disaster.

No reply to Mrs. Prouty's letter is extant, and there probably isn't one. Sylvia Plath went silent. Her calendar diary for June 9–12 is blank—an unusual occurrence. So far as is known she wrote no letters, kept no journal for those four days. Heretofore, she had recorded something for nearly every day of the year. Was she thinking over Prouty's tough words? Was "Crystal Gazer" an expression of her worst fears, facing conflict as she must, but going ahead whatever her misgivings? Is it too much to read such a portent in a single poem? Gerd, a "free-gadding hoyden" had sought the gift of second sight, to "govern more sight than given to a woman / By wits alone." She wanted to "foresee her lover's faith / And their future lot." To do so had been sacrilegious, braving a "Church curse." Sylvia had done her share of gadding about, to be sure, and had chosen, like Gerd, to remain outside of any sort of orthodoxy.

20

On June 13, 1956, the calendar diary resumed, just as Aurelia arrived in England. Over dinner the couple announced their decision to get married in three days' time. Aurelia gave no sign of disapproval and seemed utterly charmed with Ted. Sitting across from this besotted couple, what else could she do? Aurelia sometimes withheld what she really thought, sometimes putting her most private feelings into Gregg shorthand notations on her daughter's letters.[30]

Ted's friend, Lucas Myers, believed that Sylvia had hurried the marriage in London's St. George the Martyr, taking Ted prisoner, but who is to say it was not the other way around? Didn't Ted, knowing how much his friends disapproved of Sylvia, want her to himself? The world would have to get used to what he did. That is what Sylvia liked about him. They were a bold couple and would prove it!

Waiting a year to marry, as initially planned, put the fictive identity of the lovers in peril. Sylvia's daily diaries show how hard she had to work at defeating all doubts about Ted, and how he, in turn, had to act the role of the redeemed ruffian, a role that was oh so satisfying in their sweet reconciliations, just as the beast turns into the prince in *Beauty and the Beast*. Nothing must break that spell of lovers who were outside everything, as in a Cocteau film. Their specialness—how could anyone else understand it?—may also be why Hughes did not tell his parents or sister about his marriage. By telling no one, by not sharing the marriage, the couple could find—at least for a time—a respite from society and solidify the fantasy of their perfect union.

Only Warren could share the secret marriage, since it was in the family. He could take his pick of her fictive identities: "Mrs. Sylvia Hughes, Mrs. Ted Hughes, Mrs. Edward James Hughes, Mrs. E. Hughes (wife of the internationally known poet and genius." That secret would be revealed, Sylvia told Warren, in the following year at a huge Wellesley "folk festival" reception for the couple. She looked forward to Warren's meeting Ted, who would fit well into the family. To Olwyn Hughes, Ted said as little as possible, perhaps wary of his sister who had treated their brother Gerald's wife harshly.

The "folk festival" reception suggested Sylvia's powerful desire to create a community of acceptance that would slot her husband into her own sense of family destiny. For Ted Hughes, the marriage was not a family secret because he pretended it had not yet occurred. He wrote nothing at all to his parents after the wedding. In July 1956, he announced: "I am certainly going to marry Sylvia"—he thought by September, and he would bring her home then before her Cambridge term began. He told them not to say anything. Like Sylvia, he had the mistaken belief that she would not be allowed to continue her studies if she was married. He did not want his parents to worry: "Don't be frightened of Sylvia being a drag." He extolled her virtues at cooking, earning an income from writing, and a job offer to lecture at Smith. All very practical, to be sure, but nothing whatsoever about what made her attractive to *him*. The last to hear from Ted (in September) was Gerald, who received the same fiction about marrying Sylvia next June. Ted acknowledged her "influence" on him, but that was about it.

21

On July 2, 1956, in Paris, at the American Express office where she had gone so many times during the Christmas holidays in hopes of a letter from Richard Sassoon, Sylvia was handed one, as she noted in her calendar diary. What it said and what she thought are not recorded. She told Ted nothing, and he learned of the Sassoon saga only after her death. In retrospect, Ted concluded that Paris had not been theirs, and the repercussions of that discovery made its way into "Your Paris." The poem articulates the divide between them that marriage could never bridge. Her Paris reflected an American tourist's gushing over the famous sites, great works of art, and the shades of famous writers. "I wanted to humour you," he writes as if addressing her directly in a tone of insufferable condescension and superiority, since what he sees is the Paris of history, of the German occupation, in which the SS commandeered the famous cafe chairs. "I kept my Paris from you," he announces. In waiters' eyes he imagines he can see the betrayal of collaborators. He can smell the "stink of fear" in wardrobes. He said nothing about her own consciousness of history, perhaps suspended during their honeymoon that for him held no happiness that could obliterate history— even for a moment, even for love. He calls himself a "ghost watcher" thinking of Verdun and the methane escaping the graves of exhumed soldiers. Sassoon enters the poem in Hughes's reference to a sadomasochistic Plath hanging around in her chamber, "waiting / For your torturer / To remember his amusement." Hughes portrays her as walking beside him, a "flayed, / One . . . wincing / To agonies." Her gushing disguised her pain, Hughes supposes.[31] For a day Sassoon's letter may have caused her the cryptic "sick w. d. sad day" recorded in her July 2, 1956, calendar diary. But subsequent entries do not support the burden of Hughes's poem about her suffering.

He casts himself as the "mere dog . . . happy to protect you," and content to watch her drawing scenes and portraits, including of him—as if her drawing merely distracted her from suffering. The poem expresses his anger and humiliation but also, as Dave Haslam observes in *My Second Home*, an utter lack of empathy. Hughes calls himself her "guide dog," subject to her signals. Haslam sums it up well: "Plath seems elusive to Hughes, not only because he couldn't share her enthusiasms, but couldn't pin her down. She has a life beyond him." Haslam asks: "How could anyone question or begrudge her that exuberance?" Only someone never able to fully enter her orbit, even as she thought she was merging into his. In "Your Paris," Hughes treats Plath as a holdout when at the same time he did not divulge his Paris to her.

In "The Shrike," first drafted on July 3, 1956, Plath's attention and creative energy fastens on Hughes, who flies off from her in his "royal dreams" while she remains bed-bound: "Twisting curses in the tangled sheet." From the first she had worried about his tendency to wander away from his women, and she wondered what she could do to pin him down. Biographer Edward Butscher interprets the last lines of the poem as a warning from the "envious bride" with her "shrike-face" who can "Spike and suck out / Last blood-drop of that truant heart." On July 4, she told her mother another story: "the whole secret for both of us, I think, is being utterly in love with each other, which frees our writing from being a merely egoistic mirror, but rather a powerful canvas on which other people live and move." For the rest of their marriage, the disturbing dividedness of their poems seemed to subvert the equilibrium of her letters.

22

The next honeymoon stop was Madrid. Spain seems to have exhausted and unnerved Sylvia, who shared little of Ted's fascination with bull fights. He was so taken with them that he wrote a long letter to his parents barely mentioning her. Yet she wrote to her mother on July 14, 1956, that Ted agreed with her that bullfighting was disgusting. She had another story for her mother: "It is so wonderful that wherever Ted and I go people seem to love us." She enjoyed the country's violent colors and the dry heat. She had cleared out her sinuses. She omitted mentioning their fights.

After terrible sunburns, stomach upsets, and the typical travelers' maladies, they landed in Benidorm in a flat with a kitchen, bath, terrace, and balcony overlooking the sea, exceeding her "wildest, most exotic dreams," Sylvia wrote to her mother on July 14. She was "closer to the sea than grammy's place in Winthrop. . . . Day and night we hear the blessed roar of the waves on shore." She worked on a series of sketches and planned to write about local color for women's magazines while Ted composed children's fables that delighted her. Her ideal dreamscape always included the sea and the sun, living on the edge of the land. Yet Ted would write in *Birthday Letters*: "You Hated Spain." The country frightened her: "The oiled anchovy faces, the African / Black edges to everything, frightened you." He mentions she did not know the language. Well, neither did he. As in "Your Paris," he shrinks her—this time into "a bobby Sox American." He suggests that she recoils from the bullfighting, the grim Goya and Bosch paintings, because of her affinity with them: "No literature course had glamorized. / The juju land behind your African lips." It is curious that like Dick Norton, Ted Hughes fastened on her full lips as a part of herself—at least in Hughes's estimation—that she had not assimilated. He berates her because, as in Paris, she wanted to honeymoon everything.

Notice too, that like "Your Paris," "You Hated Spain" is addressed to Plath, not to us, although, of course, we are allowed to eavesdrop. In effect, Hughes's poems continue a marriage argument, as each partner honed in on the other's different perceptions, although Hughes allows himself the last word in his conflicts with *her*—not deigning to address readers directly or turn on himself for an explanation. If he had put the poems in the third person, that would have required an effort at objectivity—or at least an attempt to pull back far enough to get some perspective on how they interacted as a couple. The acidic superiority of Hughes's poems seems a kind of retaliation for what he had to put up with in Spain. He claims in his poetry that he went along with her, and yet her calendar diaries and journals show they had disagreements aplenty. He never seems to have considered how his own complicity in her moods amounted to dissimulation and dishonesty. On July 14, she wrote happily to her mother that Ted was the "male counterpart of myself." It is unlikely that he truly regarded Sylvia as the female counterpart of himself.

Of what does this Plath stand accused in Hughes's poetry? Much of their life, he implies, was a fiction of her own making that he reluctantly abetted and later regretted. He knew better, but she had to be coddled. He never seems to have contemplated his own fiction making, his way of situating himself in the retrospection of authority over what the two of them experienced. But wasn't her fantasy of togetherness his as well? Could any marriage, any person, survive without story making? "Fictions are fundamental . . . a crucial part of the human character," Jay Martin asserts in *Who Am I This Time?* Surely Hughes knew that, but he did not seem to realize that his own poetry was *his* fiction, his effort to find a way to separate himself from the powerful presence of Sylvia Plath. "We make value-ridden fictions of success, self-esteem, and social good; and in trying to bring these fictions into being we achieve power," Martin concludes. What was Hughes doing in *Birthday Letters* if not exerting his power over what it was like to be married to Sylvia Plath? Poetry, for both of them, was tied to the "fictive processes" that function, Alfred Adler believed, "at the very highest level of human aspiration and activity."[32] For Hughes to debunk in his poetry what he considered Plath's fantasies played her false, or at least left out his own contributions to their make-believe. If Hughes was not wrong about her, he certainly was not right, either. Their daily conflicts arose, it may be supposed, out of the clash of individual wills seeking to smooth out a narrative of union, to come to some accommodation as they did with the widow Mangada in Benidorm who kept fictionalizing all the luxuries she had to offer them in their seaside paradise—most of the time she couldn't get the water to run hot—even as they worked hard at believing her fiction that she had devoted herself to their needs as writers to have a quiet place all to themselves, until she broke the illusion by renting out her whole place to someone else, so that the couple had to find another abode for their holiday from reality and create their dream abode in another venue. Did he really not whole-heartedly join in her July 23, 1956, journal-celebration of their miraculous discovery of a quiet house and her vilification of Widow Mangada's noisy, filthy place by the sea? What was he doing if not perpetuating the fiction of their living together "beautifully"? As Plath put it, "Living with him is like being told a perpetual story." That meant, of course, he could later change the story.

This beautiful life was not diurnally durable: "bad evening after Ted's letter home," Sylvia wrote the next day in her calendar diary. His letter, included in an edition of his correspondence, mentions her only briefly and casually informs his parents the couple are planning to marry. It is hard to say what upset Sylvia about the letter, perhaps her minimal presence in it when he was so much the center of her writing home.

At any rate, they walked under a "wild, full, moon," toward the mountains, "sour wrongness continuing through morning of shopping—tears, synthesis & good dear love—day of recovering." At the beach they went swimming against a backdrop of "blue violent sea & reddish orange hills." This was the dialectic of their days, but so different from Hughes's subsequent accounts of fluctuating feelings that were only hers. Her journal is more grim in its report of the "mellowing of hurt, the deep ingrowing of hurt . . . hurt going in, clean as a razor, and the dark blood welling. Just the sick knowing that the wrongness was growing in the full moon." She knows she is not alone in her upset. Next to her he is not sleeping. The room, the night, is full of "wrongness." [PJ] She reports Ted asking her what is wrong. She did not tell him, but her letters and calendar diary reveal that she was exhausted after a "tiring term" at Cambridge and under an "emotional strain," she confessed to her mother, and utterly depleted from travel, the wrangles with the Widow Mangada, and the difficulty of getting the "feel of prose again"—all of which surely contributed to her disturbance. The domestic drudgery of getting meals together every day (they could not afford to eat out) and cleaning (if Ted pitched in, Sylvia did not acknowledge it) deflated her. Neither by upbringing nor other experience was he equipped to appreciate how hard it was for her to be equal to the stresses of every day. His own writing went ahead without interruptions now, and his example may well have troubled her as she fell behind. She continued to receive rejections while his work was published in *Poetry* and *The Nation*.

In "Moonwalk," the Hughes account of that night of "wrongness," he continues to be baffled, calling himself, as in "Your Paris," her faithful dog, thus relieving himself of the ability to fathom her mood. In such moments, he treated her as a problem, not really as a wife responding to him. She imagines the "murder, the killing words." Whose murder? Hers or his? Curiously her journal ends in an impasse: "Two silent strangers," not as the calendar diary does with "tears, synthesis & good dear love." This double entry bookkeeping of a life could only be resolved by a fiction, by two pregnant words, concluding the July 23, 1956, calendar entry: "our fable." To her mother, she wrote two days later: "My life has been like the plot of a movie these past years: a psychological, romance & travel thriller. Such a plot." But the pressures built up: "relieved decision to leave Spain early," she noted in her calendar diary for July 27. They were running short of money and Olwyn Hughes had not sent the $150 she owed Ted and that he was counting on. Sylvia let Warren know she wasn't happy about Olwyn: "she is evidently extravagant, always overspending, and extracting money from her is a painful job of nagging."

23

In the final two weeks of the Spanish stay, Sylvia began to rev up a story about the Widow Mangada and at the same time enjoy several successive days of making love with Ted and listening to his children's fables. It had been three years since she had written prose fiction, and her earlier stories like "Sunday at the Mintons" seemed the product of another age. Traveling, she realized, had interrupted something vital in her creative ecosystem.

Only as the end of the Spanish period approached could she seem to draw on what she had experienced. Ted, as Assia Wevill would observe much later, could write no matter what—undisturbed by playing children or daily exasperations that so troubled her and Plath. Could his uncomprehending responses to the temperaments of these two very different women reflect a sensibility that was so self-contained that anything outside of it mystified him? He could be sympathetic to Sylvia's sicknesses, making her broth and hypnotizing her to sleep, but why he was difficult to live with is actually best described by Wevill:

> Ted writing: He sits cross-legged, sideways, against Sylvia's black desk (too small for him) a mug of tea on it, sugar bowl, Theresa's sandwiches in one hand, pen in another, writing voraciously, poring through paper-obstacles, breathing through them, his nostrils flared, his hair feathery and leaping forward like a peacock's back-train in reverse, swaying a little as he writes. Rather like a great beast looking over an enormous feast, dazzled and confused by the variety. Frieda's in the bedroom, playing with my trinkets, her blanket with her, some-times leaning on Ted's knee. Murmuring to herself; saying the "light hurts"—"Make the room brown." "Nicky coming"—exciting herself by hoarding all her possessions into a mound. Ready to protect them against Nick. Ted completely immune to all the noises. My getting up, Frieda's clickety-click presence. He's in a wild fever, in the most absolute concentration I've ever witnessed. He's possessed. [AW]

Is it any wonder that Plath—or perhaps anyone—felt they could not com-pete with this giant? Is it really so hard to understand why she sometimes became distraught and he reacted with puzzlement? In the morning she could be pleased with her prose rewrites and in the afternoon, as on August 9, 1956, she fell into a depression over her inability to write poetry: "sad & sick view of uncertainties." She recovered easily—in the same day—but that intermittent sort of creativity almost never troubled him—except, as he would find out to his surprise, when Plath took him home to America. She tried to help herself out with journal exercises, describing the landscape and activities in and around Benidorm. Sometimes, as she related to her mother on August 10, Ted's ebullient creativity could be inspiring: "Every morning he tells me the wonderful brilliant dreams he has about animals and Blake and all sorts of vivid queer plots. It is like living in a fairy-tale with the dear-est, kindest, handsomest, most lovable man in the world." The good and the bad of it had to do with these powers of story telling. Ironically, she told her mother she was modeling herself after lives like the Beuschers—Ruth's

husband was also a psychoanalyst—not realizing that this wife and mother
of four children would leave a spouse who, in the end, had remarkably little
empathy for her concerns. In the cases of all three women—Plath, Wevill,
and Beuscher—they encountered men who seemed walled off from them
in the most crucial moments of their lives.

24

Out of Spain at the end of August 1956, and after a few days in Paris, where
Warren finally met Ted, and Sylvia rejoiced in the enlargement of her family,
she sequestered herself in September in what she called Ted's "wuthering-
heights" home. She sketched her summer in Spain as an aesthetic pattern
of pleasure: "Our garden itself was like a painter's palette: white daisies and
pungent red geraniums sprouted under the jagged green fronds of a palm
tree, while vivid indigo morning glories hung like a tapestry along the wall."
She did not scant the lack of comforts and conveniences Americans took for
granted—for example, cooking on a "one-ring petrol stove" with "everything
from café con leche to rich rabbit stew." In this premodern setting, people
congregated at the village pump. Spain now seemed like her "inward sun"
during a long English winter. With readers of the *Christian Science Monitor*
(November 5 and 6, 1956), she shared this rustic, seashore idyll without, of
course, any mention of the sickness or the anxiety recorded in her calendar
diary. Ted also did not let on to any sort of trouble. His September 7 letter
to his brother Gerald and his wife Joan promoted the Plath/Hughes line:
"I went to Spain with an American poetess. As a result of her influence I
have written continually and every day better since I met her. She is a very
fine critic of my work, and abuses just those parts of it that I daren't confess
to myself are unworthy." He was on board with her plan to go to America
for a year of teaching.

The first days in Heptonstall at the Hughes home, called the Beacon,
teamed with talking, meeting relatives, visiting the Brontë parsonage at
Haworth, and rejoicing in the *Atlantic Monthly* acceptance of "Pursuit" with
a check for $50—all of which seemed to seal her destiny: "sudden symbolic
rightness—renewed faith," she wrote in her calendar diary for September 1.
The drought in acceptances that had dried her out in Spain had ended. To
her mother, she described herself as now part of a "Brontë clan"—already
fictionalizing them as the characters in *Wuthering Heights*, which she read
by their fire. She stalked rabbits with Ted in a "fairy-tale wood." They were,
she said, a happy Heathcliff and Cathy.

The Brontë parsonage.

Laurence Olivier (Heathcliff) and Merle Oberon (Cathy) in *Wuthering Heights* (1939).

Plath paired the acceptance of "Pursuit" with Ted's "Bawdry Embraced," dedicated to her and published in *Poetry*. His poem, too, was a pursuit: "He trod this town a calendar / To find his bawdriste." Both poems are full of a playfulness kicked into the high gear of an erotic vehicle they reveled in creating. Yet it took only a few days for her to record in her calendar diary the return of a familiar sad cycle, with complaints about "no good love since Paris," and "fury at Ted's lack of understanding." She listened to Beethoven's heroic Emperor Concerto, she played the piano "a little," but still felt the "sterile fear in face of his [Ted's] great creativeness." High spirits would resume with nature walks and family stories by the fireside and the return of lovemaking, yet the word that recurs during her stay at the Hughes family home is "oppressed." Ted's mother had barged into their room while they were making love. Sylvia felt as if Ted had been taken away from her. Assia Wevill would later react in much the same way when she visited the Hughes home: "I feel absolutely alien to him, to them all. I expect one always does. There's nothing as chilling as being in the bedroom of someone else's family with all its secrets slammed close." [AW]

As Ted Hughes noted in his *Birthday Letters* poem "Drawing," Sylvia becalmed herself with sketching. At Haworth she noted carefully Charlotte Brontë's watercolors, needlework, and sketches. Sylvia drew her surroundings on visits to churches and chapels in Cambridge, a bull lying down near Grantchester, various buildings in Paris, a citronnade stand in Tuileries, the cliff tenements and petrol stove in Benidorm, and the various other objects she could fashion to her hand in spurts.[33] Some of her drawings appeared in the *Christian Science Monitor* to illustrate her articles. Coordinating hand and eye with pen and ink and shaping what she saw exerted her authority.

This is perhaps the right time to acknowledge the psychological burden of existence that people cope with, or try to ignore, every day. Well, what happens if you choose to face it by, say, writing a diary or journal and drawing as Sylvia Plath did for most of her life? Such bookkeeping and picture making certainly makes you hyper aware of yourself but also of how you exist in the world and what that existence is going to cost you. A good deal of what Plath felt was not actually exceptional, except in so far as she allowed herself, or pushed herself, to recognize the burden of existence, and overcome it, again and again. Ted Hughes did not, in the main, diary himself and draw himself out of danger. He wrote his poetry and stories and killed his game and later—only later—in the cunning of retrospection and the economy of memory did he allow himself to go over what it was like for him to live with Sylvia Plath.

25

Sylvia returned to Cambridge on October 1, 1956, done with what had been a harrowing time in the Hughes home and relieved by those country interludes that calm the spirit as in Frankenstein films. Jane Baltzell encountered a different Sylvia—no longer "strident" but peaceful, happy, and sweet. Sylvia admitted that marriage had been a deliverance from the "dreadful social pressure" of finding a mate. Sylvia seemed older and softer, and no longer "shooting off in all directions, trying everything." Jane did not know Ted well but was powerfully impressed with him. Baltzell did not elaborate, but she may have been responding to a quality that several of his Court Green neighbors mentioned: a calm, quiet, assured manner. [HR] Perhaps that aspect of his affect sedated Sylvia.

In spite of all those letters home about the cultural treasures of Cambridge, Sylvia was already anticipating her escape from the high castle built on her own grandiose expectations. England now seemed too small for Ted; London literati disgusted her; "writing in England is sick, sick, sick" and the magazines "dead," she wrote to Peter Davison, priming him to expect in a year or so the arrival in America of this ambitious couple. She was hoping Davison could suggest a publisher for Ted's books of beast fables for children and adults. She was going to write a novel based on her time in Cambridge. The Plath pendulum that had swung from extolling the paradise of the Mangada suite by the sea to the perfidy of the widow and the repulsiveness of her noisy abode now swung away from decadent England and toward the healthy homeland. She closed by declaring: "I find myself no literary exile, but a staunch American girl."

Yet from Cambridge the next day, she wrote to Ted, who was in London:

> Please, now, tell your dear mother and dad I love them and am thinking of them, and thank them from the bottom of my heart for making such a lovely comfortable warm home for me during my stay—how I miss the coal fires, the sherry and stories, the apple pies, the great green meadows stretching outside the windows, the black bandit-faced sheep and all the moors and valleys I tramped through. Give them both a kiss for me.

Was this mere politeness? Probably not, since what she felt depended on where she was at the moment and how clogged up her sinuses were and the state of her emotional thermometer. Alone in her Cambridge room, the company of Hughes & Co. now seemed preferable. This is a change of

mind in a life coming and going, isn't it? The making of Sylvia Plath was
an up-and-down affair—like yours, no doubt—but perhaps more so for
her because she wrote it all out. Her calendar diary for October 2, 1956,
gives you some idea of why home on the moors now seemed appealing: To
the post office, laundry, bank, food shopping, a visit to Dr. Kaplan, getting
a new bike tire, taking a watch for repair, clothes to the cleaners, a "grue-
some supper at Newnham." She consoled herself in the evening typing her
poems for the *Atlantic Monthly* and *The Nation*, reading the *New Yorker*,
and writing to her mother, enclosing a poem, "Epitaph for Fire and Flower,"
celebrating her passionate union with Ted that might have been more than
Aurelia wanted to know: "they ride nightlong / In their heartbeats' blazing wake." Edward Butscher rightly detects the doom that overtakes the
poem's celebration of lovers as the universe moves on: "Dawn snuffs out
star's spent wick, / Even as love's dear fools cry evergreen." Their love will
not last in the light of the awakening day: "the ardent look / Blackens flesh
to bone and devours them." The poem seems to contain doubts that otherwise do not spill out into her letters and journals at this point. Ted represented the "whole male principle," father, brother, husband son," she wrote
on October 5.

Ted remained with his parents, thinking it still impossible to declare
their marriage publicly without jeopardizing her Fulbright grant. His letters
were tender and playful: "Darling Sylvia Puss-Kish Ponky," saying he was
"unsettled" away from her. He was very encouraging about her poetry and
certain that it would sell. He suggested plots for her stories, including one
about a couple's desire to establish themselves in the country and find they
cannot rid themselves of city people and city ways—the change of scene
doing them no more good than the remove to Court Green would later do,
although it was Hughes then driving the plot of their lives in his mistaken
belief that away from London they would thrive. Sylvia pined for her "brute"
and wrote long letters about his work and their prospects for publication
in the States, aided by editor Peter Davison at the *Atlantic Monthly*. Ted
reciprocated with long letters, mentioning he was stopped by the police,
adding that he looked "like a strange beast unless you're with me . . . I was
just stepping up into the fish and chip shop—where we never went—when
two little girls ran out with their arms full of wrapped fish and chips, when
they saw me one let out a scream. They recovered and went off. But that's
the sort of thing which will soon dement me." There is small doubt that
Ted Hughes had become for Sylvia Plath a Promethean god as specified by
William Sheldon, "fearfully dangerous" to the populace: "When he gets
loose, fire starts, and things happen fast. There is a great healthy fear of him
deep in the remotely conscious levels of the human mind."

Ted stewed at home, awaiting word from a BBC producer who had promised more work reading poetry aloud after Ted had performed well in his audition. She reciprocated with letters calling herself an abnormality, a "gargoyle." She spoke of shunning people, which is exactly what Nat LaMar had said about her. She had no time for anyone else. Ted stood outside of institutions bending the world to his will. No wonder Sylvia had a hard time reading Augustine's *Confessions*, noting in her calendar diary: "inability to appreciate struggle for belief." She announced herself as a renegade atheist, refusing the Christian call for the subordination of self that resulted in Christ's crucifixion. Plath enjoyed the idea of taking on the whole of Western thought, inspired by her tie to Ted. "Personal love is often an entering wedge to a great development and expansion of the personality; it sometimes acts as a beginning of things on a new and broader plain." That much of Sheldon, Plath underlined, adding in the right margin "yes." But look at the next words, which she did not underline: "but far more often it becomes instead merely the end of things; a final little gasp of achievement, ushering in a life of selfishness for two or three instead of for one." That kind of danger did not occur to Sylvia as a certain viciousness plays out in her letters to Hughes, when she imagines herself in class "screaming at all the prim scholarly bitches, knocking over desks, and strangling as many as I could get my hands on." She attacked what she called "a fat vampirish monster Miss Pitt": "I have a morbid desire to cut open her fat white flesh each time I see her and see if its onion juice or what that keeps her going." She was acting on what she said was Ted's own disdain for "silly rule-mongers . . . why is everybody so banal?"

In these monstrous attacks on monstrosity, this couple portrayed themselves as in conflict with the world as they produced their prodigious Promethean work, while knowing the world, Plath said, in a "new and special way," signaled in Ted's announcement that he had secured his BBC broadcasting berth. She bolstered herself reading W. H. Mikesell's *Abnormal Psychology*, essays on manic depressive geniuses and hypnotism. Acutely aware of her own manic depressive cycles, she found herself in the good company of Byron, Beethoven, Dickens, and Tolstoy. But even more significant is what she said to her mother: "what wife shares her husband's dearest career as I do? except maybe Marie Curie?" Nothing less than a world historical match would do for Sylvia Plath, as she conceived of herself in the marital orbit of greatness: "The eyes and ears of the world are upon me," she announced in her October 10, 1956, letter to "dear darling Teddy-one." Curie's story, her coming from Poland to Paris, to one of the centers of science, had its parallel in Plath's coming from America to England, to the mother lode of literature, and to her Pierre, the husband of her ambitions. Ted abetted her conceit by affirming Freud, who said that deprived of the loved one on whom he has "built into his life, his working powers often fail temporarily." So it was: Without Sylvia he could not write. He couldn't even read. Even this man, comfortable in his rags and hardly sensitive to the sartorial, said the suit and jacket she had purchased for him were "wonderful." He said he would meet her in London "Sleek, sleek, sleek" when the date was set for his BBC program. He also looked forward, as she had hoped, to getting out of England to share her plan of a daring debut in America, winning over the colonies she had mapped out and reported on for her grade-school assignments. He cheerfully assessed her poems, praising while presenting options for improvement. She concurred: "Your words on my poems are so right, as ever; you know." But the story she sent him, "The Wishing Box," about a "dreamless woman" is transparently about her own worry that Hughes's imagination outstripped hers, since he was never in want of material, some of which indeed came right out of his dreams. She admitted as much: "my dreamless woman . . . is certainly an aspect of one of my selves now." She hoped he would not be angry that she had "plagiarized some of your magnificent dreams."

26

What was happening to Sylvia Plath? The humdrum of Cambridge that she denounced in her letters arose out of romantic love, which "stirred, transformed, ennobled," William Sheldon observed. Romantic love centralizes ambition, he noted, and Plath underlined. Romantic love becomes a "pivot about which to build a system of values." She was working out what Sheldon called the "third panel": sexual relations. The letters exchanged with Hughes exemplified Sheldon's concept that the "sex interest, when under discipline, renders available the whole energy resources of a personality as a sort of vast reservoir for warming and enriching and supporting character." Sylvia went on to underline a passage that illuminates why she felt under an imperative: "Wholehearted integration of purpose becomes a reality, and biologically the great straining of animal energies toward the unknown finds expression in an adventurous courageous, reckless upward surging of life. . . . The soul comes to find its main expression in sexual activity." Romantic love elevates sexuality to the point where a "higher feeling permeates *not only specific sexual relations but the whole range of consciousness*." Plath put a star next to what followed: "Sexual desire is life at high intensity. It lifts the whole personality up out of itself, and opens the way for transcending the self." But, Sheldon warned, and Plath underlined, the uplifting power also "carries a certain volatility." That volatility of romantic love, factored into a manic depressive cycle, would be a constant feature of her days with Ted Hughes. From Cambridge, she wrote in an effort to annihilate the distance between them: "I kneel on the couch in the pitch black and throw all my force and love in the direction, as nearly as I can discern, of your bed in Yorkshire." She was living "in a kind of chill controlled hysteria" that would not end until they were together for a London weekend to celebrate his BBC debut.

The very idea of marriage came into intellectual focus as Plath met with her supervisor, Dr. Krook, writing a paper on Augustine that took issue with the doctrines of original sin, God's omniscience, and the "low, debased view of physical love between man and woman even in 'blameless wedlock.'" Sheldon portrayed the Christian view of sex as an effort to subordinate it to morality and to a proper—that is dignified—sense of human character. Plath chafed at such inhibiting boundaries. The problem with Christianity, Sheldon argued, is that "woman is an afterthought, created from a non-essential part of the true human body." How could Plath possibly function in accord with that mythology? Christianity, as a whole, could not suffice for her because, as Sheldon declared, Prometheus had been chained to the Christian cross.

Sylvia's heavily underlined and annotated copy of Augustine's *Confessions* reads like a dialogue with an alien mind. She spoke to Augustine: "If God is immanent in all things—flesh & flowers, why not love & rejoice in them creatively? Instead of rejecting them as sinful for fleshless essence." She put two vertical slashes next to his statement: "And this is the happy life, to rejoice to Thee, of Thee, for Thee; this is it, and there is no other." To this she replied: "Yes there is!" Next to Augustine's assertion that "no one can be content unless Thou give it" she wrote in the margin "arrant lies." His conception of God as the source of perfection by which the corrupt world was measured provoked this objection: "Why create imperfection?"

In her October 16, 1956, paper for Krook, "Some Observations On The City of God,"[34] Plath expressed belief in the transcendent power of human love. She wondered why Paul and Augustine equated the union of men and women as ultimately divisive, resulting in disintegration and a turning away from God. Could it be that these men had never experienced the transcendent love of a woman?[35] So it was that they denied the exaltation that Sylvia had found in Cocteau's films and in her marriage. The very idea of transforming a beast into a prince was the miracle of human love that Paul and Augustine abjured.

27

Sylvia's letters to Ted during this time are full of frustration about rejections from editors followed by her Promethean prophecies of greatness, predicting he would win the *Harper's* prize for a first book of poetry and then going beyond that into a kind of religious fervor that Paul and Augustine would have deemed blasphemous: "I feel, in taking you to america, I am bringing, as it were, the grail to a place where it will be reverenced properly. time it may take; but in america, your voice will, increasingly, be heard. and loved." Note: This was her plan, and he went along with it. By late October 1956, she found it difficult to concentrate without him and began to think of announcing their marriage no matter the repercussions with the "authorities," as Ted called them. How did he feel about joining Sylvia? "I could crush you into my pores," he wrote, not to mention his "aching erection." London was "murderous. . . . There's no aura left here." He was coming to Cambridge to talk over their situation.

In the meantime Sylvia had "queer dreams," one of which put her and Ted into the occult service of Dr. Krook, a witch, whose power they sought to usurp. Sylvia had already transformed this Cambridge don into a kind of guru that resembled Ruth Beuscher. What Hughes made of the dream then is not clear, but later he would regard Beuscher and women like her as a threat to his own sense of the occult and mastery of his marriage. Beuscher, in turn, would, in retrospect, characterize Hughes as a warlock, with Plath remaining suspended—powerfully caught between contending parties.[36]

28

After two telegrams and Ted's visit to Cambridge on October 23, 1956, deciding he would give up the plan of teaching in Spain while Sylvia finished up at Cambridge, she went public about their marriage, telling Dorothea Krook first, before informing Cambridge officials or the Fulbright authorities. She was relieved to discover that everyone seemed happy for her and expressed no disapproval. Ted, a great success at the BBC, got paid every time his readings were rebroadcast. She did not tell her mother about flareups—like the day they apparently tortured each other about their "lurid pasts," as Sylvia put it in her calendar diary. She had the urge to tell him about her New York summer but evidently refrained—why she did not say, but she treated him as vulnerable as herself. He confessed to moments when he was "suddenly nightmarishly depressed."

In London, on October 31, 1956, all went well, meeting with Dr. Gaines in the Fulbright office, yet by the afternoon she felt "lousy" and sick on the train home to Cambridge. She was tense and insecure, and the next day no better. Cutting across her day-by-day accounting of events, her dreams dredged up an anxiety alleviated in lovemaking with Ted that nonetheless exhausted her, just as she was getting her period and the "blueness" she mentioned to her mother. Yet all seemed to fall into place as they quickly found a flat and Ted secured a teaching job at a private school while remaining in demand at the BBC.

Olwyn Hughes, who had a job in Paris, visited. Sylvia met her for the first time, describing her as "startlingly beautiful," a "changeling" who would never get old, "quite selfish" spending on extravagances and still owing Ted money. "But in spite of this, I do like her," Sylvia insisted. Not yet rivals, the two women's adversarial encounters over superintending Ted would soon emerge.

29

The attack on the Suez Canal aroused Sylvia out of her own joys and miseries, as she expressed sentiments true to what she had believed about world affairs beginning in her teenage years. She deplored Britain's bombing of Egypt and "smug commercial colonialism. . . . What joy there must be in Moscow at this flagrant nationalism and capitalism! This aggression by force, which has always been the cry of the Western Allies against totalitarians." In fact, as she noted, the West had just denounced the Russian invasion of Hungary. She hoped that her country would not side, as it traditionally did, with Britain. "How I long to come home!" she exclaimed to her mother. As she had always done, Sylvia read the newspapers and singled out the *Manchester Guardian* for its opposition to the Eden government's military operation. She took it personally, having "literally rubbed elbows" with him at a Claridge reception. "I am so emotionally exhausted after this week, and the Hungarian and Suez affairs have depressed me terribly after reading the typed last words from Hungary yesterday before the Russians took over I was almost physically sick," she wrote to her mother on November 6, 1956. She had probably been reading the *Manchester Guardian* again—Peter Howard's report, "The Last Minutes of Freedom" (November 5).

Sylvia seemed not to notice how out of it Ted was. He attributed the Hungarian uprising and the Suez crisis to "oppositions of the planets." The author of "Your Paris," who had described Plath's obliviousness to history, wrote in early 1956 to Olwyn Hughes: "I discovered the other day that one can live in Hungary even more cheaply than in Spain." In the same letter, he mused: "What is life like in Hungary? Not so many tourists as Italy etc I imagine." Subjugated Communist Hungary evidently meant no more to him than Franco's Spain. He had a passion for Hungarian poetry but was apparently incapable of imagining what had devastated his wife. If he ever had a pertinent thing to say about Suez, or about Franco, it was not included in his published letters. According to Sylvia, Ted taught Russian history and told the boys about the Nazis and the Jews, without, it is to be hoped, reverting to the misalignment of the planets.

Ted took Sylvia on calming walks. A series of rejections from the *New Yorker* dispirited her as she succumbed to one of her periodic colds and slipped a disc, drugging herself with a codeine prescription. She remained in a state of agitation over political events, mentioning in her calendar diary a "vivid dream of war on Ganges, atrocities." She wearied of her Cambridge studies, but "strong love" with her Teddy buoyed her.

Sylvia thought a good deal about her manic depressive cycles and had an opportunity to share what she had learned when her mother wrote about a depressed family friend, Steve Clark. She encouraged her mother to use her as an example: "get him to talk, break down whatever sick reserve & terror he has & even get him to let go and cry. . . . Get him to go easy on himself; show him that people will love & respect him without ever asking what marks he has gotten. I remember I was terrified that if I wasn't successful writing that no one would find me interesting or valuable. . . . Above all, don't try to be rosy; start from what he thinks is the situation. . . . He will trust you if you treat his problems as real ones."

30

In December, Sylvia wrote dreamy letters and Christmas cards about returning home and showing off Ted. "We work, we thrive," she wrote to Elinor Friedman. To Marcia Brown she described meeting and marrying Ted, adding: "He was very simply the only man I've ever met whom I never could boss; he'd bash my head in." She adverted to her struggles with the weather and English history she said was "written in dust. . . . If only you could imagine how grim England is in winter!" She would, to the end, never be able to surmount that forbidding feeling that would come over her, as if without central heating she could not maintain her core. "I sometimes feel like taking a hatchet & going out like the old foolish knights to slay the Cold," she wrote to Warren. Although she described Ted as "staunchly British," she hoped America would win him over and that they would settle there. "England is no place to bring up children—bad teeth, lousy dentists, careless overworked Mds."

31

Every life is individual, a "law until himself," as Leo V. Tepley observes in W. H. Mikesell's *Modern Abnormal Psychology*. Yet every life also has a universal pattern—whether we know it or not. Sylvia Plath—for all her accomplishments and rarity—realized that what she was now experiencing had been experienced before. She went hunting for prototypes of herself, reading a chapter in *Modern Abnormal Psychology* about the "Mania-Depression of Famous Men." What did the future author of *Ariel* make of this conjunction? —"Like Beethoven, who could feel joy and sorrow almost simultaneously, Tchaikovsky, shortly after he had reached the pinnacle of his desire to tell his suffering to the world and posterity, was laid to rest."[37] Her own daily volatility had precedent. Was it somehow related to her creativity? In the same book, she read "Tolstoy suffered long and deeply from a recurrent and persistent urge for self-destruction." Reading Plato and Aristotle she came across this sentence in *Abnormal Psychology*: "Aristotle must have known a Ludwig von Beethoven and a Leo Tolstoy when he said, 'There is no great genius without a mixture of madness.'" Her own diary meticulously documented the etiology of manic-depression in *Modern Abnormal Psychology*: "The daily wear and tear of the body physiology frequently brings on an attack of manic depression."

But was Plath's volatility abnormal? Did she have a personality disorder? A good deal of what she felt—her frustrations and desire to get on with her life were part of what Gail Sheehy in *Passages* calls the "trying twenties": "how to take hold in the adult world. Incandescent with our molten energies, having outgrown the family and the formlessness of our transitioning years, we are impatient to pour ourselves into the exactly right form—our own way of living in the world." Isn't this why certain readers connect with Plath—because she has documented this transitioning? For a poet and a young woman, finding "exactly the right form" became paramount. She was readying herself for what Sheehy calls the "bigger, bullying arena." Her letters often are accounts of contests, as she entered herself and Ted Hughes into the highly competitive literary world. It had all started in her youth with poems and jingles designed to win prizes.

32

Sylvia's first days at Cambridge reflected a search for a mentor that she did not find until the end of her first year in the figure of Dorothea Krook. "The tasks of this period," Sheehy notes, "are as enormous as they are exhilarating: To shape a dream, that vision of one's own possibilities in the world that will generate energy, aliveness, and hope. To prepare for a lifework. To find a mentor if possible. And to form the capacity for intimacy without losing in the process whatever constancy of self we have thus far assembled." Between Krook and Hughes, Plath believed she had found her equilibrium, and yet by the end of a day, or at the beginning, she could go to sleep or wake up wondering: "One of the terrifying aspects of the twenties is the conviction that the choices we make are irrevocable," Sheehy points out. Plath tried to put a lock on her life, to steady her purpose, by constantly, in letters and conversations, extolling Hughes in Sheehy's terms: "'Perfect' is that person we imbue with the capacity to enliven and support our vision or the person we believe in and want to help." Plath was not that special: "And to what degree does the young woman invent the man she marries? She often sees in him possibilities that no one else recognizes and pictures herself within his dream as the one person who truly understands. Such illusions are the stuff of which the twenties are made." It was hard work—all that typing for Ted!—to get the world to know him as she did. If she got upset on this day or that it was all about "trying to stabilize—that is what the twenties are about," Sheehy observes. The trouble—and the trouble would come a few years later—is that, in Sheehy's words: "Early marriage often short-circuits young people's work on themselves as they slip under a grid of obligations to act as spouses and parents." Sylvia would admit as much in the last months of her life. It had been up to Ted to protect her—that is what he would say to his friends who complained about her. She aligned with the man in his twenties who, as Sheehy puts it, "finds it easier to believe that all those protective powers are carried by her mate."

Heading into 1957, in letters to her mother and friends, Sylvia put on what Sheehy calls the "armor of optimism"—the necessary protective gear for the trying twenties. Sylvia noted for good measure: "the planets point to a magnificent successful year for us both, & we will work to make it come true." Regular writing hours in the morning and getting to bed by ten fueled their sense of accomplishment. She made light of their "violent disagreements" that were dissolved in their common aims. Ted chimed in with a letter to Aurelia and Warren thanking them for Christmas presents and extolling Sylvia's collection of poems she hoped to get published: "Her book is startling. The individual poems are dazzling and disturbing enough, but more than that, they add up to each other—most books of poems stale their effect because the poems somehow break each other down, betray each other, outyell each other—Sylvia's are cumulative. This is especially surprising because her individual poems have such a brilliant and emphatic finish." To his brother Gerald and his wife Joan in Australia, he wrote, "Sylvia is my luck completely."

33

What to do with her head perplexed Plath—the clay head that Mary Bailey Derr had made of her and fired up in a Smith art class. The model had been "knocking about & I didn't have the heart to throw it way, because I'd developed a strange fondness for the old thing with passing years," Sylvia told her mother. Ted suggested they should leave the head in a tree overlooking cow pastures and the river in her beloved Grantchester, the scene of so many soothing walks. The idea of putting herself to rest had intense appeal as the head gazed out "over the lovely green meadows with the peace that passes understanding. I like to think of leaving my head here, as it were." She called it a monument now twining with leaves and ivy, becoming a thing of nature. Yet that is not how she ended "The Lady and the Earthenware Head," which she enclosed in a letter to her mother. The head in the poem is an "unlovely conversation piece," with a "Half-blind" and "derisive pout," a "rude image" treasonous to its life model. The unidentified male urges her to throw it out, but she has an atavistic feeling of a bond between herself and this "coarse copy," even though it is a frightening effigy that menaces her in a dream, reminding her of "that vast stellar head / Housed in stark heavens, whose laws" ordain her existence. To be rid of it, in other words, would be to get rid of herself. No place is safe to store a head that rules her psyche. "At the mere thought her head ached." Even the idea of submerging the head in a "murky tarn" arouses images of it emerging out of its "watery aspic, laurel led by fins." Had Sylvia seen *The Creature from the Black Lagoon* (1954)? The poem proposes Ted's solution, putting the "mimic-head—in a crotched willow tree, / green-Vaulted by foliage." But instead, in the poem,

The Creature from the Black Lagoon (1954).

the head endures "shrined on her shelf" and "Refusing to diminish / By one jot its basilisk-look of love"—a serpent's love that is like a chilling scene in a horror movie. It is understandable why Plath could not do without that ending, since as so often in her poetry, what remains unresolved is what she thought she could resolve in her life. The poem is a kind of rebuke to Ted's belief that her head could be transubstantiated in an anodyne nature. Nature in the poem is not the benign force in Sylvia Plath's letters, nor can the atavistic Plath deny her own "simulacrum . . . Lewdly beckoning."[38]

34

On February 23, 1957, a telegram arrived announcing *Hawk in the Rain* had won the Poetry Center First Publication Prize, including a *Harper's* contract.

Plath pointed out to her mother that it is the "anniversary of the fatal party where I met Ted! . . . Genius will out! . . . I am more happy than if it was my book published! . . . There is no question of rivalry, but only mutual joy." So it seemed and yet Sylvia was already conceiving of a plan that Ted had no part in but that she thought he would welcome: her "long-range project of making Ted love America." Although he had declared several times that England was "dead," he never supposed that America—except as temporary place holder—would be the alternative to home. That alternative had been Australia and a life with his brother before the meeting with Sylvia that had derailed his departure. In a February 24 letter to Gerald, Ted still held out the possibility of a trip there.

At the same time, in her journal, Plath plotted out a novel drawing on her own effort to find herself in Cambridge, going through several lovers (including Richard Sassoon) before encountering Ted's "big, blasting dangerous love." She conceived a three-hundred-page work that would read like a memoir and could be submitted for one of the *Harper's* or *Atlantic Monthly* contests. But she was still not able to settle on a coherent narrative. She escaped into domesticity, reading the *Joy of Cooking* "like a rare novel." She felt linked to Virginia Woolf, who had suffered her share of rejections and killed herself, yet Sylvia declared herself "apple-pie happy." She was reading D. H. Lawrence, a favorite of Dorothea Krook's, and believed she could batter through the conventionality that conquered so many women.[39] The marriage to Ted was part of a mission, which included raising a "batch of brilliant healthy children!" This would have been news to Ted who at best indulged Sylvia's dynastic dreams without, as he later admitted, really expecting to act on them. He remained, she thought, the "perfect male counterpart to my own self." She knew that it sounded "so paragon," but it was so she insisted, and at their dinner celebrating his award he gave her no reason to think otherwise. Then she returned to sketching out her novel that would deal with the depressing days in Paris without Sassoon and the inadequate companionship of Gordon Lameyer. She seemed headed toward a story that would redeem her suffering with the advent of Ted Hughes, whom she seemed about to get to in what she called in her journal the "Pivot-point of decision."

The joy over Ted's award did not last a day. They got into an argument that included his criticism of her Earthenware Head poem. Why he objected to it, Sylvia did not say, but the poem's horror-film ending mocked his effort to alleviate her dread. Her head, in his view, was not where it was supposed to be. His own poem titled "The Earthenware Head" is evasive, concentrating on her reaction to the "evil" head, but again, as usual, occluding his own part in the story. Or was he, as his biographer

Elaine Feinstein suggests, simply bewildered by the woman who said he was her counterpart?

Sylvia overlooked how Ted diverged from her. On February 27, 1957, she wrote: "Dear Ted's mother & dad!": "Isn't he wonderful!" Winning the first book contest had occurred almost exactly a year after she met him, confirming her "intuitive vision" that he could be a "great poet." The contest judges, "three of the greatest living poets today!"—Marianne Moore, W. H. Auden, and Stephen Spender—were not piddling poets "scared" to acknowledge Ted. She had met all three, which in itself implied that she had taken Ted into her impresarial orbit. But it was more than that. It was a dynastic achievement: "What a wonderful family we are!" she wrote to Warren. Ted let Sylvia gush in that letter to his parents. He wrote to Olwyn Hughes dispatching the announcement of the award and its significance in a few paragraphs. Then he discussed his current writing, nowhere making the slightest nod to familial pride—on his side or Sylvia's. The letter he sent the next day to his brother Gerald and his wife Joan does not even mention the prize.[40] Sylvia had a habit of saying in her letters that Ted shared her feelings, that her family was his family, yet his letters rarely show as much.

35

In her final year at Cambridge, Sylvia wrote weekly papers on Augustine, Hobbes, Hume, Bentham, Mill, Coleridge, Chaucer, Locke, Blake, and others, but lamented: "I am stymied, stuck, at a stasis. Some paralysis of the head has got me frozen." Her novel was "atrocious." The prospect of her end of May exams oppressed her. Her dilemma: how to write about the "voyage of a girl through destruction, hatred and despair to seek and to find the meaning of the redemptive power of love. But the horror is that cheapness and slick-love would be the result of the thing badly written. Well-written, sex could be noble & gut-shaking." Without Ted, she mused, she might just write a second rate novel and be done with it. With Ted, she had to be more exacting. Her studies of philosophy and fiction under the guidance of Dorothea Krook seep into this March 4, 1957, journal entry: "But I must get back into the world of my creative mind: otherwise, in the world of pies & shin beef,[41] I die. The great vampire cook extracts the nourishment & I grow fat on the corruption of matter, mere mindless matter. I must be lean & write & make worlds beside this to live in."

36

On March 12, 1957, Sylvia wrote to her mother: "Hold on to your hat for some wonderful news: I have just been offered a teaching job for next year! AT SMITH!" The news came as an enormous relief after her worries about her Cambridge exams, the strain over her novel, and Ted's exhausting schedule at the boys' school, where he had just spent even more time directing a play. She told her mother: "I never want Ted to have to undergo a year of strain like this again. I don't care if he only gets a part time free-lance job this next year, I want him to write above all." Sylvia did not share with Ted her dream that they would settle permanently in America: "one must never push him: he'll come around of his own accord."

"The Snowman on the Moor" provides quite a contrast to Sylvia's giddy letters of triumph: "We are going to catapult to fame, I predict." In the poem, a woman rushes out of the coal-fired house vowing to "win / Him to his knees." She taunts the man: "Come find me," but he remains "guarding his grim battlement." She encounters a snowman with the "sheaved skulls" of ladies whose wit "made fools / Of kings." The chastened woman hies home, "brimful of gentle talk / And mild obeying." That was the trouble with Ted: He would not come at her command. The pattern would be repeated—her walking out on Ted until, in the end, she had to tell him to go.

In the main, though, they were a team, with Ted putting up a big chart on the wall for Sylvia to keep a clear chronology of the periods and figures she had to write about in her late May exams. She spent days and nights in the library studying "2000 years of tragedy," she told her mother, concentrating on Corneille, Racine, Ibsen, Strindberg, Webster, Marlowe, Tourneur, Yeats, Eliot. Ted hypnotized her to relax, dried the dishes, took country walks with her. She looked forward to a Yorkshire visit, she wrote to his parents: "You have no idea how forward I look to living at the Beacon again. I catch myself daydreaming about the moors, with the mad-eyed moor sheep, & then the wonderful view from your livingroom windows over the green fields which always makes me think of living on top of the world."

37

Ted's unusually expansive letter to Gerald and Joan Hughes comes close to Sylvia's own celebration of their union:

Well, my life lately is splendid, wonderfully repaired from what it was. Marriage is my medium. Also my luck thrives on it, and my productions. You have no idea what a happy life Sylvia and I lead or perhaps you have. We work and walk about, and repair each other's writings. She is one of the best critics I ever met and understands my imagination perfectly, and I think I understand hers. It's amazing how we strike sparks. And when we're fed up of that we walk out into the country and sit for hours watching things. We sit by the river and watch water-voles and when they come near Sylvia goes almost unconscious with delight. She's the most responsive alert creature in the world, about everything.

"America is waiting with arms open," he exulted. His arrival would be heralded by the Poetry Center in New York, where he would make the kinds of contacts with fellow poets that would further his career. He dismissed London's "literary nabobs," saying "America has as it were snatched me from under their nose." Sylvia-America amounted to much the same thing as he joined his wife in a kind of fairy tale romance.

Sylvia still thought she could finish her novel, now called "Hill of Leopards." She expected the book to be controversial, exposing a "lot of people and places" while emphasizing a theme that came straight out of *Psychology and the Promethean Will*: the "positive acceptance of conflict uncertainty, & pain as the soil for true knowledge and life."

38

Exams were grueling: "I have honestly never undergone such physical torture as writing furiously from 6 to 7 hours a day (for the last two days) with my unpracticed pen-hand: every night I come home and lie in a hot tub massaging it back to action," she told her mother. Ted said her typing had made her a victim of evolution. He had been a "saint: making breakfast & heating water for a daily tub, meeting me at 4:30 after exams & last night (I was very exhausted & aching) served me with steak mushrooms & wine on a tray in bed, doing the dishes afterwards."

Sylvia marked her one-year wedding anniversary with a letter to her mother saying she could not remember not being married to Ted: "our horoscopes read, when Leo & Scorpio marry, they feel they've known each other forever in a former life." In the bracing air of the moors she began reading the works on the Smith syllabus she would teach, thrilled also that

Ted had dedicated his first book to her. She had slotted two weeks for a visit home and socializing, with the rest of the summer in a Cape cottage devoted to their own writing, which included her novel, now titled "Falcon Yard." She expected to have her second novel finished by the age of 27 and to begin having the first of three or four children. Thinking this far ahead overwhelmed Ted, but he would not be willing to say so until she had banished him from Court Green, sending him into a kind of royal exile that befitted his treacherous transgression of her dynastic design.

But right now: "Our deep Cambridge fatigue is all gone & we are healthy & fine. . . . Coming home with Ted will be like discovering a new country & seeing it all through his eyes," she wrote her mother from Waterloo Station on June 20, 1957. She wrote at the same time to Ted's parents, saying they were on their way and she would write more from America. She had encouraged Aurelia to do the same, wishing for a union of the crowns on both sides of the Atlantic.

Ted's letter to Olwyn Hughes told a different story. "Don't criticise Sylvia too badly about the way she got up and came after me. After her exams etc I suppose she felt nervy—she did, that was obvious." There had been an altercation between these two women around the throne of Ted Hughes, with Sylvia walking out as Olwyn asserted her sovereignty. Ted would in the days to come make his excuses for Sylvia—in this case noting that the Beacon was "too small for five or six people—especially if one of them has an obsession about resting. And everyone was walking in and out & up and down continually." She had been similarly disturbed at the second-floor noisy tenants in Cambridge who played music too loudly. Ted assured Olwyn that Sylvia admired her, and Olwyn should not be put off by Sylvia's "smarmy" manner. In fact, in her panic she said "stupid things then that mortify her afterwards." He treated her as a somewhat delicate specimen with a "miserable past," which he would tell his sister about "gradually." In effect, he was saying Sylvia could not help herself. He was already creating a kind of deterministic view of her fate, elaborated in *Birthday Letters*.

39

Aboard the *Queen Elizabeth*, Sylvia spent her time people watching. Ted extolled the food "steak, steak steak. . . . Greens & fresh fruit" until surfeited, followed by a black depression alleviated by watching movies and the "bows towering up into the sky and towards the empty horizon." Sylvia recorded the "fierce wind" and spray "folding back from bow like white rich curd." For Ted it was a choppy sea of white horses out of which emerged what Sylvia called a "wake of rainbows" and he called "a great clear rainbow" all along the edge of the spray. [PJ, THL]

Sylvia sketched out a story, "The Great Big Nothing," about a New York City secretary, Gertrude Twiss, on the *Queen Elizabeth* in a June crossing to America: "Mood: failure, misery, lemon-acid." Like women Plath observed aboard ship, Elizabeth has staked everything on finding a man. She has quit her job for a trip to Europe that she discovers is a "great big nothing": nasty men in Rome and English decadence, and cruelty on the cruise. "If you don't catch a man on this ship, you never will," a waiter tells Elizabeth. A French doctor is for her the epitome of grandeur, glamor, and the love she cannot have. The Statue of Liberty looms as an ironic "imprisonment of self," since her liberty has resulted, yet again, in a "great big nothing." [PJ] That's as far as Plath got with her fictional conceit, unable to conceive of what would happen next to her heroine. Plath's own marriage seemed miraculous and apparently explainable only in the length of a novel. For the longest time, though, she had thought she might never get beyond the Elizabeth stage of existence. This abortive story might well have been one of those ventures for the slicks that Sylvia could not quite bring off. In a July 21, 1957, letter to Elinor Friedman, Sylvia mentioned biting her nails "over tripe" and banging on the "doors of the Saturday Evening Post." Might she have gone further with *Post* stories and the like with Val Gendron aboard to encourage her? Instead, she looked to the high art of Virginia Woolf for inspiration. In her diary, she put the thrust of her projected Cambridge novel into a single phrase: "American innocence on the saturated spot of history."

40

In several letters, Sylvia had relished returning to a land with so many conveniences, yet on their arrival, Ted conveyed a different impression: "The thought of settling to a comfortably housed life gives Sylvia the jimjams almost as badly as it does me." Had he misread her, or had she misled him? He was already deploring the "rat-race," the indiscriminate friendliness of Americans, the huge cars, the opulence of Wellesley that made him want to "practice little private filth," spitting and peeing on shrubbery "just to keep in contact with a world that isn't quite so glazed as this one." Mostly he liked the birds and the kindness of the people with none of the sulkiness of British literary life.

Of course, Sylvia had to make adjustments after two years away from home: "Everything seemed immensely sparkling & shiny & fast-paced & loud after my bucolic existence on the Backs and the Bronte moors," she wrote to Lynne Lawner on July 1, 1957. She summed up what it was like to reenter the country by describing the customs inspector suspiciously going through a book crate. She told him she was going to be a college teacher. "Yeah," he said looking her up and down, "you're too young to get a job like that."

41

During seven weeks in a Cape Cod cottage Sylvia enjoyed baking in her landlord's oven. But the couple "got down to business," as she liked to say in her childhood diary. Even though writing again was "awkward and painful," it was the "prime condition" of their happiness. They wrote in the morning, swam in the afternoon, read in the evening. "You could have done nothing more wonderful than giving us these seven weeks," she assured her mother. In fact, Ted felt uneasy about Aurelia's largesse and the thought of being in her debt. Sylvia wrote happily in letters about returning to Smith, but "bad dreams" told another story: "diabolically real: Haven house, the feet of Smith girls past the room, which becomes a prison, always giving out on a public corridor, no private exits." She would come to see Smith as a dead end. "Why these dreams?" she asked herself in her journal. "These last exorcisings of the horrors and fears beginning when my father died and the bottom fell out."

On July 15, 1957, in a remarkable moment of reckoning, Sylvia wondered if she had put her suicidal trauma behind her: "still the dreams aren't quite sure of it. They aren't for I'm not. And I suppose I never will be." Work, she hoped, would be her salvation. Ted is not mentioned in this crucial moment that she apparently did not share with him. Instead, she turned from her bad dreams and dead ends to her novel, described in her journal now as "FALCON YARD: central image: love, a falcon, striking once and for all: blood sacrifice: falcon yard, central chapter of book: the irrefutable meeting and experience. Emblem: lord & lady riding smiling with falcon on wrist. Get impersonal into Judith, create other characters who act in their own right & not just as projections of her." Not just—that was the trouble, how to make it real? The novel did not jell. Why? She thought it was because her earlier fiction had been "slick," and what she wanted to write now could not easily encompass the last five years. Fragments of what would become *The Bell Jar* sifted through her reveries about events leading up to her suicide attempt and to "earthy Dr. Beuscher." She also considered a story, "The Day of Twenty-Four Cakes," about a married woman and mother at "loose ends," suicidal, baking cakes to steady herself, with a husband returning home to a "new understanding" and beautifully baked cakes. [PJ]

42

On July 22, 1957, Ted reported to Lucas Myers: "The real world retreats a bit here. Sterilised under cellophane." His letters suggest that he spent most of his time in his head, showing little interest in his surroundings. A curious passage in this same letter suggests that Sylvia had conned him into her scheme of things:

> When I consider how my affable familiar has sabotaged my every attempt at a normal profession, and sabotaged my whole life while I constrain it so, and how very affable & very magically helpful & luck-bringing it is when I entertain it & its inventions, its fantasticalia, its pretticisms and its infinite verballifications—then I think it would be the best & most sensible course to make a career of humouring it.

There it is: what Ted would say more plainly to Plath after he left their home in Devon: He had been humoring her. It is often the case in marriages bound to break up that one or both parties sense they are trapped but go on, as Hughes did, because, in his case, of the magical and helpful and congenial ways the marriage seemed to be working even while he felt controlled. The "its" in Hughes's letter proliferate, as if he is caught in the vague syntax that bound him up with Plath. But she was *his* familiar, which meant a double of himself, an alter ego, a personal demon. Why not say something to Sylvia if he felt that way? "If you humiliate your devils," he confided to Myers, "they avenge themselves, by paralyzing your outer efforts." The only solution, at least then, was to not "nose into other folk's affairs" and write.

With Olwyn Hughes, Ted would be more circumspect and defend his wife, but with Myers, no fan of Sylvia's, Ted could share his plight. Sylvia seemed oblivious or perhaps was simply making her mother feel good about her visit to the Cape cottage: "Ted and I loved every minute of your stay and it was great fun planning for it." She was, however, working on a story, "Trouble-making Mother," and began to get into the rhythm of writing.

"We dream: and my dreams get better," she wrote on July 20 as Ted saved her from a "tiger-man."

43

In late July and early August 1957—two "black lethal" weeks—she could not write. It was like the summer of her suicide. But in this case she worried about a pregnancy that would wreck her writing and teaching plans. Finally the "hot drench" and "red stain dreamed for" arrived, but then her book was not chosen for the Yale Younger Poets series. She wrote in her journal about the "misery of knowing half of the poems, published ones, weren't any longer, or in two years would definitely not be, passable in myself because of their bland ladylike archness or slightness." She called her gift "little" compared to Ted's but vowed to stoically carry on. Fortunately Ted cared not at all for "flashy success." In an August 22 letter to Olwyn Hughes he had already made up his mind: America was a "temporary expedition."

44

By September 5, 1957, they had moved into a Northampton apartment, with Sylvia handling all the details and describing herself as "manager of the exchequer." No comment required on this journal entry for September 6: "Story: woman with poet husband who writes about love, passion—she, after glow of vanity & joy, finds out he isn't writing about her (as her friends think) but about Dream Woman Muse." No comment required, *yet*.

In preparation for teaching, Sylvia had been reading *The Sound and the Fury*, which perhaps inspired her idea for "Four Corners of a Windy House," set in *Wuthering Heights* territory, with four characters, described in her journal as "each seeing different facets of absolute reality—which is nearest truth?" The characters: "Evi (egoistic actress), Leroy / Curt (realist prosaic artist), William (creative poet—half-dust, half-deity), Sibyl (dreamy pale medium of spirit forces)—The house stood. The black stones cast no shadow. Vary tones of voice, style, observations of others—Leroy—he-man Curt → Evi (her beauty, vivid life—Sibyl too pale, ethereal)." The story expresses Sylvia's own veering from the poetic to the prosaic, from slick fiction and high art, from the conflicts and tensions arising from the flesh and the spirit that she had probed in her sessions with Dorothea Krook.

She was exploring her own tendency to idealize, to do more than report on what she saw, to turn it into something visionary, mythic, in the figure of William whom Evi hopes will create beautiful words and roles for her even as Sibyl, another alter ego for Sylvia, "assumes responsibility, pain & suffering."

45

Sylvia's four-day teaching schedule (65 students total), plus three office hours by appointment and department meetings, took up lots of time, especially for a conscientious instructor. Ted helped out making breakfast and doing the dishes. She followed her mother's advice and went on some "morale boosting" clothes shopping. But it was not enough. To her journal she confided a "soul-annihilating flux of fear. . . . The groaning inner voice: you can't teach, can't do anything. Can't write, can't think." But she vowed to fight "from day to day" to be a better teacher. She realized her quest for perfection was a "murdering" self, an inner demon demanding a "paragon." William Sheldon could have told her that she was on the right track: "When a person has lifted his Promethean conflict well up into full consciousness, and has insight into his own temperamental quality of mind, he is well insured against the chaotic inner doubt which is often so characteristic of middle life." It was not so easy for Plath, of course, but she did go on, closer to her middle life than she could have imagined. Why Ruth Beuscher recommended Sheldon to her becomes obvious in what she now wrote in her journal: "I have a choice: to flee from life and ruin myself forever because I can't be perfect right away, without pain & failure, and to face life on my own terms & make the best of the job." She did not hide her pain and failure, admitting to Lynn Lawner, now at Cambridge experiencing a dark Plathian period, that she had been "going through a black spell" after her fifth week of teaching three sections of freshman English.

Ted Hughes was doing no better and subject to the same manic-depressive cycles that plagued Plath. "I sit for hours like the statue of a man writing," he confided to Lucas Myers. He had "never known it so hard to write. I have never, of course, tried to write before." Writing had just come to him, as Sylvia had noticed with some envy. He already felt like a shipped-out convict: "Two years will be our stretch in America." Smith held no interest for him—not even the young women, whom he dismissed as "Chromium dianas," one about the same as the other. The highlight for him was his debut (a reading and reception) at The Poetry Center in New York to celebrate the publication of *The Hawk in the Rain*, but he was disappointed that none of the big names in poetry showed up. So far America did not deliver on the great big welcome that Sylvia had forecast, although she said they were "terrifically excited" about all his positive reviews.

Both poets stalled as Sylvia identified the crux of her problem, explaining to her mother that she could not confide in her Smith colleagues and say "how I begrudge not sitting and working at my real trade, writing, which would certainly improve rapidly if I gave it the nervous energy I squander on my classes." In fact, at least one faculty member would have understood. Newton Arvin, one of Smith's most prized professors—author of renowned biographies of Hawthorne and Melville—had spent decades regretting the time spent in the classroom that he should have spent writing.[42] Sylvia had taken his course on Hawthorne and Melville in her senior year, and he had written a recommendation for her when she applied to graduate school, noting that in his thirty years at Smith he had never taught a better student. [MGL] The retiring Arvin, who kept his life as a gay man hidden, would have been a difficult colleague to befriend, even though Sylvia would work as his paper grader. But they both functioned in an environment that had a narrowing impact, making it impossible for them to fully reveal themselves. It was still a culture of reticence with a kind of formality that few could breach—unless you were someone like Alfred Kazin, an independent critic, picking up a check but not committed to the institution or concerned about what colleagues thought of you. In short, like Arvin, Plath had to watch herself carefully and observe the conventions that Ted scorned but had to put up with for the sake of his spouse.

Did Plath even know that Arvin was gay? In her journal, she notes a supper with Arvin and Ned Spofford, both of whom would be involved in a scandal that led to their prosecution a few years later. She described them as a couple but made no comment other than this vivid description: "Newton Arvin, bright, balding, a strange, quirked lovely man, pink, in his brown suit, & classical Ned Spofford with his thin responsive face, black Indian-short crew-cut and black sparking eyes, pale, pointed face, giving out light, and his hawk-hooked nose." But women were not a part of their circle, and only a few male professors—Daniel Aaron and Albert Fisher—were aware of their friends' sexual proclivities. An entry in Plath's journal suggests she had no inkling, listening to her friend Ellie with "idle curiosity to hear about how these queer people live—lesbians & homosexuals—I couldn't care less."

Arvin, in fact, was still married then, and his "big, placid" wife did not appeal to Sylvia. She enjoyed his lectures, even when he seemed to get a little lost. She did not mention his mental breakdowns and apparently did not know that it was sometimes an agony for him to teach, the same agony, in fact, that she had experienced in her first weeks at Smith. She seemed comforted by his presence and mentioned a department meeting without him that was like an "old lady's meeting." One of her descriptions of him, "eyes & mouth dry slits as on some carved rubicund mask," suggests that here was someone in hiding like herself. But Ted interfered with her perception of the man: "Ted does not like Arvin: I sense an acrid repulsion between the two men—he senses a lizard, snakiness & I, half-caught in this vision, see Arvin: dry, fingering his key-ring compulsively in class, bright hard eyes red-rimmed, turned cruel, lecherous, hypnotic & holding me caught like the gnome Loerke held."[43] In her second semester of teaching, he disappointed her by reading from notes of lectures she had heard in 1954, her last year at Smith. Arvin later invited her and Ted to Yaddo, the writer's colony, but they do not seem to have had any more contact with him. Sylvia never knew about the strain on Arvin, even though they socialized, or that he had attempted suicide twice and had been treated with a dozen electric shock treatments. Elizabeth Drew, alone among his colleagues, sensed the "fullness of Arvin's futility," according to Arvin's biographer.

The hidebound 1950s made the link that might have been forged between Plath and Arvin virtually impossible. She called life on the Smith campus "airless." Sylvia and Ted had already thought about decamping to Boston after her year of teaching. She felt oppressed at playing the "returned and inadequate heroine of the Smith campus," she wrote to Warren. She did not want to teach about novels but to write them, and teaching was getting in the way.

Through much of the first semester at Smith, Plath felt "deathly nervous," she confided to Warren and in a "cold twitch" in early November when colleagues began visiting her classes. She was apparently a better teacher than she let on, and had heard she would be invited to stay another year at Smith with a promotion. But she had already fallen in with Ted's belief that they could never be "tame campus poets," as she put it to her brother in a late November letter. She continued to think ahead to a year in Boston devoted solely to writing poems, stories, and a novel. The prospect scared her more than she would admit to anyone. She had spent most of her life bound to an academic schedule that gave her a structure. Now she would have to create her own, and stand on her own, vowing not to complain to Ted or share her anxieties, no matter how comforting it might be to confess her misery. Professors like Newton Arvin did not dare to leave Smith, even though he did not think that much of Smith students and longed to be alone with his writing. Arvin's fate—decades of a sinecure—would stale her creativity. The prospect of getting away from campus life seemed to galvanize Ted, bringing him out of a dry spell with several good poems.

46

In early January 1958, an elated Plath told her "sorry and surprised" department chair that she would not be returning the following year. In spite of a cold and "battle fatigue," she expected to delight in her last semester of teaching, knowing it was her last, as she prepared to teach *Crime and Punishment*. Not only was Ted in good form writing poetry but they could now save money for the next year in Boston, since he had secured a one-semester teaching job in Amherst at the University of Massachusetts. She knew she was in for it as soon as she decamped from the Smith campus, observing in a January 4, 1958, journal entry: "It will take months to get my inner world peopled, and the people moving. How else to do it but plunge out of this safe scheduled time-clock wage-check world into my own voids. . . . I dream too much of fame, posturings, a novel published." But the alternative, staying at Smith—as her colleagues wished—would be a kind of relapse: "How I can go, meeting & exorcising my own ghosts here!" she exclaimed in her journal. Yet she felt relaxed enough to appreciate her classes: "I do feel I am building up a pretty good relation with most of my students and am feeling some rather well-placed conceit as one of the more favored of the freshman English teachers. They are really good girls."[44]

47

How much of his interior life Ted shared with Sylvia is hard to gauge. Certainly his critical views of England (repressive) and America (opportunistic) did not make their way into her letters or her journal. This man was biding his time, wishing to travel abroad but unwilling to essay the life of an exile. Sylvia never seems to have shared with anyone how she came to terms with his rejection of her homeland—perhaps because she was moving away from it herself as she revolved in his orbit. She had supposed he would conquer the new land and that, in turn, it would conquer him, and they would stay, with periodic trips abroad. Now she could see

ahead no more than the year in Boston. The flatness of his prose suggests his lack of enthusiasm: "The truth is, that I have taken a job. As a
teacher," he wrote to Lucas Myers. "I am a little weary of this place—New
England—and work at my life here as one takes satisfaction in walking with
a lame leg." None of that sour attitude can be found in Sylvia's letters to
his mother. "I shall not quickly be caught in a small American town again,"
he vowed to his friend. He did rejoice, however, in her disenchantment
with Smith. "Now she sees what an utter kindergarten the whole place
is, and she is really a different person." Her journal of this period affirms
as much.

In one entry, she departs for Newton Arvin's lecture after the "sweat
and fury of the bed." Sometimes, she noted in her journal, quarreling
with Ted was like being in a Strindberg play. She watched the students
"spoiled faces, sweet faces, ugly faces," feeling some nostalgia for her "lost
Smith-teacher self." The college was already behind her. Does some of Ted's
brusque dismissal of people infect her journal, or is it just that she now had
no compunctions about letting loose? She describes an outing with the
Roches to see a film of *Pickwick Papers*. Paul: "adonis-boy looks lost, seedy,
coarse-pored with skin too-bright orange & seamed as if grease-paint were
cracking"; Clarissa: "blonde & sullen, her hair down, sheened metallic gilt
in the dim light." Sylvia revels in a "new sense of power & maturity growing
in me from coping with this job, & cooking & keeping house" that "puts
me far from the nervous insecure miserable idiot I was last September." The
faculty could not believe she would give up what she told Olwyn Hughes
was a good teaching schedule, "lively faculty," and "bright, eager" students, but the pressure of teaching great works was detrimental to creating
her own.

In a letter to Jane Baltzell, Sylvia reported teaching the drama she read at
Cambridge. Smith was a wonderful place to teach, so it was "with a double-
self very regretful that I resigned, although there was this pressure, as in
a high-grade aluminum cooker, for me to stay on. And on." But teaching
interfered with writing. Sylvia felt "much more partisan about Cambridge
than I ever did about Smith: it seems one of those primitively mystic places,
saturated with spirits of the past and whatever." She remembered the misery
of it, the "sodden slovenly weather," but still endowed it with the "light of
gone, very gone youth, or whatever." She was still trying to capture all that
in a novel but not getting very far with it.

Sylvia and Ted did a lot of socializing in their last months at Smith. She
took an art class, but no one—not even new friends like Paul and Clarissa
Roche—seemed to satisfy, although Sylvia would draw closer to Clarissa on

her return with Ted to England. The parties loosened Sylvia up, but it was the future away from the classroom that riveted her attention.

48

In late February 1958, Plath seemed in an especially transitional mood, looking ahead to going away from "this glass-fronted, girl-studded and collegiate town." At the same time, the images of what she called her cocooned childhood appeared in her journal:

> every casual wooden monkey-carving, every pane of orange-and-purple nubbled glass on my grandmother's stair-landing window, every white hexagonal bathroom tile found by Warren & me on our way digging to China, becomes radiant, magnetic, sucking meaning to it and shining with strange significance: unriddle the riddle: why is every doll's shoelace a revelation? Every wishing-box dream an annunciation? Because these are the sunk relics of my lost selves that I must weave, word-wise, into future fabrics.

There was no precise model for what she wanted to become. She envisioned "taking my place beside Ruth Beuscher & Doris Krook in theirs—neither psychologist-priestess nor philosopher-teacher but a blending of both rich vocations in my own worded world." It is as if in such journal entries, she was trying to build a platform for her future, which would include the suffering and conflict that William Sheldon said were integral to the ambitions of the Promethean personality: "I shiver in a preview of the pain & the terror of childbirth, but it will come & I live through it." But Ted remained an inspiration: "I am married to a poet: miracle of my green age. Where breathes in the same body, a poet and a proper man, but in Ted?"

In rejecting Smith (her colleagues thought of it that way), she was following the path that Alfred Fisher's second wife, Helen Eustis (1916–2015), had taken, later writing a novel, *The Horizontal Man* (1946), which Sylvia had read.[45] The novel reveals why a woman or man of Plath's temperament might find Smith insufferable. Eustis had been just one of Fisher's Smith students that he had married. Charles Finch's Foreword to the Library of America edition of *The Horizontal Man* (1947) points out how Eustis "anatomizes the varieties of complacent self-satisfaction, anxious ambition, and feverish neurosis found on that kind of campus." If Eustis ever read Plath's journals, she would have discovered a kindred spirit. One of

Eustis's characters, reminiscent of Newton Arvin, dreads the "grinding efforts of talking to students, chattering with imbecile colleagues, lecturing to classes." Hungerford, like Arvin, is a writer of great talent and yet has stifled himself in college routines. He forms an attachment to a younger colleague, Kevin Boyle, urging him in "deadly earnest": "You must get away from here. . . . If you want to be a poet, you must not stay. You will be wrung dry." Boyle replies: "I'll stay yet a while. I've nothing to lose, and three square meals a day plus a pleasant life to gain." The bluff Boyle hides his doubt, and the result is that he loses his life when his head is bashed in with a fireplace poker. Plath had picked up on the tensions between faculty members, the veiled animosity, that disturbed her and that as a junior faculty member she could not discuss. She saw the menace that might otherwise be attributed to her own paranoia. A February 10, 1958, journal entry: "weary, depressed: am I getting a persecution-complex from Sears' & Bramwell's obvious snubs, Monas's knowing mock-deferent looks? so that when Tony Hecht rattled off: 'O-you-energetic-girl-coming-to-campus-when-you-don't-have-classes' with a pale monkey-sneer I took it as calculated mockery? The second time he said it: once or twice too many."

Was Plath wrong to suppose that Anthony Hecht's condescension—from a fellow poet no less—was meant to put her in her place? Hecht's biographer, David Yezzi, reveals that Hecht regarded Plath as self-absorbed. He later rejected her "confessional" brand of poetry, never realizing, it seems, how much they had in common in their obsession with the Holocaust. Like Plath, he would leave Smith, rejecting an atmosphere that stifled him as a poet.[46]

Near the end of her teaching year, her yearning for a larger life became overwhelming. She had underlined why in Sheldon's book:

> At moments there comes to perhaps every human being a well nigh painful sense of the nearness of richer and broader human happiness. We deeply feel that some relentless, invisible, yet not quite insurmountable barrier bars the way to an inexpressibly better life. . . . But in a few minds, it becomes a dominant mood as the hour of the splendid urge. Another always calls it the voice of Prometheus, and minds in which it is dominant he calls Promethean minds.

In this poetic passage "he" is identified only as a "voice" continually whispering, "No, this is not good enough, there is somewhere something better." Plath underlined Sheldon's Shelleyan declaration: "One mind develops where many merely adapt to circumstance." Sylvia wrote to her mother,

Shelley statue near the Elan Visitor Center, Elan Village, Wales.

who spent a lifetime tied to teaching jobs: "Now that I write 'March' it seems close to real spring and liberation."

49

Her novel continued to bedevil her: "So this American girl comes to Cambridge to find herself. To be herself. She stays a year, goes through Great Depression in winter." She planned to include scenes in Paris and Rome in which the American girl "runs through several men—a femme fatale in her way." Sylvia named Richard Sassoon and Gordon Lameyer as candidates for characters, but also "stolid Yale man critic Kraut-head Gary Haupt," a Yale graduate and Fulbright student she had seen "a great deal of" at Cambridge. He had made an initial good impression, she reported to her mother: "my most analytical and intelligent friend from Yale," who had "offered to do an hour of Rilke a week with me!" She noted in her diary his calming influence. Later, in a letter to her mother, she called him "sweet, if pedantic." He had seen her through "a rather traumatic experience yesterday at the casualty ward of Addenbrooks Hospital." A cinder had to be surgically removed from her eye, and later in a poem, "The Eye-mote," she feared she would be "Blind to what will be and what was / I dream that I am Oedipus." Gary was there to entertain her, reading from James Thurber. In another journal entry she called him "distressingly pedantic." Yet in Paris he had suddenly appeared during her agony over Richard Sassoon. She described Haupt as "blond blue-eyed solid"—a contrast to the effete, "sickly" Sassoon. She "fell upon" Haupt with "cries of joy," being "so grateful for his simple presence & friendly escort, after wielding off men as dusk came." He remained a recurring character in her novel, essential to her creations of the "time & space of Cambridge." She dreamed about him: "refusing to speak and passing by with a stiff accusing and sallow face as if he smelt something bad."

Something about Gary Haupt triggered her and tied him to her own ups and downs. Did she know he was manic-depressive? It would seem so, given a cryptic calendar diary reference on March 16, 1956, to "mill race talk." Did they discuss the ending of *The Mill on the Floss*, in which Maggie Tulliver and her brother Tom drown, reconciled at the last moment in an embrace, fulfilling the novel's Biblical epigraph: "In their death, they were not divided." The brother and sister bond is fraught with tension that may have reminded Plath and Haupt of their clashes of temperament, their conflicts and reconciliations. On March 19, she would mention in her calendar diary a quarrel with Haupt. Later, in June of 1956, she noted receiving a "nasty letter" from him. Yet in September 1958, she wrote to Dorothea Krook about her visit to the States: "Did you have the opportunity to see Gary Haupt at Yale on your visit here? I know he was a great admirer of yours and a fine student in his own right. How is he, and how is his career progressing?"

Haupt eventually taught at Memphis State University. An aide at the Tennessee Psychiatric Hospital and Institute in Memphis took care of him.[47] When the down part of Haupt's cycle "set in," the aide remembered, Haupt would

go into his room and laugh like a goat braying, but when he was lucid he was brilliant and insightful. He explained some of the meaning of the complexity of Faulkner's writing to me quite well and we also talked about Shakespeare. I liked him very much. A few years after I knew him [1979] I was saddened to read in the paper that he took his life by jumping out of the 6th floor window of a hotel room downtown.

Haupt never mentioned Sylvia Plath. The aide remembered him saying "I am the most distinguished professor in the history of Memphis State. . . . And he would say this in a kind of frustrated manner as if he was unappreciated." Is that how Sylvia made him feel? Unappreciated? Is that part of what she meant by his pedantry, his Kraut-headedness? Ted would make a point of telling his parents about Sylvia's German ancestry, and it is possible

that in Gary Haupt she saw the brotherly but dogmatic side of her sensibility, an authority figure she both admired and abjured, who expressed the
dictatorial strain in "Daddy" that she would send up.

Cambridge and life abroad with Ted Hughes had broken the Smith College spell, the parade of learning that Gary Haupt evidently represented, the
Kraut-head hierarchy of higher education, exacerbated by the experience of
teaching and abetted by Ted's own feeling of being trapped in the classroom.
She wondered if the move to Boston would be any better. "What is it that
teaching kills? The juice, the sap—the substance of revelation: by making
even the insoluble questions & multiple possible answers take on the granite
assured stance of dogma." She felt a "forcing to formula the great visions, the
great collocations and cadences of words and meanings." She would need
more energy than she had to be creative as a teacher. "America wears me,
wearies me. I am sick of the Cape, sick of Wellesley: all America seems one
line of cars, moving, with people jammed in them, from one-gas-station
to one diner and so on." She longed for the moors and the Spanish Medi-
terranean, the "old history-crusted & still gracious, spacious cities; Paris,
Rome." Was she reading too much into her description of Alfred Kazin,
a dinner guest: "broken, embittered & unhappy: greying, his resonance
diminished." What had happened to the Promethean who had set himself
apart from other faculty members and most students and inspired her? At
the same time, Ted was going through what looked like a psychosomatic
disorder manifested in his pale and "raggle-haired" appearance, coughing
and sweating and nauseated. She was falling apart physically with fatigue.
Her nails were "splitting and chipping. A bad sign." It all sounded rather
like an O'Neill drama, a strange interlude indeed—wrestling through "slick
shellacked façades to the real shapes and smells and meanings behind the
masks." Her chronic fatigue and anxiety were, according to Sheldon, signs
of the "disorientation" that "prevails into middle life."

The Sylvia Plath who delighted in recording every hour of her Smith
student days now wrote: "O how my own life shines, beckons, as if I were
caught, revolving, on a wheel, locked in the steel-toothed jaws of my schedule." Newton Arvin made her point for her when she heard him deliver the
same lecture on *Mardi* she had heard four years ago. She cut his next class
and asked herself "why not?" Quarreling with Ted had turned her life into
the Strindberg plays she was now teaching. One of her dreams at Smith
evokes the murderous atmosphere of *The Horizontal Man*: "Deep sleep
last night and queer nightmares—fragmented rememberings at breakfast:
of Newton Arvin: withered, mysterious, villainous."[48] Another nightmare
featured Joan of Arc's face "as she feels the fire and the world blurs out in a
smoke, a pall of horror." [PJ]

Sylvia recovered her good spirits by writing poems about the work of painters. In a March 22, 1958, letter to her mother, she included two poems inspired by Paul Klee, "Battle-Scene from the Comic Operatic Fantasy *The Seafarer*" and "Departure of the Ghost." Both brought back her childhood delight in art, to what the latter work calls the "Point of Eden" and children's dreams: "To the loud-cuckoo land of color wheels"—which she had first played with as a twelve-year-old in school. A poignant, lyrical Wordsworthian child is father of the man spirit inhabits the poem. Eight more poems followed in quick succession.

After weeks of worry about her writing and weary of teaching, she had broken through with Ted's help. He was "right, infallibly, when he criticizes my poems & suggests, here, there, the right word." The spurt of creativity resulted in her claim to the throne:

I think I have written lines which qualify me to be The Poetess of America (as Ted will be The Poet of England and her dominions). Who rivals? Well, in history—Sappho, Elizabeth Barrett Browning, Christina Rossetti, Amy Lowell, Emily Dickinson, Edna St. Vincent Millay—all dead. Now: Edith Sitwell & Marianne Moore, the ageing giantesses & poetic godmothers. Phyllis McGinley is out—light verse: she's sold herself. Rather: May Swenson, Isabella Gardner, & most close, Adrienne Cecile Rich—who will soon be eclipsed by these eight poems: I am eager, chafing, sure of my gift, wanting only to train & teach it—I'll count the magazines & money I break open by these best eight poems from now on. We'll see.

Ted wrote to Olwyn Hughes in late March ratifying Sylvia's achievement. She was in an ecstasy of creation, writing twelve hours "at a stretch . . . too excited to sleep," in a manic, Promethean outpouring.

"The Disquieting Muses," one of those eight poems written in eight manic days, has been given much attention in discussions of her poetry and biography[49] as one of the markers of her incipient greatness. It is also a harrowing upheaval of her childhood, of the wonder world she had created in her earliest diaries about building snow caves and huts, playing games, excelling in school with well-drawn maps of American history, taking field trips to plays and museums, and, always, with her mother hovering around Sylvia's joyous times, telling her stories, reading to her and Warren, working at every moment, it seemed, to make her children's world worthwhile. The poem supposes the mother has contrived a realm that excludes the "illbred aunt" and the "unsightly cousin" who are not invited to the child's christening. When the hurricane comes, the mother teaches her two children to chant: "Thor is angry" but "we don't care!" Shifting to adolescence, the scene of a dance pictures the schoolgirl "heavy-footed," standing aside "In the shadow cast by my dismal-headed / Godmothers." Mentioned too are piano lessons and the daughter's technique: "each teacher found my touch / Oddly wooden in spite of scales / And the hours of practicing." This mother world is rebuked by what the daughter learns "elsewhere, / From muses unhired by you, dear mother." The mother's "soap bubble" existence is evanescent as her daughter is brought back to earth. But these are the words of a poem not to be shared with "Mother, mother," in the many letters Sylvia sent home perpetuating her mother's fantasy: "no frown of mine," the poem ends, "will betray the company I keep."

Aurelia read "The Disquieting Muses" and was hurt, pointing out after her daughter's death that some of the experiences in the poem, like the heavy-footed dancer, were actually her own and that in fact Sylvia enjoyed playing the piano. The daughter may well be revising history so far as her mother is concerned, since Sylvia's meticulously kept diaries reveal not the slightest resistance to those piano lessons or to her mother's presence.

The poem may also be about the poet's rejection of the world restricted for her not only in childhood but at Smith as well. While "The Disquieting Muses" is full of a pent-up anger about the prevarications of a parent about the nature of the world, the poem also reveals the dualism Plath had to practice at Smith, displaying the pleasant and academically proper mien while behind the mask she seethed as faculty members observed her classes. The restraints Smith put on her person were another form of in loco parentis that infantilized faculty and students alike—as Ted liked to point out to her.

Sylvia mined her life and that of others for symbolic purposes—in this case also drawing on Giorgio de Chirico's painting with the same title and on the three witches in *Macbeth*, who appear as "three ladies / Nodding by night around my bed, / Mouthless, eyeless, with stitched bald head,"[50] and not as the witches the poem's mother bakes into gingerbread. The poem is a declaration of independence against the tyranny of good intentions. Edward Butscher deems "The Disquieting Muses" the birth of Plath's "artist self."

That birth of the artist's self seems connected to the recognition of evil that is shielded from the child, and to Sylvia's crucial decision to forsake the security of Smith. She is Sheldon's Prometheus "penetrator of the future who, heedless of his own world of present comfort, eternally yearns to discover new knowledge." The journal of her last few months at the college is relentlessly fixated on her future and how it is not to be bound by the protocols of institutions like Smith. She sensed the resentment of certain faculty members when she announced, with some anxiety, her decision to leave, which for some of them was like forsaking Eden, complete with its own Paradise Pond. Why not just write in the summers, was the "patronizing tone of George Gibian." [PJ] Plath marked out the following passage in Sheldon about the Promethean quest for knowledge, calling it "lovely": "In so doing he [Prometheus] eternally endures the resentment of the other side of the mind, projected as the righteous hatred of the gods, who have always seemed a little unreasonable about the tree of knowledge." The mind in conflict with itself becomes, in "The Disquieting Muses," the poem in conflict with how the self has been nurtured to evade the Promethean quest by doing what the gods—the powers that be—command.

Ted Hughes deserves the crucial credit for turning Sylvia Plath so resolutely toward a Promethean path. He had stood aloof, alone, in all manner of circumstances—at Cambridge, in London, now in Northampton, never conceding anything to institutional imperatives, always intent on developing his own voice. Even initial skeptics, like Mrs. Prouty, had been won over. Sylvia proudly reported her mentor's response to Ted's public reading of his poetry. In "loud clear tones," she declared, "Isn't Ted wonderful?!" It is one thing to talk your principles, another to actually embody them and bring the world along with you. That is what Ted Hughes had done, and his impact on Sylvia Plath was profound. He really did not care what others thought. She counted on "Ted's being himself, and me, one hopes, my own self." [PJ] He was his own authority, and that is precisely the power she sought for herself. He did not want to be pampered and cosseted but was also quite willing to perform such functions for his wife. She desired and he delivered a full measure of devotion without ever compromising himself—or so she believed. In fact, as he would later admit, after about two years of marriage, he had begun to fake it and to feel the strain of perpetuating her heroic image of him. How much he really felt this inauthenticity is hard to say and probably would have been difficult for him to articulate then. Only in retrospect would the next three years seem to him a struggle to maintain the Promethean pitch that Plath prized.

Ted did have his moments of pique, objecting to the way Sylvia dressed him up. They quarreled when he discovered she had thrown out some old clothes and cuff links. They both went out to sulk. She spotted him in Childs Park, and she recorded in her journal the result: "He paused, stared, and if he weren't my husband I would have run from him as a killer." This passing remark led to nothing and did not linger, evidently, since the same day they went out to an amicable dinner. Perhaps it was Sylvia's notion to title a book of poems *Full Fathom Five*; that is the origin of Ted's belief, expressed in *Birthday Letters*, that she had imprisoned him in her mythology as the "buried male muse & god-creator risen to be my mate in Ted." [PJ]

50

The manic energy that had produced eight good poems now gave way to lethargy as Sylvia's dreams would not let go of the hold that schooling had had on her for so long: "Felt, as usual, exhausted this morning & fell back into those horrid dreams of getting up to make a school deadline, waking up & being still in the dream & it being still later." [PJ] She treated Ted as the antidote to her anxieties and depressions: "This is the man the unsatisfied ladies scan the stories in the Ladies' Home Journal for, the man women read romantic women's novels for." Other men bored her with their "partialness." But how to make him in her novel sound "special" without sentimentality? She summed up her departure from Smith, her unfulfilled novel, and herself as "between two worlds, one dead, the other dying to be born."[51] For the first time, Sylvia noted in her journal that her mother's own insecurities made Aurelia fearful of their decision to renounce teaching and rely on their writing to support themselves.

In a May 14, 1958, journal entry, Sylvia referred to her "highstrung depression." It seems to be another way of describing manic depression. What excited this description? What she felt seems of a piece with Sheldon's account of the swing of feelings in the transition from the early to the middle years, from in Plath's words her "five-year distinct adolescent success in writing" and her "hamstrung" present, with nothing to show "but a handful of poems." She was hung up on what Sheldon posited as the arc between the Promethean sensibility and the "waster," the type of person who expends too much of himself in his emotions: "After the flush of youth is gone, either his appetite or his materials are forever giving out, and the waster then pays for the upper euphorial range of his cycle with recurrent periods of profound depression and frustration. His life is an alternation of extremes. In mental pathology he tends to become the *manic-depressive* of the psychiatrists." That last sentence encapsulates Sheldon's own straddle of the psychological and mythological binary of his book, which describes the conflicts inside and outside of individuals, between the Promethean and the Waster, as both psychological and sociological phenomena. At precisely this point in her journal, Sylvia was working out this conflict between herself and other selves—notably in her criticism of the Roches, whom she treated as characters in a novel, wondering what roles they were playing. Paul seemed a fraud doing bogus translations relying on a lexicon and the translations of others, and Clarissa, sulky and sociable, exhibited different personas that resembled the shifting affects of O'Neill characters. Interacting with the Roches became a study: "We go to see them to learn more—to 'place' them for they have places, queer, but none-theless, places."

Then came the famous blowup, preceded by this curious passage in her journal, in late May 1958, calling Ted a "liar and a vain smiler," like herself. "I confided my faith in Ted and why is the wife the last to see her husband's ulcer?" Because of "blind faith," she answered. She had been waiting for him to meet her after that last class she would teach at Smith, and he had not shown up. Then, walking out of the library, she had "one of those intuitive visions. I knew what I would see": Ted "coming up the road from Paradise Pond where girls take their boys to neck on weekends." He was smiling, broadly and intensely, in the company of a doe-eyed "strange girl," who appeared to Sylvia in "several sharp flashes, like blows." The girl ran away when she saw Sylvia, and Ted professed innocence: "He thought her name was Sheila; once he thought my name was Shirley. . . . I am no smiler anymore. But Ted is." What set Sylvia off was the look of adoration in the girl's eyes, and how Ted happily absorbed it. She saw she was not so special. Ted could bestow himself on other women. Sylvia had witnessed Ted's dalliance—for that is what she projected into the scene—even as she was thinking about how Albert Fisher had gone through generations of Smith girls as mistresses and wives. She grouped Fisher, Richard Sassoon, and Ted together: all had the "brand of male vanity." She rejected his excuses but refused to contemplate jumping out of a window, or driving into a tree, or

Paradise Pond, where Plath saw Hughes walking with another woman.

filling a garage with carbon monoxide, or slitting her wrists. Instead, she would maintain her integrity and dignity. She wondered how she could trust Ted.

It took three weeks before Sylvia could write in her journal about a physical fight resulting in her sprained thumb and Ted's "bloody claw-marks." But: "Air cleared. We are intact. And nothing—no wishes for money, children, security, even total possession—nothing is worth jeopardizing what I have which is so much the angels might well envy it." She wrote to Warren, turning her diatribe against Ted into quite a different sort of fiction:

> Oh we have rousing battles every so often in which I come out with sprained thumbs & Ted with missing earlobes, but we feel so perfectly at one with our work & reactions to life & people that we make our own world to work in which isn't dependent on anyone else's love or admiration, but self-contained: our best pleasure is writing at home, eating & talking & walking in woods to look for animals & birds.

The myth of self-containment proved hard to relinquish and would require a retreat from Paradise Pond to Boston. "I like Boston as much as any city I've been in," Ted wrote to Olwyn Hughes sometime in June 1958. He believed Sylvia was making advances in her poetry.

In her letter to Warren, Sylvia enclosed a poem, "Mussel-Hunter at Rock Harbor," an account of fiddler crabs she and Ted had used for fish bait the previous summer on the Cape. She wanted Warren, an innovator in theoretical and computational linguistics, to tell her if he found "anything inaccurate about the crabs" and explained that the poem was written in "'syllabic verse,' measuring lines not by heavy & light stresses, but by the number of syllables, which here is 7," which gave the poem a "speaking illusion of freedom (which the measured stress doesn't have) as stresses vary freely." This technical information seemed her way of showing her brother that she, too, worked with "strict form," a kind of precision that could be called scientific. Warren loved puns and word play, and like Sylvia had a "lifelong fascination with the natural world."[52] She would often voice in her letters the hope that Ted and Warren would become close, although they never fulfilled her expectations.

The poem has a deceiving slackness quite unlike her usual careful, polished formalism. It is easy to picture a scene that as a child she could easily have experienced with Warren: "I'd come for / free fish-bait: the blue mussels / clumped like bulbs at the grass-root / margin of the tidal pools." It is a beautiful, exquisitely observed performance, centered on a Columbus crab

"Intact, strangely strayed above / His world of mud . . . no telling if he'd / died recluse of suicide." This entrancing look into a world "absolutely alien" to human thought nonetheless spoke to Sylvia as she thought it would speak to Warren, remembering their earliest days by the sea that she associated with her own nativity. The poem is presented to Warren with an invigorating freshness, with so much for him to observe and savor—a rare gift from his sister that is perhaps why he never felt able to share their intimacy with an inquiring world. Such poems were for *him*, and what others made of them would not be his concern. Sylvia had also strayed far from the sea and had also been beached like the "headstrong Columbus crab," finding herself facing, like Columbus, a new world, or looking for one, as children do. How much Warren, as much of an innovator as his sister, relished this poem we will probably never know.

And what did Warren make of the reference to suicide, and the poem's identification of the speaker with the "headstrong Columbus crab?" Far from her earliest years with Warren in Winthrop, Sylvia had crawled into the space beneath her Wellesley house to die, and Warren had crawled inside that dark place and brought her back into the light. "To survive a suicide attempt is to be alive in a different way from everyone else," observes Plath biographer Ronald Hayman. That different way is manifest in "Mussel-Hunter at Rock Harbor," in which a creature is given a human name and even motivations—at least as a matter to muse upon. Sylvia wanted to get the scientific observation of the scene right for Warren even as she wrote of grass that can grow claws, drawing Warren back, perhaps, into the child's imaginative effort to comprehend nature.

Did the letter and poem arise out of what Sylvia wrote in her journal on June 20, 1958: "It is as if my life were magically run by two electric currents: joyous positive and despairing negative—which ever is running at the moment dominates my life, floods it." Warren, her playmate and witness, had seen as much. She had begun her letter: "It was fine to get your good letter. I am so happy you are coming home in only two months. Life here has been such a holocaust that I lost all sense of timing and have been a frightful letter writer as my work began to go round faster & faster like a merrygoround . . . I realize, as I start to write, how many letters I've written you in my head & how much I've missed you. There are so very few people in the world I really care about, & I guess you and Ted are the closest of all." And she ended her letter: "Don't follow my example: write soon! And I promise to answer." What was Warren to her that she wanted to hold him close? I think he provided a perspective and even a kind of serenity that she counted on when despair began to drown her. Toward the end of her life, she ached for him—or even a simulacrum of him in the form of his new wife—to bolster her when Ted bolted. So she wrote Warren, and in her journal expressed a "longing to revisit my first hometown: Winthrop."

51

Now she found herself on the brink of what she had wished for: fourteen months of freedom to write unhampered by a lifetime of scheduling her school days. The very expansiveness of this time paralyzed her. It was not so different from her depression after that heady *Mademoiselle* month in New York City. She had to "make up my demands" and produce a book without the option of blaming outer forces for delaying her. She vowed not to resort to that other way of putting off the payload of poetry and fiction by waylaying herself with a baby. [PJ]

Her first *New Yorker* acceptance on June 25, 1958, propelled her out of her funk. She shared the "VERY GOOD NEWS" with her mother, although without the customary salutation: "dearest mother." Sylvia felt her decision to live by her writing had been vindicated. The long poem and another, "Nocturne," would bring in something like $350, paying for three months rent in Boston. It was also "well over 3 times as much money as I got for half a year of drudgery in that American lit course, correcting exams, and well over a month's salary for a week's work of pure joy." Take that, mother! Mrs. Prouty also received the good news—and Warren, who she hoped would visit them in September at the Beacon Hill apartment: "I feel we should get to know each other again, we've been abroad so much!" To Olwyn Hughes, Sylvia wrote: "Our Boston apartment is minute, but aesthetically fine with its light, air, quiet & superb view. The city is a delight to walk in."

"Nocturne," set on the moors, complements "Mussel-Hunter at Rock Harbor" in setting human consciousness against the elements of nature: "The whole landscape / Loomed absolute as the antique world was / Once in its earliest sway of lymph and sap, / Unaltered by eyes." The woman dwelling on this purity of existence thinks it is enough to "snuff the quick / of her small heat out," and so she turns back before the "stones and hills of stones could break / Her down to mere quartz grit in that stony light." The poem speaks to Sylvia's desire to decommission all the paraphernalia of her past life and approach an uncontaminated state—though she, like the woman in the poem, "turned back"—reverting to the person she could not escape.

The other side of Sylvia Plath remained political: "Tell us more about deGaulle," she wrote on June 30, 1958, to Olwyn Hughes (working in Paris).

That kind of news almost never interested Ted, even if Sylvia included him in "us." She was the poet who wrote journalism, attended political talks, sailed with Anthony Wedgwood Benn, and worried about who her more conservative mother would vote for. The state of the world, like the state of nature, shaped her moods and outlook. The full historical dimension of her poetry had yet to emerge, although it was there, in embryo, in poems such as "Bitter Strawberries."

In letters to family, Sylvia promoted the idea that poetry would sustain the marriage economically and esthetically. She knew this was, to most people, a dubious proposition. In Sheldon's chapter titled "A Working Picture of the Mind," she underlined his observation that the "maturest and most developed minds frequently lack sufficient economic security to free energies for intellectual pursuits." This is how "matters are arranged," he concluded, and that is what the Promethean mind had to confront. The "maturing of a social culture," he argued, depended on "guaranteeing" a distribution of money to "more highly cultivated, responsible minds," yet "almost the opposite of this ideal actually prevails"—to which Plath replied in the book's left margin: "yes!"

Sheldon divided his working picture of the mind into five panels, the first being concerned with economics, with the "acquisition and possession of things with the wealth and property relations of a mind." Plath starred Sheldon's conception of what the possession of money meant psychologically: "a release from the necessity of expending energy in the pursuit of basic wants." Plath's emphasis on homemaking, including cooking, indicated, of course, her enjoyment of such activities, but also her belief that it sustained her own idea of property and material existence. She wrote Warren that Ted's royalties from his book and her sale of poems to the *New Yorker* had netted over $2,000. Aurelia also received accounts of how poetry paid.

Sheldon's second panel had to do with the "political and social arrangements of society," with "social dominance and submission." Self-protection in the Sheldonian universe meant that Sylvia had to keep a lookout. She bracketed his acknowledgment: "[It is well known that the more intellectual and the kinder a personality becomes and the less concerned with its own protection it grows, the more threatening is the danger of exploitation at the hands of watchful opportunists. This is the source of the Promethean tragedy.]" Hence her careful sizing up of her contemporaries, her wariness of the competition, her wishing to hold her family in her carapace. Learning about De Gaulle was no idle matter in learning about the dominance/submission nexus of society. In her journal for July 4, 1958, she noted: "Independence day: how many people know from what they are free, by what they are imprisoned."

In letters to Ted's parents, Sylvia maintained what might almost be called the party line, repeating what she told Olwyn Hughes: "Ted & I both thrive while working at writing & nothing else." She mentioned how much Aurelia loved getting their letters and that her mother wanted to visit The Beacon someday. The family, for Plath, was a kind of polity that helped her govern and protect her own life. Otherwise she left herself vulnerable. So she put a star next to this underlined dictum: "in the case of individuals the sensitive and relatively fragile one is forever in danger of being caught out alone, and bullied or destroyed by a *gang* of less imaginative beings." That could happen even at Smith when she believed her colleagues were ganging up on her in an effort to keep her in place.

Ted wrote to Aurelia with a rare insight into what "poetry writing" was like for both of them: "bringing your style to unity with your experience. It would be easy if your experience weren't continually outgrowing itself. As it is one's style is always just a bit out of date." But he brought home the point that Sylvia was so eager to impress on her mother: "We are both about twice as industrious as were were at teaching, the way it should be."

Sylvia's journal told another story. She could not write, she could not sleep, and she recognized the symptoms—the same reaction in her "two months of hysteria" before beginning to teach at Smith. "My danger, partly, I think, is becoming too dependent on Ted. He is didactic, fanatic—this last I see most when we are with other people who can judge him in a more balanced way than I." She did better when he was "off for a bit," building on her "own inner life . . . without his continuous 'What are you thinking? What are you going to do now,'" which prompted her to "stop thinking and doing." She did not want to complain since she thought they were "amazingly compatible," but he kept giving her orders on what to read and how to read it. "His fanaticism & complete lack of balance & moderation is illustrated by his stiff neck got from his 'exercises'—which evidently are strenuous enough to disable him." This journal entry is instructive for those who have depicted Plath as the demanding one, never giving Ted enough space, enough freedom, to be himself. His dictatorial tendencies later informed the denunciations in "Daddy." But it would be a mistake to suppose that she thought of him as suppressing her. By virtually every measure he had enlarged her life and made her feel safer and more a part of the world. What she said to Warren in her July 9, 1958, letter seems to be true: "I am all for foreign relations: it is extremely pleasant to have extended my own affiliations & to feel I have also a permanent home in England, especially in such a beautiful moor-top place."

Without question their outings to observe nature and to nurture it brought Sylvia and Ted closer together. They lost a week of sleep tending to an injured baby bird before putting it out of its misery by gassing it in a box. She confided to Warren: "it was a shattering experience. Such a plucky little bit of bird. I can't forget it." She admitted in her journal that in the aftermath she clenched when she tried to write prose. She had fragments, character sketches, but could not drive the narrative forward, and the slump continued into August, although the appearance of "Mussel-Hunter at Rock Harbor" and the prospect of a "beach-week" on the Cape before they moved from Northampton to their Boston apartment cheered her.

52

The first days of the September 1958 move to Boston were exhilarating, as she vouchsafed to Elinor Friedman: "Now that we are here, in our minuscule & marvelously aesthetic two-room furnished flat, I don't know how I stood living in Northampton for a year. Nobody here has heard of Smith, or us, which is magnificent." Just looking out the window was expressive of the liberation she experienced: "We have an enormous view—the Charles river, sailboats, reflected lights from MIT—the moving stream of car lights on Riverside Drive—the hotels & neons—red, blue, green, yellow, above the city—the John Hancock building, weather tower—flashing—rooftops, chimneypots, gables—even the tree tops of the common from the bedroom." [PJ] The "richer and broader happiness" conceived in Sheldon's Promethean mind now seemed on the horizon.

53

Living with Ted Hughes still required adjustments and admonitions: "I would like to squander money on hair styling, clothes. Yet know power is in work and thought. The rest is pleasant frill. . . . No criticism or nagging. Shut eyes to dirty hair, ragged nails. He is a genius. I his wife." [PJ] This sounded noble, but was it necessary? Did Sylvia really need to deny herself the pleasures Ted thought were frivolous? He had no real conception of style outside of his own poetry. A good part of Sylvia Plath had to be put aside to please him and to convince herself she was a serious poet. She would burst out in her journals in asides that had no place in his frame of reference: "Liz Taylor is getting Eddie Fisher away from Debbie Reynolds who appears cherubic, round-faced, wronged, in pincurls and houserobe—Mike Todd barely cold. How odd these events affect one so. Why? Analogies?" [PJ]

Just then, at the approach of autumn, for all the exuberance of her letters, Sylvia confided to her journal: "we both bogged down in a black depression." They listened late at night to Beethoven and brooded. We know what bothered her: the absence of "twenty-five years of school routine," but what was up with Ted Hughes? He nagged her about writing exercises from his "superior seat," as she put it in her journal. But might the nagging also be a sign of his own upset? He never seems to have realized as much even as Sylvia wondered: "Do we, vampire-like, feed on each other?" This is what psychologist Kay Redfield Jamison calls "assortative coupling," when someone seeks a partner who also experiences manic-depressive cycles.[53] What, after all, was his obsessive physical and mental exercising about—other than to create a schedule of effort to control his anxieties, which multiplied away from his homeland, and which he suppressed by transforming his doubts into strictures for Plath.

Sylvia sent out letters to family that were like feel-good Hollywood press releases: "Dear Ted's mother & dad . . . Ted & I are both extremely happy here in Boston." His depression continued well into the rest of September 1958. On September 27, she wrote in her journal: "I diagnosed & Ted diagnosed my disease of doldrums—& I feel better." Ted, as you see, went undiagnosed: two "acrid fights" with Ted. "I feel his depression . . . only he is not articulate about it."

Sylvia could not tell what was behind Ted's moods, and perhaps he could not say himself or did not make the effort to do so. She was counting on him, the supposedly stronger one. Did that begin to distress the stalwart, hypnotizing hero? He could not let her down without jeopardizing the role she had destined him to play. In her journal, Sylvia lamented: "I am too ingrown—as if I no longer knew how to talk to anyone but Ted—sat with my face to a wall, a mirror." It was all on him. Aurelia could not help: "must keep clear of any confiding in mother: she is a source of Great Depression—a beacon of terrible warning," Sylvia admonished herself. And so Ted Hughes would later regard Aurelia in the struggle to control Sylvia's legacy.

54

Then Sylvia secured a part-time job in a psychiatric clinic at Massachusetts General. She typed cases of patients with paranoid delusions of various kinds involving family members, hideous violent dreams, obsessions with death, feelings of persecution, and rape fantasies. She believed "my objective daily view of troubled patients through the records objectifies my own view of myself." What that meant exactly, she did not say, but it can be supposed she gained some perspective on what worried her, realizing that her own afflictions could be managed.

At the same time, Sylvia resumed sessions with Ruth Beuscher. A December 12, 1958, journal entry recorded the results: "Better than shock treatment: 'I give you permission to hate your mother.'" Sylvia reacted as though a burden had been lifted and she could finally jettison the cocoon her mother had cosseted her in. Sylvia acknowledged her mother's "hard life: married a man with the pre-thirty jitters on her, who was older than her own mother." Aurelia hated Otto and treated the children as her salvation, projecting a happy future for them, making sure they had the best of everything she could afford. Aurelia's announcement of Otto's death was tantamount in Sylvia's mind to having killed the "only man who'd love me steady through life." She conceded her father was "an ogre. But I miss him. He was old but she married an old man to be my father. It was her fault. Damn her eyes."

But it wasn't old age that killed Otto. Did Sylvia in her anger forget that? He had stupidly neglected his health until it was too late. Sylvia's revisionist account of her childhood is startling when read against the exuberance of her teenage diaries. Nothing like this attack on the mother or yearning for the father appears in her entries. But the happiness she experienced, it seems, had been acquired at too great a price. Perhaps that is why she starred and underlined a passage in Sheldon about the few who "live more for the second than the first half of life. They are happier and stronger in old age than in youth. Their lives suggest the uneasy intuition that where youth is a disproportionately happy period, life is perhaps a great failure."

Sylvia's diatribe against her mother signaled her continuing effort to liberate herself: "I have done practically everything she said I couldn't do and be happy at the same time and here I am, almost happy." The "almost" was telling, since Sylvia could not quite beat back feeling guilty for not doing what her mother wanted. Sometimes Sylvia got so mad she wanted to strangle Aurelia. Instead she had "tried to murder myself: to keep from being an embarrassment to the ones I loved and from living myself in a mindless hell." She struggled to take her life back from her mother. In short: "She wants to be me: she wants me to be her: she wants to crawl into my stomach and be my baby and ride along. But I must go her way." Now the reasons for Sylvia's growing desire for children emerged: they would be part of her separation from her mother: "I'll have my own babies thank you. I'll have my own us and thank you."

If Sylvia said all this to Ruth Beuscher, or some version of same, Beuscher tried to slow down the Ted bandwagon, asking (as reported by Sylvia): "Would you have the guts. To admit you'd made a wrong choice?" Sylvia brushed past the question all too categorically, announcing she had made the right choice, delineating her husband's warmth, bigness, humor, stories, smell, with a body that seemed to have been made in the same shop as hers. All other men she found wanting. He was the epitome of her uncompromising search for the complete man. Nowhere in this encomium did she recur to her initial response to him: that he was thrilling, sure, but dangerous. The closest she came to it was her acknowledgment that her mother worried she was happy with "something so dangerous." Beuscher's contacts with Ted in Boston did not leave her with a favorable impression, even though, according to Sylvia, he supported her therapy sessions. Beuscher may well have held her fire, since, judging by Sylvia's journal, she was hardly prepared to listen to any dissent on the subject of Ted Hughes. As Sylvia noted, Beuscher "won't tell me what to do." The therapist said Sylvia would have to learn that by herself.

55

The major work of this period, "Johnny Panic and the Bible of Dreams," draws on Sylvia's own institutionalization and her recording of patients' dreams. She turned the story into a parable about the panic of existence: "Well, from where I sit, I figure the world is run by one thing and this one thing only. Panic with a dog-face, devil-face, hag-face, whore-face, panic in capital letters with no face at all—it's the same Johnny Panic, awake or asleep." The "from where I sit," is no throwaway. The narrator says she is working in a mental institution and has dedicated herself to surreptitiously copying *all* the dreams in the psychiatric clinic's files. By the end of the story, however, the Johnny Panic grapevine has alerted Johnny Panic's panicked "top priests," who take her into custody. The clinic Director calls her "Naughty naughty," as she tries to dodge the box, "copperhead-ugly . . . its coil of electric wires, the latest model in Johnny-Panic-Killers." This is the electric shock machine that kills the panic but is a killer in a broader sense as it infantilizes patients.

Modern psychiatry has been turned into a religion with "masked priests"—attendants and "votaries" engaging in a protest that is also a "devotional chant" expressing their contradictory mission: "The only thing to love is Fear itself. / Love of Fear is the beginning of wisdom. / The only thing to love is Fear itself. / May Fear and Fear and Fear be everywhere." FDR's famous declaration comes to mind: "the only thing we have to fear is . . . fear itself—nameless, unreasoning, unjustified terror which paralyzes needed efforts to convert retreat into advance." This call to action and courage, which Plath would have heard in her childhood, has been perverted in the grotesque communion of those who crucify their patients: "The crown of wire is placed on my head, the wafer of forgetfulness on my tongue." Electric shock results in memory loss, a short-circuiting that may be temporary but is an interruption nonetheless of brain function and control over one's own history. The narrator observes one patient leaving the institution: "The pure Panic-light had left his face. He went out of the office doomed to the crass fate these doctors call health and happiness."

The dreams in the story include those Sylvia recorded at Massachusetts General: the man who "dreams every night how he's lying on his back with a grain of sand on his chest" that "grows bigger and bigger till it's big as a fair sized house and he can't draw breath." This is the weight of an asphyxiating incarceration, or in another's dream: machines are running over or eating people. These dreams are absorbed into the narrator's "dream of dreams" of a "half-transparent lake" of people's minds trickling to "one borderless reservoir" and ending in the "sewage farm of the ages." Call it "Lake Nightmare, Bog of Madness." It's what happens when the narrator's dream is, in effect, everyone's dream.

The story breaks down the distinction between doctor and patient, positing a panic that is universal and familiar. The meaning of the word "Johnny" is manifold: a short hospital gown; a way of describing an unimportant person, a type; in Hebrew: God is gracious; an enemy: Johnny Reb; an affectionate diminutive (Johnny Appleseed); movies: *Johnny Eager* (1941), *Johnny Belinda* (1948), *Johnny Guitar* (1954).[54] The name, like the condition, is ubiquitous. Fear, as the story reveals, can assume all sorts of guises, just like Johnny.

It is crucial that Sylvia, at this point, was meeting Ruth Beuscher outside of an institution, and that both regarded their exchanges as far more than a doctor-patient relationship. Sylvia did not feel like the object of treatment in Beuscher's care so much as an aspirant looking for guidance, as she had done with Dorothea Brooke in Cambridge. As a result, she felt freed from the "Panic Bird on my heart and my typewriter." [PJ]

By December 16, 1958, Plath was sending out this "queer and quite slangy story," which seems to have lifted her spirits by realizing that her fears were not hers alone. "Have been happier this week than for six months," she wrote in her journal. She recognized that "paralyzing fear" got in her way: "Once that is worked clear of, I will flow. My life may at last get into my writing. As it did in the Johnny Panic story." The story put fear into a compact compass: "The Novel got to be such a big idea. I got panicked." Two months before she wrote the story, Sylvia had admitted: "A panic absolute and obliterating."

At Smith, she had periods of "complete and horrible panic." At Cambridge, while reading O'Neill, she noted: "sometimes, in panic, mind goes blank, world whooshes away in void, and I feel I have to run, or walk on into the night for miles till I drop exhausted. Trying to escape? Or to be alone enough to unriddle the secret of the sphinx. 'Men forget.' Said Laughing Lazarus." [PJ] The reference to *Lazarus Laughed* is pertinent to "Johnny Panic," because O'Neill's play is about existential panic that Lazarus acknowledges and by doing so is reborn.[55] The elements of her story had been roiling in Sylvia for some time in disconnected journal passages: "I wonder if, shut in a room, I could write for a year. I panic: no experience! Yet what couldn't I dredge up from my mind? Hospitals & mad women. Shock treatment & insulin trances. . . . Faces and violence." The story liberated her: "I feel I could crack open mines of life—in my daily writing sketches, in my reading & planning, if only I could get rid of my absolutist panic." What is the narrator in "Johnny Panic" doing if not cracking open the mines of life? In another entry: "don't panic. Begin writing, even if it is only rough & ununified." The "quite slangy" style of the story has a roughness to it, and a brash narrator that goes about her dream-collecting business until the authorities anesthetize her as a threat not so much to herself but to their own ministry of fear. Society shuns and shuts down the Promethean mind, Sheldon maintained. Society favored arbitrary resolutions of conflict and attempts to "kill a problem" rather than resolve it. "Johnny Panic" demonstrates Sheldon's exposure of society's effort to "civilize the dominance and submission relationships between human beings."

The Promethean narrator in "Johnny Panic" is a thief, stealing by copying and assembling a bible of dreams, which is tantamount to taking control away from the institution's gatekeepers. She works her own hours and establishes her own regimen. "The Promethean is necessarily rare," Sheldon observes, because "no society can support very many of him and remain cohesive." The narrator exposes the chaos of dreams that bog down the world and swamp it in terrifying nightmares. The narrator is heroic in the sense that she refuses to adapt to the institution's regime. Such a Promethean, Sheldon concludes, is "most often classed among 'thieves and radicals,' and almost never recognized for his true nature."

Sylvia's reading of Shirley Jackson's *The Bird's Nest* may have had an impact on "Johnny Panic."[56] Kevin Wilson's summary of the novel's theme applies as well to Plath's story: "The threat of the world around us and the even more potent threats inside us cannot offer much in the way of happiness." Jackson's work is set in a museum, an "enormous seat of learning," with a sagging foundation, leading to "little wry jokes about disintegration." Elizabeth Richmond, who does copying and routine correspondence for the museum, is a fragmented self with multiple personalities. Like Jackson, Plath exposes the fault line of society over which are built institutions purporting to shore up the sagging self. What bothered Sylvia, she realized, also bothered a lot of other people who were carted away and isolated from society and then rewired, so to speak, for reentry on society's terms. She could have been writing the premise of an O'Neill play when she wrote in her journal at the beginning of 1959: "A great, stark, bloody play acting itself out over and over again behind the sunny facade of our daily rituals, birth, marriage, death, behind parents and schools and beds and tables of food: the dark, cruel, murderous shades, the demon-animals, the Hungers."

Perhaps brooding on the powerfully complacent and conformist society that stifled the singular imagination is what turned Sylvia away from her own country and back toward England where, as she wrote to Ted's parents, he wanted to return. No longer did this couple dismiss his native land as decrepit and corrupt. "Ted has got set on living in England," she told his parents, and that was that, apparently. "I am as fond of England as any place, which is lucky," she concluded. Not exactly a tribute. But a visit to Winthrop, the site of her first ten happy years, which she loved "better than any place I've been," could not suffice: "I wouldn't want to bring up a family there." She was not the first American writer to think a change of scene, and a removal to England, might do for her what it had done for Stephen Crane and Robert Frost: "England seems so small and digestible from here," she wrote in her journal for February 19, 1959. On March 11, she wrote to fellow poet Lynne Lawner that the English had "many companies, small, idiosyncratic . . . and seem to publish vast amounts of unknowns."

Yet she would be "a "good bit in exile," and Ted, it seems, would drop his disguise. She wrote his parents about his wearing a wolf mask for a New Year's 1958 masquerade party and her own red caped appearance as Red Riding Hood. It is a devouring tableau vivant: "one day" that mask would "stick, and his nails will grow." What did Ted's mother, steeped in the lore of witchcraft,[57] make of this masque of a marriage?

56

A return to childhood and memories of a grandmother now dead suffuse the melancholic "Point Shirley," written during this interregnum between one side of the Atlantic and the other: "I would get from these dry-papped stones / The milk your love instilled in them." The grandmother's "labor of love" disintegrates in the poem's evocation of the sea that "Eats at Point Shirley." Her other Winthrop revery, "Suicide off Egg Rock," seems to connect with Sylvia's attempts to end her life in a crawl space: "No pit of shadow to crawl into." She imagines, like Emily Dickinson, flies buzzing in the "vaulted brain chamber." Is the suicide a writer, a victim of the writer's block that bedeviled her? "The words in his book wormed off pages. / Everything glittered like blank paper." The suicide has "walked into the water / The forgetful surf creaming on those ledges." However attached she had been to Winthrop and the sea, her poetry dramatizes why she could not return to that early ocean-blue bliss, which, in itself, took on a very different coloration—like the "ocherous salt flats" of "Suicide off Egg Rock" as she made plans with Ted to return to England.

Sylvia recorded a visit (perhaps her first) to her father's grave, expressing a yearning to dig him up just to prove he existed. [PJ] In "Electra on Azalea Path," the poet as Electra has buried herself and the knowledge of his death: "The day you died I went into the dirt, / Into the lightless hibernaculum." After twenty years, her visit to the grave, going through a "field of burdock," has been an awakening. The heart-shaped leaves of this plant, used for a wide range of medicinal purposes and attractive to wintering bees, converge with her own "wintering," her refuge from remembering him. The burdock field leads to the path of the past, and to the Plath-poet's recognition of how she

Point Shirley, where Plath's grandparents lived.

put her father into hibernation. The young girl who had loved to play with dolls now describes her former self as "Small as a doll in my dress of innocence." This Electra has returned to the grave of the father that Clytemnestra has slain, the father that in Sylvia's journal is murdered by Aurelia. But the poem tells another story of this Electra's obsession with her father's death: "my love that did us both to death." This allusion to Sylvia's own suicide attempt is made explicit when this Electra refers to herself as the "ghost of an infamous suicide." The poem's Clytemnestra tries to absolve Electra saying "gangrene" ate him "to the bone," and he "died like any man." The mother tries to dispel the daughter's mythologizing grandiosity with the literal truth, which is of a piece with this Electra's admission "I borrow the stilts of an old tragedy," as if to acknowledge she is different from the Electras in the tragedies Plath studied in Cambridge. As Tim Kendall observes: "This is a poem loudly in conversation with itself, interrupting and drowning out its various voices, wildly swerving in its registers, desperately ambitious in its scope, and puzzled about how to resolve the conflicts between emotion and artifice, the personal and the mythical, and the poet and the poetic voice."[58] It also seems like a poem deriving from a therapy session, with the back-and-forth, call and response, of an analysand: "Got at some deep things with Beuscher: facing dark and terrible things: those dreams of deformity and death. If I really think I killed and castrated my father may all my dreams of deformed and tortured people be my guilty visions of him or fears of punishment for me? And how to lay them? To stop them operating through the rest of my life?" Was the poem a preliminary, unresolved effort to disengage from the mythology of the father by asking him, in the last lines, for pardon, describing herself in contradictory/complementary terms as "your hound-bitch, daughter, friend"? She has haunted him as he has haunted her, but can there be a rapprochement? It's the kind of question a therapy session might well address.

Sylvia Plath's life and work reflect a split between those heady happy days of childhood that now seemed haunted by her father's death, and her mother's efforts to gloss over his absence with all those Wellesley projects and pursuits—the demanding, exhilarating school work, camp outings, stamp collecting, scouting, piano and viola lessons, and all those New England coastings and slidings and snowball fights that regularized her childhood. At twenty-four, in *The Bird's Nest*, Elizabeth Richmond, a seemingly well-adjusted, if rather dull, young woman goes missing, as Sylvia did. Elizabeth, who is watched over as diligently as Aurelia monitored Sylvia, is in search of her dead mother who is associated with her lost happy childhood. In Shirley Jackson's story, Elizabeth splits into three other selves: the sociable and empathetic Beth, the raucous Betsy, whose vulgar acting out mocks her two other good-girl selves—almost like Sylvia's own mocking, hostile turn of mind evident in her journals even as letters to her mother were so sedate, so Elizabeth-like. A late entrant, Bess, seems an amalgam of all these conflicting selves that Sylvia played out in a variety of episodes. The trauma of a mother's loss in *The Bird's Nest* seems akin to the fraught reckoning with childhood that had just begun to emerge in "Point Shirley," "Suicide off Egg Rock," and "Electra on Azalea Path."[59] Sylvia Plath, like the fictive selves Jay Martin describes, modeling their behavior on what they have read, began to turn her childhood into the literature she read and wrote and into a new biography of herself.

57

Seeing Ruth Beuscher during the first half of 1959 was essential, even if, at times, it proved frustrating: "getting nowhere with RB," her March 20 journal entry reported. So it is for Elizabeth Richmond via her Betsy self who thwarts her therapist Dr. Wright even as another of Elizabeth's selves, Beth, is compliant with his requests and responsive to his questions. Sylvia's own ambivalence about the value of therapy that Beuscher was barely able to overcome became paramount even as Sylvia bonded with her. Sylvia's showdown with herself and with the very conception of therapy had been developing over more than six years, beginning on August 27, 1952, when she read *The Story of My Psychoanalysis* by John Knight, the "pen name of a famous scientist who was sick and unhappy and didn't know why." His story "could be YOURS," announced the Pocket Book edition, published in June 1952. The book first appeared in October 1950, but it is likely that Plath read the twenty-five-cent paperback. This story of redemption and recovery is part of Plath's preparation for what she initially called her potboiler novel, *The Bell Jar*. Knight's book claimed to discover a secret self in a "startling confession" that leads to a "new and better life through psychoanalysis."

The Story of My Psychoanalysis is not supposed to be fiction, yet it contains dialogue—some of it extending over several pages—so that what purports to be fact seems like a fiction by John Knight, who, in this respect, is kin to Victoria Lucas, the pseudonym Plath chose for her novel. Writing with a pen name presumably separated the author of *The Bell Jar* from the elements of her own life that could be read into the novel, but choosing to write as Victoria Lucas also created a character/author and gave free reign to invent rather than simply report a life. So it may also have been for John Knight, doubly disguised not only because he was a chemist who did not want his true identity discovered but also because "John Knight" represented a switch to a gentile name that his Jewish father had assumed so as to assimilate into an anti-Semitic society. The "story that could be YOURS," in other words, had to be told—captured—in the boundaries of a book that could not be traced to its origins.

The Story of My Psychoanalysis is not in Plath's library, so we cannot know what she might have underlined or annotated. But toward the end of the book there emerges a hatred that she recognized in herself as the result of her own therapy, what Knight calls the "discharge of the deepest and most hostile impulses," the "murderous drive," and the "killing of ourselves when the murderous impulses happened to be directed inwardly." He equates these feelings of hatred, which have exacerbated his life-threatening ulcers, with the Holocaust and realizes that what he repeatedly calls his "overreaction" to the slightest expression of anti-Semitic sentiments triggers his own bestiality, his desire to hurt others. Through therapy, he realizes, as well, that the "same factors which led to the bestialization of a great nation under Hitler can operate among ourselves." It is exactly that dealing with bestialization that Plath would dramatize in "Daddy."

Knight's self-incrimination brings to mind the declaration in Plath's poem "Daddy": "every woman adores a fascist," and also *The Bell Jar*, which begins with the "summer they executed the Rosenbergs." When Esther Greenwood says to Hilda in the magazine office, "Isn't it awful about the Rosenbergs?" Hilda answers, "Yes!" And Esther thinks "at last I felt I had touched a human string in the cat's cradle of her heart." But no, Hilda nonchalantly adds: "It's awful such people should be alive." Hilda yawns, her "pale orange mouth opened on a large darkness. Fascinated, I stared at the blind cave behind her face until the two lips met and moved and the dybbuk spoke out of its hiding place, 'I'm so glad they're going to die.'" That is the story of psychoanalysis that John Knight reiterates—those demonic forces that are beneath the surface of polite society, the ulcerating tensions that may have led to those operations Aurelia Plath suffered to repair a fragile intestinal tract that became a constant worry for her daughter.

Ruth Beuscher had no trouble recognizing herself as Dr. Nolan in *The Bell Jar* and never seems to have felt any need to object to her portrayal or to correct the record in any significant respect. She remained, as in therapy itself, a projection of her patient's perceptions—much as Dr. Maxwell appears in *The Story of My Psychoanalysis*. Just as John Knight is surprised that the psychiatrist does not argue with him or express shock at some of Knight's hostility toward others, Esther is disarmed by Dr. Nolan's equable response to her patient's rejection of her mother: "'I hate her,' I said, and waited for the blow to fall. But Doctor Nolan only smiled at me as if something had pleased her very, very much, and said, 'I suppose you do.'" Why is Dr. Nolan pleased? Because, as Beuscher told biographer Harriet Rosenstein, it had taken weeks to get Sylvia to admit she bore any hostility toward her mother. In *The Bell Jar*, Esther shuts down when several "strange men" try to treat her. Only after several sessions with Dr. Maxwell is Knight willing to confess how much he hates his father. In both cases, the psychiatrist creates the conditions in which the patient no longer feels judged or expects that punishment will follow an expression of patricidal or matricidal emotions. But Knight, like Plath, has to repeatedly overcome his resistance to the therapeutic enterprise. Even after many weekly sessions with Beuscher, Plath recorded on May 13, 1959: "Bothered about RB: I seem to want to cover everything up, like a cat its little crappings with sand . . ."

We don't know, of course, if Plath compared Ruth Beuscher to Dr. Maxwell, or if Dr. Maxwell in any sense provided an inspiration for the creation of Dr. Nolan, but the novelist may have been struck by the absence of jargon and psychiatric buzz words in the treatment John Knight received. Dr. Maxwell eschews Freudianisms. "I never talked about Egos and IDs with Doctor Nolan," Esther Greenwood recalls. In both cases, the therapy is not programmatic. Neither Dr. Maxwell nor Dr. Nolan initiates what their patients are supposed to talk about.

Both John Knight and Esther Greenwood recover a sound sense of themselves, but they are not cured, since no cure is possible. At the termination of treatment Dr. Maxwell sums up the good results but also Knight's "weaknesses and danger spots," noting we can aspire to perfection but never attain it. Upon her release from treatment Esther notes: "I had hoped, at my departure, I would feel sure and knowledgeable about everything that lay ahead—after all, I had been 'analyzed.' Instead, all I could see were question marks."

The way ahead is fraught with doubt, and with possibilities that every human being encounters. Knight quotes Tolstoy on the circulatory system of human identity:

Men are like rivers: the water is the same in each, and alike in all; but every river is narrow here, is more rapid there, here slower, there broader, now clear, now cold, now dull, now warm. It is the same with men. Every man carries in himself the germs of every human quality, and sometimes one manifests itself, sometimes another, and the man often becomes unlike himself, while still remaining the same man.

Esther Greenwood reads from *Finnegans Wake* about how "riverrun, past Eve and Adam's, from swerve of shore to bend of bay, brings us by a commodius vicus of recirculation back to Howth Castle and Environs." Vicus, a word of Roman origin for a village within a rural area, is part of the riverrun, the hundreds of years of humanity that Tolstoy describes, and that Joyce sees as never ending. The small letter that begins the riverrun of a sentence "might mean," Esther supposes, "that nothing ever really began all new, with a capital, but that it just flowed on from what came before." Eve and Adam's was Adam and Eve, of course, but it probably signified something else as well. The "something else," she hazards, is "maybe . . . a pub in Dublin." Joyce is a lot to unpack, but so is Plath. She is here, I think, playing with concepts of the universal and the particular, with Adam and Eve and a pub, with places and persons, rivers and humanity.

It is possible, of course, that *The Story of My Psychoanalysis* had no impact on Plath, except to say that she did, after all, make a river of her reading, and that everything she read ran over the borders of a book's pages and into marginalia and into her imagination and spilled out into her life, as she created characters unlike herself and yet remained the same Sylvia Plath.

58

Approaching the spring of 1959, Plath enjoined herself: "Must use Beuscher to the hilt," and get rid of "baby feelings" and ties to "Mother Academia." She wished to break out of her "glass caul," already recognizing the bell jar of her existence. Ted, an inspiration, was daunting: "Must try poems. DO NOT SHOW ANY TO TED. I sometimes feel a paralysis come over me: his opinion is so important to me." [PJ] More than two weeks went by before she resumed writing in her journal.

Part-time work typing up lecture notes and letters for a professor at Harvard and then Robert Lowell's Boston University poetry class provided some of the structure Plath craved. Lowell recognized her talent, but he devoted himself to Anne Sexton, and Plath knew why: "She has the marvelous enviable casualness of the person who is suddenly writing and never thought or dreamed of herself as a born writer: no inhibitions." Sylvia seemed less envious than energized by Sexton's example. Sexton's influence came just when Plath was breaking out of her highly controlled, metaphoric and mythic poetry, chastising herself in her journal to get real, get down to the specifics of existence she describes in "Suicide off Egg Rock": "hotdogs split and drizzled / On the public grills . . . / Gas tanks, factory stacks—that landscape / Of imperfections." In her journal she noted Lowell set her up with Sexton, "an honor, I suppose. Well, about time. She has very good things,

and they get better, though there is a lot of loose stuff." Sylvia thought she
herself needed some loosening up. Sexton thought so, too, saying later that
she was not that impressed with Plath then and did not foresee the poet
who emerged in *Ariel*.[60]

Plath wrote to fellow poet Lynn Lawner: "I have been doing some poems
this month, as always happens when spring nears, but they are grim, antipoetic (compared to the florid metaphorical things I had in Poetry, Chicago) &
I hope, transitional." She wanted to know about Lynn's pleasures and bothers. "I feel an odd sisterly bond, partly because I feel, as I think and suspect
you may, a dim doppelganger relationship with the few women I know
who are very much physically & psychically akin to me." Sylvia sought to
align the world inside the self with the world outside that could be brought
closer to her own experience. In *The Bird's Nest*, Betsy constantly refers to
her place inside of Elizabeth and Betty's struggle to reach the outside world.

Sylvia did not have that much to say about the atmospherics of Lowell's
class, but fortunately Kathleen Spivack, in attendance, evokes the high
church atmosphere presided over by the priest of contemporary poetry. As
Spivack puts it in *With Robert Lowell and His Circle*, it was like "edging into
a pew, trying not to call attention to oneself, and waiting for the service
to start"—a few hellos but mostly silence awaiting "what was to come."
Sylvia was no different from other students: "pleasant but noncommittal."
Spivack sometimes detected her agitation even as she remained perfectly
still. As Lowell entered, Plath stiffened. Spivack remembered her dressed in
pleated skirts and long-sleeved shirts or "liberty" blouses, a "frozen woman
student's uniform."

Spivack could not know then, of course, about Plath's periods of paralysis
and how she looked to fellow poets like Lowell to help her thaw. So determined was she that Spivack could discern "absolutely no sense of humor."
Sylvia could be scathing about the work of her fellow students: "I would
never have guessed that she taught her own classes at Smith College, since
she did not have an encouraging warmth that prefaced her critical comments." But Sylvia was not in charge and she took her cue from Lowell, as
did the others who knew, in Spivack's words, that he would "bite our heads
off if we say the wrong thing. We're all afraid." Ted reported one of Lowell's
outbursts: "Usually he is very quiet, shy, whispers (a real mad whisper) but
this time he burst in, flung the tables into a new order, insulted everybody,
talked incessantly." In "Elegy in the Classroom," Sexton captured Lowell's
aura: "your face / was noble and your words were all things" transmogrified
"like a hunk of some big frog" and still remain "gracefully insane."[61]

Spivack confirms Plath's own impression that Lowell seemed much
more interested in Sexton, although he always treated Plath courteously.

She invited Spivack to her Boston flat, and with Ted seemed to put on a show, performing a marriage, complete with Britishisms like "Rubbish" and "Nonsense." To Spivack, they acted like contestants, vying for supremacy.

Apparently Sylvia saved the humorous side of herself for the rollicking rides to the Ritz for drinks with Sexton and George Starbuck, an editor-poet. What did Plath and Sexton talk about? They were both from Wellesley and had rejected its restraints. "It seems unlikely Plath and Sexton would not talk about their mother-daughter relationships," Gail Crowther speculates in *Three-Martini Afternoons at the Ritz*: "Did they gossip about their husbands and dramatic marriages over their third martini at the Ritz while these very husbands were at home waiting for them to return?" Certainly Plath's later letters to Sexton suggest an intimacy that few other female poets shared with her. The bold Sexton was a split-off of Plath, another potential self, like Lynn Lawner, with whom Plath craved a closeness, as if Lawner might divulge what might be possible for Plath as well. What did Sexton, often suicidal, make of "Suicide off Egg Rock"? We know very little about what these two poets said to one another, but enough to imagine their sisterhood. It seemed to be a relief and a deliverance for Plath to be in Sexton's presence after the intensities of dealing with the patriarchal, unpredictable, and sometimes menacing Robert Lowell. Crowther sums up so well this feminine convergence: "When Plath first read Sexton, she realized the strength of Sexton's work lay in the ease of expression, her honesty, and ability to get straight to the point. Not only that, she envied Sexton's subject matter: madness, motherhood, sex, parents, therapy, death, suicide. These topics were a breakthrough, not just for poetry in general but for women operating in a male-dominated discipline."[62] When Sexton's affair with Starbuck heated up, Plath noted in her May 3, 1959, journal that she "felt our triple martini afternoons at the Ritz breaking up."

59

While Plath and Hughes were preparing for a summer cross-country trip to California, she had "pressure points" to bring up with Ruth Beuscher, including suicide, Olwyn Hughes, writing, and "lack of children." At one point, she had thought of herself as pregnant, writing "Metaphors," a poem full of the expectation that both poetry and childbirth could bring her. She worked on a children's story, *The Bed Book*, and dreamed of her childhood play with dolls. But she still seemed stalled, put out with Ted's hectoring, and wondering what to do with her anger. She would ask Beuscher. In the meantime, she dissipated some of her hostility during a violent session of rug braiding, calling the result an "anger rug."

Besides torment about her own work, what was there to be angry about? "Ted is thriving. He is handsomer than ever," Sylvia wrote to his brother and sister-in-law. "If he has any faults they are not shutting the icebox (a kind of subconscious revenge on American appliances) and knotting his clothes up in unknottable balls and hurling them about the floor of the room every evening before retiring. Oh yes, and the occasional Black Moods." She was not very specific, except for suggesting he was upset with the state of the world. It is remarkable how she rarely examined his depressions the way she did her own. Why was that? Since he would not talk about his feelings the way she did with herself and her therapist, we can only guess. For sure, she had to maintain her belief in his stalwart character. Were their fights a result of her momentarily giving way to criticism of him, perhaps when it became just too much to untwist him? It would be useful to know how these fights started. Did he interpret her fastidiousness as nagging, the way Hemingway did when he said Gellhorn expected her man to have the probity of Cardinal Newman and the organizing capacity of Henry Kaiser? Or did Sylvia and Ted sometimes argue about his absolutely dismissive view of her country: "I can't describe the terrifying lack of inwardness about America," he wrote to Daniel Huws on May 15, 1959. Or were those "Black moods" inexpressible to her because he could not share his sneering at the "brainless American romanticism" he mentioned in a letter to Lucas Myers four days later? He finished off with quite a diatribe that seems to have the Beats, Norman Mailer, and the approaching 1960s in mind as the "modern literary syphilis—verseless, styleless, characterless all-inclusive undifferentiated yelling assertion of the Great simplifying burden-lifting God orgasm—whether by drug, negro, masked nympho, or strange woman in the dark. And the obverse of this—damning of all constructed civilisation, including all poetry that has not been gasped out with vomit or orgasm." What more Hughes might have said is cut off with ellipses in Christopher Reid's bowdlerized edition of the letters.

Such missives from America may have been Ted's only outlet since, unlike Sylvia, he had no interest in figuring out why he felt this way. It was enough for him that he did. With such a withholding man—you can be sure if he had let himself go there would be some evidence of it in her journals, no wonder Plath turned to Beuscher and to her journals as at least a partial way of sharing and exploring herself. Too often she had to remind herself not to overburden Hughes with her feelings. It never seemed to occur to her that hiding what she experienced did damage both to her and to their marriage. He, in turn, had quite enough of her worries, thank you very much, and could only, as he supposed, put up with them, as he confessed much later. In the meantime, it would be writing exercises and hypnosis that would be his way of dealing with her traumas.

60

A May 31, 1959, journal entry announced a triumphant return to prose with summaries of essays, sketches, and stories to come: "I feel this month I have conquered my Panic Bird." The month started well with a piece in the *Christian Science Monitor*, "Kitchen of the Fig Tree," comparing her kitchens in Boston, Spain, and England. From her sixth floor flat she had a view all the way to the Charles River. Accompanied by gulls' cries she was "lifted from her position of a prone housewife at a stove: I became a voyage on the deck of a ship, an airplane passenger looking down at a familiar map of streets and parks, poised high above it all." She thought of her modern American appliances and yet still yearned even for her cramped English kitchen with its primitive icebox and stove, but with access to a kitchen garden that scented her life in warm weather with apple blossoms and roses that "mingled with spicy odors of pies and stews." In Spain, conditions were even more primitive with her landlady showing her how to scrub dishes with straw and cold water from a well inside the house; the view included a fig tree set against the panorama of mountains and the "pink and orange tints of the sun rising over the sea." In August she could pick her dessert from that tree and "eat it from the nature plate of the leaf." She would ideally have a composite of all three kitchens; otherwise, she would choose the "Kitchen of the Fig Tree," and obtain from the farmer next door whatever was in season. Call Plath's *Monitor* article a trifle, a diversion, yet it took her out of the binaries and black moods that she succumbed to with her assortative mate, who nonetheless would never have thought of writing such a piece precisely because of its antipoetical, prosy, qualities.

Within a week Sylvia was brooding over another rejection of her first book of poetry. She had been proud of her looser, rougher poetic line, yet she had been deemed "antipoetic. My God." [PJ] She went through a period of worrying about her ovulation. She thought her barrenness would weaken her tie to Ted, not realizing, as he later confessed, that he was not ready for children—they had never been a part of his plan. She felt incomplete, calling intercourse without conception a "dead end." [PJ] Unlike Ted, she thought of family as an organizing principle for life, and she sought, in her reading, confirmation of how lives ought to be governed.

61

On June 10, 1959, Sylvia read the first part of David Riesman's classic sociological study, *The Lonely Crowd*. She underlined his distinctions between "*tradition-directed people*," "*inner-directed people*," and "*other-directed people*." What she thought of these categories she did not say, but she was coming from a three-generation home, with grandparents, parents, herself, and brother who reflected the three categories Riesman identified. Rather than thinking of Riesman's terms abstractly as they might apply to society, think of how they may have been brought home to Plath, whose life encompassed a reverence for and internalization of tradition while traveling well beyond the conditions that had shaped her grandparents and parents. When she underlined what Riesman said was "tradition-direction": "ritual, routine, and religion to occupy and to orient everyone," was she thinking of her childhood attendance at Sunday School, her enrollment in Scouts, her participation in clubs? When she underlined Riesman's observation that "inner-direction" involved "character types who can manage to live socially without strict and self-evident tradition-direction," did she see the second phase of her life?

Her decision to forsake the confines of the Smith campus came into play in the passage she marked with a vertical slash: "The inner-directed person becomes capable of maintaining a delicate balance between the demands upon him of his life goals and the buffeting of his external environment." Did she see herself in the passage she starred and wonder if it explained the economy of emotion that she experienced with Ted?: "The American is said to be shallower, freer with his money, friendlier, more uncertain of himself and his values, more demanding of approval than the European." Riesman quoted Erich Fromm as an authority, as did Ruth Beuscher.

Even before Sylvia met Ted, she was in the process of measuring herself no longer simply by what she had learned at home but against her fellow writers like Adrienne Rich: "What is common to all the other-directed people," she underlined in Riesman, "is that their contemporaries are the source of direction for the individual—either those known to him or those with whom he is indirectly acquainted, through friends and through the mass media." It is hard to see Ted Hughes reading *The Lonely Crowd*, or seeing the need of it, since he always considered himself in a class by himself, as did those cronies at Cambridge who followed him.

Sylvia had friends who admired her, but it was not quite the same thing as the Hughes brotherhood, and she would need a level of support that she associated with her own family and the family she planned to populate: "the major agency of character formation in societies dependent on tradition-directions," Riesman concluded, "is the extended family and its. environing clan or group." What Sylvia missed after she left home was that "environing clan or group." She underlined that Riesman summary, as if to emphasize her plight and her project, which had begun in her earliest diaries,[63] and which perhaps accounts for the vertical slash in the margin next to this passage: "the drive instilled in the child is to *live* up to *ideals* and to test his ability to be on his own by continuous experiment in self-mastery—instead of by following tradition."

Teaching at Smith probably drove home Plath's reaction to Riesman's comments on social mobility: "it depends less on what one is and what one does than on what others think of one—and how competent one is in manipulating others and being oneself manipulated." It is a passage in Riesman that she decorates in the margin with a huge exclamation mark. To his proviso: "one must always ask whether in changing oneself, one is simply adapting to the world as it is without protest or criticism," she remarked in the margin "good point!"

Sylvia underlined Riesman's interview with a twelve-year-old girl who said, "I like Superman better than the others because they can't do everything Superman can do. Batman can't fly and that is very important." Sylvia had, in a sense, flown away with Ted, abandoning what Riesman calls, and which Plath underlined, the "brooding omnipresence of the peer-group." She underlined passages about the liberating role of popular culture, such as the reading of comics and going to the movies, that accorded with her own experience, as noted in her diaries, when she went to see *Cynthia*, for example. Young people used movies to "learn how to look, dress, and make love," Riesman observed. Women's magazines (she underlined his mention of *Mademoiselle*) "dealt largely with modes of manipulating the self in order to manipulate others, primarily for the attainment of intangible assets such as affection." Magazines, including the *Ladies' Home Journal*, ran counter to what Sheldon had said about conflict, which in the magazines involved "neither risk nor hardship but only the commodities—interpersonal effort and tolerance—that the other-directed person is already prepared to furnish." Her own life in that starred passage could not fit such a formula, even though she would continue to yearn for copies of the magazine when she later moved to Court Green and would continue to champion Ted as the hero "standing out, in violent integrity," taking all to the "heights of fame"—the words are Riesman's description of Ayn Rand's architect hero in *The Fountainhead*, words that Plath underlined.

62

Plath's journal shut down for business by June's end as the couple drove westward into a jubilant July. Ecstatic letters and postcards to her mother and Warren made it seem as though the somber Sylvia of the journals had vanished the way Elizabeth's Betsy-self gives way to her more sprightly self in *The Bird's Nest* and bursts out of her aunt's confining house on a road trip to New York City. In Sylvia's case, it was fishing and nature trails in Ontario, the "unspoiled green wilderness" areas of Wisconsin, the hugeness of Lake Superior, the "reddish" deer that licked Ted's face, the "marvelous endless prairies, rich with cows & unpeopled" of the Dakotas and the Badlands, the "yellow wheat & black earth fields stretching in alternate ebony & gold bands to the purple mesas on the horizon" in Montana. They counted nineteen bears at Yellowstone. "Neither of us have seen such wonderful country anywhere in the world. Flowers everywhere, & animals & snow," she wrote home.

Toward the end of July 1959, both Sylvia and Ted wrote letters detailing their harrowing, exhilarating encounter in Yellowstone with a bear that smashed their car's rear window and gobbled up their food. Their accounts dovetailed, but then Sylvia turned it all into a story in which the bear kills the husband.[64] In *Birthday Letters*, Hughes turned their joint experience into another instance of an "emergency angst" they both felt, but he pointed out she was "more used to . . . death in disguise." Suddenly the trip, in his view, fulfilled the great "nothing there" in the American landscape, "except death / I saw her dead face—unmoving & still / I didn't write it down." But he says he told Sylvia about this vision of emptiness, and that she confirmed his own sense of dread. For Hughes, the campers killed by bears reflect their mindless Disneyland delusions about animals. It is the incident that confirmed their decision to leave North America, he claims. But right after their bearish night, Sylvia wrote to her mother and brother: "Well, we are fine, and both of us tanned, and having the experience of our lives." Was she temporizing about the terror, or was Hughes, in retrospect, projecting too much into her temporary upset? In *Birthday Letters* he never lets up in his deterministic account of their lives together any more than Plath relents in portraying their trip as perfectly spectacular. As usual, she said Ted shared her mindset. To his parents, she wrote: "Ted looks the best I've ever seen him!"

63

Sylvia extolled their fall at Yaddo, the famous refuge for the rejuvenation of writers, including the beauty of the estate and the sumptuous meals, even though she was nauseated (the beginnings of her pregnancy) and depressed about her work in prose and poetry, wondering what happened to the tyro who had produced so much writing with such confidence. Decades later, writer Helen Humphreys stayed in the third floor studio Plath occupied, with skylights through which the tops of pine trees towered. What could be more conducive to composition? Yet, the "old fall disease" plagued Plath, she wrote in her journal, which expressed anxieties about moving to England— allayed by a dream of Marilyn Monroe who appeared as a "fairy godmother" who gave her beauty advice, an expert manicure, and asked Plath to visit her during the Christmas holidays, "promising a new, flowering life." The maternal side of Monroe, on display in *River of No Return*, and in her very public desire to have children and a career, held obvious appeal to Plath, who included Hughes in her dream of fulfillment when she told Monroe, "almost in tears," how much "she and Arthur Miller meant to us." Monroe had landed in England in July 1956 on her honeymoon with Miller and for her work on *The Prince and the Showgirl* with Laurence Olivier. She had broken her Twentieth Century-Fox contract and formed her own production company. Plath was unusual at the time for her serious treatment of Monroe, regarding a meeting with her as an "occasion of 'chatting' with audience much as the occasion with Eliot will turn out, I suppose." She put Eliot, not only a great poet but a literary editor and director at Faber and Faber, Hughes's publisher, together with Monroe on the same level in the commerce of culture that she wanted so much to conquer.[65]

Plath also sought poetic inspiration in Ezra Pound, Elizabeth Bishop, and in Iris Murdoch's novels. She summed up her plight in one sentence: "When will I break into a new line of poetry?" A rejection from Harcourt, she noted in her journal: "Ted says: You are so negative. Gets cross, desperate." Even so, "Ted is the ideal, the one possible person," she insisted. Would children humanize her? Make her more productive? [PJ] She thought that constantly receding novel that she could not write might be done in England: "My tempo is British," she confided to her journal. Her rationalizations began to mount up: the "fastness and expense of America is just about 50 years ahead of me," she told her mother. She went to see a Bergman film, *The Magician*: "America cannot make such films. Why? The corruption of the capitalist civilization? The lack of any knowledge of deep humanity?" She seems to have adopted Ted's line, so prevalent in his letters, of a superficial country unable to plumb the depths.

While waiting for her new line of poetry, Plath put long descriptions of her surroundings into her journal, as if to keep a hand in, so to speak. She also read Mavis Gallant's novel *Green Water, Green Sky* (1959) about the breakdown of a young woman in Europe, the fraught relationship with her mother, and the husband who finds it impossible to succor his wife. The novel seems to have banked itself in Plath's imagination, accruing in value two years later as *The Bell Jar* quickly unblocked the obstacles to writing long fiction.

In the meantime, drawing seemed a soothing emollient for writer's block. She published her pictorial work in the *Christian Science Monitor* on October 19, 1959, as "Explorations Lead to Interesting Discoveries," featuring a still life of shed, stove, trunk, tire, wheelbarrow, and washing machine, captioned as "A colorful pattern of rounds and oblongs, knobs, and wheels, legs and handles." The scene is of a partially recovered past, the parts of which do not cohere, but which she would shape to her quest for order. The article ends: "One does not need to become a buyer of antiques to savor those age-polished, wear-smoothed jugs, and barrows and boxes and stoves and sleighs. One can try to capture them with a few lines of the pen, or, lacking cupboard space, store them in a niche of words." Plath thought the drawings "came out well." [PJ]

On November 1, 1959, five months pregnant, she dreamed of giving birth to a beautiful and healthy boy: Ted called it the rebirth of her soul. Even while complaining of paralysis and her failure to make good on her early promise, Sylvia wrote seven poems in quick succession, including "The Colossus," which begins: "I shall never get you put together entirely." Allusions to her father are fitful in her diaries, letters, and journals, and the poem seems a product of those fragmentary efforts at restoration going on, as the poem reveals, for close to three decades, with the poet "none the wiser." She had tried to build a monument to her father, but like that "crazy statue in the snow" of Hitler she had tried to construct as a child, what had been a forbidding figure in the popular imagination becomes unmendable, a ruin, "pithy and historical as the Roman Forum." Perhaps not enough has been said about Plath's desire to adorn her life with history, which keeps breaking out in the allusions to the ancients and what "The Colossus" calls the "old anarchy." History looms so large in the figure of the father that

Film poster for *Colossus of Rhodes* (1961).

the poet can "squat in the cornucopia / Of your left ear, out of the wind."
The poem's evocative Greek ending suggests the hour of revelation that has
not come and that the poet now supposes will never arrive: "No longer do
I listen for the scrape of a keel / On the blank stones of the landing." It is
easy enough to say in biographical terms that Sylvia was haunted by her
father's absence, but perhaps less obvious to realize that she viewed her plight
not only as personal and Promethean but historical.[66] "The Colossus" was
written in a period of profound anxiety as Plath sought to find her bearings, to climb down off not only the statuary authority of her father[67] and
poets like Robert Lowell and her own Hughes, but to see in history itself
what Sheldon called the "deepest *orientational* nature of the restlessness and
uncertainty of the educated mind."

PART THREE

THE LATER YEARS

1

On December 9, 1959, the couple sailed for England. On the way, Ted wrote to Lucas Myers: Sylvia, six months pregnant, had composed a dozen spectacular poems that reflected an entirely new phase—all done as wild monologues: "I've already stolen several things from them." She had done the Promethean Sheldon proud.

Plath brought the critical sensibility of "The Colossus" with her to Yorkshire, where she spent the Christmas holidays of 1959–60 with Ted's family. The poet who had dispatched the "barnyard" bray of the father figure posing as an oracle deplored Mrs. Hughes's poor housekeeping and cooking, admiring the stylish, sardonic Olwyn Hughes as an "ally." For Aurelia's delectation, Sylvia presented a Dickensian cosy scene, sitting by the coal fire in "great armchairs" among a "loving & closeknit" family. It was very important that Sylvia perpetuate the ideal of family harmony: "Olwyn is very nice, a beautiful blond slim girl, my height & size, with yellow-green eyes and delicate graceful bone structure: looks 21, not 31. I get along with her much better now that she's really accepted me as Ted's wife & like her immensely."

After an arduous search for a flat that was not filthy or cramped, Sylvia and Ted signed a three-year lease on a small but tidy unfurnished Chalcot Square place, near Primrose Hill, a neighborhood that seemed like a village to Sylvia. They planned to paint and paper and furnish their new home with a gas stove, a bed, and bookshelves that Ted would make. They welcomed furniture given to them by poet W. S. Merwin and his resourceful wife, Dido.

England was still recovering from war, which accounts for some of Sylvia's very American reactions: "the English are the most secretly dirty race on earth." Daniel and Helga Huws were very kind, with Helga cooking German dishes and hosting Sylvia and Ted while they fixed up their Chalcot Square flat, which she described in detail to Marcia Brown, adding: "Day by day things get better as I get the routines under control . . . in another week I shall feel human again. I may even read a book." She was getting used to the idea of a midwife: "that's the way they do things here." She attended relaxation classes for home births, a risky venture in Sylvia's mind, since her American doctor had warned her against natural childbirth at a time when most American babies were born in hospitals. Sylvia wanted Marcia to write to her at least once a month. Thus began a pattern of attempts to hold on to friends and family as Sylvia negotiated her life in a new land. At the same time, she had been trying to keep on good terms with Olwyn Hughes, writing to her on October 8: "I don't think either of us has sustained such a prolonged period of crammed exhaustion & despair before—& physical cold, hunger & all the misères. . . . My one prayer is that the saws, nails & sawdust are out of the tub tomorrow, along with the workmen."

The great event that made the move worthwhile was the signing on February 10, 1960, of her first book contract for *The Colossus and Other Poems*, to appear in the fall published by Heinemann in England, with her editor seeking an American publisher. She now felt more settled, fully moved into the Chalcot Square flat, baking banana bread and sounding positively lyrical about her midwife who spoke to her in a "lovely lilting voice," seeming "both kind & warmhearted & extremely practical & capable." At such moments, Sylvia enjoyed the domestic, familial, and professional success she had sought so diligently. A first book, a first child—now it all seemed to be her destiny: "I think I shall be a very happy exile & have absolutely no desire to return to the land of milk & honey & spindryers," she wrote to Lynn Lawner on February 18.

Sylvia never said how much her decision to leave the United States was in fact predicated on her husband's state of mind. Hughes treated their departure as vital, writing on December 3, 1959, to Daniel Huws: "Another year in America would have worked a permanent petrifaction on my glands. As it is I'm recovering already—more vitality & zest than I've had since I left England." His letters support Sylvia's account of their early days in London and their high expectations for their marriage and family. He easily slid back into the circle of his English friends. Sylvia was keen to keep up correspondence with American friends: "PLEASE do write in answer." One way to hear her own voice was to receive these letters: "say something," she urged Lawner, then in Rome: "About you, men, the Tiber, the color of things."

Sylvia presented her marriage to her mother as one of equals: "Ted & I are alternating, one day each a week, until we are fully recovered from the strain of the last months & the settling in. He had his Day Sunday: the one in bed orders what is desired for meals, reads, writes & sleeps." She had underlined a passage in Riesman approving of men who did their domestic share. The birth of their child might coincide with publication of Ted's second book, *Lupercal*. This couple looked for such signs of their creative destiny. But it was quite a different world for a pregnant mother, expected to put up with company, as she confided to her mother: "Ted is, if anything, too nice to his relatives and friends, and I got weary sitting for 8 hours at a stretch in our smokefilled rooms waiting for them to leave—impossible to nap or relax with so many people around."

So much has been made of Plath's mood swings that Hughes's delicate condition, which she worried about, is overlooked: "Ted is back at work at his desk, much happier. He gets almost nervously sick when he hasn't written for a long time, & really needs careful handling." She speaks of fighting to give him the time and space in which to write. That fragile side of her titan is absent from his letters and poems, which never account for how Plath propped him up. But he was there for her, nonetheless, cooking and washing when she came down with a cold.

It thrilled Sylvia to be noticed even as Ted got his A. Alvarez *Observer* review praising his "immensely assured poetic skill." Also in the paper a "note about <u>me</u> 'his tall, trim American wife. . . . who is a New Yorker poet in her own right.'" But that was nothing like the thrill of childbirth. On April 1, 5:45 a.m., Frieda Rebecca arrived "white as flour with the cream that covers new babies, little funny dark squiggles of hair plastered over her head, with big dark eyes." Ted, there "the whole time," held Sylvia's hand, rubbed her back, boiled water, while the baby "pink & healthy," fell sound asleep. Sylvia wrote her mother:

> We can't imagine now having favored a boy! Ted is delighted. He'd been hypnotizing me to have a short easy delivery—well, it wasn't "easy," but the shortness carried me through. Less than five hours labor, the midwife announced: "A wonder child!". . . Well, I have never been so happy in my life. The whole American rigmarole of hospitals, doctors' bills, cuts & stitches, anesthesia etc. seems a nightmare well left behind.

Imagine the astounding scene, at a time when most men paced hospital corridors and were of practically no use to their wives. Imagine how Sylvia felt confirmed in her decision to come to England, with a National Health Service doctor and midwife in attendance upon her instead of an institutional medical staff putting her through their procedures. Imagine having a husband who had *prepared* for this moment that simply could not have been replicated in her native land, which still had not offered up a publisher for her first book. It was all positively Promethean. In effect, Plath had dared to be reborn, given herself a second birth—of the kind that Sheldon, relying on William James's *The Varieties of Religious Experience*, had projected and that she had underlined: "The second birth is really the breaking and resetting of the orientational backbone." Sylvia had "shuddered" at the first mention of a midwife, and yet she had overcome her fears, renounced the cosseted campus life and the ministrations of her mother, and had reoriented herself and her world.

Ted's letter to Lucas Myers recounting the hours leading up to the birth adds details that show he attended to the intervals of pushing, the starting and stopping over which his wife had considerable control with the midwife's guidance. At the same time, he detached himself, saying "the business is like backing a lorry round a tight bend in a narrow alley of parked cars." He achieved an exquisite equilibrium between empathy and dispassion that served his wife well just when she went into labor, depressed that she might be in agony for twenty hours or more. Frieda, born in his prose, is alive as herself, giving a "little sneeze" and "muttering to herself and moving her fingers." Sylvia saw the same thing, telling her mother: "The midwife didn't slap her when she came: she just caught her breath, sneezed & there she was." At that point, all three coalesced: "Sylvia was amazed. So was I," Ted recalled. He liked to think his "hypnotisings" had worked: "For the past month I've been putting her to sleep at nights—telling her to lose her toes, release her feet, so on, up her body, telling her she's getting sleepy, can't open her eyes etc, to relax & relax & relax, & that she's going to have an easy short delivery, that she can leave it all to the spirit who has it in hand etc." Putting together the Plath and Hughes accounts of the birth is the only way to complete the scene of what they had created.

Sylvia had read about hypnosis,[1] as did Ted,[2] but he put it into practice, and she was sure, she told Olwyn Hughes, he had made a huge contribution to the rapid delivery of their child. In modern medical accounts of hypnosis, emphasis is placed on the patient's suggestive state of mind, including her willingness to be hypnotized, her trust in the procedure, and her understanding that, in effect, she is in charge by voluntarily submitting herself to a state of concentration that makes her susceptible to suggestion. Plath knew all of this from reading Robert A. Rothchild's "Suggestion and Hypnosis" in *Modern Abnormal Psychology*. But a curious phrase in Hughes's account suggests something more, when he adds that "she can leave it all to the spirit who has it in hand etc." Are there hints of the occult, of the world of spirits that they had conjured with their ouija board? Was Ted invoking what Rothchild calls Mesmer's early supposition of "connecting forces between the universe and mankind"? How much Sylvia was willing to "leave it all to the spirit who has it in hand" is impossible to say, but she and Ted shared—at least to some extent—an inquiry into a higher power, out of which their life and work ensued. Some kind of spirit matter—a contradiction in terms, I know—seemed to move them in their greatest moments of solidarity that convinced Sylvia they could never be parted. "Both of us are thriving, doting parents," she wrote to Philip Booth on May 31, 1960.

2

The first months of the English return were taken up with the couple's delighted, if exhausting, focus on Frieda and with the burgeoning of Ted's reputation at the BBC and at Faber, where he was photographed alongside the publisher's three generations of poets: T. S. Eliot, Stephen Spender, W. H. Auden, and Louis MacNeice. "Of course I was immensely proud. Ted looked very at home among the great," Sylvia wrote her mother on June 24, 1960. To another correspondent she wrote: "I am becoming an Anglophile, what with U-2's,[3] the boom of biological & chemical warfare plants in Maryland, the Chessman execution[4] & Dick Nixon to keep me beating my head for my homeland." But such sentiments were balanced by letters yearning for news from home and deploring the inadequacies of English domestic life, softened by the sound advice and help from the Merwins. Aurelia sent baby clothes and Sylvia responded: "You have no idea how much it means to me to dress her partly in American clothes." This is the voice of displacement that cries out, as Dante did: "All that you love the best, which is the bolt / That exile's bow shoots first."[5] The very help the Merwins offered ameliorated the onset of another down cycle. "I am at the depressing painful stage of trying to start writing after a long spell of silence," Sylvia admitted to her mother.

Sylvia consoled herself with her husband's growing fame, with what the exile craves: the "response he will receive from readers . . . his dreams; his yearning for a speedy acknowledgement of his prestige; his awareness of his destiny." The words are Jay Martin's applied to Dante, but they resonate in Hughes's triumphal return from the land he had exiled himself from, and in Plath's need, like Dante's, "to throw himself on the protection of others," which will, as in the case of the Merwins, be regarded as "full of grace."

How to situate herself in a foreign domain became a preoccupation of sorts, starting with that first visit to Ted Hughes's Yorkshire, which Sylvia could identify with as Wuthering Heights Land. She took possession of it in her imagination, drawing the artifacts she observed in the Brontë museum.

Now, in London, she latched on to another landmark, telling her mother on June 30, 1960: "Something odd happened to me today which both elated & depressed me": She had her first look at Fitzroy Road where Yeats lived and where she imagined living with Ted in a future home. "Ted, of course, is much more hesitant than I to commit himself." What a portent in that "elated & depressed" reaction that would rock her final days. She reveled in the very idea of commitment, later extolling her Devon neighbor, Elizabeth Compton, a "committed woman." That kind of commitment Ted did not have it in him to offer.

3

Sylvia had a seasonal sensibility. A rainy and raw July 1960 brought on the fever of homesickness and a longing for "days that start out blue & clear & stay that way." She missed "being tan, as I have always been in the summer. I am a horrid pale yellow. O England," where a day did not "stay that way." She missed clean New England beaches when they visited the mucky beaches of Whitby,[6] near Ted's parents, although ten days of resting up while his mother babysat, and long walks in Yorkshire, refreshed her.

During the summer and fall, Sylvia's letters say almost nothing about her writing and are almost solely concerned with domestic life, the joys of Frieda, making baby clothes, and touting Ted's successes. She mentioned a diary, but that has never been located, and working on women's magazine fiction. Missing, too, is much about the anxiety of not writing. She felt a "cabbagey calm," she told her friend and fellow poet Lynn Lawner. Was this period quite so pacific? A turned-up diary might tell that story. What we do have is Ted's account of a restorative trip to Yorkshire to stay with his family. He had become fed up with London literary life, too inbred and careerist, and both of them, according to Sylvia, had tired of the Merwins whose helpfulness had transformed into what felt like patronage now, with the Merwins dropping in on Sylvia and Ted and expecting them to perform like "domestic lions." Sylvia made a point of returning the furniture the Merwins had loaned to them. Dido, as her memoir in Anne Stevenson's Plath biography demonstrates, had taken against Sylvia as a brash, entitled American, while remaining fond of Ted, whom she regarded as a much put-upon husband.

In a letter to Aurelia and Warren, Ted relished Sylvia's ability to talk to his father and get him to reminisce about World War I: the "past is raked up as something intensely interesting & highly amusing. It isn't that they live in the past at all, but the whole past is kept alive & very present. It's the sort of thing I miss very much when we're in London, and now Sylvia's getting addicted to it."

By the end of the year, a relieved Ted reported to Aurelia and Warren that Sylvia had resumed writing poetry. He also thought writing for women's magazines would help her jettison the vestiges of an academic style, forcing her to learn "how to write about life directly and boldly and full-scale." He continued to appreciate her as an astute critic of his work. His long letter in late December 1960 to Sylvia's mother and brother suggests that Sylvia was right in saying he cared about what her family thought and wanted to include them in an understanding of his work. Sylvia's late December letters were now full of her references to stories she had written and plans for more.

Sylvia's effort to maintain the family romance ended during the Christmas holidays in Yorkshire. "Olwyn made such a painful scene this year that I can never stay under the same roof with her again," Sylvia told her mother. Olwyn Hughes had

> never hidden her resentment of me, & her relation to Ted is really quite pathological—I think they slept in the same bed till she was 9 years old & probably this is one of the reasons she never married. In any case, she has never spoken to me, asked me one personal question or done anything but ignore me & make it plain she has come to see Ted. Naturally, this hurt me very much, but I never crossed her, because I knew Ted was fond of her.

The two women had a confrontation after Olwyn complained that Sylvia was critical of everyone, and that she was an interloper in the Hughes home. It wasn't just Sylvia that Olwyn rejected. She had done much the same with Joan, Gerald's wife. Ted wasn't willing to do anything about Olwyn, confirming Sylvia's belief that his sister dominated him. In fact she quoted him to her mother: Olwyn had "always bossed that house shamefully & as Ted says, her outburst derived from an idiotic jealousy." Sylvia would later go over impressions of Olwyn with Ruth Beuscher, who relayed the result to Harriet Rosenstein. Sylvia suggested that "Ted had engaged in an incestuous relationship with his sister . . . and was perhaps continuing to do so."

4

On February 6, 1961, Sylvia miscarried. "I lost the little baby this morning & feel really terrible about it," she wrote to her mother. The doctor could not explain it, except to say that one in four mothers miscarry. Sylvia planned to "plunge into work" as a cure for "brooding." A troubling appendix impeded her progress. At the end of the month she had it removed and recovered quickly, although she remained in hospital for nine days, treating it as a sort of holiday, reading Agatha Christie mysteries, enjoying a break from child rearing, and welcoming the angelic Ted's visits with steak, tollhouse cookies, and a visit with Frieda. She felt more rested and refreshed than she had for months. She made notes about the patients, figuring she might make a story out of her convalescence.

The hospital stay seems to have allowed Sylvia to acknowledge how run-down she had become, or was it just the hindsight of late March 1961 that led to the catalogue of wretchedness overcome that she penned to friends? To Philip and Margaret Booth, she wrote: "a manic-depressive winter full of flu, miasmas, near bankruptcy, nights full of teething yowls from our changeling, topped off by my grateful departure from my very nasty tempered appendix several weeks ago." She had recovered her "American plateau of fearsome health." She veered from Gothic to gregarious in a life that she liked to present as a fairy tale.

By mid-April 1961, Knopf, one of the best American publishers, expressed interest in *The Colossus*, provided that Plath eliminate certain poems. Those poems were considered too much under the influence of Theodore Roethke, to whom she announced the news and enclosed "Tulips," written just after her appendectomy. The poem evokes the sudden reversal of winter woe as the patient lies watching the whiteness of hospital walls and admiring the "too excitable tulips," springing up in her "snowed-in' condition," "learning peacefulness." All striving departs as she conceives of herself as a "nobody" with "nothing to do," consigning her name and clothes to the nurses. This is a scene of rebirth and renewal that requires, to begin with, a renunciation, as she gives away her "history to the anesthetist" and her "body to surgeons." Watching the nurses pass "the way gulls pass inland in their white caps," she is lulled into a sea-like serenitude of waves, which Plath always associated with her earliest memories of the safe harbor of childhood. The patient loses herself in the numbness the needles bring, setting herself loose from husband and child, and the body that she likens to a "thirty-year old cargo boat," swabbed of its "loving associations," as if she has taken a vow to be a nun, never having been so "pure" before. This state of freedom is a kind of peaceful daze interrupted by the "too red" tulips that remind her of the "redness" of her wound, making it difficult to "efface myself." The tulips bring her back to the excitements of life, the "red blooms" of love seated in water that she imagines tastes like the warm salt of the sea, coming from a country "far away as health." The last words are those of a patient still in recovery of herself.

The poem is a kind of presage of oblivion, of what it would feel like to submerge the self, and forsake the punishing pace that Plath set for herself as poet, mother, and wife. "Tulips" is aswim in the competing and complementary elements of her Promethean life, evoking the great weight on her psyche of all she had wanted to accomplish, and of what it felt like, for a short while, to relinquish all ambition, which the excited tulips arouse, and to which her wound resonates in the redness of the blood signifying both creativity and death. A reader of poetry might well think of Amy Lowell's marching tulips, of the poetry of influence that propelled Plath to write to Roethke as one of the progenitors of her work, enclosing a poem that she believed freed her of his authority, so that she could proudly stand on her own, paradoxically learning to be herself out of poetry he had fathered in her.

Ted Hughes identified with the swings of mood his wife experienced because they were his own. "It's not true that only women have children," he wrote to Aurelia and Warren: "I think the general psychological upheaval is quite as severe for the father. This was complicated, as an illness might be." Frieda's arrival had caused a "profound inner revolution" that came at the same time as he was becoming a much in demand public figure. Sylvia's letters are full of all the invitations he accepted and rejected as they struggled to make time for themselves and their child. He compared his involvement in literary life to entering "a small windowless cell"—not a life at all, in other words, but a form of incarceration with "millions of invisible eyes . . . watching through the walls." Like Sylvia in hospital, he experienced through both Frieda's birth and his emerging fame a kind of out-of-body episode, making it difficult to be just himself. He adored Frieda and was not then prepared to see that now it would be increasingly difficult to tend to himself, which is an experience that any parent—more or less—understands. For Sylvia, it was enough to have a respite, those ten days in hospital, but for Ted seeking relief from family and the world that tried to get at him would become increasingly paramount. He would try to manage his desire to escape through holidays and, soon, a home in the country, but all that would not suffice. In early 1961, he wrote Lucas Myers: "Last year was a sort of death-march, except for Frieda." He was exhausted with "nervous tics of all the kinds I had always thought impossible for me, came from my turning from a youngest son into a father of sorts. Did you go through any of that?" In some ways, with the world's attention not yet up to the pitch that pestered Ted, Sylvia, drained of the poisons in her appendix, had been liberated. In late April 1961, Ted wrote to Aurelia and Warren: "Sylvia's been writing at a great pace ever since she's been out of hospital & has really broken through into something wonderful—one poem about 'Tulips.'"

Something else had happened in hospital, which Sylvia noted in her journal: After surgery, she had spoken with a fellow patient about her breakdown and "mis-applied shock treatments." That patient became, in effect, the first auditor of *The Bell Jar*, which Plath had conceived during negotiations with Knopf. To Ann Davidow and her husband Leo, she confessed: "the dykes broke and I stayed awake all night seized by fearsome excitement, saw how it should be done, started the next day." The novel is "chock full of real people. . . . It's probably godawful, but it's so funny, and yet serious, it makes me laugh."

It had been Plath's plan to write a novel about a young woman's education at Cambridge, having rejected the idea that she could write a sustained fiction about her suicide attempt and its aftermath. Now she realized that she needed to back up, to a time before her arrival in England, and to the events that had resulted in her first rebirth. In her letters home she had contrasted her cheerful treatment in an English hospital to previous, lugubrious American hospitalizations. It seems that the suffering of those earlier days could finally be depicted in a novel by tying the punishing personal trauma of her protagonist to a punitive society. Perhaps in an English hospital, Sylvia was finally able to put together the inchoate elements of a novel that had stymied her for several years. A model of what to do was at hand.

Florence, the protagonist of Mavis Gallant's novel *Green Water, Green Sky*, isn't well, and like Esther Greenwood in *The Bell Jar*, this young woman struggles with her divided self. Her cousin thinks of her in "twin pictures, love and resentment . . . always there, one reflecting the other, water under sky. . . . She had always been a moody girl with an unpredictable temper." At the heart of Flor's distemper is her mother: "their closeness had been a trap, and each could now think, If it hadn't been for you, my life would have been different. If only you had gone out of my life at the right time." Flor pretends to be "perfectly all right," saying what her mother, Bonnie, "wanted said." Flor's friend Doris tells her: "Everybody makes someone else pay for something, I don't know why. If you are as awful to your mother as she says you are, you are making her pay. . . . All children eventually make their parents pay, and pay, and pay." Yet Bonnie also believes her daughter worships her, making it even harder for Flor to assert herself. Flor gravitates to a man she marries who can save her, since she lacks, in Europe, an "emotional country," a home for her feelings. Plath's own sense of displacement, even as she shifted her novel's time frame to the period before Ted Hughes, remained an abiding aspect of Esther Greenwood's alienation.[7] Flor confesses: "I can't leave my mother, and she won't go. Maybe I don't dare. She used to need me. Maybe now I need her. What would I do at home?

My grandmother is dead. I haven't got a home. I know I sound as if I feel sorry for myself, but I haven't got anything." Flor has lost, in fact, what she had, what sounds very much like Sylvia Plath's adolescence: "she was a high-spirited attractive girl," Bonnie recalls: "She could have had any one of a dozen tremendous men." What Flor no longer has is a sense of herself. She has apparently succumbed, as William Sheldon suggested, to a midlife ennui that has followed hard upon happy, cosseted, but illusory early years. Flor hungers for the oblivion of sleep, a cessation of the consciousness that comes to haunt Esther Greenwood.

Esther Greenwood, in New York City, can no longer believe in herself as a success story. She thinks of how "all the little successes I'd totted up so happily at college fizzled to nothing outside the slick marble and plate-glass fronts along Madison Avenue." The city seems impossible for Esther to penetrate, just as Europe leaves Flor stranded. Esther, more articulate than Flor, and more ambitious, finds the accelerated competition of Manhattan utterly debilitating. "After nineteen years of running after good marks and prizes and grants of one sort and another, I was letting up, slowing down, dropping clean out of the race."

Esther looks around for relief and latches on to the bold Doreen, who stays out late and takes risks with men that no young lady of her generation and station, society said, should countenance. Esther wonders why "I couldn't go the whole way doing what I shouldn't, the way Doreen did, and this made me even sadder and more tired." Flor cannot even get out of bed. Esther is forced to move according to the timetable of magazine publication.

Women in *The Bell Jar*, except for the rare Doreen, seem projections of male desire and domination. In the childbirth Esther witnesses when boyfriend Buddy Willard takes her on his medical school rounds, the mother is put into a kind of "twilight sleep," and afterwards Esther comments: "I thought it sounded just like the sort of drug a man would invent." Sylvia's own experience at home with midwives seems to have heightened her sense of what she had escaped. It would come as such a shock later, when Ted, who had been so helpful, admitted that children had never really been part of his plan. When Esther says that she did not "feel up to asking" Buddy "if there were any other ways to have babies," it is as if Sylvia was saying to her readers: "There must be another way." Finding that other way, perhaps, is what gave her the perspective to write *The Bell Jar*.

Esther is incensed when she learns that Buddy Willard, who expects her to be pure, has had sex. Disgusted, she remembers her mother and grandmother saying that he was a "fine clean boy," from a "clean family," and how "clean Buddy was the kind of person a girl should stay fine and clean for." Imagine Sylvia Plath, in her London flat, with Ted—not always so clean, as she sometimes regretted—nevertheless sharing a life of creativity that the bogusly antiseptic Buddy Willards of the world could not imagine.

Creating Buddy Willard may have given Sylvia Plath an enormous lift and feeling of gratitude that she had left the confinement of a culture that closed in on Esther. Quentin Compson comes to mind, horrified that his sister is no longer a virgin, when Esther comes to the conclusion that Buddy's innocence has been an affectation: "From the first night Buddy Willard kissed me and said I must go out with a lot of boys, he made me feel I was much more sexy and experienced than he was and that everything he did like hugging and kissing and petting was simply what I made him feel like doing out of the blue, he couldn't help it and didn't know how it came about." Buddy was a pretender—unlike Caddy Compson who refuses to pretend to her brother that she is an innocent.

Think also of Sylvia's shock, not so long after *The Bell Jar* was completed, when she learned that Ted, too, was a pretender, a breaker of the faith that Esther and her creator wanted to maintain, a faith that relied on a level of trust and honesty that broke their hearts when their men destroyed the fiction of their fidelity. As Esther puts it, Buddy led a "double life," perpetuating the ruse that he is "superior to people." That recognition of duplicity is what Sheldon said made idyllic childhoods such a poor preparation for adulthood. Esther concludes that she was only "purely happy" up to the age of nine, as she sums up the experience that Sylvia enjoyed: "After that—in spite of the Girl Scouts and the piano lessons and the water-color lessons and the dancing lessons and the sailing camp, all of which my mother scrimped to give me, and college, with crewing in the mist before breakfast and blackbottom pies and the little new firecrackers of ideas going off every day—I had never been really happy again." The scholarships, the prizes, the striving for that kind of success is at an end: "I felt like a racehorse in a world without racetracks or a champion college footballer suddenly confronted by Wall Street and a business suit, his days of glory shrunk to a little gold cup on his mantel with a date engraved on it like the date on a tombstone."

Coming home from the devastating month in New York City, Esther reenacts the depression that Sylvia felt: "I stepped from the air-conditioned compartment onto the station platform, and the motherly breath of the suburbs enfolded me. It smelt of lawn sprinklers and station wagons and tennis rackets and dogs and babies. A summer calm laid its soothing hand over everything, like death." Esther's mother is waiting, and Esther feels smothered by it all, in what she calls a "private totalitarian state"— not unconnected from the politics of the novel, in which the execution of the Rosenbergs hardly even registers on the consciousness of Esther's New York cohort.

Quentin Compson smashes his watch. Esther follows "the green, luminous course of the second hand and the minute hand and the hour hand
of the bedside clock through their circles and semicircles, every night for
seven nights, without missing a second, or a minute, or an hour." She cannot
sleep anymore than Sylvia could sleep that summer of her death-watch. "I
wanted to do everything once and for all and be through with it." At least
death has a finality, a conclusiveness to it.

Sylvia Plath, in London in 1961, was composing the words that in the
summer of 1953 she could not write about herself and that now could be
invested in her character who can get no help: "Doctor Gordon twiddled
a silver pencil. 'Your mother tells me you are upset.'" His blandness, as he
sits across an "acre of highly polished desk," is the problem—not Esther's.
He keeps tapping his pencil. Is he bored? Is he even listening? He has
"features . . . so perfect he was almost pretty," Esther observes. No wonder
she hates him. How could she connect with someone who lived in such
an immaculate, ordered world. She had hoped for a "kind, ugly intuitive
man." Esther's brutally administered electric shock treatments make her
wonder "what terrible thing it was that I had done." In short, this "therapy"
is torture, a punishment. Institutionalization, to Esther, is the same as being
hidden away.

It all changes for Esther when she meets Dr. Nolan: "I was surprised to
have a woman. I didn't think they had woman psychiatrists. This woman
was a cross between Myrna Loy and my mother. She wore a white blouse
and a full skirt gathered at the waist by a wide leather belt, and stylish,
crescent-shaped spectacles." This is Ruth Beuscher who had style and who
really listened. Esther, so aware of the esthetics of existence, is right to be
surprised that a woman is treating her. There were not many women then
trained, as Beuscher had been under William Sheldon, to be prepared for
someone like Sylvia Plath, for someone like Esther Greenwood, who sees
every aspect of her life determined by male prerogatives. The Myrna Loy
reference is no throwaway. Consider the aplomb she displays in all those
movies with the suave William Powell, holding her own, with a critical yet
warm sensibility. As Lee Kravetz imagines in *The Last Confessions of Sylvia
Plath*, for Beuscher to have succeeded in such a world required a bold and
canny intelligence that even a misogynist like Sheldon had to acknowledge,
however maladroitly. What Dr. Nolan and Dr. Beuscher show is another
way for Esther, and for Sylvia, to survive.[8]

Dr. Nolan's "crescent-shaped spectacles" signal Esther's rebirth, a burgeoning development of the self, like the crescent moon that can excite
feelings of hope, an emergence of something new. At the same time, Esther
realizes she is a phenomenon, acknowledged by Joan Gilling, who tells

Esther she has read about her. "I've got a pile of clippings somewhere." As for Sylvia, so for Esther, she is made to feel her significance—that the world is watching. That Esther is not impressed with the suicidal Joan is almost beside the point since what is important is that Joan is there to give the clippings to Esther for her scrapbook, the sort of record of a life that Sylvia herself liked to compile. Joan may be the "beaming double of my old best self, specially designed to follow and torment me," yet the very recognition of same shows Esther's difference from Joan, who never makes the transition to health that Esther makes by coming to terms with her "old best self."

Dr. Nolan says exactly the right thing when Esther asks her how many shock treatments she must undergo: "That depends . . . on you and me." Dr. Nolan's role is get Esther to take the next step, to recognize "I was my own woman." Esther recovers when she no longer feels bound by the conception of others. Sylvia Plath was able to write *The Bell Jar* when she felt the same way, with the proviso: "How did I know that someday—at college, in Europe, somewhere, anywhere—the bell jar, with its stifling distortions, wouldn't descend again?"

5

Every morning in the spring of 1961, Sylvia repaired to the study the Merwins had set aside (they thought for Ted). They were miffed to learn she was using it and were "oddly spiteful."[9] Plath did not seem to detect their animus, but their alienation from her would later contribute to her sense of isolation and her quest for allies.

Sylvia boasted to her mother about how much she was writing, although remaining careful not to say *anything* about *The Bell Jar*, which would later grieve Aurelia because of its send-up of her, Mrs. Prouty, and so many others. Sylvia's letters home were about her mother's forthcoming visit, including plans to nestle her in the Merwin's "grand bedroom" and to equip Aurelia to babysit for a few weeks while Sylvia and Ted toured France and stayed at the Merwins' farm, resting, eating well, and sunbathing. Her letters reveal that taking care of Frieda had been exhausting for the couple, and that the hospital scene of "Tulips" presaged how much Sylvia yearned for a release from responsibility even as she prepared to return to mothering. Ted's letter to Daniel and Helga Huws complained: "I wish we had gone almost anywhere else." He did not say much about the visit to the Merwins, who did little to conceal their dislike of Sylvia.

6

By early August 1961, Sylvia and Ted were preparing to move to Court Green in Devon, agreeing on a purchase price for house and land of 3,600 pounds with a 10 percent deposit. Aurelia had loaned them $1,400. "Ted is in seventh heaven," she wrote her mother, saying she looked forward to fixing up the house, which need a lot of refurbishing. To John Sweeney, who had recorded her at Harvard, she provided a succinct picture of an "antique thatched house, barn, stables, orchard, vegetable garden on 2½ acres of walled land." Moving to the country was momentous, exciting, and disconcerting. She had acclimated to London and had to accede to Ted's pressing wish to liberate himself from the claustrophobia of literary life. Yet she took to their pastoral idyll with enthusiasm, reveling in her spacious house:

Advertisement for a Bendix washing machine, 1957.

Her "whole spirit" had "expanded immensely." A cleaning lady, a local doctor and midwife nurse, and the prospect of a Bendix washing machine made
her feel all was in place for the birth of her second child.

The move to Court Green coincided with completion of *The Bell Jar*.
Sylvia claimed to Ruth Beuscher that she wrote the "serio-comic" novel in
two months,[10] "about my New York summer at <u>Mademoiselle</u> & breakdown,
fictionalized, but not so much that doing it & coming back to life is due so
much to you that you are the only person I could dedicate it to."[11] The "not
so much" related to the novel's fidelity to her experience, however much it
strayed from factuality. At that moment, she believed she had control of her
life, which is perhaps what made the novel possible to write, whereas a second
novel, taking up her life from Cambridge onwards, had yet to be.

7

The poems Plath wrote in September 1961 seem to emerge from a state of
mind alien to the cheerful, busy letters to her mother and the business of
publishing her poems. The persona of "Wuthering Heights," "Blackberry-
ing," "Finisterre,"[12] and "The Surgeon at 2 a.m." is isolated, undone, exposed.
The Romans believed that Finisterre was the end of the earth, a surgeon
looks at a body as a garden with a lung-tree and snaky organs, part of a
"purple wilderness," the architecture of the body reminding the surgeon of
Roman aqueducts and the Baths of Caracalla: "The body is a Roman thing"
a ruin under repair, just as Sylvia and Ted were getting the worms out of
ancient Court Green, cleaning up, and gardening. She confessed to Ruth
Fainlight that she missed the city and its cultural attractions. "Wuthering
Heights" is about feeling hemmed in: "The horizons ring me like faggots,"
the poem begins. Court Green's surrounding spaciousness also seems to
have represented a lack of center—as suggested in the first line of "Black-
berrying": "Nobody in the lane, and nothing, nothing but blackberries."
What is a refuge is also a void. These poems are the laments of a displaced
person. On October 22, 1961, she wrote to her mother asking for copies of
the *Ladies' Home Journal*: "It has a special Americanness which I feel the
need to dip into, now I'm in exile."

Exile becomes a cul-de-sac in a forbidding poem, "The Moon and the
Yew Tree," completed the same day Sylvia wrote to her mother: "The trees
of the mind are black . . . I simply cannot see where there is to get to." The
moon is stripped of its romantic associations, appearing "White as a knuckle
and terribly upset." The "Gothic shape" of the Yew forms a "message" of

"blackness and silence." The next day, Sylvia completed "Mirror" portraying the self swallowed whole in its reflection, rewarding the "I" with "tears and an agitation of hands." In the poem, in the mirror, in "me she has drowned a young girl" and coming toward her is "an old woman" surfacing "day after day, / like a terrible fish." It is hard to say exactly why such disturbing poems broke through to the surface of Sylvia's daily celebrations of deliverance from the cramped life of London. Perhaps spreading out at Court Green with its ancient mound of a buried past and house that no one knew how old, unearthed a primal anxiety that her poetry had to affirm. Perhaps her craving for the intimate female companionship of Ruth Fainlight, Suzette Macedo, and Helga Huws—to whom she wrote invitations to visit—were the signals of her bereft state. She never stopped wishing for family members to visit her. She would say that all she needed was her work and Ted and Frieda, but the poems suggest otherwise. Sylvia joked about turning thirty and never mentioning her birthday again. In Augustine's *Confessions*, she had underlined: "And lo, I was now in my thirtieth year, sticking in the same mire, greedy of enjoying things present, which passed away and wasted my soul."

The poems seem also to presage the change of seasons, and a dread of the next five "grim" months of "dark evenings closing in in midafternoon." She wished for a red carpet that would "keep me forever optimistic," she told her mother. All her life she had been a weathervane. It has often been said that Sylvia told her mother what her mother wanted to hear: Everything was not only all right, it was super. But those letters are just as likely expressions of Sylvia's own bifurcated sensibility, expressed one way in her letters and another way in her poems and journal. To say the poems are the reality and the letters are not is, then, misleading. Sylvia was a split personality that she was aware of and read about in Mikesell's *Abnormal Psychology*. When she first entered McLean, she had "All the classic signs of schizophrenia," according to Ruth Beuscher: "Sense that there was a body inhabiting her body among them." [HR] Such split in the self may well be one reason why Shirley Jackson's work appealed to Plath.

The syndrome of schizophrenia—as it is called in Mikesell's book— fascinated her. It is likely that the idea of double and of alternative selves appealed to her because in her writing she seemed to split off from her everyday self. In Mikesell, she read about the schizophrenic who believed he was "one person at night and another during the day." Augustine had said as much in her underlined copy of *Confessions*: "And yet there is so much difference betwixt myself and myself, within that moment wherein I pass from waking to sleeping, or return from sleeping to waking." Another Mikesell schizophrenic spoke of his good and evil selves. She read about changes in puberty, marriage, or childbirth that could exacerbate schizophrenic episodes. Sylvia was more than six months pregnant and did not complain of sickness except for fatigue, but depression can be associated with hormonal changes, although she cycled through manic depression at various stages in her life.

All Ted knew to do when his wife seemed down was to hypnotize her, wait on her, and advise her to write, write, write. His own state of mind, judging by his letters, was opaque—perhaps even to himself. But a phrase in a letter to the rock-climbing Al Alvarez, written in late 1961, suggests he shared some of Sylvia's bleak moods and desire for company: "When you next come climbing King Arthur's cliffs you must apply your brakes at about Taunton, which should slow you down sufficiently to turn in at our gate & come in & stand on our bare cheerless floors for a while, & maybe eat an apple. We'd be very glad to see you."

In *Birthday Letters*, Hughes poses as psychobiographer, boldly announcing in "Apprehensions": "Your writing was also your fear" that all would be taken away—not only her husband but her dreams, her children, and even her typewriter and sewing machine. All that is missing from his catalogue of "terror" is her Bendix. Hughes was well read in psychology and had years to reflect on his wife's behavior, attuning himself to her manic-depressive phases, described in Mikesell's book by a patient who declares: "As well as I know the sun, the air, and the earth, I have known death. . . . Fear dominated my character." For Sylvia, her brooding mental landscape fixated on the moon: "The day-moon lights up like a sorry mother" ("Sleep in the Mojave Desert");" "the moon too abases her subjects" ("The Rival"); "The moon is my mother. She is not sweet like Mary" ("The Moon and the Yew Tree"); "The moon also is merciless" ("Elm"). The "cancerous pallors" of the moon in "Purdah" reflect the troubled topography of thinking and feeling in Plath's poems, and also in *The Bell Jar*: "My mother's face floated to mind, a pale, reproachful moon, at her last and first visit to the asylum since my twentieth birthday." In "Apprehensions" (May 28, 1962) Plath asks, "Is there no way out of the mind?"

Sylvia was never quite convinced of the sway of the planets, yet something in her makeup made her particularly susceptible to the tides of the universe that made hers a tidal life. Swimming inside her was a child whose weight was making her feel ponderous. She wrote to Ruth Fainlight: "Life here is very pleasant in spite of absolutely black weather & huge winds." Except when it (life) wasn't. Another title for a Plath biography—borrowed from Kierkegaard: *Either/Or*.

Winter in an old house numbed her: "it's so bare & cold with just the boards." She wrote her mother about ordering two more electric heaters and carpets. The Saxton grant for fiction did not add to pressure on her because she had a draft of *The Bell Jar* that she could divide up and send in with her reports to the foundation. She still had not told her mother about the novel, referring to it as a "batch of stuff." Olwyn Hughes only got the positive spin: "I can't imagine living anywhere else now nor can Ted." So there.

In spite of aches and pains, including a weird tendency for her arms to feel heavy and tingly as if punctured with needles, pregnancy soothed Sylvia who felt lazy and "cowlike," as she did with Frieda. If writing really induced the fear that Ted evoked in his poem, "Apprehensions," pregnancy proved a respite, since she no longer even pretended to be working in her study. To her mother she presented a picture of a community awaiting the arrival of the baby. The doctor, midwife, shopkeepers, townspeople—all seemed on her side. She baked for Ted and Frieda, storing up goodies for them during the time she would need to recover from childbirth.

8

The child arrived on January 17, 1962, with a great gush of water that drenched Sylvia, Ted, the midwife, and the doctor. She seemed elated and already, it seems, revising her earlier depiction of herself as placidly cow-like, writing to the Macedos on January 31:" I am always so broody before a baby is born I say nothing." One reason Sylvia Plath will always deserve yet another biography is her polyvalent personality.

As she approached the age of thirty, she was entering a period of special concern for the Promethean personality. In a Sheldon footnote, she underlined his reference to Jung who also believed the thirties were a sort of "critical threshold for emotional life."[13] She marked out Sheldon's prognostication: "It seems to be a general principle that if the Promethean personality can hold out and remain true to itself past the thirty-fifth year, the second half of life is likely to be immensely happy." Certainly, Sylvia had a tendency to project beyond the present in plans for large family and her own establishment as mother, wife, and writer. She never thought of herself as alone, as a career woman—to use her word—so that her happiness depended on a family destiny, which is why she always included Warren, and then his wife Margaret, and the other Plath relatives, plus Ted's family, in a kind of empire of self.

Both Sylvia and Ted were entering a new passage: "Satisfaction with marriage generally goes downhill in the thirties (for those who have remained together) compared with the highly valued, vision-supporting marriage of the twenties," Gail Sheehy observes. A reduced social life and care of the children resulted in restrictions that chafed Ted, who began to succumb to what Sheehy calls "a vague but persistent sense of *wanting to be something more*." In the transitional stage of the thirties, with some men and women, a desperate urge is expressed in the "tearing up the life one spent most of his twenties putting together." Divorce is often the outcome. At the same time, Ted was feeling the full strength and attractiveness of his success. In Sheehy's words, men become aware of "their own social and sexual powers and quite satisfied with themselves." Women, on the other hand, approach their thirties "*less* sure of themselves than they had been as young adolescents when they were far ahead of the boys."

Plath and Hughes were on a devastating trajectory that neither of them had yet to recognize, let alone understand. Sheehy explains: "Until very recently in our culture, most men and women spent a good part of their twenties and thirties living one of two illusions: that career success would make them immortal, or that a mate would complete them. (Even now, those illusions die very hard.) Men and women were on separate tracks. The career as an all-encompassing end to life turned out to be a flawed vision, an emotional cul-de-sac. But did attaching oneself to a man and children prove to be any less incomplete as life's ultimate fulfillment?" To be sure every life and every biography is different, but nonetheless they can seem, in some respects, all the same. Already, by October 27, 1960, Sylvia was writing to Olwyn Hughes: "I've been having a lovely birthday week to console me for catapulting so swiftly towards thirty"—not to mention that line in "Tulips" about the "thirty-year-old cargo boat / Stubbornly hanging on to my name and address."

The birth of a second child floored Ted Hughes. He admitted as much in a letter to Esther and Leonard Baskin: "I was flat." Sylvia noticed he did not take to Nicholas as he had done to Frieda. Both had been expecting a girl, but Sylvia got over her disappointment quickly and could not figure out what had caused Ted to pull away. He would later tell her that it was all too much, this second birth had awakened his anxieties. Winifred Davies, Sylvia's midwife and confidant, noticed that after the birth of the second child, the writing schedule for husband and wife no longer seemed so simple as taking turns minding Frieda. "Sylvia used to interrupt his train of thought with cooking or the children," she told Harriet Rosenstein, and he "resented the interruption."

Suzette Macedo, who had seen the couple both in London and at Court Green, claimed, in retrospect, to have detected Ted's restlessness. He behaved like a "trapped animal." Harriet Rosenstein reported Suzette's comments that "he had a way of—sort—of—(here she glances sidelong very swiftly)—looking for an exit." Suzette said she spoke often on the phone to Sylvia, who reported that after Nicholas's birth, Ted referred to him as "the usurper."

In retrospect, in "The Rabbit Catcher," using the same title Plath had used for her poem, Hughes paused to glimpse a reckoning with himself, but then he shifted the burden to her: "Had you caught something in me, / Nocturnal and unknown to me? / Or was it / Your doomed self, your tortured, crying / Suffocating self?" Even though Hughes had been depressed during his time in America and yearned for home, he never seems to have factored in just how much exile and climate depleted Plath: "chilblains undid me . . . I got very grim," she wrote to Paul and Clarissa Roche.

Sometime after Nicholas's birth, Sylvia let loose in an undated journal entry that hearkened back to the New Year's Eve party before her baby was born. She described sixteen-year-old Nicola, the fetching daughter of bank manager George Tyrer and his wife Marjorie. To Sylvia, it seemed that Nicola was putting in an "obvious bid for Ted's interest." Ted thought of "educating" her: "He wanted to give her 'Orlando.' I groaned and gave her 'The Catcher in the Rye.'" Sylvia observed his "Biblical need to preach." The scene aroused in her a "curious desperate sense of being locked in among these people." She longed for London, a "big world." She envied Nicola's "complete flowerlike involvement in self, beautifying, opening to advantage. This is the need I have, in my 30th year—to unclutch the sticky loving fingers of babies & treat myself to myself and my husband alone for a bit. To purge myself of sour milk, urinous nappies, bits of lint and the loving slovenliness of motherhood." [PJ] A talk with neighbor Marjorie Tyrer about childbirth and babies resulted in Marjorie confessing she never really wanted babies, disliked "cooking, housewifery," and was happiest living in London. An undercurrent of dissatisfaction for both Sylvia and Ted had yet to break out into the open. Nicola began showing up at Court Green with various excuses for visiting—at least that is how Sylvia saw it. One evening she spotted Nicola and Ted standing together "at opposite sides of the path under the bare laburnum like kids back from the date, she posed & coy." [PJ]

9

On January 31, 1962, Sylvia wrote to her mother: "I have got awfully homesick for you since the last baby—and for the Cape & deep snow & such American things. Can't wait for your visit." Sylvia's letters, so full of domestic details and child care, portrayed Ted as endlessly patient with her milk fevers and moods—which she alluded to in the "small things" that still loomed "very large. I get so impatient with myself, chafing to do a hundred things that have piled up, and barely managing one or two." The constant familial responsibilities wore away at a restless man whom Al Alvarez told me was more of a prowler than a patriarch. Imagine the exhausting daily routine as Sylvia reported to her mother: "Ted is still taking the brunt of Frieda—she needs watching every minute. Her favorite trick is peeling our poor wallpaper off the wall, there are so many cracks she can get her fingernails in."

Sylvia was doing no writing. This was not the woman Ted had wanted, and she knew it: "How I envy girls whose mothers can just drop in on them. I long to have a day or two on jaunts with just Ted—we can hardly see each other over the mountains of diapers & demands of babies." Nothing stopped him from writing, and Sylvia continued to extol his work, but that was just it: Writing was his *alone* now, and even if that was a temporary change, he believed he would never get back the Sylvia Plath that he had had all to himself. She was regressing, in his view, talking of home and the recipes her mother and other families members made. "I am getting very sentimental about family things. For instance, someday I hope to be well-off enough to send for grammy's desk. I'd like it to be Frieda's little desk," she told Aurelia. She was effusive over issues of the *Ladies' Home Journal* that she read "cover to cover." Her letters to her mother announce all this homesickness in the most bland terms that took no account of the toll on Ted. She craved "bits of personal detail about the people I used to know."

While Sylvia fed Frieda and Nicholas, cooked and baked, mended and washed clothes and shopped, Ted made frequent trips to London via Exeter to do his BBC broadcasts. In early March 1962, a snowfall delighted Sylvia but it had melted by midday—a fitting picture of her fleeting homebound feeling. Perhaps she remembered the ice sliding and snow huts she built with friends when winter was still a wonder to be recounted in exhilarating detail in her diaries. Having children—more children—could bring that childhood back to her.

As Sylvia made Court Green more and more hers, Ted heard some version of what Sylvia told her mother: "I think having babies is really the happiest experience of my life. I would just like to go on and on." She wanted to plant American corn seed. It was an orderly household, remembered housekeeper Nancy Axworthy: "Her herbs and spices were lined up like little regiments of soldiers." For Ted, that kind of order was too much. [HR]

10

By March 1962, the cold had turned to damp, and Sylvia suffered what she called the "March megrims," relieved only by a sunny day. Toward the end of the month she seem to pluck up, poised between memories of childhood piano lessons and musing on a new activity: horseback riding, both of which her children might eventually desire. "Life begins at 30!" she exclaimed to her mother—repeating the phrase as well to friends—as she scrupulously returned the sum Aurelia had advanced toward the purchase of Court Green. She was nearing completion of one of her most ambitious poems, a short verse play: "Three Women: A Poem for Three Voices," set in a maternity ward.

The first voice sounds like the exuberant Plath of pregnancy: "I cannot help smiling at what it is I know. / Leaves and petals attend me. I am ready." The second voice, a second self, miscarries, as Sylvia did, declaring: "I saw death in the bare trees, a deprivation," and asking, "Is this the one sin then, this old dead love of death?" The third voice comes in somewhere between the other two: "the face / Went on shaping itself with life, as if I was ready." What face? The face of the unborn child but also the faces of governments, parliaments, societies, the "faceless faces of important men." Such men flatten the world, the second voice declares, because they are flat (without the curvature and fecundity of women), as are the doctors who "hug their flatness like a kind of health." Giving birth in this poem is, in part, participating in the monstrousness of the world. The mother of the first voice describes the "center of an atrocity. / What pains, what sorrows must I be mothering?" The birth is a drain: "It milks my life." With the birth of Nicholas, Sylvia said she felt broken to bits, yet survived without a scratch. "I am breaking apart like the world," the first voice announces, as the voices blend into one another. "Three Women" seems to emerge out of Nicholas's wondrous, troubled arrival: "this blue, furious boy, / Shiny and strange, as if he had hurtled from a star?" Frieda's had been an easy birth, but the boy is "looking so angrily!" Yet the voice softens into acceptance of his guileless innocence: "May he keep so."

The three women are, by turns, hopeful and despondent, obsessed with what is happening to their bodies and yet at the same time all too conscious of what a destructive world might make of them. Carrying children and caring for them was an uneasy Eden for Plath, not sure "how long I can be a wall around my green property," poised, as the second voice says, between town and country, despair and hope: "The city waits and aches. / The little grasses / Crack through stone, and they are green with life." Had any poem before "Three Women" treated childbirth as an epic, as another act in the history of the world that the mother perpetuates with both promise and dread?

On March 27, 1962, Sylvia wrote to Ruth Beuscher, describing the move to Court Green after feeling cramped in London and house hunting in

Devon: "I have never felt the power of <u>land</u> before." She mentioned the grim winter and the "Dickensian disease" of chilblains, Nicholas's birth after a worrisome miscarriage the previous year, gardening, cooking, house repairs, and finishing a novel in under two months. All seemed in place, as she concluded the letter to her lifeline: "It is an immense relief to me to feel I can write you every so often; it heartens me no end to feel you are <u>there</u>, whether I talk to you or not."

11

April 1962 weather proved not much better than March, bludgeoning Sylvia's spirit. Ruth Fainlight, wife of novelist Alan Sillitoe, who had recently given birth to a boy after three miscarriages, would understand. Fainlight called her feeling for Sylvia "friendship at first sight." They were both literary women married to prominent writers. These two Americans were keen to share their parallel lives. [HR]

In "Elm," dedicated to Fainlight, a female voice says "I know the bottom . . . I know it with my great tap root." That voice does not fear the bottom: "I have been there," she says. Was Sylvia thinking of Ruth, who had written about miscarriage in "Sapphic Moon"? The "she" is a tree, who speaks, presumably, in the voice of the woman who addresses it: "I have suffered the atrocity of sunsets. / Scorched to the root," a "wind of such violence." Are the clouds that "pass and disperse" the "faces of love"? The words of "Three Women" (atrocity, faces) infect the "I" (tree or person) of "Elm": who questions "this face / So murderous in its strangle of branches?" This is a tree of life and of death, of romance and mordacity with "snaky acids" that "kiss," forming an "isolate," an extract of elm Plath may have studied in botany but is here also an expression of a separation into "slow faults / That kill, that kill, that kill."

The great elm that stood outside Court Green, and that also makes an appearance in "Three Women," seemed to serve as totem of a history of conflicting feelings that could not be expressed in letters home, to London friends, or even, it seems, to her husband. Sylvia often said that her Court Green neighbors were nice and friendly, but they were not friends to confide in. John Avery, a North Tawnton Ironmonger, remembered her coming into his hardware store "just dressed out of this world" in long dresses "way above us, as far as modern trends went." She amazed everyone, he said, and she reveled in it. He did not think she realized that some people snubbed her: "It takes a long time for someone to be accepted." [HR]

Sylvia Plath was indeed an isolate. She had grown up on Elmwood Road in Wellesley known for the elms that lined its streets, spent her first year in Haven House on Elm Street, frequented a campus with a botanical garden that included elms, attended Maureen Buckley's coming-out party at her estate, The Elms, and now had her own elm-enveloped manor built who knew when. She wrote on an elm plank meant for a coffin lid, and on which she drafted more than a dozen versions of "Elm." How much did she know about elms, an ancient species mentioned in Homer? The first woman in Norse mythology is made from an Elm. In tarot, the tree is emblematic of human development. This is a poet who saw her own plight writ large in the ages of the world and the very elements of nature.

Biographers naturally want to see the poem as a premonition of Hughes's infidelity in lines such as "Love is a shadow" with the departed lover "gone off / like a horse." They want to see the after effect of electric shock in the tree's scorched roots. Maybe. But the poem seems larger than any misgivings about a husband or modern medicine. So far Ted had not given much sign of an impending departure, and for all her skepticism about doctors, Plath relied on them, whatever their moral or male failings. Could it not be that in Sheldon's work on the Promethean personality, she realized that what troubled her troubled the world? Could it be that her poems make of her own psychology a work of ontology, with the elm, in this case, being the object of study that is about being?

Sylvia's life seemed to be turning, moment by moment, in sentences like this one, written to her mother on April 25, 1962: "On Easter Sunday the world relented & spring arrived." Sometimes she felt and acted as though the world was against her, like Stephen Crane's man who tried to get the attention of the universe. The upkeep of the house, the children, the gardening (catching up with planting as the weather improved), the writing, including reviewing for the *New Statesman*—and putting it all in some order led to letters like this on April 30 to friends Marvin and Kathy Kane: "No no we are not dead. . . . Only exhausted." After putting their noses to the earth all day, they fell like "great stones into bed."

Twice in May 1962, recovering from spring planting and reveling in warmer, sunny days, Sylvia drew back and looked at what they had wrought and pronounced it their own Eden. Ted called it "Cape Cod August weather." Sylvia had turned brown, as she had for so many American summers. Ted mentioned their rhubarb, a vegetable that was often on the table during Sylvia's childhood. He had no doubt that the weather had lifted her spirits. Did he exaggerate, though, reading more of himself into her when he told Aurelia and Warren: "Since she left America, she's lost the terrible panic pressure of the American poetry world—which keeps them all keeping up on each other."

12

With the visit of David and Assia Wevill on May 18, 1962, the atmosphere at Court Green changed, although to David nothing seemed amiss when he returned to the Chalcot Square flat sublet from Sylvia and Ted.[14] What happened on that visit remains somewhat occluded, with some accounts portraying Assia as pursuing Ted and others emphasizing that he took the initiative, later showing up at her advertising firm in London. Nothing in Sylvia's letters or calendar from this period suggests she was disturbed by the visit. She usually mentioned visitors in letters to her mother, but she made no reference to the Wevills. If she kept a diary, it has gone missing.

After three weeks of silence, Sylvia wrote to her mother, mentioning work on a tapestry: "Wonderfully calming." She did not say that Assia Wevill had sent her the materials. On June 8, 1962, Al Alvarez visited Court Green and saw nothing amiss. The day before she had written to Aurelia: "This is the richest & happiest time of my life." Not so in "The Rabbit Catcher," completed on May 21: "Tight wires between us." The poem ended: "The constriction killing me also." In "Event," completed the same day, we seem to enter their bedroom with the "child in the white crib" while the couple lie, their backs against one another in the very posture of bereaved estrangement: "Love cannot come here." It seems a third party is involved: "Who has dismembered us?"

In his own "The Rabbit Catcher," Hughes seems to begin where Plath's poem ends: "What / Had bared our edges . . . / Bleeding each other?" Characteristically, he is "baffled," thrown off by her "dybbuk fury." He treats her comments as a mood, in which she decries "English private greed / Of fencing off all coastal approaches. . . . You despised England's grubby edges." How is her reaction different from his own screeds against American greed? Her own extremity of exile is pictured only as a woman out of control, at the mercy of her "furies." And then he has to nationalize her feelings, referring to her "Germanic scowl." It's Hemingway all over again calling Martha Gellhorn a "kraut." As Sylvia takes apart a rabbit trap, he sees a desecration of his heritage of the hunt in her cries of "Murderers!" It is not the rabbits but her rage that is the issue, he insists, in a scene right out of *The Misfits*, when Monroe calls the cowboys capturing wild mustangs murderers.

There never seems even a moment when Hughes stops to consider the impact of Plath's deracination on her psyche. She felt the pressure to remain a happy prisoner of Court Green, trapped as surely as those rabbits. Yet Hughes would soon say that life there was suffocating him, projecting his self-repression all onto her "Suffocating self." But to her the rabbits in traps "waited like sweethearts. / They excited him." In *Birthday Letters*, he ignores what those lines portend about the lover and his snares. In *Her Husband*, Diane Middlebrook puts it well: Plath had divined "a practice that he pursued for the rest of his life: the creation, alongside his marriage, of a kind of inner game preserve," with women, I would add, as his prey.[15]

Perhaps the "hot blue days" of June 1962, the kind of weather that made Sylvia sing with health, momentarily screened her misgivings. The cooking, baking, washing, planting, painting, and sewing that are recorded in her calendar, the work of the day, has to be balanced against poems that subvert the busy bee keeping empirical happiness of her household. The physical hard work in the garden exhausted her into euphoria: "I don't know when I've been so happy or felt so well," she wrote to her mother on June 15. It reminded her of all that toil at Lookout Farm the summer before she matriculated at Smith. In her Eden, she walked with her mate in the strawberry patch, the rhubarb, and radishes, taking in the "progress of our rows." At the same time, can anyone imagine Ted Hughes writing this kind of letter to a BBC producer?—"I have a very crammed day at the BBC Tuesday 26th and can't really manage to arrange the infinite complications of babysitters, wipers & minders twice in the same week."

All seemed well in the first ten days of Aurelia's arrival: An end of June 1962 report to Marvin and Kathy Kane: "My mother is a blessing. We are writing again, both of us, and she gets on beautifully with the babies, minds them, bakes cookies. O it is lovely. We are writing a few poems. And manage a mad morning at the BBC (working for train fare & a flight back so I can feed the baby) once in a great while."

On July 6, 1962, Sylvia arrived, along with a sulky Ted, to celebrate Elizabeth Compton's thirty-fourth birthday. Perhaps it was Elizabeth's own outgoing nature that brought out something similar in Sylvia, who enchanted houseguests with her "vivid storytelling about small stuff." She was "alive, sparkling," and "absorbed in conversation, in talk of others." She sat "like a jackknife just opened—hands thrown over her knees: 'Tell me about that!'" There was no "shop-front" about her, Elizabeth observed. She "really pierced into you." [HR]

13

On July 9, 1962, everything "went queer."

"Words Heard, by Accident, over the Phone," written two days later, declared that Sylvia was sure: It was Assia's voice coming over the line like mud, "how fluid!— / Thick as foreign coffee." Sylvia felt her house had been defiled as the voice inquired: "Is he here?" Good question. The phone call signaled to Sylvia that he had not been there all along as they counted up their rows, which in the acrimony of her suspicions became rows between them. Aurelia witnessed part of it: Sylvia burning some of his work and hers, including a novel in which he would have figured as the lionized hero; Sylvia ordering Ted out of the house.

Winifred Davies remembers how Sylvia's distress filled the house. She would "open her mouth and howl as a child would howl. Poor Frieda was terrified." [HR] Sylvia wrote to Ruth Beuscher: "I honestly hope you feel you can answer this letter by return, as I am suddenly, after all that happy stuff I wrote you some while ago, at sea, and a word from you I could carry around with me would sustain me like the Bible sustains others." The buildup to the breakup began when a restless Ted started talking about experiencing "everybody & everything." He seemed to be in a hypomanic phase—not so different from the initial stages of Sylvia's own arcing emotions.

The Wevills' visit had confirmed her suspicions. John Avery, the local ironmonger, said "it was obvious" that Ted had affairs: "He's got a real gift with women. He's the sort of man that commandeers women."[16] [HR] With Ted's constant lying about the affair Sylvia could not sleep or eat. Could she ever trust him again? Yet she considered her marriage the "center of my being." He told her: "Why should I limit myself by your happiness or unhappiness?" It was impossible to speak with her mother about this, so to Ruth Beuscher: "I do need word!"

The proofs of *The Bell Jar* "saved the day . . . I roared and roared, it was so funny and good." For the next several days Sylvia, all business, wrote to friends and fellow writers. By July 20, 1962, her letter to Beuscher exuded a new calm: "Well, we are 30. We grow up slowly, but, it appears, with a bang." Mainly she wanted practical advice on how to proceed and to maintain "my own woman-morale from day to day. And toughen myself." On July 21, she wrote to Al Alvarez about "Event," "Rabbit Catcher," and "Elm." She wanted his frank opinion: "don't be ginger." She consoled herself with visits to Elizabeth Compton, a mother with her own young children. Anyone who spent some time in Elizabeth's company, as I did, remembers the sparkle of her generous spirit. It was impossible to leave her without feeling invigorated.

On July 30, 1962, Sylvia wrote to Ruth Beuscher: "I have been at a nadir, very grim, since my last letter [July 20] to you." Headed toward writing "Daddy," she was pursuing "father-feelings from my relation with Ted" to rid herself of "little girl desires & fears." To a London friend, the writer Jillian Becker, Sylvia confessed that meeting Ted was like having her father "restored to her," but that "after Ted 'turned Nazi,' she believed that she had to 'kill' them both." [HR] Her other impulse was to say: "O fuck off, grab them all." Ted said to her: "this would either kill me or make me, and I think it might make me. And him too." She needed advice about how to handle Ted. He was writing a radio play, *Difficulties of a Bridegroom*,[17] and had been asked to rewrite the part about a femme fatale, making clearer what is real and what is not. "A nice parable illustrating your point about the reality of this woman," Sylvia concluded, still in doubt as to what Assia really meant to him. Unfortunately, she did not realize that Assia was having the same problem: gauging the level of Ted's commitment to her.[18] Plath thought Assia was confidently bedding Ted and not having the doubts that, in fact, both women felt about his loyalty.

14

On August 13, 1962, Sylvia completed "Burning the Letters," ridding herself of their "death rattle." As they burn she wonders what "they know that I didn't." How had things come to such a pass and what were the markers along the way, the trail that biographers, too, try to track. Her allusion to the "eyes and times of the postmarks" reflects what it is like to think of one's life as an archive and to clean it out before it comes back to the surface like a "dumb fish" caught in someone else's line. Carbonizing these old letters might fuel a new self while destroying the old one.

15

By late August 1962, Ted remained most of the time in London. Sylvia said she did not believe in divorce but would seek a separation from a liar and adulterer who had no business living with her children. He had told her he did not have the courage to say he didn't want children, and then he tried to convince her doctor that she was "unstable." Aurelia had unwittingly contributed to the impression Ted conveyed by telling Winifred Davies, one of Sylvia's midwives, that Sylvia had had a nervous breakdown. Sylvia believed her husband had a better self but chose not to behave well. She wrote to her mother and to his parents to announce the separation. She was hoping for a visit from Warren and his new wife Maggie, and fortifying herself with weekly visits to the Comptons. She managed to write, no matter that she had never before been so sick, having lost considerable weight and even now, on September 8, felt "still very wobbly, but better."

Sylvia needed a "health trip" to Ireland, she told Elizabeth Compton. She told Marvin Kane that she was going to Ireland to "heal herself by 'the wild sea.'" [HR] When Sylvia thought of reconciling with Ted, she believed it should occur away from Court Green, away from the children, and near the sea. Saying nothing about an estrangement from Ted, she wrote to poet Richard Murphy who ran a hooker out of Cleggan, an Irish fishing village: "The center of my whole early life was ocean and boats, and because of this, your poems have been of especial interest to me, and I think you would be a very lovely person for us to visit just now." She remained, however exhausted, a wit, wanting to read David Compton's new mystery novel: "it looks just the thing to cheer me up, all about murder."

16

The trip to Ireland devastated Sylvia. Ted left her without a word in Richard Murphy's cottage.[19] She went to London to see a solicitor about the separation agreement, telling Kathy Kane: "the end has come. It is like amputating a gangrenous limb—horrible, but one feels it is the only thing to do to survive"—a revealing choice of words for a woman whose father had lost a limb to diabetes in an effort to survive. To Ruth Beuscher, she wrote about freeing herself, of resuming "my own sweet life," separating from an "infantile" and "dangerously destructive" Ted, a "vampire on my life, killing and destroying all. We had all the world on tap, were even well off, now this insanity on his part will cost us everything."

Sylvia began, as well, to create a fiction about Assia Wevill as the other woman, a malign temptress, not realizing just how aggressive Ted had been in his pursuit of a new lover.[20] Sylvia, driven to her last extremity, did not realize what she had in common with her supposed nemesis, the "beautiful and barren" woman she mentioned to Mrs. Prouty.[21]

17

By early October 1962, Sylvia's feelings were escalating. She had decided to take her therapist's advice and make a clean break. "I am getting a divorce, and you are right, it is freeing," she wrote to Richard Murphy: "I am writing for the first time in years, a real self, long smothered. I get up at 4 a.m.

when I wake, & it is black, & write till the babes wake. It is like writing in a train tunnel, or God's intestine."

By October 12, Sylvia had completed her signature poem, "Daddy." Whatever you believe about the symbiosis of a writer's life and her work, this poem shows she was in full control of her feelings, casting them into a dramatic monologue that rivals anything Robert Browning wrote. The speaker is a character who draws on many aspects of Plath's life, and yet the poem remains its own thing, separable and inseparable from the woman who wrote it—as she said: the expression of a "real self, long smothered." The speaker is declaring her escape from the very suffocated self that Hughes claims in *Birthday Letters* overcame her. The "real self," she seemed to be telling Murphy, is the poetry.

The opening lines of "Daddy" reflect the exuberant letters Sylvia wrote to her mother and brother about packing Ted off by train to London. At that moment all seemed settled. She had burst the self-imposed confines of her domesticity, which the woman of the poem likens to living "like a foot" in a black shoe for thirty years, "poor and white." All those years of calculating expenses, and of living in the cramped feelings about her father, are released, so that he too is getting packed away. Scenes of Sylvia's childhood by the sea populate the poem, the father looming "Big as a Frisco seal" but also a "head in the freakish Atlantic." The freakishness of her own moods filters through a woman who prayed to "recover you," the German father, born in a Polish town, that she now regards with disgust: "Ach du." All through her days at Court Green she was listening to BBC German lessons and still claiming she wanted to learn the language well enough to speak it. But it appears in the poem only as staccato syllables that reflect this woman's struggle to achieve her own "I": "Ich, ich, ich, ich," with the same guttural sound as ick, the English expression of disgust. Her life had been a concentration camp of the self—a conceit that has troubled those who see Plath as appropriating the Holocaust, especially in the line: "I think I may well be a Jew." But was it wrong to incorporate the Holocaust into her own family's history and sense of self—this still young woman who wanted her German pen pal to tell her about the costs of war? Would it be better to leave the Holocaust only to those who suffered and to their descendants? Isn't Plath allowed to portray history as a personal experience?

Elinor Friedman, Smith classmate and friend, thought Sylvia had a romantic notion of Jewish identity that seemed so much richer than the arid, complacent wealthy world of Wellesley:

I think that the idea of these people who went through great trials and who wandered a great deal and yet had a central core on which they could rely was a big source of fascination. Jews seemed to have a relationship to self that I think she always felt was missing. Whether it was despising herself for her whiteness, the blond hair and white skin and the blue veins—her total waspy self that she was always trying to dissipate, leave somewhere else, by feigning freedom of it in some kind of way. [HR]

In this view, "Daddy" is yet another kind of liberation poem.

Yet this identification with Jewry is hard to square with Sylvia's letter to her mother about the "Yorkshire-Jew miserliness" of the Hughes family. Sylvia had it all wrong, but that is beside the point, really. Her atavistic racism remains even as the poem rises above it and personifies her father as a commanding Nazi, the kind of neat, "bright blue" sort of Aryan man who thrusts a boot in the face, exerting a violent authority that leads to overstatement: "Every woman adores a Fascist." The woman speaker of the poem, all worked up, universalizes her plight and fright that seem straight out of a horror movie and that segue to another racist trope: about the "black man who / Bit my pretty red heart in two." Remember, this is a poor, White woman, and this is *her* feeling.

Approaching thirty in a matter of days, Plath created a persona transitioning from a kind of slavery to freedom. She said as much in letters to her mother. She would not return to America, the site of her suicide attempt, which in the poem occurs at twenty when the woman seeks to "get back, back, back to you"—the Black man, in this case the vampire dressed in black calling up images of Bela Lugosi in *Dracula* (1931), the "vampire who said he was you / And drank my blood for a year / Seven years, if you want to know."

As the Ted of a seven-year marriage and her father merge into a composite figure that is neither one of them, a biographer feels compelled to point out that at just this time Sylvia said Ted began to taunt her, to drain their bank accounts, to say her luck had run out, even as she took those early morning hours to write great triumphal poems. In her letters, Sylvia complained that Ted was living off of her, spending her grant money, but encouraged by a solicitor to clean out her joint accounts with her husband, she began to recover what she had lost. The poem can be read as a similar exercise in recovery, which transcends that desire to "get back, back, back to you."

There she was in Court Green, miffed at the locals who she said were "leering and peering" at her. Perhaps that is why she took to wearing dark glasses. John Avery remembered seeing her wear them and that her face was "very drawn, very yellow." People sympathized, he said. They didn't like Ted. He would ignore people, and you do that only once in a village like North

Bela Lugosi in *Dracula* (1931).

Tawton, Avery observed. Sylvia talked to everyone and often gave Avery a day's worth of thought after talking to her. [HR] The Ted Avery describes appears at the end of "Daddy" in the poem's closing lines about the villagers who "never liked you," and are now "dancing and stamping on you. They always *knew* it was you." This exorcism ends: "Daddy, daddy, you bastard, I'm through." The poem works in a way life cannot. On October 12, 1962, Sylvia Plath felt the exhilaration of her husband's leaving Court Green, but that did not end the story, or her feelings, and even the poem as protest might leave a reader wondering who is through.

Both the confidence and the extremity of "Daddy" is understandable if Plath is taken at her word: "Ted has said how convenient it would be if I were dead, then he could sell the house & take the children whom he likes," she wrote to her mother on October 16, 1962, adding: "I am a genius of a writer, I have it in me." She had never before said anything like this about herself or her work. As if arising right out of the voice of "Daddy," she declared: "Ted is dead to me." But she knew something was missing: She needed the armory of a family member with her and still yearned for Warren, Margaret, or her Aunt Dot to appear beside her: "I am fighting now against hard odds and alone," Sylvia wrote her mother: "Please have a family powwow & answer this as soon as possible!"

Any family member would do, it seems, except her mother, the "eely tentacle" of "Medusa," a jellyfish also known as an Aurelia, as well as a poem often treated as a companion to "Daddy." Unlike her father, "you are always there"—in the imagination of a mind that "winds to you," like an Atlantic cable. "I didn't call you," the poet insists, but "You steamed to me over the sea." But Sylvia did call, cable, and write home incessantly, telling her mother how much her summer visit would help her daughter, until the pliable (jellyfish-like?) Aurelia's presence did not help at all, since she was there to witness Ted's departure and the paralyzing sting of her daughter's deprivation. "Medusa," however, is less about what Aurelia actually did than it is about her daughter's Declaration of Independence, begun in "Daddy."[22] "Medusa" ends as ambiguously as "Daddy," announcing: "There is nothing between us." No rapport? Nothing any longer to share? It is hard to say how much the poem is an expression of itself and of the woman who wrote it. Judith Kroll sums up the strategy of "Medusa" and "Daddy": "canceling her historical parents and banishing from the portrait the affection which would only keep her tied to the past, and thereby undermine her resolve to affirm a new birth."[23]

It bothered Sylvia, more than the poem let on, to do without her mother, and she continued to write to Aurelia, for reasons she underlined in Sheldon: "One of the most important experiences, if not _the_ most important, in a child's life, is constituted in the feeling of rapport in the mutual enthusiasm and affectional interests that tie his mind to that of both his mother and father. Here above everything else in the world, is needed the influence of an adult mind the dominant quality of which should be _child-like_ enthusiasm and candor." Sheldon believed those ties to parents superseded the "contemporary relations" built up over a lifetime. What mattered to Sylvia is what should matter, according to Sheldon, and what should matter to every daughter and son is what troubled the poet and the person. In psychology, in Sheldon, she read about what ought to be the template for her existence, and she measured her own distress against that template. "Medusa" reflects, in the poem and the person, a mothering the poet could not do without in the very act of rejecting that mothering. Robin Peel is right, of course, to call the voice of "Medusa" a "contrivance,"[24] but it is Plath's contrivance. What do you think of Peel's suggestion that the voice in "Medusa" is also the voice of America? At the time of writing this poem, Plath was resisting the very idea of returning to her native land. She had gone so far away from what she had read in her school textbook *The Rise of a Free Nation.* That "Atlantic cable" in "Medusa" is the link that Plath once thought she could use to communicate between two countries, that Ted would profit from, and that would make their own link all the stronger.

That American link, whatever you make of "Medusa," was very powerful: Sylvia again proposed that Warren's wife Maggie visit for a few weeks, since Sylvia dreaded dealing with Ted alone and needed a defender from "<u>home</u>." To Mrs. Prouty, on October 18, 1962, she explained why she was so fearful of her husband's return: "he was furious I had not committed suicide—evidently he and his new flame had discussed this, in view of my old nervous breakdown." What to think of the way she describes her husband's cruelty? It is reminiscent of the film *Gaslight,* from which the term gaslighting derives. As Gail Crowther notes, to be gaslit is to make you

Scene from the film *Gaslight* (1944).

believe that your feelings are the problem.[25] Hughes, as Crowther also notes, need not have been aware of himself as a gaslighter. In *Birthday Letters*, he never reflects on the import of his lying, and how, like Charles Boyer in the film, he charmed his beloved—to begin with anyway—telling her how wonderful she was. When she turned against him, he treated his wife as a mental case, and in Plath's case, as a woman doomed to die. For Hughes, Plath's securing a solicitor and demanding her own terms—when all along she had accommodated his every wish to live where he liked—ran counter to his view of her as suicidal, as someone who would collapse as soon as he removed his support. Calling him out made her, in his view, unreasonable.

Far from suicidal, Sylvia was setting up a new household, replacing a nasty nanny with a sweet-tempered twenty-two-year-old children's nurse, Susan Roe. Sylvia had been asked to organize an "American night" at the Royal Court Theater. She was also looking forward to establishing the "Salon that I will deserve." To Ruth Beuscher, on October 22, 1962, she summarized in a sentence the explosive nature of her life: "everything has blown up, blown apart, and settled in a new and startling places," abetted by Beuscher's own advice to get on with life, leaving Ted behind her. "I love you for listening," Sylvia concluded: "Each of your letters is so rich, they last like parables." It is a suggestive reaction since poems like "Daddy" are so allegorical.

The best evidence of an exhilarating rebirth is to be found in "Cut," ostensibly about cutting her thumb "instead of an onion," with the "top quite gone," the dismembered digit beheaded like a "Little pilgrim" with an axed scalp. The high spirits of those first days when Ted left, which felt like such a victory, flow into the blood of the poem, which becomes a "celebration," as the defeated Redcoats, millions of them, run. This was an American victory over the English, no matter the odds against the colonists, and the odds that Sylvia fought against. She had overthrown oppression. She was feeling especially American just then, surrounded by her Devonshire neighbors—even suspecting she was watched, telling Clarissa Roche that someone had been looking in Court Green windows. [HR]

But Sylvia was also attuned to the devastations of war as she covered her thumb, which reminded her of a "Babushka" and, perhaps, her childhood war game of "Russia" mentioned many times in her diaries.[26] She saw in the gauze bandage the Ku Klux Klan of terror that came right into people's houses as it had done entering Court Green. Surviving Ted's onslaught she had become the "Trepanned veteran," with a hole in her head, pulped by war but also a "Dirty girl" and "Thumb stump"—the literal and metaphorical expression of a remnant, no matter how disabled, no matter how dirty, no matter how small, no matter.

The "girl" is important: "Cut" brought her back to childhood, to her first understanding of history, and to her depiction of the world in maps of North America, of the Albany Plan of Union, of the northern colonies, of the United States and its possessions, of her part of Massachusetts, in drawings of the Continental Congress, and a map she titled: "The Story of the American Revolution." She copied part of the Declaration of Independence into another map, worked on a "Treaty of Peace" map, but also on maps of Europe and Australia. One of the highlights of a school field trip had been to the Christian Science Monitor building's maparium: "We learned that it was made of over 600 pieces of 1/4 inch thick stain glass," she recorded in her diary. In social studies, she won first prize for her drawing of the Monroe Doctrine. She had watched one of her teachers as he "crooked up the corner of his mouth in a heart warming smile and said, 'That is a wonderful map and the drawings are beautiful.'" As with those maps, she made something beautiful out of "Cut."[27]

In the thrilling aftermath of "Cut," Sylvia's confidence rose. She contented herself with the prospect of Warren and Maggie visiting her in the spring, no longer needing, apparently, a bulwark against Ted's depredations. For the first time outside her poetry, in a letter dated October 25, 1962, she took square aim at her mother:

> It's too bad my poems frighten you—but you've always been afraid of reading or seeing the world's hardest things—like Hiroshima, the Inquisition or Belsen. I believe in going through & facing the worst, not hiding from it. That is why I am going to London this week, partly, to face all the people we know & tell them happily & squarely I am divorcing Ted, so they won't picture me as a poor, deceived country wife.

Sylvia sought to transform her plight into heroic terms for her progeny: "One thing I want my children to have is a bold sense of adventure, not the fear of trying something new. She planned to spend winters in London, summers at Court Green, on her horse: "I'm 'rising to the trot' very well now. . . . My riding mistress thinks I'm very good." She would take on the world, much as her childhood writer adventure hero, Richard Halliburton, had done, and those others heroes on horses, like the Lone Ranger, one of Plath's favorite radio programs.

To Mrs. Prouty, Sylvia went even further: "I shall forge my writing out of these difficult experiences—to have known the bottom, whether mental or emotional is a great trial, but also a great gift." Sylvia felt that Mrs. Prouty, her literary godmother, "will feel as proud of my independence

as I am." The writing of "Lady Lazarus" (October 23–29, 1962), with its famous line, "I eat men like air" expresses her commanding persona, signaled,
as well, by her decision to forego Ireland for London, to brave the literary
world she was determined to conquer. The poem is a "comeback" story, a
saga of rebirth, the "skin and bone" of the persona like Sylvia's own, arising out of the ash of a former life, defying the will to death that Ted had
marked out for her. She seemed almost recklessly alive, which is, perhaps,
to skirt the edge of death, a different kind of "Suicidal"—to adopt the word
in "Ariel" that has the poet atop her horse, riding into the red "Eye, the
cauldron of morning," the dawn of the poems that kept coming at four in
the morning.

18

By early November 1962, it seemed like destiny: She had found the flat
W. B. Yeats had lived in, not far from Primrose Hill and the neighborhood
near her "old doctors" and the shops she had frequented. It was not a sure
thing, yet she was sure she could secure a lease. Her new high-topped hair
with a coronet from the back declared her reign: Men stared at her in the
street and truck drivers whistled, and by summer, with her appearance in
the American program at the Royal Court, she would be a "knockout."
Neither Ted nor his "girl" (Sylvia never named Assia) seemed to bother
her now.

But Elizabeth Compton, who saw Sylvia for the last time in late November, described her lively, engaging friend as drained. Harriet Rosenstein put
Compton's words in all caps:

HER HAIR WAS LIFELESS AND THERE WAS A THIN QUAL-
ITY TO THE WHOLE PERSON. SHE WASN'T REALLY THERE
IN THE ROOM WITH YOU. ONE WAS NOT IMPORTANT
TO HER. YOU COULDN'T BREAK IN ON THAT. YOU
COULDN'T BREAK THROUGH IT SHE HAD GONE SO
THIN. SHE WAS PALE BUT THERE WAS A DARKNESS
AROUND HER EYES AND A DARKNESS ABOUT HER THAT
WAS VERY FORBIDDING. ONE FELT SHE WAS COMMUN-
ING WITH SOMETHING ALL THE TIME THAT WASN'T YOU.
GETTING THE CUPS READY. CONCENTRATING ON THE
THINGS SHE WAS DOING WAS REALLY NOT IT. THERE WAS
A DIALOGUE GOING ON THAT ONE COULDN'T KNOW,

COULDN'T SEE, BUT THAT MADE ONE SUPREMELY IRREL-
EVANT. SHE TRIED TO MAKE THE SOCIAL NOISES AND
SMILE BUT YOU WEREN'T REALLY THERE.

Sylvia had lost twenty pounds during a flu siege, but it was more than that. She appeared to be almost a ghost or communicating with ghosts.

And yet she seemed resilient. So much had changed so swiftly in a matter of a few years—from Chalcot Square to Court Green, to her return to a London flat. As Sylvia wrote to Ruth Fainlight: "My life seems to be spent furnishing a new place every year!" Ted now did not seem to stand in her way. He was telling her about work she could do for the BBC, including a program titled "Landscape of Childhood." To Mrs. Prouty, she wrote: "My dream is selling a novel to the movies and eventually buying the house from the present owner. I am applying for a 5 year lease, the longest I can get." She hoped to take possession by Christmas, which seemed destined to be after she opened a copy of his plays and read: "Get wine and food to give you strength and courage and I will get the house ready." When Ted met her at the train station in her new hairdo and wardrobe, he did not recognize her: "I am going to leave all my old Smith clothes in Devon & just take these new ones to London. I want my life to begin over from the skin out," she wrote to her mother. She described her second novel, "Doubletake": "about a wife whose husband turns out to be deserter and philanderer although she had thought he was wonderful & perfect." Fran McCullough, later Ted's American editor, heard the novel was "wicked, funny, nasty, precise—about Ted & Assia." [HR]

19

On November 29, 1962, Sylvia wrote to her mother that she expected to move into her new London flat by December 17, with Aurelia as the "guarantor" since Sylvia had no regular employment. A year's rent in advance secured the lease. An exasperated daughter told her mother: "for goodness sake don't say 'unless you are safe & reasonably happy, I can't live anyway'! One's life should never depend on another's in that way. Why do you identify so with me? That sort of statement only makes one chary of confiding any difficulties in you whatsoever, as I am sure you will see if you think of it." If Sylvia had a point, so did Aurelia, who, after all, was asked to be a "guarantor." Like Aurelia, Sylvia liked to project the future for her children, seeing them as an integral part of the mark she was making on the world.

She was more like her mother than she ever wanted to admit, but also so much more ambitious for herself than Aurelia was for herself, which is part of what Sylvia held against her. It was never enough for Sylvia to invest all her hope in her children, since her own writing meant so much to her. Living for her children, in itself, could never suffice—which became even more plain to her in the last days of her life.

At any moment, life could seem perfect: "When I get safely into this flat I shall be the happiest person in the world." She had come to terms with a cooperative Ted about a divorce, and they were "friends as much as can be at times like this." She persisted in portraying Assia as the femme fatale, writing to Mrs. Prouty: "This woman, who is still dangling her 3rd husband, has brutalized Ted beyond belief—taught him it is 'clever' & 'sophisticated' to lie & deceive people and so on."

The move went well, except for a "comedy of errors," about getting a gas hookup and electricity. For the next few weeks Sylvia immersed herself into furnishing the flat. "Having to close up that big house & open this flat has given me an immense pleasure in businesslike dealings, I feel to have grown up a great deal in the process," she wrote to Mrs. Prouty on December 15, 1962. Sleeping pills had helped her to prepare for each day of frenetic activity. Her letter to Aunt Dot, who had sent a $700 housewarming gift, exuberantly describes the friendly village-like atmosphere of this London neighborhood, but home and all she missed was never very far from her mind: "You have no notion how much your cheery letters mean!"

The title of her novel-in-progress, "Doubletake," suggests she had in mind her delayed reaction to Ted's perfidy, how she had misjudged him and had consequently formed a false conception of her marriage and happiness. Some of that theme made its way into a poem, "Amnesiac," which Sylvia described to Mrs. Prouty as about a "man who forgets his wife & children & lives in the river of Lethe. Guess who!"

20

By December 21, 1962, Sylvia seemed in a manic phase, extolling her new life in a celebratory letter to her mother: Everything was just right: the flat's furnishings, new clothing, socializing: "You should see me nipping round London in the car! . . . Now I am out of Ted's shadow everybody tells me their life story & warms up to me & the babies right away. Life is such fun." The weather was "blue & springlike & I out every day with the babies." Blue was her new royal color. Tellingly, she had to feel as if she reigned over a new dispensation, noting that Ted never liked the color blue. The next day Sylvia painted three bureaus, yellow for her bedroom and kitchen, red and blue for babies' room, pink for au pair's room, transforming her domain into the color wheel she had worked on in her earliest art classes. Creating an esthetic space, almost like an art studio, helped her to materialize her aspirations. She wanted her mother to *see* how she lived, incorporating past and present: "My bedroom has yellow, & white wallpaper, straw mat, black floor borders & gold lampshade—bee colors, & the sun rises over an 18th century engraving of London each day."

Less than a week later: "Dear mother, I wish you could see me sitting here in my gorgeous front room." Would it have made a difference if Sylvia could have used FaceTime to connect to the homebound world that she sought to recreate but also to share with those from home? She spared telling her mother how Christmas without family had troubled her, confessing only to getting "a bit homesick." Sometimes it seemed that she lived on letters from home and from her few friends in England—like those from Daniel and Helga Huws, who hosted Sylvia and Ted when they had been looking for a flat. Sylvia wrote that Frieda, Ted's pet, was coming out of her "regression" after his departure. She expected Ted to visit them once a week and take the children to the zoo. As to his behavior, she agreed with Daniel: "His guilt alas makes him very hard & cross & hurtful, and you can imagine the public humiliations one has to face, being in the same work & Ted being so famous."

It didn't help matters that Ruth Fainlight would not return to London until end of February 1963. They had bonded as mothers and poets and Americans. Sylvia again understated the devastation of her Christmas, calling it a "bit of a large gap & I'm very glad to get rid of it." In retrospect, Fainlight rued her decision to stay in Morocco, where she had befriended writer Jane Bowles. Fainlight had fled London, looking for a warmer companion and clime, feeling, as Plath did, the chill of London's literary society. Fainlight thought it just possible that her presence might have prevented—at least for a time—Plath's decision to end her life.[28] Did Sylvia feel, with Ruth not scheduled to return to London until sometime in March 1963, even more isolated? She probably knew about Jane Bowles and her husband Paul, celebrated for hosting writers in Tangiers. Did Sylvia feel betrayed by Fainlight, who sought the warmth of another woman, another climate? We cannot know, but certainly by Fainlight's own account, she came to feel that she had let Plath down.

How hard this new regime was on Sylvia she could hardly say—even to her old friend, Marcia Brown: "I guess you can imagine what it's like coping with two infants, free lance jobs, painting & decorating acres of floors &

haunting sales for curtaining etc. Toute seule!" Yet she insisted that after "six months of unique hell," she was "fine now."

On December 26, 1962, Sylvia attended a dinner party at Catherine Frankfort's. They shared the same physician and had become friendly. To Catherine, Sylvia appeared gay, but her mother-in-law, who engaged in a long conversation with Sylvia, remarked after Sylvia left: "what a sad person she is," complicated and "tortured." [HR]

21

At any moment, all could seem lost: The weather turned on her as abruptly as she could turn on herself. The first weeks of January were "ghastly." Everyone came down with the flu. After nearly a two-week gap in letter writing (unusual for her), on January 16, 1963, Sylvia, still recovering, admitted to her mother she was exhausted and "cross." The huge snowfall had resulted in narrowly rutted frozen streets that made Sylvia feel stuck without even a phone that she had now been expecting for two months. Troubles with finding a good au pair exasperated her stranded sensibility. She had been too weak to cook much, which had always been a solace and pleasure. These trials and responsibilities she experienced as a direct assault: "I just haven't felt to have any identity under the steamroller of decisions & responsibilities of this last half year, with the babies a constant demand." Ted's visits put her in a shaky state. He came once a week and was, by turns, "nice" and "awful." According to Suzette Macedo, Sylvia said Ted talked incessantly about Assia, including intimate details, telling Sylvia that he preferred Sylvia to Assia sexually. He proposed they reconcile, and she agreed, then changed her mind, rejecting Suzette's suggestion that Sylvia give Ted a chance. [HR] How could Sylvia trust him? Everything she had worked for seemed undone: "It is the starting from scratch that is so hard." It was life interrupted by power cuts, dinner stopped, "mad rushes" for candles. In such circumstances, the light of the world seemed a flickering thing.

Sylvia had always cherished letters from home, but now they meant something more: "How good to get your letters! They are like soul letters to me," she wrote to Mrs. Prouty on January 22, 1963. She yearned for Ruth Beuscher, but her letters were not the same as "those hours of talk." How could they be? Sylvia missed the spontaneity and sudden insights of their sessions together, the reciprocal feeling of their exchanges that no one else, *no one*, could possibly supply. Sylvia was succumbing to a starvation of the spirit and flesh. Susan Roe, taking care of the children, had made it possible for Sylvia to be "alone with myself," but that was two months ago, and now she felt the "keenest torture, this lack of a centre, a quietness, to brood in and grow from. I suppose, to the writer, it is like communing with God." Sylvia did not say so, but Beuscher had believed in the spiritual dimension of therapy, that she was ministering to her patient's souls. Sylvia's use of that word in her letter to Beuscher demands our attention because it suggests an existential suffering.

Sylvia hoped that writing about her childhood would restore that ebullience so in evidence in her earliest diaries. She could not resume work on a novel until she had overcome her dread, made worse by Frieda's anxiety about her father's fitful visits, expressed in cries "Daddy come soon." Mother and daughter felt tortured. Sylvia would have to write, no matter what, but the outlook appalled her: "I must just resolutely write mornings for the next years, through cyclones, water freezeups, children's illnesses & the <u>aloneness</u>. Having been so deeply and spiritually and physically happy with my dear, beautiful husband make this harder than if I had never known love at all." She made it clear, though, that "my dear, beautiful husband" was a character that Ted no longer resembled. She was not suggesting she wanted him back, or he, as such, was the cause of her woes, except in so far as the result of his departure had set her back, in a manner of speaking, because she felt so disestablished. In her happiest moods, Sylvia had felt blessed, "spiritually and physically happy." Now body and soul were disintegrating as quickly as she had lost those twenty pounds during the flu. This was her winter of struggle. She felt she was writing poems in her own blood.

Tim Hancock has suggested that the "main emotional booster that had been powering" Plath's forceful poems until January 1962 had "burnt itself out. Transcendent, motile imagery of launches, ascensions, and soaring passages gives way—in the poem "Sheep in Fog"[29]—to "stillness," a sense of being distanced from "people or stars," and the chilling imminence of envelopment by "vacuous black," as "the far / Fields . . . threaten" to let her "through to a heaven / Starless and fatherless, a dark water." [BHSP] Plath projected an inner emptiness, of having played herself out, into the nothingness of the universe. She could no longer envision a world elsewhere, a new terrain, a salon. On February 23, 1956, from Cambridge, she had mentioned to her mother how much she missed a "constellation of friends" from home that could orbit around her. Just before beginning her last semester at Smith, she wrote to her mother about a plane ride to New York City: "I kept my nose pressed to the window watching the constellations of lights below as if I could read the riddle of the universe in the braille patterns of radiance." The universe no longer lit itself up for her.

On February 4, 1963, Sylvia admitted to her mother that she had gone silent: "I just haven't written anybody because I have been feeling a bit grim—the upheaval over, I am seeing the finality of it all, and being catapulted from the cowlike happiness of maternity into loneliness & grim problems is no fun." Returning to America seemed inconceivable, since the only hope of supporting herself by her writing came from BBC commissions and magazine work not available to her elsewhere. Frieda, still distraught over her father's absence, would suffer terribly from more uprooting. The only way to make Ted feel responsible for her was to ensure his visits by remaining in his proximity. Wellesley had "always stifled" her: "I shall simply have to fight it out on my own."

A neighbor, Lorna Secker-Walker saw Sylvia in her last week and remembered her exhausted look, her saying, "Oh, I feel so weary." Lorna also noticed what Jillian Becker also detected: Sylvia, under tremendous strain, seemed "slightly cut off from her children," saying she could not devote all of herself to them or to her work. On the Friday Sylvia went to stay with the Beckers, she called Lorna to say everything has been resolved and she was calling to say "good-bye." Only in retrospect did Lorna think that "Sylvia was announcing her intention to die." [HR] To Elizabeth Compton, Sylvia had appeared as a woman "so alive, so vivid," living every second: "to look at her own extinction . . . wasn't a <u>wish</u> to be dead. It was, I think, that life to her in that last week had become just something she couldn't support alone." [HR]

Without her native home, the diurnal person plummeted. "Your letter was like a shot of brandy or a shot in the arm," Sylvia wrote to her friend and former roommate Marcia Brown. On the same day Sylvia wrote her mother, she confessed to Marcia: "Everything has blown & bubbled & warped & split." Sylvia was caught in transit, in "limbo between the old world & the very uncertain & rather grim new." She looked upon Marcia's visit as a rescue. She condensed the trouble with Ted's appearances in a phrase: He was an "apocalyptic Santa Claus." He had become the very word for a world that had been destroyed even as he came and went, bestowing upon Frieda, and occasionally Sylvia, his overwhelming attention that only resulted in their severe withdrawal symptoms when he departed. The diary he kept during the last week of his wife's life shows that whatever he meant to do by way of succor actually tormented her.[30]

Sylvia seems to have put all her last effort in these February 4, 1963, letters. She wrote to Father Michael Carey about "creeping" out of a "post-flu coma," still writing poems at dawn. The poems kept her alive; the poems took the life out of her. They were a kind of last stand as she determined to go down fighting. Suicide, in the minds of many, reflects a surrender, a weakness, but for others, in a state of inconsolable despair, it can be an act of courage, saving others, including one's own children, from the tremendous burden of their mother's affliction. In her copy of *Confessions*, she had marked the reference to the Stoic belief in suicide as the "last and greatest fling of the brave heart."

Sylvia had known what it had been like to be tied—it seemed forever—to her mother. Shouldn't children be permitted to get on with their own lives without the drag of a parent's troubles? In Sylvia's mind, there was only one way to show Ted that he had to come home—to his children at least. That seems to the meaning of several letters in which she deplored his living only for himself and his desires.

No extant poem or letter can stand as Sylvia's testament to suicide. She left no note—at least none that has been revealed. There is only her February 4 letter to Ruth Beuscher and Jillian Becker's and Trevor Thomas's accounts of Sylvia's last distraught weekend.[31] Judging by her letter to Beuscher, she diagnosed herself as suffering the consequences of "idolatrous love," making Ted husband, lover, and father. On October 5, 1956, in the early, heady days of their marriage, she had written to him that he represented the "whole male principle," father, brother husband, son.

Sylvia feared the return of "madness," a "vision of the worst" leading to a "cowardly withdrawal" that returned her to "a mental hospital, lobotomies." She kept slipping into a "panic" and "deep freeze," writing great poems that verged on the "edge of madness," which perhaps is part of what is displayed in one of her last poems, "Edge," evoking a dead woman who is "perfected," with a "smile of accomplishment, / The illusion of a Greek necessity." What is striking about the poem is how studied it is and shrewd. It is about a state of mind seen from the outside, as if the woman is observed by another who is, perhaps, skeptical of the "smile of accomplishment"—hence the word "illusion." Sylvia did observe herself in her letter to Beuscher: "I'm scared to death I shall just pull up the psychic shroud & give up." Daily life tortured her as she thought of what she had not accomplished at thirty—that crucial transitional moment when a life might go either way: toward its demise or rebirth. She spoke with Jillian Becker about the "dreadful milestone" of turning thirty. She did not feel she had done enough. [HR]

She knew she needed help. Dr. Horder, her physician, estimated that he had seen Sylvia between twenty and thirty times—for never less than twenty minutes—in the last three months of her life, and every day during her last week. Sometimes she relied on him almost daily to help sort out the practicalities of her life, including child rearing. The children, he hoped, might help to keep her alive. The children were also the reason why institutionalizing her was problematic. Admission to the right hospital, in any case, was difficult. "There are so few that give a person the privacy that they need and the understanding that they need." Institutionalization could well make her "more depressed," he told Harriet Rosenstein.

In Dr. Horder's view, Ted was no help and did not seem upset about her condition. A failed marriage did not mean the same to him as to her, because of her "expectation that she be more successful in all things."[32] Her thoughts of suicide, Horder thought, were more pronounced than she gave him reason to suppose. "I think she did take us in to some extent," he concluded. [HR]

On her last weekend, Dr. Horder had engaged a female psychiatrist to see Sylvia on Tuesday, February 12, 1963, which turned out to be the day after she died. It had been Horder's idea that Sylvia spend that last weekend with the Beckers. At the time of her death he told the attending police officer that he had been treating Sylvia for "mental depression," but that in the last few days she had seemed "much brighter." [HR] But in her letters she keep returning to her "self-induced freeze," which was her way of saying she could not see a way to go forward: "let me just die & be done with it." That urge to complete herself, as in "Edge," may have been part of what she had in mind in her last hours of life, and not out of place in the world of the Promethean spirit.

When Harriet Rosenstein interviewed Ruth Beuscher on June 16, 1970, seven years after Sylvia's death, the biographer concluded the therapist felt "very guilty about Sylvia's suicide." Sylvia wanted to stay with her in an arrangement that would probably have been something like Ralph Greenson's unconventional treatment of Marilyn Monroe: taking the actress into his home and making her one of his family. Beuscher knew that her orthodox psychiatrist husband would not countenance that level of involvement in a patient's life. When Beuscher related Sylvia's appeals to Rosenstein, Beuscher cried. "She feels it was the greatest error of her life," Rosenstein reported. Ruth, ten years older than Sylvia, was like a sister, the biographer observed. Perhaps because of her intolerable grief, Beuscher destroyed many of Sylvia's letters.

Sylvia was taking a drug cocktail, as Heather Clark puts it, that included amphetamines, barbiturates, and an opioid (codeine) producing a variety of reactions: increased depression and suicidal feelings, but also, in some cases, increased energy. Her autopsy report disclosed she had recently suffered a very painful ruptured ovarian cyst that had added to her suffering. Whatever impact drugs had, it seems they did not cause but perhaps exacerbated her conflicting emotions and wavering responses to Ted's own hypomanic behavior.[33] Organized to the end, she left her flat "clean and tidy." [RC]

Sylvia preserved the lives of her children, trying as carefully as possible to stuff up any apertures in their room into which the oven gas might seep. She could still conceive of a future for them as part of that dynastic design she had originally projected for herself and Ted. She thought about death often—and not as a morbid occupation. Any child who loses a parent is hard put not to dwell on the torment of mortality: "funny thing about pain: it annihilates one's pride completely," she wrote to Philip McCurdy on April 28, 1954: "if we could be clairvoyant and see the date of our own doom, the bloodclot in the vein of our existence—how differently we might proportion our own time." In the end, Sylvia proportioned her own time to thirty seconds, the time it took for the gas to asphyxiate her after she put her head in the oven. It was a season of suicide, with 213 of them recorded in England for the winter of 1962–63, far in excess of the usual number.[34]

As early as a journal entry for November 26, 1950, written in her Haven House room, Sylvia realized

> no matter how enthusiastic you are, no matter how sure that character is fate, nothing is real, past or future, when you are alone in your room with the clock ticking loudly into the false cheerful brilliance of the electric light. And if you have no past or future which after all, is all that the present is made of, why then you may as well dispose of the empty shell of the present and commit suicide.

This was not said in despair, but in a kind of wonder at the nature of existence and how that existence can seem at different times. Sylvia stood in the hallway electric light the night before she died and asked the tenant below her for some stamps to airmail to America, still thinking of the home she could not have. She was alone in the same sense Joseph Conrad's Decoud is alone on his boat and confronts a nothingness he has been able to decoy with all the temptations of the society in which he has thrived. There was no Smith infirmary, no way station, campus cocoon, to steady her—only the prospect of institutionalization, the snakepit of the spirit. Like Goethe's Werther, another victim of idolatrous love, Sylvia was an enthusiast and broke her heart on the wheel of unrequited love.

Jillian Becker, a writer who had often engaged in sessions of storytelling with Sylvia, and saw her, on average, twice a week after the move to Fitzroy Road, knew many of Sylvia's friends, as well as Ted Hughes. Becker believed that Sylvia Plath was "engaged in making her life an inescapable, ineluctable history, the novelist's shaping with one inevitable outcome. Life as fiction." Becker thought of Plath as "the last Romantic. Whether vivacious

Goethe's Werther.

or despairing," she went at everything with a "Romantic's intensity." As for
Ted, Becker said he wanted "that part of her to be the whole of her." [HR]

Something of Sylvia's predicament finally broke through to Ted in
January 1962. A remarkable journal entry reflects an awareness that never
manages to infiltrate *Birthday Letters*: "I am completely responsible for
S's fixation on me, I demanded it." He acknowledged his "weakness with
women," and how hard it was to be "rational & disciplined" about them.
He deplored his "yielding to whatever I may think is their whim." It was
"ruining—has probably already ruined my life. And in the end it leads
to disaster for them too, meshed in my falsity. . . . My unwillingness to
hurt women, my incredible indulgence toward them is simple reflection
of the same attitude toward myself. My fear of rebuffing & feeling ends
in the utter callousness of my dealings with S."[35] Sylvia could hardly have
said it better—except that understandably immersed in her own suffering, she did not see she was not alone. Ted said he was unwilling to hurt

women, and yet he hurt them, as the collected writings of Assia Wevill manifest. [AW]

Thomas Carlyle said Werther stood for a "class of feelings deeply important to modern minds but for which our elder poetry offered no exponent, and perhaps could offer none, because they are feelings that arise from passion incapable of being converted into action." He could have been describing the work of Sylvia Plath, by which I mean both the person and the poetry. Like Plath, Werther keeps a diary of his feelings, a series of letters to his friend acknowledging "my sudden transition from sorrow to immoderate joy, and from sweet melancholy to violent passions." It is this "too eager interest in everything" that makes a Wertherian incapable of self-exculpation, knowing "I have entangled myself step by step . . . seen my position so clearly, and yet to have acted so like a child!" Sylvia had endured, to use Werther's words, "a certain degree of joy, sorrow, and pain" but it was her nature, human nature, he says, that "becomes annihilated as soon as this measure is exceeded."

At the Beckers on her last weekend, Sylvia tried to break out of the exile that Werther tried to explain to his friend: "observe a man in his natural, isolated condition; consider how ideas work, and how impressions fasten on him, till at length a violent passion seizes him, destroying all his powers of calm reflection, and utterly ruining him." Sylvia kept repeating "I'm ill, I'm ill." She refused to let them call Warren or anybody else. Sylvia hardly had the energy, or the interest, to look after her own children. [HR] The Beckers tried to console Sylvia, but as Werther observes: "It is in vain that a man of sound mind and cool temper understands the condition of such a wretched being, in vain he counsels him. He can no more communicate his own wisdom to him than a healthy man can instill his strength into the invalid, by whose bedside he is seated."

How many readers in their impatience with Plath have reacted as Werther predicts:

Shame upon him who can look on calmly, and exclaim, "The foolish girl! she should have waited; she should have allowed time to wear off the impression; her despair would have been softened, and she would have found another lover to comfort her." One might as well say, "The fool, to die of a fever! why did he not wait till his strength was restored, till his blood became calm? all would then have gone well, and he would have been alive now."

The summer Sylvia worked on a truck farm, earning a little extra for her first year at Smith, she slept soundly after all the physical labor and saw what a relief from sorrow and joy that kind of strenuous occupation provided. As Werther says: "Many a time and oft I wish I were a common labourer; that, awakening in the morning, I might have but one prospect, one pursuit, one hope, for the day which has dawned." It is not so for those whose hopes are many. Werther posits: "For is not this anxiety for change the consequence of that restless spirit which would pursue me equally in every situation of life?" Out and about, forming a salon, as Sylvia wanted to do, associating with other people, as Werther did, made him "far better satisfied with myself," and prone to think "our happiness or misery depends very much on the objects and persons around us."

What Sylvia Plath missed in her last days was not Ted Hughes per se, but what Werther identified: "It is the greatest and most genuine of pleasures to observe a great mind in sympathy with our own." This loss was coupled with a sensibility highly critical of others, which Aurelia had deplored. Werther acknowledged what was also true of Sylvia: "that want of esteem for others with which I had often been reproached." This class of feelings and people, whom Carlyle had identified, had trouble finding an outlet for the excessive energy poured into their work and their lives. Werther observes: "Naturalists tell of a noble race of horses that instinctively open a vein with their teeth, when heated and exhausted by a long course, in order to breathe more freely. I am often tempted to open a vein, to procure for myself everlasting liberty." So it seemed as well for Sylvia Plath.

Werther and Sylvia are psychic compatriots, sharing similar "happy dreams" of childhood" with a mother, after the father's death, retreating to "immure herself" in a "melancholy town," or a stifling one, as Sylvia would have it in her final verdict on Wellesley. But New York, in that *Mademoiselle* summer, had proved to be no antidote, as she returned, like Werther, from "that wide world" with disappointed hopes and unsuccessful plans. Futurity, in the eyes of a Werther, or a Sylvia Plath, is a "dark gulf . . . when everything shall dissolve around me, and the whole world vanish." What did that future portend, especially if it was in a mental institution, the equivalent of what Werther dreads in the last words of his life: a "cold, monotonous existence."

Sylvia had told Dorothea Krook that the cold "reduced and diminished her, she felt herself humiliated, degraded, by it." Krook thought again of what it would mean to Sylvia when her faith in her marriage collapsed, and like a drumbeat in her head, Krook kept hearing Othello's "piercing words":

> But there, where I have garner'd up my heart,
> Where either I must live or bear no life,
> The fountain from the which my current runs
> Or else dries up; to be discarded thence

Or keep it as a cistern for foul toads
To knot and gender in . . .

"To be discarded thence, discarded, discarded, discarded," Krook seemed
to cry out: "I seemed to see the word burning her heart to ashes in her last
days in the freezing London flat."[36]

POSTSCRIPT

For years after Sylvia Plath's death, her friends and family tried to come to terms with her life, and especially with her suicide. Many of them provided Harriet Rosenstein with elaborate psychological interpretations of Plath's personality, creating the pathology that Heather Clark rebukes in *Red Comet*. Jillian Becker, for example, thought of Plath as a Romantic who could not come to terms with reality, with life's disappointments and rejections. In Becker's view, Plath did not want to live beyond her suffering; the suffering, was, in a sense, the point, and it should not be set aside with the suggestion that she could get over it. This intense Romantic absorption in the self meant that not even caring for her own children was enough to ensure her survival—as Dr. Horder had hoped.

Aurelia Plath blamed her daughter's death on the dogma of psychiatrists who put all sorts of fraught Freudian concepts into her head, she told Harriet Rosenstein. This reaction is rather common, repeated to me by Marilyn Monroe's friends who denounced her psychiatrists and method acting that made her dwell on her traumas.

More than one interviewee told Rosenstein that Sylvia Plath's suicide was an act of revenge, or that she was irresponsible, leaving behind her children. A few, like Al Alvarez, clung to the idea that it was an accident and that she was expecting to be saved.

Elizabeth Compton, later married to William Sigmund, thought otherwise. Given the right circumstances which of us might not consider suicide? So for Elizabeth, the suicide was situational. Some combination of an intense personality and her wintry surroundings conspired against her. In effect, Elizabeth's position is that we cannot judge, cast blame, attribute Sylvia's death to some innate personality defect, childhood trauma, or hereditary proclivity toward self-annihilation.

That Plath was depressed seems undeniable. But is that, in the end, the right word for her plight? In *One Friday in April*, Donald Antrim describes his own suicidal behavior as unwilled, as an overwhelming urge that overtook him, and that he could not explain. He begins his book with an epigraph from Sir William Osler: "Ask not what disease the person has, but rather, what person the disease has." Plath objectified her own encroaching death as a coldness that came at her—as an advancing nemesis. Antrim describes suicide as having a "natural history, a disease process, not an act or a choice or a wish." He does not deny the psychological factors in suicide: "trauma and isolation . . . deprivation of touch . . . neglect, in the loss of home and belonging." Certainly Sylvia Plath experienced the withdrawal of love and the touching that comes with it, and her letters demonstrate the devastating "loss of home and belonging." She knew enough of her kind of suffering to also know it would likely last a long, long time. "My sickness lasted years," Antrim notes, as he details "more than fifty rounds of electroconvulsive therapy" and "long hospitalizations." He thought of throwing himself off of the roof of his apartment building, and he even hung on to the fire escape, letting go but then reaching back to save himself. That scene of five hours on the roof is equivalent to his cycles of "recovery, relapse, and recovery." He admits that he was holding on to the fire escape so long that he was beginning to lose his grip and might easily have fallen. "Up on the roof, I felt as if I had been dying all my life."

This may well have been the perilous grip that Sylvia Plath had on her own life during her last weekend. She may have felt, as she did when Warren found her under their house, what Antrim articulates: "it would be better for others, for all the people who have made the mistake of loving you, or who one day might, if you were gone."

Grief, sadness, or despair do not adequately explain suicide, Antrim argues. "Suicide did not seem like a choice to me, but an eternal state, like the eternity of death." He would tell friends he felt better, as Sylvia did during her last days, and perhaps she felt, as he did: that he was "hoarding death. It became omnipresent. The notion that we choose death over pain, fundamental to our current thinking on suicide, suggests . . . some part of us exists outside the illness, unaffected, taking in the situation and making rational decisions." In such a decisionless state, what is there to share with others? "Coherent bonding is difficult for those of us who 'lose our minds.'"

It is understandable that Sylvia's friends and families would want to sort through what happened to her and even—as Becker did—want to say that Plath should have been able to take responsibility for herself, to, in effect, grow up. Sylvia herself used those words in a letter, and so did Ted. And she may well have blamed herself for not getting beyond her grief. But should we?

NOTES

AW: Julie Goodspeed-Chadwick and Peter K. Steinberg, editors. *The Collected Writings of Assia Wevill*. Louisiana State University Press, 2021.

BHSP: Anita Helle, Amanda Golden, and Maeve O'Brien, editors. *The Bloomsbury Handbook to Sylvia Plath*. Bloomsbury Academic, 2022.

CR1: Carl Rollyson. *American Isis: The Life and Art of Sylvia Plath*. St. Martin's Press, 2013.

CR2: Carl Rollyson. *The Last Days of Sylvia Plath*. University Press of Mississippi, 2020.

CR3: Carl Rollyson. *Sylvia Plath Day by Day, Volume 1: 1932–1955*. University Press of Mississippi, 2023.

CR4: Carl Rollyson. *Sylvia Plath Day by Day, Volume 2: 1955–1963*. University Press of Mississippi, 2024.

HR: Harriet Rosenberg Papers, Stuart A. Rose Manuscript, Archives, and Rare Book Library, Emory University.

LWM1: Linda Wagner-Martin. *Sylvia Plath: A Biography*. St. Martin's Press, 1987.

LWM2: Linda Wagner-Martin. *Sylvia Plath: A Literary Life*. Palgrave Macmillan, 1999.

MGL: Andrew Wilson. *Mad Girl's Love Song: Sylvia Plath and Life Before Ted*. Scribner, 2013.

PC: Sylvia Plath. Personal calendars. Special Collections, Smith College.

PJ: Sylvia Plath. *The Unabridged Journals of Sylvia Plath*. Edited by Karen V. Kukil. Faber and Faber, 2000.

RC: Heather Clark. *Red Comet: The Short Life and Blazing Art of Sylvia Plath*. Knopf, 2020.

AUTHOR'S NOTE

1. In some cases, as in the library of books Plath underlined and annotated, Hughes probably never did a study of what she was thinking and imagining, which is the work of biographers.

2. See MGL for an account of Plath's reading of Nietzsche, which began at the age of seventeen.

3. Plath recorded the events of her life in a variety of journals, diaries, and calendars. See *Sylvia Plath Info Blog* by Peter K. Steinberg, "Sylvia Plath's Calendars," February 11, 2022, https://sylviaplathinfo.blogspot.com/2022/02/sylvia-plaths-calendars.html.

4. An "imagining of rivalry" with whom? Perhaps with Ted's proprietary sister, or with Ted himself.

5. This occult experience cannot be dismissed as only Plath's. CR2 reports similar instances of others whom Hughes haunted.

6. Later in the book, I will draw on Gail Crowther's dissection of Hughes's gaslighting. See GailCrowther.com, "What Sylvia Plath Can Teach Us about Gaslighting," August 10, 2020, https://gailcrowther.com/2020/08/10/what-sylvia-plath-can-teach-us-aboutgaslighting/.

7. "Idolatrous love," a phrase Thomas Carlyle ascribes to Werther, will figure in the conclusion of this biography.

8. Mention should be made of Hughes's sister, Olwyn, who superintended Anne Stevenson's biography of Plath and took extreme measures to bully other Plath biographers and scholars.

9. I could not, for example, obtain from Indiana's Lilly Library archive a copy of a paper Plath wrote at Cambridge University because Ted Hughes's widow had the power to veto such requests. I sent a request (acknowledged by Faber and Faber), but Carol Hughes never responded. Another example of the private hoarding of Plath's work was recently unveiled at the New York Antiquarian Book Fair (April 4–7, 2024): "Many of these items have never before been seen publicly," says Rebecca Romney, co-founder of Type Punch Matrix. "For decades most were in the private collection of a friend of Plath's mother, Aurelia, and he acquired them directly from her. We're excited to give people the chance to see these items in person for the first time." Among the most significant is a copy of Karl Jaspers's *Tragedy Is Not Enough* (1953), a book Plath used for one of her first classes at Cambridge in 1955. "'It's heavily underlined and annotated by Plath throughout,' explains TPM co-founder Brian Cassidy." See "Sylvia Plath Collection Coming to New York Antiquarian Book Fair," Newswire.com, March 21, 2024, https://www.newswire.com/news/sylvia-plath-collection-coming-to-new-york-antiquarian-book-fair-22272950.

10. Beuscher resumed her family name of Barnhouse after divorcing her husband, which is why her Smith College archive is listed as the Ruth Tiffany Barnhouse papers.

11. As one of the epigraphs to this book suggests, Plath was profoundly influenced by the work of William Sheldon. I have used his book, *Psychology and the Promethean Will*, as one of the foundational texts in Plath's understanding of herself and the world, a text which no other Plath scholar has acknowledged. As a result, it may seem that I am suggesting that *only* Sheldon should be consulted, thus diminishing the impact of other texts on Plath's sensibility. That is not my intention. Many Plath scholars have given readers ample exposure to other authors who shaped Plath, especially, for example, Nietzsche, discussed by Andrew Wilson (cited in note 2), and D. H. Lawrence, whom I discuss in CR1. In addition, I mention several other texts in this book that have a bearing on Plath's thinking and behavior. Readers of CR3 and CR4 will be able to gauge what one peer reviewer calls the "vast range of reading and influences Plath engaged in." I am not trying to "pin Plath's motivations to one text," as one peer reviewer supposed, so much as I am saying that Sheldon affirmed her motivations. As Plath's annotations reveal, Sheldon articulated what she already had sensed and confirmed when she wrote "Yes!" in the margins of his book, signaling his agreement with *her*.

PREFACE

1. For my review of Heather Clark's *Red Comet: The Short and Blazing Life of Sylvia Plath* (Knopf, 2020), see SimplyCharly.com, December 26, 2023, https://www.simplycharly.com/read/reviews/red-comet-the-short-life-and-blazing-art-of-sylvia-plath#.YyHi-copAWU. See also my interview with Clark published on SimplyCharly.com, "Not So Silent: Heather Clark Attempts to Restore Sylvia Plath's Rightful Place in American Literature," February 14, 2021, https://www.simplycharly

.com/read/interviews/not-so-silent-heather-clark-attempts-to-restore-sylvia-plath-rightful-place
-in-american-literature#.YyHhm8opAWU. See also my podcast, *A Life in Biography*, "Episode 41:
Heather Clark on Her New Plath Biography," January 9, 2021, https://anchor.fm/carl-rollyson
/episodes/Episode-41-Heather-Clark-on-her-new-Plath-Biography-eoofn8.

2. More about Plath's reading of *The Lonely Crowd* is to come in this book.

3. See CR2 for more details about Beuscher's European experience.

PART ONE: THE EARLY YEARS

1. A reviewer of this book's manuscript asked whether Mel Woody is "another man in Plath's
life pontificating on his perception of the father/daughter relationship."

2. The photograph is included in CR1.

3. HR includes Otto Plath's account of this experiment and the review of his book *Bumblebees
and Their Ways*.

4. An FBI report also depicted Otto Plath as a loner; see Dalya Aberge's "FBI Files on Sylvia
Plath's Father Shed New Light on the Poet," TheGuardian.com, August 17, 2012, https://www
.theguardian.com/books/2012/aug/17/sylvia-plath-otto-father-files.

5. Harriet Rosenstein wrote to Otto's first wife and received the following reply on July 12,
1975: "My life with Otto Plath became a closed book when we were divorced; and so under no
circumstance would I give out any information about him."

6. Nathan Bailey told Harriet Rosenstein that Otto taught only one laboratory course and
had no laboratory of his own.

7. Ruth Beuscher interview with Aurelia at McLean Hospital in September 1953. [HR]

8. For more on Plath's proclivity for Superman and the Lone Ranger, see CR1.

9. Plath's attitudes did not change much even after she met Nat LaMar, an African American
writer studying at Cambridge University during her Fulbright term of residence.

10. In *A Passion for Life: The Biography of Elizabeth Taylor*, Donald Spoto notes that the situation of a young woman struggling to overcome a sheltered life "mirrored her own" and led to a
"poignantly affecting" performance.

11. No other mention of the contest appears in Plath's diaries.

12. *Motion Picture Herald*, October 18, 1947 (courtesy of Kathleen Spaltro).

13. For details about the Totem Pole, see the *Goldendaze-Ginnie* blog, "1951 . . . Dancing at
the Totem Pole Ballroom," June 5, 2007, http://goldendaze-ginnie.blogspot.com/2007/06/1951
-dancing-at-totem-pole-ballroom.html.

14. See Carl Rollyson, *Nothing Ever Happens to the Brave: The Story of Martha Gellhorn*
(St. Martin's Press, 1990).

15. A reviewer of this book's manuscript suggests Plath's reaction may have been "fear or shock.
A guy turning up unannounced on your doorstep is more than a bit stalker-ish, Plath wrote in
her journal fear of being a woman alone at night etc. She knew the risks. The word she uses about
him turning up is 'shaken'—it is more likely her perceived rudeness was fear." Another reviewer
protests: "It's not abnormal that Plath was taken aback by an unplanned, unannounced visit from
a total stranger, especially in 1951. She was also well within her rights to feel uncomfortable or
unsafe not getting immediately into his car for a long drive with him. To ask her to be otherwise
in a culture that treated women who dealt with strange men as promiscuous is to hold her to

a double-standard." These criticisms have merit; however, Eddie Cohen was hardly a "total stranger." From his point of view he had shown considerable sensitivity in his letters and Plath had welcomed his observations.

16. For more on the importance of Eddie Cohen, see CR1.

17. For more on Dawson's novel *The Ha-Ha*, see CR2.

18. A reviewer of this book's manuscript observes that Hughes "left out anything she wrote before meeting him or assigned it to the Juvenilia section [of *Collected Poems*] thus beginning his myth that her genius started with his influence."

19. Quoted in Luke Ferretter, "Gender and Society in Plath's Short Stories," in *Sylvia Plath's Fiction: A Critical Study*. (Edinburgh, 2010; online edition, Edinburgh Scholarship Online, Sept. 20, 2012), https://doi.org/10.3366/edinburgh/9780748625093.003.0006.

20. Lee Kravetz, a therapist and author of the novel, *The Last Confessions of Sylvia Plath* (Harper, 2022), provides a convincing portrayal of the way Beuscher had to manipulate both Lindemann and Plath to accept the therapeutic value of electric shock treatments. See my review of the novel in the *New York Sun* "Novelist Takes an Intriguing Fresh Approach to the Sylvia Plath Story," March 16, 2022, https://www.nysun.com/article/novelist-takes-an-intriguing-fresh-approach -to-the-sylvia-plath-story; see also my podcast interview with Kravetz, "Talking with Lee Kravitz about His Fresh Intriguing Depiction of Sylvia Plath and Her World," March 27, 2022, https:// anchor.fm/carl-rollyson/episodes/Talking-with-Lee-Kravetz-about-his-fresh-intriguing-depiction -of-Sylvia-Plath-and-her-world-e1gb5a5.

21. For more on Beuscher's background, see CR2.

22. The New Directions edition of the play includes an afterword by Williams dated June 1, 1953. Williams's biographer, Ellen Brown, responding to my query, notes that the announcement of the play's publication first appeared in the *Publishers Weekly* "Weekly Record" on October 24, 1953, with one of the earliest newspaper reviews in the *Cincinnati Inquirer* on November 8, 1953.

23. William Faulkner also saw this play, commenting "I think it is the best. . . . *Camino Real* was—it touched a very fine high of poetry, I think." In a discussion with University of Virginia students he used the phrase, "Kilroy was here," as an expression of the human desire to make a mark, of the writer's quest to have an impact on the world. See Frederick L. Gwinn and Joseph L. Blotner, editors, *Faulkner in the University: Class Conferences at the University of Virginia 1957–1958* (University Press of Virginia, 1959).

24. William Faulkner spent most of his life celebrating flyers and owned his own plane, then confessed in his last years that he was now afraid of flying.

25. I'm indebted to Ellen Brown for showing me an early draft of her Williams biography and allowing me to quote from it.

26. Judy Denison took the photograph of Plath in a tree on the Smith campus that is on the cover of CR1. I asked her about Lawrence House meetings.

27. For more on Sassoon's story, see MGL and RC.

28. See Cuke.com, "Richard Sassoon," http://www.cuke.com/people/sasoon-richard.htm.

29. For Sassoon's obituary, see Legacy.com, "Richard Sassoon, 1934–2017," https://www.legacy .com/us/obituaries/dailycamera/name/richard-sassoon-obituary?id=8463368. The obituary does not mention suicide, but his friend, Sharon Adams, who is working on a biography of Sassoon, told me about the nature of his death.

30. "Suspend This Day" was retitled "Midsummer Mobile" and included in *Collected Poems*.

31. Barnes graduated from Smith in 1956. Later from England, Plath wrote to Klein asking if it was true that Barnes had signed a contract with Columbia Pictures. Barnes was also a poet and achieved recognition at Smith for her writing. She continued to write and appeared in more than twenty films and numerous television productions. She is now retired. See Wikipedia, "Joanna Barnes," https://en.wikipedia.org/wiki/Joanna_Barnes.

32. For a discussion of this topic, see Maeve O'Brien, "Centering Whiteness: Sylvia Plath's Literary Apprenticeship," BHSP.

33. For more on Plath's thesis, see CR1.

34. For an explanation of the tripos, see Holly Ranger, "Sylvia's Plath's Greek Tragedy" in BHSP.

35. See my discussion of "Circus in Three Rings" in CR1.

36. Bard Hall refers to a residence hall at Columbia University that housed medical students.

37. Sheldon invented the now discredited somotypes: ectomorphs (thin, tall, sometimes fragile, introverted), endomorphs (overweight and outgoing), mesomorphs (athletic and physically demonstrative). See Sheldon's obituary from the *New York Times*, "William H. Sheldon, 78; Correlated Physiques and Traits of Behavior," September 18, 1977, https://www.nytimes .com/1977/09/18/archives/william-h-sheldon-78-correlated-physiques-and-traits-of-behavior.html. There is no evidence that Beuscher applied this scheme to Plath, although Sheldon's interest in how the body's constitution affected human psychology clearly fascinated Beuscher.

38. Sheldon's note is from June 4, 1952. His letters to Beuscher are in the Ruth Tiffany Barnhouse Papers at Smith College. There were not many women therapists, and it may be wondered if Beuscher took Sheldon's remarks as a backhanded compliment. In *The Last Confessions of Sylvia Plath* (Harper 2002), Lee Kravetz provides an imaginative portrayal of the male hierarchy Beuscher had to surmount.

39. Plath's underlined and annotated copy of Sheldon's book is in Special Collections, Smith College.

40. See Enclopedia.com, "Stefan Wolpe," updated June 8, 2018, https://www.encyclopedia.com /people/literature-and-arts/music-history-composers-and-performers-biographies/stefan-wolpe.

41. See the website for the Babson Centennial, 1919–2019, "Babson World Globe," https:// centennial.babson.edu/past/babson-world-globe/.

42. The story "Platinum Summer" exists in two versions at Lilly Library, Indiana University, and in Special Collections, Emory University.

PART TWO: THE MIDDLE YEARS

1. Quoted in Jad Adams, *Tony Benn: A Biography* (Biteback, 2011). Benn makes no mention of Plath in his published diaries. I did not know of Benn's tea with Plath when I interviewed him for my biography *To Be a Woman: The Life of Jill Craigie* (iUniverse, 2009). Part of my interview also appears in *A Private Life of Michael Foot* (University of Plymouth Press, 2015). In my experience, Benn manifested a keen desire for dialogue and a curiosity about his interlocutor that would have appealed to Plath, who would be as responsive as Benn was inquisitive.

2. Plath's copy of *As You Like It* is in Special Collections, Smith College.

3. As documented in CR3, Plath played the piano several times a week for an hour or more, amounting to several hundred hours between 1944 and 1950. She also played viola and kept careful

track of the hundreds of hours she worked on that instrument. She could play the first movement of Beethoven's Moonlight Sonata, a favorite, and enjoyed listening to Toscanini's radio concerts. Her diary entry for September 14, 1955, mentions a "piano escape" in a friend's apartment and reading *Psychology and the Promethean Will*.

4. See "Education: The Hidden Ones," *Time*, March 4, 1957, http://content.time.com/time /subscriber/article/0,33009,862482,00.html. LaMar later worked as an editor for New York City trade houses, and lists himself as a freelance editor and writer on Linkedin. See Linkedin.com, "Nat LaMar," https://www.linkedin.com/in/nat-lamar-99717831/.

5. In the early 1970s, in a pharmacy in Cape May, New Jersey, where I was working, a salesman told me he could not stock southern drugstores with the Lincoln pipe tobacco he was giving me to display.

6. By "religious," Sheldon did not mean a belief in God. The religious experience, in his view, had to do with this sense of oneness and unity, and not with any particular denomination or dogma. Plath underlined his declaration: "Intense atheists are also intensely religious." In the margin, she wrote "Yes!" In a letter to her mother Plath described herself as an "ethical culturist" and "close to the Jewish beliefs in many ways."

7. Plath's diary for January 1, 1955, notes that a story, "Christmas Encounter," had been sent to *Good Housekeeping*. The story does not seem to be extant.

8. Stewart's comment was not unusual. One of Plath's professors, Kay Burton, said she was surprised when Sylvia, always so neatly turned out, married "crude" Ted: "he seemed much too rugged and he'd been about rather a lot and we were certainly aware that he'd been a bit promiscuous, to put it mildly." [HR]

9. Strahan, a student of modern and medieval languages at Cambridge, dated Plath.

10. See CR1 for an interpretation of "Pursuit."

11. I learned about Sassoon's reaction to "Pursuit" during a conversation with his friend, Sharon Adams, who is writing his biography. Sassoon told Richard Wertz the same thing. [HR]

12. Quoted in CR1.

13. Norman Mailer brilliantly identified this Napoleonic strain in Marilyn Monroe: the desire to conquer, the will to suicide.

14. For a full discussion of the impact of *The Man Who Died* on Plath, see CR1.

15. I quote from the typescript Krook sent to Rosenstein.

16. I have transcribed this passage from Krook's typescript exactly as she typed it. The ellipses are hers, as is the punctuation.

17. For Myers's overdetermined dislike of Plath, see CR2.

18. For more on Shirley, see CR2.

19. See CR1 for more details about Anderson's visit to Cambridge and what Plath said about Hughes.

20. See CR2 for more evidence of Hughes's penchant for violent sex.

21. See Carl Rollyson, *Rebecca West: A Modern Sibyl* (iUniverse, 2008).

22. Quoted in AW.

23. See the entries for this period in CR4.

24. Rosenstein's ambulatory talk with Wober occurred on December 7, 1973. He never answered my letters.

25. See Carl Rollyson and Lisa Paddock, *Susan Sontag: The Making of an Icon* (revised and updated, University Press of Mississippi, 2016).

26. For this deep immersion in worlds elsewhere, see the diary entries in CR3.

27. Nikolai Bulganin (1895–1975) was Premier of the Soviet Union under Nikita Khrushchev.

28. Plath did continue to think about LaMar, asking her friend Lynn Lawner for news about him in a May 16, 1957, letter. Plath had heard that Nat had finished the first draft a novel, and she asked Lawner, if she saw Nat, to say "Ted & I might see him when we come home this summer." No such meeting seems to have occurred.

29. I am quoting Jay Martin's paraphrase in *Who Am I This Time?* of Anna Freud's concept in *The Ego and the Mechanisms of Defense.*

30. See Catherine Rankovic's fascinating account of reading Aurelia's shorthand notes: "Medusa's Metadata: Aurelia Plath's Greg Shorthand Annotations," BHSP. See also Rankovic's blog *Studying Aurelia Plath*, https://aureliaplath.blogspot.com.

31. Heather Clark reports that Sassoon's friends Mel Woody and Dick Wertz said his letter expressed regret for losing Sylvia and that it took him years to "get over Plath, who had been his first love." Clark goes on to say his letter "must have been deeply discomfiting for Sylvia," upsetting her "equilibrium and helps explain the melancholy she noted in her calendar that July." But the calendar is not clear about the cause of her sadness, which could just as well have had to do with Hughes, or with, as she told her mother, the frustrations and weariness of travel—documented in her calendar diary. Beware of "must have been"—the biographer's dodgy coverup for what she does not know. It is possible, for example, that Sassoon's letter angered Plath since it came too late for her to switch course, as her poem "The Shrike" makes apparent. "Must have" forecloses other possibilities. We may think we know our subjects, but they can surprise us.

32. The words are Martin's paraphrase of Adler.

33. See Frieda Hughes, *Sylvia Plath: Drawings* (Faber & Faber, 2013); Kathleen Connors and Sally Bailey, *Eye Rhymes* (Oxford University Press, 2007).

34. The paper is in Special Collections, Lilly Library, Indiana University. For the content of what Krook taught Plath, see Dorothea Krook, *Three Traditions of Moral Thought* (Cambridge University Press, 1959).

35. What did Krook make of this resort to biography on her pupil's part? In *Three Traditions of Moral Thought*, Krook believed that the ideas of a philosopher/theologian could not be separated from the style in which they are expressed. But her book, at least, does not venture into biography. As to Augustine's position on sex and marriage, Krook seems to have agreed with Plath, observing: "It is plain that, for Augustine, the sexual act is never anything but concupiscential. Love has no power to transform it in any significant way; there is no essential difference between the bare biological act of sex and the act of sex which is the physical consummation of a union of hearts and minds."

36. The rivalry between Beuscher and Hughes is explored in CR2.

37. Plath had this book in her library, but as Peter K. Steinberg notes, it was sold at auction to a private party, so what she may have underlined or commented upon in the book is not available. But we do know which chapters she read from the auction catalogue and from her letters.

38. *The Creature from the Black Lagoon* (1954) features a geology expedition gone wrong as it encounters a piscine humanoid. See Wikipedia, "Creature from the Black Lagoon," https://en.wikipedia.org/wiki/Creature_from_the_Black_Lagoon. I have quoted from "The Lady and the Earthenware Head" as rendered in Plath's letter to her mother, which differs from the version in *Collected Poems.*

39. For Lawrence's profound influence on Plath, see CR1.

40. Perhaps Ted had more to say that is not included in THL, which is inadequate not only because it is so selective but because the editor sometimes presents only parts of letters. The first book award given by three distinguished poets along with a contract from a trade book publisher is a momentous event that is mentioned in just a brief note in THL.

41. Shin beef is a cut from the lower leg of a cow.

42. See Barry Werth's *The Scarlet Professor: Newton Arvin: A Literary Life Shattered by Scandal* (Doubleday, 2001).

43. Loerke is a reference to D. H. Lawrence's *Women in Love*.

44. For more on Plath in the classroom, see CR1.

45. Elinor Friedman told Harriet Rosenstein that Plath discussed the novel with her.

46. See David Yezzi, *Late Romance: Anthony Hecht—A Poet's Life* (St. Martin's Press, 2023), and my review "Getting the News from Poets, in This Case Sylvia Plath and Anthony Hecht," published in the *New York Sun*, April 3, 2024, https://www.nysun.com/article/getting-the-news -from-poets-in-this-case-sylvia-plath-and-anthony-hecht.

47. The aide wrote to me and does not wish to be identified.

48. There is no record of Plath reading *The Horizontal Man*.

49. See, for example, the discussion of "The Disquieting Muses" in LWM2.

50. Plath recorded her reading of *Macbeth* in her calendar diary for February 19, 1956, and in her journal the next day.

51. She is paraphrasing Matthew Arnold in "Stanza from the Grand Chartreuse."

52. These details about Warren are from his obituary, available at Legacy.com, "Warren Plath, 1935–2021," https://www.legacy.com/us/obituaries/nytimes/name/warren-plath-obituary?id =33131668.

53. For more discussion of assortative coupling see CR2.

54. Plath does not record seeing these films, and they have no direct connection to the story. I cite them because Johnny characters are so diverse that it is no wonder Plath settled on "Johnny" as a way to evoke the many different manifestations of panic that could be personified in the name.

55. For more on *Lazarus Laughed*, see Carl Rollyson, "Eugene O'Neill: The Drama of Self-Transcendence," in *Critical Essays on Eugene O'Neill* (G. K. Hall, 1984), and "O'Neill's Mysticism: From His Historical Trilogy to *Long Day's Journey into Night*," *Studies in Mystical Literature* 1 (Spring 1981).

56. According to her calendar diary, Plath read *The Bird's Nest* on January 15–16, 1956. For more Plath–Jackson affinity, see Ruth Franklin, *Shirley Jackson: A Rather Haunted Life* (Liveright, 2016).

57. See CR2, in which the occult and witchcraft is explored in some detail.

58. See Kendall's *Sylvia Plath: A Critical Study* (Faber and Faber, 2001).

59. Am I the only reader who is tempted to call the poem "Electra on Aurelia Plath"? Perhaps not so farfetched given Gail Crowther's comment about the Freudian Electra Complex "dealing with the daughter's psychosexual competition with the mother for possession of the father." See William K. Buckley, ed., *Critical Insights: Sylvia Plath* (Salem Press, 2013).

60. See Linda Gray Sexton and Lois Ames, eds., *Anne Sexton: A Self-Portrait in Letters* (Houghton Mifflin, 1977).

61. Robert Lowell's *Memoirs* (Farrar, Straus & Giroux, 2002) have nothing to say about Plath in the classroom, and do not convey his personal impressions of her.

62. For more examples of how Sexton's work influenced Plath's, see CR2, and Gail Crowther, *Three Martini Afternoons at the Rita: The Rebellion of Sylvia Plath and Anne Sexton* (Gallery Books,

2021). See also my review of Crowther on SimplyCharley.com, https://simplycharly.com/review s/three-martini-lunches-at-the-ritz-the-rebellion-of-sylvia-plath-and-anne-sexton; and my podcast "Talking with Gail Crowther about Her New Book" May 8, 2021, https://anchor.fm/carl-rollyson /episodes/Talking-with-Gail-Crowther-about-her-new-book-on-Plath--Sexton--Three-Martini -Afternoons-at-the-Ritz-e1ogg5e.

63. See CR3 and CR4 for Plath's extraordinary number of diary entries that deal with tradition and self-mastery.

64. For more on her bear story, see CR1.

65. For more on Plath and Monroe, see CR1.

66. Steven Gould Axelrod, *Sylvia Plath: The Wound and the Cure of Words* (Johns Hopkins University Press, 1990) neatly sums up different responses to the poem.

67. In "Sylvia Plath and the Cycles of History," *Sylvia Plath; New Views on the Poetry*, ed. Gary Lane (Johns Hopkins University Press, 1979), Jerome Mazzaro notes: "The impossibility of reconstructing that bronze 'wonder' [the Colossus of Rhodes] of the ancient world, felled in 225 B.C. by an earthquake, foreshadows the poem's concluding failure." Over one hundred feet tall, the ruins of Rhodes colossus "lay on the ground for centuries . . . attracting visitors from far and wide," Teresa Marie Laye notes in "Sylvia Plath: An American Poet," *Critical Insights: Sylvia Plath*, ed. William K. Buckley, (Salem Press, 2013).

PART THREE: THE LATER YEARS

1. She mentions in an October 7–8, 1956, letter to Hughes reading about hypnosis in *Modern Abnormal Psychology*, edited by William Henry Mikesell (Philosophical Library, 1950).

2. See his letter to Olwyn Hughes in THL, late March 1958.

3. A U-2 spy plane was shot down over the Soviet Union on May 1.

4. In the months leading up to the execution on May 2, 1960, of Caryl Chessman, in prison for robbery and rape, a widespread protest against capital punishment arose that involved many public figures.

5. Quoted in Jay Martin, *The Psychologies of Political Exile* (2021).

6. One reader of my book manuscript protests: "I do find Plath's description of Whitby unfair—it is a stunning town. She is kinder to the place in her published short story, "The Perfect Place," which is a much more accurate reflection. Perhaps worth noting Whitby is not just a seaside resort, it is an always has been a working port and fishing town."

7. The husband in Gallant's novel has no parallel in *The Bell Jar*, but Plath might well have got to that part of the story in her second novel.

8. Flor also has a psychiatrist, but he does not seem to do her much good.

9. The "oddly spiteful" comment was made by a reader of this book's manuscript.

10. Did Plath complete the novel in two months, as she wrote to Ruth Beuscher on March 27, 1962? In an email to me, Plath scholar Peter K. Steinberg points out that in a letter to Ann Davidow, Plath said she started the novel during her negotiations with Knopf for an American edition of *The Colossus*, which occurred in early April 1961. A note in her journal indicates she finished the novel in August 1961.

11. It is not clear why Plath did not, in fact, dedicate the novel to Ruth Beuscher and, instead, dedicated it to Elizabeth and David Compton.

12. Finisterre is a port in France Plath and Hughes visited, but there is also a Cape Finisterre on the west coast of Spain.

13. On the connection between Plath and Jung, see the appendix in CR1.

14. My communication with David Wevill is documented in CR1.

15. See CR2 for details about Hughes's post-Plath depredations.

16. Avery reported the gossip to Harriet Rosenstein, but he also had several dealings with Ted and watched him come and go with "friends," mentioning one, Brenda Heddon, who later became one of his lovers—and more, although one is not supposed to talk about that. One reader of my book manuscript reminded me that in an interview with Harriet Rosenstein, Winifred Davies "more or less confirms" that two of Heddon's children looked "just like Shura Wevill," the daughter Hughes fathered with Assia.

17. See CR2 for more discussion of *Difficulties of a Bridegroom*.

18. See AW.

19. After Plath's death a guilty, remorseful Ted Hughes told Anthony Waite about his abandonment of her in Ireland. [HR]

20. See CR2 for more details about Ted's campaign to woo Assia as well as Assia's own account in AW.

21. See my review of AW, "The Other Woman," *Plath Profiles* 14 (Fall 2022).

22. For Aurelia's point of view, see Catherine Rankovic, "Medusa's Metadata: Aurelia Plath's Gregg-Shorthand Annotations," in BHSP.

23. See Kroll's *Chapters in a Mythology: The Poetry of Sylvia Plath* (Sutton, 2007).

24. See Peel's *Writing Back: Sylvia Plath and Cold War Politics* (Fairleigh Dickinson University Press, 2002).

25. See GailCrowther.com, "What Sylvia Plath Can Teach Us about Gaslighting," August 10, 2020, https://gailcrowther.com/2020/08/10/what-sylvia-plath-can-teach-us-aboutgaslighting/

26. See CR3.

27. For a detailed accounts of Plath's childhood school activities, see CR3.

28. See Heather Clark's essay, "'Not Mrs. Hughes and Mrs. Sillitoe': Sylvia Plath and Ruth Fainlight in the 1960s," in BHSP. See also Fainlight's own account, "Jane and Sylvia," available on the Poetry Society of America website, https://poetrysociety.org/assets/homepage/Jane-and-Sylvia.pdf.

29. "Sheep in Fog" was completed on January 28, 1963.

30. For more on the Hughes diary, see CR1

31. For more on Jillian Becker, see CR1, CR2, and her memoir, *Giving Up: The Last Days of Sylvia Plath* (St. Martin's Press, 2003); Trevor Thomas's self-published *Sylvia Plath: Last Encounters* (1989). Harriet Rosenstein also interviewed Becker and the results are in her archive at Emory.

32. When Rosenstein showed Horder her notes from their conversation, he asked her to take out the remarks about Ted.

33. See RC and CR2 for more discussion of Sylvia's pharmaceutical plight.

34. This was the testimony of a Dr. Goodall who obtained documents relating to Plath's suicide, conveyed them to Jillian Becker, who shared them with Harriet Rosenstein.

35. This remarkable journal entry is quoted in RC.

36. See CR2 for an extensive discussion of what the cold meant to Plath.

INDEX

ABOUT THE AUTHOR

Self-portrait courtesy of the author

Carl Rollyson, professor emeritus of journalism at Baruch College, The City University of New York, has published biographies of Marilyn Monroe, Lillian Hellman, Martha Gellhorn, Norman Mailer, Susan Sontag, Rebecca West, Jill Craigie, Michael Foot, Dana Andrews, Sylvia Plath, Amy Lowell, Walter Brennan, William Faulkner, and Ronald Colman. His reviews of biographies appear every Wednesday and Friday in the *New York Sun*. He has a podcast, *A Life in Biography*: https://anchor.fm/carl-rollyson.